P9-CJG-674

The Enemy at the Gate

*Habsburgs, Ottomans and the
Battle for Europe*

The Enemy at the Gate

*Habsburgs, Ottomans and the
Battle for Europe*

ANDREW WHEATCROFT

BASIC
BOOKS

A MEMBER OF THE PERSEUS BOOKS GROUP
NEW YORK

Copyright © 2008 by Andrew Wheatcroft
Published in the United State 2009 by Basic Books,
A Member of the Perseus Books Group
Published in Great Britain 2008 by The Bodley Head, Random House

Extracts for T.S. Eliot's "Little Giddling" and
"The Dry Salvages" reproduced by kind permission of
the Estate of T.S. Eliot and Faber and Faber Ltd.

All rights reserved. Printed in the United States of America.
No part of this book may be reproduced in any manner whatsoever
without written permission except in the case of brief quotations embodied
in critical articles and reviews. For information, address Basic Books,
387 Park Avenue South, New York, NY 10016-8810.

ISBN-13: 978-0-465-01374-6
Book Club Edition

For
Denise Gurney Wheatcroft
1914–2007

Mutter, *du* machtest ihn klein, du warsts, die ihn anfing;
dir war er neu, du beugtest über die neuen
Augen die freundliche Welt und wehrtest der fremden.
Rainer Maria Rilke, 'Die dritte Elegie'

Contents

Maps   viii
Illustrations   xiv
Acknowledgements   xv
Preface   xix

Introduction: The Terror in the East   1

PART ONE

1 A Call to Arms   13
2 Turks and Tartars   35
3 A Plague on the Land   55
4 Taking the Road to War   77

PART TWO

5 The Adversaries   97
6 'Rise Up, Rise Up, Ye Christians'   119
7 The Pit of Hell   145
8 'A Flood of Black Pitch'   162
9 A Holy War?   188
10 Storming Buda   201

PART THREE

11 The Age of Heroes   227
12 Myth Displacing History   245

   Coda   266

   Notes   269
   Bibliography   301
   Index   327

The Road to War, 1683

← Ottoman forces approaching Vienna and Tartar raids into Austria (see also inset)

— H.R.E. boundary

N O R W A Y

Oslo (Christian...

North Sea

SCOTLAND

• Edinburgh

DENMARK

Copen...

IRELAND

Dublin

WALES

ENGLAND

London

Calais

Amsterdam

UNITED PROVINCES

Brussels

Aachen

Cologne

Münster

Hamburg

HANOVER

Hanover

BRANDENB...

Magdeburg

Elbe

Leipzig

SAX...

P...

BRITTANY

NORMANDY

Seine

Paris

Luxembourg

Frankfurt

Nuremburg

Stuttgart

BOH...

LORRAINE

Strasbourg

Danube

BAVARIA

Munich

Nantes

Tours

Loire

FRANCE

Lyon

Bern

SWISS CONFEDERATION

TYROL

ST...

Bordeaux

Garonne

Rhône

SAVOY

Turin

PIEDMONT

GENOA

Milan

Po

REP. OF VENICE

Venice

Toulouse

Avignon

Genoa

Florence

TUSCANY

PAPAL

STATES

Rome

Marseille

CORSICA
(to Genoa)

PORTUGAL

Duero

SPAIN

Madrid

Tagus

CASTILE

Guadiana

Ebro

ARAGON

Barcelona

Valencia

Balearic Islands

SARDINIA

Naples

Lisbon

Seville

• Cordoba

Granada

GRANADA

Tangier

M e d i t e r r a n e a n

Palermo

SICI...

Algiers

Tunis

A T L A N T I C   O C E A N

0   100   200   300 miles
0   100   200   300   400   500 km

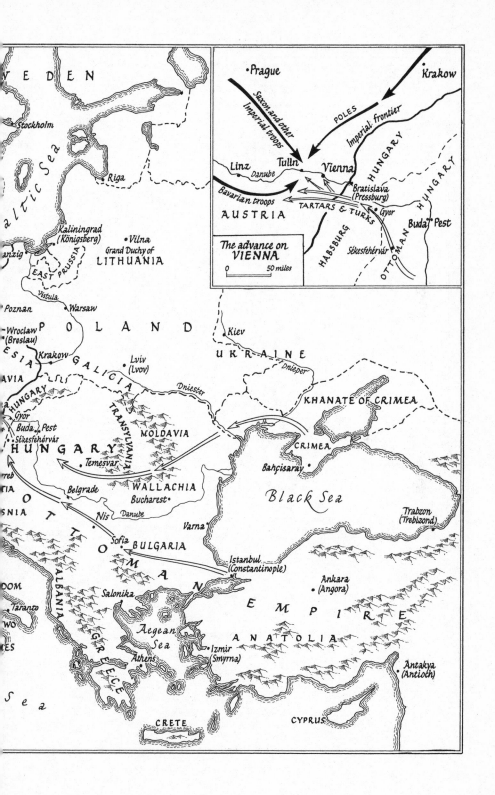

SWEDEN

Stockholm

Baltic Sea

Riga

Danzig

Kaliningrad
(Königsberg)

EAST PRUSSIA

Vilna

Grand Duchy of
LITHUANIA

Vistula

Poznan

Warsaw

POLAND

Kiev

Wroclaw
(Breslau)

SILESIA

MORAVIA

Krakow

GALICIA

Lviv
(Lvov)

UKRAINE

Dnieper

Dniester

HUNGARY

Gyor

Buda   Pest

Székesfehérvár

HUNGARY

TRANSYLVANIA

MOLDAVIA

KHANATE OF CRIMEA

CRIMEA

Bahçisaray

Black Sea

Temesvar

Zagreb

CROATIA

BOSNIA

Belgrade

WALLACHIA

Bucharest

Trabzon
(Trebizond)

OTTOMAN

Nis

Danube

Varna

KINGDOM OF
NAPLES

TWO
SICILIES

Taranto

ALBANIA

Sofia

BULGARIA

Salonika

Istanbul
(Constantinople)

Ankara
(Angora)

EMPIRE

GREECE

Aegean
Sea

Athens

Izmir
(Smyrna)

ANATOLIA

Antakya
(Antioch)

Sea

CRETE

CYPRUS

The advance on
VIENNA

0   50 miles

Prague

Krakow

Saxon and other
Imperial troops

POLES

Imperial frontier

Linz

Danube

Tulln

Vienna

HUNGARY

HUNGARY

Bratislava
(Pressburg)

Gyor

Bavarian troops

TARTARS & TURKS

Buda   Pest

AUSTRIA

HABSBURG

Székesfehérvár

OTTOMAN

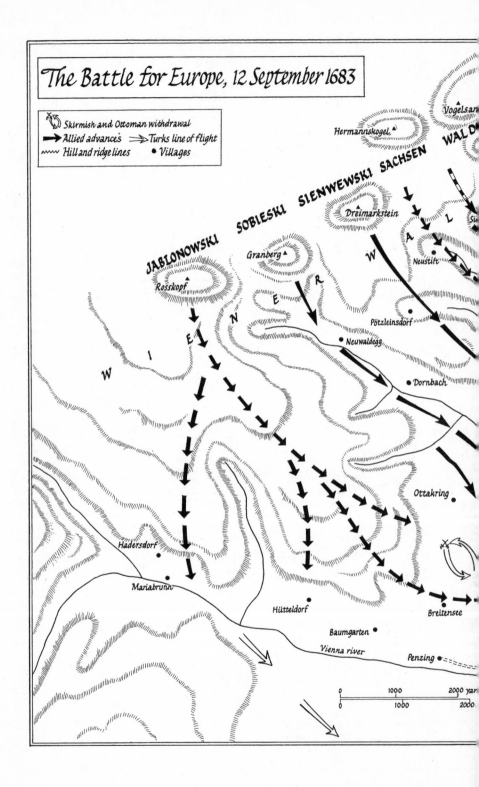

The Battle for Europe, 12 September 1683

🦅 Skirmish and Ottoman withdrawal
➡ Allied advances   ⇨ Turks line of flight
〰 Hill and ridge lines   • Villages

Vogelsan

Hermannskogel

WALD

JABLONOWSKI   SOBIESKI   SIENWEWSKI   SACHSEN

Dreimarkstein

Granberg

W A L

Neustift

Si

Rosskopf

Pötzleinsdorf

W I E N E R

Neuwaldegg

W I E N E R

Dornbach

Ottakring

Hadersdorf

Mariabrunn

Hütteldorf

Breitensee

Baumgarten

Vienna river

Penzing

| 0 | 1000 | 2000 yar |
| 0 | 1000 | 2000 |

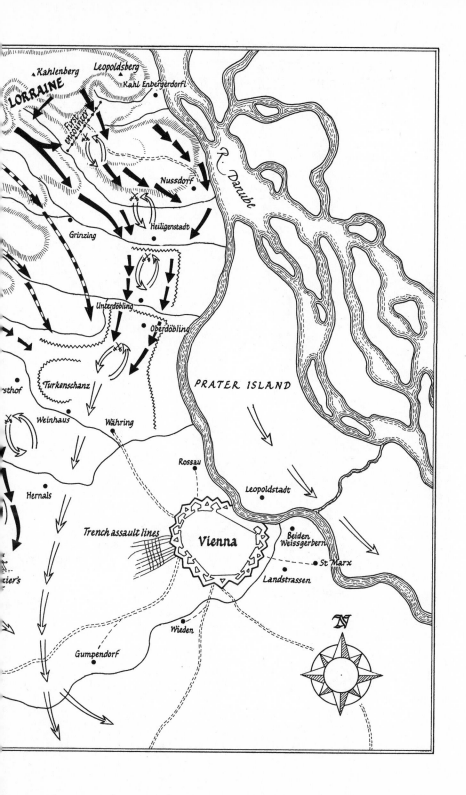

LORRAINE

▲ Kahlenberg   Leopoldsberg ▲
              ● Kahl Enbergerdorfl

R. Danube

Fürst Lothingen

Nussdorf ●

Grinzing ●

Heiligenstadt ●

Unterdöbling

Oberdöbling ●

PRATER ISLAND

Turkenschanz

...sthof ●

Weinhaus ●   Währing ●

Rossau ●

Leopoldstadt ●

Hernals ●

Trench assault lines

Vienna

Beiden
Weissgerbern

...zier's   ● St Marx

Landstrassen ●

Wieden ●

Gumpendorf ●

N

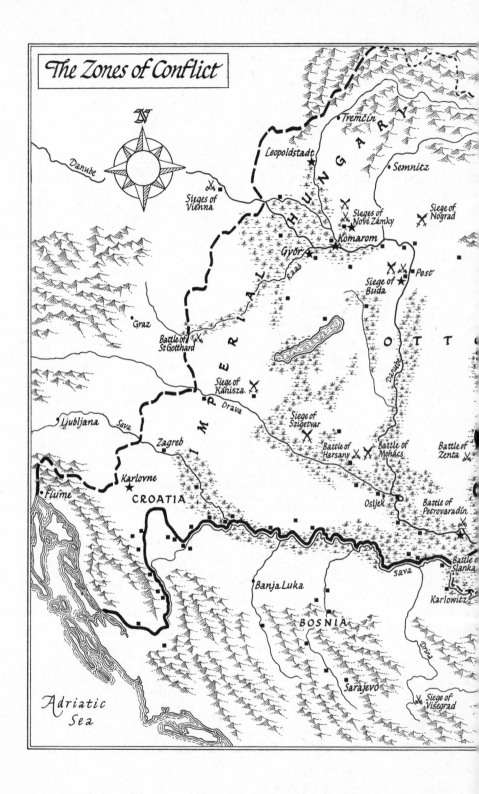

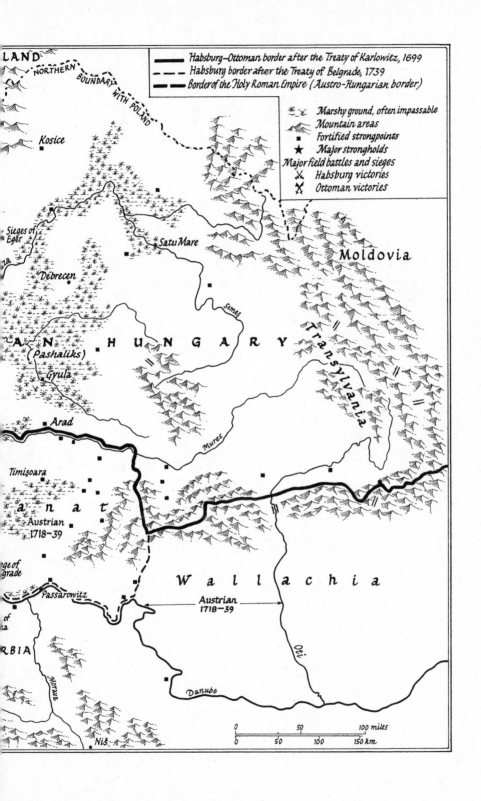

——— Habsburg–Ottoman border after the Treaty of Karlowitz, 1699
– – – Habsburg border after the Treaty of Belgrade, 1739
▬▬▬ Border of the Holy Roman Empire (Austro-Hungarian border)

🌿 Marshy ground, often impassable
🞕 Mountain areas
■ Fortified strongpoints
★ Major strongholds
Major field battles and sieges
⚔ Habsburg victories
⚔ Ottoman victories

LAND

NORTHERN BOUNDARY WITH POLAND

Kosice

Sieges of Eger

Satu Mare

Moldovia

Debrecen

Somes

HUNGARY

Transylvania

N (Pashaliks)

Gyula

Arad

Mures

Timișoara

a n a t

Austrian 1718–39

ge of grade

Passarowitz

Wallachia

Austrian 1718–39

of a

RBIA

Olt

Morava

Danube

Niš

0   50   100 miles
0   50   100   150 km

Illustrations

For permission to reproduce illustrations author and publishers wish to thank the following: akg-images: 10 and 16; Belvedere, Vienna: 9; Bridgeman Art Library: 2, 11, 15 and 18; Magyar Nemzeti Galeria, Budapest/Tibor Mester: 1.

Acknowledgements

The *Enemy at the Gate* has been slowly growing for almost the entirety of my writing life. In a sense, the idea for this book began with one conference and ended with another. In 1972, Geoffrey Best and I organised a meeting at the University of Edinburgh in the then-new field of War, Peace and Peoples. We had both switched from other interests to the study of war and society; Geoffrey has gone on to be much more productive in the field than I have been: his friendship has been a constant in all the years since then.

In the late 1990s I picked up the threads of this subject which had been in abeyance over fifteen years. By then I had written other works on the Habsburgs and the Ottomans, and felt confident enough to take up the main questions which are the subject of this book: why did they fight each other for so long – and why did they finally stop fighting? In 2007 I had almost finished the text and then attended another conference, at the University of Reading, on 'Crossing the Divide: Continuity and Change in Late Medieval and Early Modern Warfare. Whereas at Edinburgh we had quite rapidly assembled a hand-picked group who met, talked and argued (sometimes fiercely) day and night for four days, Frank Tallett and David Trim had spent two years organising a much larger and more open meeting of experts: it was a huge success. The battlefield is not my preferred territory; descriptions of war and suffering can still cause me a very real sense of revulsion. Yet both Edinburgh in 1972 and Reading in 2007 demonstrated to me that war and conflict are central to our understanding of the past.

I want to thank those who have been both an inspiration and, like all good friends, a practical help. I have boldly dispensed with titles in listing them here.

John Keegan was in our Edinburgh group in 1972, and I have valued both his friendship and his work ever since. We have written books together and he was the first person to encourage my interest both in the Habsburgs and in the use of visual material in the study of history. For this book I have tried to apply some of the insights contained in his groundbreaking work, *The Face of Battle*.

John Brewer flits invisibly through these pages. He has been a trail-blazer in almost every topic that I have covered. *The Sinews of Power* showed the economic consequences of war in developed societies; and the huge collective work, *Consumption and the World of Goods*, edited with Roy Porter, provided the superstructure for my work on images and networks of communication. Now, with the final chapter of his book A *Sentimental Murder: Love and Madness in the Eighteenth Century*, John has again introduced me to ideas and material I would never have found for myself. Over the decades – in Florence, Los Angeles, Oxford and London – John and Stella have been the best of friends; neither of them can know how much their constant support has meant to me.

Writing this book has created a new passion for Hungary. I only wish that I could read and understand the marvellous sinewy language beyond a few words and phrases; my colleague Díana Káli has assured me that it is now too late to begin. I am very grateful for her help by translating material from the Hungarian, including a marvellously spir-ited version of the last section of Miklós Zrínyi's epic *Szigeti veszedelem* (The Peril of Sziget), published in 1651 and never translated into English.

I now can entirely understand the old Latin tag *extra Hungariam non est vita, si est vita non est ita* – there's no life outside Hungary, and if there is, it's not life. My guide in this discovery has been Stephen Pálffy who, with the spirited support of Annamaria Almásy, has introduced me to the Hungarian way of life – from perfect food and wonderful wine to a sheer joy in life – and has provided often complex answers to my endless questions. I have benefited especially from Stephen's extraordinarily broad knowledge of the issues and the personalities I encountered in the course of writing this book. Since Pálffys have appeared for generations on these battlefields, this has been invaluable.

Budapest has become for me a quintessence of scholarly excellence. Thanks to Gábor Ágoston in Washington D.C., who smoothed my path, I met Pál Fodor and the group of erudite and immensely active Ottomanists at the Hungarian Academy of Sciences. Terza Obórni in turn introduced me to Agnes Sálgo Wojtila at the National Széchényi Library, which houses the best researched collection of images I have encountered anywhere. Her kindness and expert knowledge have been a very great help. Opposite the Library, a Habsburg palace on the castle hill – the scene of so much bloodshed in this book – now contains the National Gallery of Art, a treasure house of nineteenth-century history paintings; next door to it, the City Museum is home to a huge collection of material on the siege of Buda in 1686. From their resources I have culled some of the paintings and images that appear in these pages.

Other parts of this book have been researched in Vienna, Graz, Edinburgh, London, Washington DC and Philadelphia. In Vienna, I consulted the Wien Bibliothek, the Österreichische National Bibliothek and the Wien Museum; in Graz, the Joanneum; in Great Britain, the British Museum, the London Library, Cambridge University Library and the National Library of Scotland; in Washington, the Library of Congress and the Folger Library. In Stockholm Henrik Andersson showed me the unique printer's manuscript of Marsigli's last work in the collection of the Livrustkammeren; in Philadelphia, Earle Spamer helped me with the volumes of the Lindsay manuscripts held by the American Philosophical Society. I especially appreciated the kindness of Peter Parshall, who introduced me to the extraordinarily rich collection of engravings and woodcuts in the National Gallery of Art, Washington DC.

To Claudia Fabian at the Bayerische Staats Bibliothek in Munich, I owe a great debt of gratitude. She was the first person to understand how my pursuit of images in books could 'add value' to the great digitisation projects in European libraries. She joined in setting the direction of our research project – the Printed Images Research Consortium – by James Knowles, Gerald Maclean, Agnes Sálgo Wojtila, Sylvia Mattl Wurm, and the project manager, Susanne Peters. No one has provided more input into this book than Susanne. She has read every word through endless drafts, tactfully suggested changes, more firmly excised some of its excesses, loaned me books, and provided a stream of ideas. I do not think a simple 'thank you' could ever express my gratitude. Gerald Maclean, both in writing and in conversation, has been the stimulus of much that finally appeared in these pages. He and Donna Landry have also helped me to understand much better a world that centred on the horse, and by implication its role in the eastern war. At times, they must have dreaded my simplistic interrogations.

I also want to thank Peter and Barbara Geymeyer for their extensive hospitality in Bavaria, and Peter for his exceptional knowledge of Austrian engraved images. His book collection, for example, provided in an instant the detail of where Bosnian regiments were stationed before 1914, turning a supposition into a historical fact. That Graz features repeatedly in these pages is partly because it should, for good historical reasons, but also because Peter and Greta Kocevar entertained me, and proved a wonderful source of arcane information about Styria: a magical region and the heart of old Austria.

Working on the text with Tessa Harvey has been thoroughly enjoyable and fruitful. Her unerring sense of what works on the page taught me a great deal; I can still hear her voice: 'Don't give the story away *yet*.' I would like to thank Lara Heimart and her team at Basic Books, who have been effective, fun to work with, attentive to every detail, and above all, most wonderfully encouraging.

It may seem bizarre to acknowledge a place – Craigieburn. This book is about borders and boundaries: living in this very old house, writing at the top of a Scottish border tower first burned out by reivers in 1570, makes this history of raiding and border warfare along another, far distant frontier very real. It has always been a contested and debatable land, much like the territory fought over by Habsburgs and Ottomans. It was a land of war and skirmishing, but now it exemplifies amity.

My wife Janet is at the centre of this book and of everything else. She has found time to work with me on this project, with advice and recollections of places we had been to and which I had forgotten. Most valuable of all has been the half-expressed 'no', saving me from many fine messes.

Andrew Wheatcroft
Craigieburn House
April 2008

Preface

I first set foot in Vienna in late August 1963 from the Belgrade train.[1] The dingy 'hotel' that I found not far from the station was the worst I have ever stayed in, surpassing in awfulness even a workers' hostel in Seville, with its bedbugs and cockroaches. But it was all I could afford. Other dejected occupants came and went carrying their cardboard suitcases strapped up with rough string, but none of them stayed long. I did, because there was a good local (*Beisl*) in the next street and I could live off soup and bread and sometimes, every few days or so, a redemptive glass of rough white wine.

In 1683, exactly 280 summers before, a vast Ottoman camp had occupied the same spot: the Turks were besieging Vienna, for the second time in history. They had been there before, during the first siege in the autumn of 1529. Of course, there was no sign or memory of either ferocious struggle and in 1963 I had barely heard of them. What you could see were traces of a much more recent assault. In 1945, the Soviet 3rd Ukrainian Front armies had fought for twelve days street by street with the Nazi Waffen SS, finally taking the city on 13 April. Eighteen years later, high up on the façade of a long apartment block, I could still see the tell-tale spatter of bullets.

Just a few months earlier I had seen those same marks on the park walls behind the Humanities Faculty (Facultad de Filosofia y Letras) in Madrid; within the buildings where we studied, in the early winter of 1936 the Republicans had fought desperately, retreating from floor to floor, but still successfully holding back General Franco's Army of Africa. Seeing those pockmarks in Vienna produced an instant frisson: I knew what they meant. So from those first moments, submerged beneath the more normal responses to Vienna's exuberant life of food, drink, art, music and culture, I also had an uneasy sense of war, violence and mortal struggle.

For an eighteen-year-old, fuelled with his Austro-Hungarian grandmother's romantic pre-1908 memories, Vienna was both enticing and a little depressing. But those pitted walls, in some places like a huge, ugly rash, were what stayed in my mind. Next time I came, I at least knew about the Turks besieging the inner city in 1683. My guide was John Stoye's then-new book *The Siege of Vienna,* published in 1964, and every day I traced an identical path through streets of the Inner City, trying to relate what had happened in 1683 to the buildings that now stood there. The street plan in most places had remained much the same, but there were then (before the days of 'heritage') no signs or plaques that suggested what had happened centuries before.

Nevertheless I soon created my own landmarks: a butcher serving wonderful fresh sausages with a plate of sauerkraut and a glistening potato salad; a seedy bar that had good cheap wine, best during September and October. I later found much better wine by taking the tram out to the wine villages like Grinzing or a local train to a *Lokal* in the shadow of the great abbey at Klosterneuburg. But through the subsequent decades, my old haunts began to vanish, although more slowly than in other European cities. The building of the Underground (*U-Bahn*) in the 1980s, Vienna's most spectacular construction project since the demolition of the ancient walls and the building of the Ringstrasse a century before, was the end of the old pre-1914 world.

Or so it seemed. In fact, it promoted a rediscovery. The ancient walls and bastions, supposedly demolished, are still present, at least in their trace and foundations, just below the surface of the new nineteenth- and twentieth-century city. A few months before I finished this book, I told a friend of seeing some excavation work close to the National Theatre (*Burgtheater*). The builders were digging the foundations for a new office block, and had exposed what looked like some old vaults. The colour of the walls and rubble was odd, rather pale, and I was not sure whether it was brick or stone. He believed he knew what I had seen: the walls of Vienna. When the builders of the Ringstrasse removed the fortifications, stone by stone, from the 1850s onwards, they were only taken down to just below ground level, providing a solid foundation for the new buildings of the great project. So the walls of Vienna are still there, or at least the vestiges of them, just as the more recent marks of the Russian assault on the city were still there in 1963, if you knew where to look.[2]

Knowing where the events took place was important. Walking the ground was a good idea, but often the landscape had altered irrecoverably. Nevertheless, as the story took shape, and grew inexorably, there were more trips to battlefields and to other places we would now call sites of memory. In fact more often than not they were sites of oblivion. No one there knew or could even suggest where some long-forgotten battle had taken place. Sometimes I had more luck. Above the site of the Battle of St Gotthard, on the modern frontier between Austria and Hungary, near the village of Mogersdorf, there is a low hill overlooking the battlefield. On it a local enthusiast and the community have created a little memorial museum.[3] That battle was the most historic thing that ever happened in Mogersdorf, and the people there have made, in effect, a war memorial.[4] But that memorial records only an instant in a long and complex history, out of context. It is just one disconnected element in a long story.

★   ★   ★

This, then, is not a straightforward *history*. With something so evanescent and imponderable as fear, my main topic, I had no idea what would be relevant or useful. Late on in my quest, one of the finest historians of Ottoman Hungary, Pál Fodor, gave me a clue why this should be. One day, walking out of the Academy of Sciences in Budapest, he told me that we know a great deal about many terrible incidents that had taken place in Ottoman Hungary. We might know where an outrage had occurred; we might even know who had suffered or what had happened to them. But none of these horror stories created a universal, a stereotype, that could be generalised for every similar occasion. Each event was *sui generis*, unique, unless we could realistically suggest otherwise.[5] History is messy, and usually manages to surprise us.

By chance I had stumbled into a huge and only partially cultivated field. A huge amount of fine work had been done on the fifteenth and sixteenth centuries, very much less on the seventeenth and almost nothing on the eighteenth.[6] For this reason, I have concentrated on this later period, with the Siege of Vienna in 1683 as its centre piece until the final period of conflict between the two imperial powers.[7]

To keep the book manageable, I have had to exclude other partici-
pants in the struggle with the Ottomans, discarding the material on
the role of Venice and the campaigns in the Peloponnese, the islands
and the Mediterranean. Then a huge tranche on the Crimea and
Russia's eventual expansion eastward into the khanates of Central Asia
went the same way. I had to set aside, regretfully, my long excursus
about China.[8]

On the later Ottoman–Habsburg military struggle the most recent
sources were still those written in the nineteenth century. Plainly, the
last phase of the Holy War had fallen off the historical map after occupying a central position for so long. In the years after my first coming
to Vienna, my path had led not to seventeenth- but nineteenth- and
twentieth-century military history. Work in the archives centred on
the Austrian role in the international arms trade, and I spent weeks
(happily) in the small town of Steyr with contemporary logbooks and
inventories. From there I would make visits to the *sanctum sanctorum*
of the Kriegsarchiv (War Archive) in Vienna. Yet all the time, and in
many of the records, there was an underlying sense of fear: fear that
competitors or rivals would overtake the Austro-Hungarian monarchy;
of being unprepared, of being left behind technologically, outsmarted.[9]
As, eventually, I moved on to other Habsburg topics, there was still
evidence of this taint of anxiety more or less ever-present. Where
could it have come from?

★   ★   ★

Most books require a number of preliminary explanations. First, a set
of intellectual debts – a kind of paternity in the ideas. This book only
became possible, although I had wanted to write it for a long time,
with the publication of Rhoads Murphey's *Ottoman Warfare, 1500–1700*
in 1999 and Caroline Finkel's *Osman's Dream: The Story of the Ottoman
Empire 1300–1923* in 2005. I had never believed the ineradicably negative
tone of contemporary publications on the 'Turk'. Although I could
explain how one negative idea after another proliferated in the West,
through books, pamphlets, paintings, prints, even teacups and tiles, it
was impossible to suggest what an alternative might be. Murphey and
Finkel demolished some of the stereotypes, but, more important, they
also diminished the pragmatic differences between the combatants.
Because western polemicists took the 'Turk' out of the normal span

of human behaviour – by being cruel, lustful and driven remorselessly by the power of blind faith – they presented, in effect, a race of psychopaths. Ottomans could almost never behave in any different manner: for example, humanely. This image simply did not match the evidence, which, when approached forensically, exhibits constant and disturbing ambiguities that undermine the stereotypes.

The other debt of origin was to an Austrian social anthropologist, Andre Gingrich. Most of the material and the deeper study of the events I was making did not fit any framework. Gingrich described what had developed to the east of Western Europe as 'Frontier Orientalism', which developed out of the peoples and cultures of the region. I tried and tested this concept against my material covering a much longer period than Andre Gingrich described. It worked. It has provided me with an underlying matrix into which the pieces of evidence can fit like a jigsaw puzzle. I think historians will find 'Frontier Orientalism' an immensely valuable idea in the future.

This book is not based on manuscript sources, except in one or two instances. It is written from contemporary published sources, from the sixteenth to the eighteenth centuries, the material which must have informed people at the time, providing most of what they knew of these events. These are materials with which I have been working for more than twenty years; I am still making discoveries and also changing my mind about what I have researched already. It is impossible, now and then, to know how people form their opinions. But we can understand how the material comes before them. Things have not changed much since the fifteenth century. Like the book before you now, someone decided to publish it and hoped to make money from it. Some books and pamphlets were printed with other motives, but most of the material I have used was frankly commercial. They were products in a market, and printers (the publishers of their day) sought to make them as saleable as possible to the potential customers. One of the key ways to achieve this was to illustrate them with engravings and woodcuts. This was especially valuable in an era when full literacy was relatively limited.

One way of knowing if a text reached a broad audience was how many editions were printed, and over how long a period. Equally, if a book was translated and published into another language, it must have reached a new and different group of readers. Slowly, we are beginning to trace these networks. Some texts formed opinion across the whole European continent. Sir Paul Rycaut's books were published in many editions, and translated into French (twice), Dutch, German, Italian, Polish and Russian; Johann Peter von Vaelckeren, the lawyer who lived through the siege in Vienna, wrote a short book that was published during 1684 in Brussels both in French and Latin editions; in Linz in a German edition; in Vienna, Venice and Naples in Italian; in Cracow in Polish; and in London in English. Some other books simply plagiarised the published texts and produced the same stories under different names. A handwritten manuscript was most common, quite a restricted form of communication, but a printed book, a printed woodcut or engraving, or a pamphlet, was something that existed to be bought and sold on a wide scale, a marketable commodity. In that sense what sits on the rare printed book collections is often more revealing of public attitudes and opinion than the contents of the great archives' manuscripts.

How can we understand what actually happened? We could look at it in grandiose *Clash (and Failure) of Civilisations* terms. That falls apart at the first testing of the evidence. We could look at the *Muslim Decline* argument: a long spiral downwards from the grand triumphs of the early Middle Ages. I do not find that persuasive either. This book uses different terms. I talk about the [Ottoman] 'Turks' and not 'Muslims'. Ottomans were good and faithful Muslims, but they also had a specific Turcic heritage *in addition* to Islam that suffused the empire which they created. These days historians do not use the word 'Turk' on the grounds that Ottomans considered a 'Turk' as a rustic fool, and were hence grossly insulted to be called a 'Turk'. True enough: yet at the same time they gloried in their Turkish ancestry and origins. Ultimately, it was a Turcic identity that provided the ideology for Kemal Ataturk's new nation, the Republic of Turkey.

The Habsburgs emerged by chance as the Ottomans' principal long-term adversary in the west. There are different and equally significant Polish and Hungarian histories of conflict with the Ottomans separate from this Habsburg story. However, the confrontation between Ottomans and Habsburgs was between two *empires*, both claiming the same kind of power and authority. They had more in common. Both these old empires were decrepit (in the eyes of their competitors) long before their final demise after the First World War. This perception

of their common decrepitude, their archaic ceremonials, the slightly
amused tolerance of their senility in the late nineteenth century, was
false in 1900, but it also falsified their past. This book begins at the
start of their conjoined history and ends at the point that they stopped
fighting each other. The test of war is a revealing kind of diagnosis,
a refractive prism that breaks up complex intertwined issues into their
essential elements. It has helped historians to ask (and answer) the
question: why did the Ottoman state fail? Oddly, the same question
has been asked less insistently about the Habsburgs' failed state.[10] This
is not a military history but rather seeks to understand how societies
meet this primal challenge. We need to know the Ottoman 'face of
battle', to borrow Sir John Keegan's transforming idea, if we are to
understand what happened.

Finally, a problematical terminology. There are sometimes German,
Turkish, Hungarian, Croat or Serb names for the same place or event.
Using one or another version systematically inevitably suggests a particular sympathy. But there must be some consistency for the sake of
the reader. I have mostly used the names (with a few exceptions) as
they are today – Czech or Slovak for some, German, Hungarian,
Bulgarian, Romanian, Croat, or Turkish for others. These modern
names are also cross-referenced in the index to those used in the
past. For internationally known events, like battles or treaties, and
for places with English variants of the local name – Vienna and
Munich, for example – I have used the English name. Hungarian
names are written as *first name* followed by *last name* to avoid confusion for non-Hungarians. I have also used 'Turk' and 'Ottoman'
in the unselfconscious way they were applied in the seventeenth and
eighteenth centuries. Although the number of punctilious Ottomans
still left alive must be quite small in number, I hope this will not
cause any affront.

Introduction:
The Terror in the East

In the fiftieth chapter of *The History of the Decline and Fall of the Roman Empire*, Edward Gibbon tells us: 'After pursuing, above six hundred years, the fleeting Caesars of Constantinople and Germany, I now descend . . . on the eastern borders of the Greek monarchy.' He describes the 'genius of the Arabian prophet' and how the 'spirit of his religion' led to the decline and fall of the eastern empire. Gibbon concludes that 'our eyes are curiously intent on one of the most memorable revolutions which have impressed a new and lasting character on the nations of the globe'.

Yet this Arab, Muslim dominion, which at its greatest extent stretched westwards from Arabia to the Atlantic and northwards into the deserts of Central Asia, lasted for roughly three and a half centuries.[1] What replaced it came from much farther east. Both Christian and Muslim legend were agreed about its origins: a land ruled by two giant kings, Gog and Magog, a kingdom where the mountains were full of terrible and deadly warriors, 'the number of whom is as the sand of the sea.'[2] The universal hero Alexander the Great had preserved the civilised world from their ravages by building a great wall pierced by only two huge iron gates. This was all that saved the west from catastrophe.

This story appears both in the Qu'ran and in the *Alexander Romance*, written in Greek in the sixth century CE, and it is possible to sense historical roots for the myth. There really were *great walls* in China, designed to keep out the nomads, and there is ample justification for the successive waves of barbarian peoples migrating westwards. Alexander's rampart and the Iron Gates was a plausible explanatory fiction.[3] The terror from the east was nomadic Turks from the steppes. They first entered the world of Persian civilisation, then overwhelmed the Byzantine empire and finally pushed on into the south-east of

Europe. The Turks were mysterious in a way that the Arabs were not. The Romans had known about Arabia, divided it into Arabia Felix and Arabia Deserta, and marked Arabia on the map. But the vast eastern world north of Parthia and Persia was an unknown.

For Rome these eastern peoples had all been 'Scythians', numberless, menacing riders mounted on shaggy ponies. Gibbon wrote of

> the Turks or Turkmens, against whom the first crusade was principally directed. Their Scythian empire of the sixth century [BCE] had long since disappeared; but their name was still famous among the Greeks and Orientals; and the fragments of the Scythian nation, each a powerful and independent people, were scattered over the desert from China to the Oxus and the Danube: the colony of Hungarians was admitted into the republic of Europe and the thrones of Asia were occupied by slaves and soldiers of Turkish extraction . . . a swarm of these northern shepherds overspread the kingdoms of Persia: their princes of the race of Seljuk erected a splendid and solid empire from Samarcand to the confines of Greece and Egypt; and the Turks have maintained their dominion in Asia Minor till the victorious crescent has been planted on the dome of St Sophia [in Constantinople].[4]

★   ★   ★

In the summer of 2005, an exhibition at the Royal Academy in London depicted *Turks*. It was *A Journal of a Thousand Years* from the sixth to the seventeenth centuries.[5] Looking at the extraordinary objects displayed – carvings, painting, friezes, ornaments, bronze doors, it was immediately clear that these many tribes of Turcic-speaking peoples had a culture in common. This was not solely an Islamic culture – it was the tenth century before the Turkmen tribes began to accept Islam – and they carried into their new faith many remnants of the old folk beliefs. We regard, perhaps following Gibbon, the Arab world as sempiternal, the powerhouse and the heart of Islam. Yet by the eleventh century, Arabs were no longer the dominant and dynamic force. Arab scholarship certainly remained a powerful intellectual force, notably in science, mathematics and invention, but the power that sustained Muslim culture was now Turkish.

The impact of Islam upon the Turcic peoples was both dramatic and profound, but it did not obliterate all the social and cultural patterns that had survived among the Turks from earlier times. Islam, in practice rather than theology, displayed many local variations. The Turks, like all the Central Asian peoples, grew up on the edge of the Chinese cultural zone, something that is evident in many of their earliest artefacts; Arab culture by contrast had grown up on the fringes of the Hellenistic world, and there were numerous Christian and Jewish Christian settlements in Arabia before the coming of Islam. Turks were latecomers into Western Asia, and had little in common with the cultures that bordered the Mediterranean – Arab, Greek, Roman. The Turks who entered the Middle East possessed a distinct, double heritage: first, by their origins which they traced back to the mythical Oghuz Khan, and beyond him to Noah; and, second, to their rebirth as Muslims, from the eleventh century. We need to understand this complex double nature, if the Ottomans are to become intelligible.

* * *

This book is first of all about Europe's fear of the Turks and then, by the end, about fear itself. To understand this process, it is important to know that the Turks did not suddenly appear out of nowhere in 1453. The point that Turks entered the European memory was almost four centuries earlier: we can place it exactly – after the Battle of Manzikert in eastern Anatolia, close to Lake Van, on 19 August 1071. Carole Hillenbrand, who has already transformed our view of the crusading period, has now identified the true significance of Manzikert and its echoes through history.[6] The shock of the battle was captured by an eyewitness, the historian Michael Attaleiates:

> It was like an earthquake: the shouting, the sweat, the swift rushes of fear, the clouds of dust, and not least the hordes of Turks riding all around us. It was a tragic sight, beyond all mourning or lamenting . . . the entire imperial army in flight . . . the whole Roman state overturned.[7]

The Turks' entry into Western Asia came in phases. First it was as slaves or mercenaries. The Seljuk Turks, victors at Manzikert, went on to capture Jerusalem, which prompted Pope Urban II's call for the First Crusade in 1096. Other Turks, the slave soldiers of Arab rulers, rebelled against their masters and founded the Mamluk sultanate that ruled Egypt from 1250 to 1517, only to be replaced by still another set of Turks, the Ottomans. With the rise to power of the Ottomans, a kind of state organisation which was at the same time both uniquely Turcic and distinctly Islamic eventually ruled a territory equivalent in scale to that of the Roman empire; and proved almost as enduring.

The sense of the Turk as the enemy of Christendom antedates the arrival of the Ottoman Turks in Europe in 1354. One channel of communication was through Hungary. In the twelfth century the kings of Hungary already had close connections with the politics of Constantinople. They were closely allied with the Byzantines by marriage and common interests. The stories of Manzikert and of another Byzantine defeat almost a century later at Myriocephalon (1176) in western Anatolia were transmitted to the west via Hungary: Bela III, King of Hungary, had been educated at Constantinople and sent his own troops to the failed campaign of 1176. There had even been plans for the union of Byzantine and Hungarian kingdoms. In March 1180, the ten-year-old Alexius, the son of the Emperor Manuel Comnenus, was married by proxy to the daughter of King Louis of France, so there was a second channel of communications to the west.[8]

From Manzikert onwards, Western Europe was aware of the rising Turkish power in the east. Four centuries after the battle was fought, one of the miniatures painted by the French artist the Maître de Rohan for Boccaccio's *De casibus virorum illustrium* (*On the Fates of Famous Men*) showed the moment that the Byzantine Emperor Diogenes Romanus was taken prisoner by the Seljuk Turk leader Alp Arslan. Although he painted the Turks wearing western plate armour – having had no notion what Turkish armour would look like – he did at least know that the Turks carried curved sabres quite unlike the straight European broadswords. The bottom half of the image shows the Byzantine emperor on all fours, being used by Alp Arslan as a foot-stool to mount his horse.

The Ottomans, meaning the *sons of Osman*, were one of the minor Turkish tribes that had followed the Seljuks into Anatolia.[9] In 1324, Orhan, Osman's son, was a client of the Seljuks, and granted land in the far west of their domain, close to Constantinople. Being in close proximity to a dangerous enemy made this a perilous frontier posting.

But the Ottomans thrived as border warriors, *gazi*, sparring with the Byzantines, and slowly increasing their territory, as well as impressing their enemy with their military prowess. The connections between Orthodox Byzantines and Muslim Ottomans soon became more direct. By 1346, Orhan had married the daughter of Emperor John VI and in 1352 the Ottomans were invited to garrison Gallipoli, on the European side of the Sea of Marmara, for the Emperor. By 1360, the Ottomans held more land on the European shore than they did in Asia. In that year their capital was moved to the city of Hadrianopolis, which they renamed Edirne.

Within forty years of their first settlement in north-west Anatolia, still overshadowed by Byzantine might, the Ottomans had turned the tables. Now Constantinople was in fear of its belligerent Turkish neighbours. So, too, were the Christian principalities inland like Bosnia, Albania and Serbia; many Christians accepted the new Ottoman Sultan Murad I as their overlord instead of the decrepit and enfeebled Byzantines. In 1389 Murad and his Christian vassals defeated Lazar, the Prince of Serbia, in an epic battle on the field of Kosovo Polje. But while the battle was in progress the Sultan was murdered by a Christian pretending to be a renegade and when the Serbs were defeated, Lazar was executed as a reprisal. Western Europeans were quickly informed as to the rise of a new power in the mountainous regions (*Balkan* in Ottoman Turkish) of the south-east.[10] Two years after Kosovo, the Turks reached the Danube and captured the fortress of Nicopolis; Europe reacted by launching a crusade.

The Crusade of Nicopolis in 1396 was disorganised and badly led: the result was a catastrophic defeat. However, it was the aftermath of the battle which produced the greatest impact in Europe. Jean de Froissart described in Book 4 of his *Chronicle* how, after the battle, the Sultan ordered the execution of many of his noble prisoners, harsh recompense for the slaughter of Ottoman prisoners by the French. A miniature in one edition of Froissart shows the bodies of the decapitated men beginning to pile up before the Sultan, who wished to make an example that his enemies would not forget. The watercolour in Loqman's sixteenth-century Ottoman court history, like Froissart, shows the Turk as a fearsome enemy. By the time the Ottomans finally captured Constantinople in 1453, the image of their implacable cruelty had been formed and reinforced over almost three generations. The fear had its roots even farther back in time, on the field of Manzikert in the summer of 1071, so far back indeed that it was in *time out of mind*. Yet it had not been forgotten.

★　　★　　★

An old Roman military road ran from Constantinople through the Balkan mountains to Belgrade (Singidunum) on the Danube. Upriver was Buda (Aquincum), and still farther upstream Vienna (Vindebona). The sense of 'being Roman' remained long after the empire had vanished, but the visible evidence of Rome's long presence – like the remaining pillars of 'Trajan's Bridge' across the Danube near the Iron Gates – was a reminder of the empire. The Christian states of the Balkans and Hungary and the Ottomans all regarded themselves as the inheritors of the Roman past. For the Ottomans as for the Seljuks, the Roman empire belonged to them by right of conquest, and had, they believed, become their patrimony. In *Europe: A History* Norman Davies points to the 'daring' of Murad in claiming the title *Sultan i-Rum*, which his successors bore until the end of the Ottoman Empire in the twentieth-century.[11] In conquering Constantinople in 1453, Murad's descendant Sultan Mehmed II 'the Conqueror' believed that he was restoring the former unity of the eastern Roman empire, *Rum* in Ottoman Turkish, in both Asia and in Europe.

Ottomans regarded the Holy Roman Emperors of the west as usurpers to a title which belonged by right to them. They would refer to the Habsburgs as mere dukes of Austria, or, at best, as a petty king. This curious mirror image – of two rival claimants to the same estate – underpinned the developing rivalry between the two dynasties. The Habsburgs believed that their duty lay in restoring 'Rome' eastwards, for one of their proudly borne titles was King of Jerusalem; the Ottomans believed that it was their destiny to reclaim the Roman empire westwards, from Constantinople. This gave an added potency (or virulence) to the contest.

This definitive struggle between East and West was rooted in the claim to be the heir to a long defunct empire. Explanations based on *realpolitik*, economic rivalry, or competing ideologies (religious faith) might seem a lot more intelligible, but in the context of the fifteenth century, which is where it began, it was a significant issue. Both Ottomans and Habsburgs were new to power, and both claimed authority from their ancient origins. Their carefully constructed genealogies both led back to Noah, and beyond: they were necessary fictions. The Habsburgs only began their long continuous tenure of the imperial title when Frederick IV, Archduke of Austria, was crowned Frederick III, Holy Roman Emperor, in Rome by Pope Nicholas V, with the crown of Charlemagne. That was on 16 March 1452. Just over a year later, on 24 May 1453, the young Sultan Mehmed II took Constantinople by storm. At that point, despite his imperial title, Frederick was a powerless nonentity while the Ottomans were rapidly becoming a dominant military power in the east.

The contest was delayed because at the time that the Habsburg Frederick III and the Ottoman Mehmed II both assumed the supreme title of Roman Emperor, a powerful state still separated them. Between Vienna and Constantinople was the Kingdom of Hungary, ruled by one of the most skilful generals of the age, a Transylvanian noble named John Hunyadi, but known as the 'White Knight' because of his highly polished armour that gleamed like silver. When Mehmed advanced to attack Belgrade three years after the capture of Constantinople, it was Hunyadi's well-led army that threw him back in disarray in July 1456. However, the White Knight died of plague three weeks after the battle, and his second son, Matthias Corvinus (his eventual successor), was only twelve years old.

It was 1458 before Matthias was elected King of Hungary and for thirty-two years under his leadership Hungary expanded its territory in both east and west: both Habsburgs and Ottomans were cowed by him. But after his death in 1490, the power of Hungary crumbled and in the second decade of the sixteenth century the Habsburgs and Ottomans for the first time faced each other directly. Two young and supremely ambitious rulers committed themselves to the struggle.

In January 1519 the old Emperor Maximilian I had died and was succeeded by his grandson, Charles of Habsburg, already ruler of Spain in succession to his other grandfather, Ferdinand of Aragon, and beneficiary of the rich lands of Burgundy and the Low Countries. With Maximilian's death Charles also inherited the Habsburg lands in Austria and Germany. In the following year, Sultan Selim I, who had conquered the Levant, Egypt and the Arab lands for the Ottomans, died, leaving his only son Suleiman I to succeed him.[12]

Selim had already proclaimed himself 'the conqueror of the world' and his son intended to make good that claim. Suleiman was six years older than Charles, but they shared an imperious sense of destiny. In a letter to Sigismund I, King of Poland and Lithuania, Suleiman described himself as the ruler of a vast domain

> *Padishah* [King of Kings] of the White [Mediterranean] and the Black Sea, of *Rumeli* [the 'Land of the Romans], Anatolia, Karaman, the provinces of Dulkadir, Diabakir, Kurdistan, Azerbaijan, Persia, Damascus, Aleppo, Egypt, Mecca, Medina, Jerusalem, and all the lands of Arabia, of Yemen, and of the many lands conquered with over-whelming power by my noble father and magnificent grandfathers.[13]

Charles V had stated his own claim a few years earlier:

> Roman King, future Emperor, *semper augustus*, King of Spain, Sicily, Jerusalem, the Balearic Islands, the Canary Islands, the Indies and the mainland on the far shore of the Atlantic, Archduke of Austria, Duke of Burgundy, Brabant, Styria, Carinthia, Carniola, Luxembourg, Limburg, Athens, and Patras, Count of Habsburg, Flanders and Tyrol, Count Palatine of Burgundy, Hainault, Pfirt, Roussillon, Landgrave of Alsace, Count of Swabia, Lord of Asia and Africa.

At least three of these – Jerusalem, Athens and Patras – were firmly in the possession of Suleiman. The obvious areas of conflict would be the Mediterranean, and in the huge Hungarian kingdom, overripe for takeover. Its young king Louis, King of Bohemia and Moravia, elected ruler of Croatia and Dalmatia, lacked the resources of his powerful neighbours to both west and east. No crusade would be mounted to save Hungary from an Ottoman assault.

★   ★   ★

In a secular age there is perhaps a temptation to diminish the religious dimension of the struggle between Christendom and Islam, as Suleiman I (with some anxiety) prepared to launch his war of conquest. Yet the Habsburg–Ottoman contest was a clash of faiths: Charles V was the leader of the Christian world (eventually sanctified by papal coronation). Suleiman was the leader of most of the Muslim world, protector of the holy shrines of Mecca and Medina, possessor of the emblematic treasures of the Prophet Mohammad. Late in his life he would have the following inscribed upon the mosque that bore his name in Istanbul-Constantinople:

> Sultan Suleiman has drawn near to God, the Lord of Majesty and Omnipotence, the Creator of the World of Dominion and Sovereignty ... who is His slave, made mighty with Divine Power, the Caliph, resplendent with Divine Glory, who performs the Command of the Hidden Book and executes its decrees in all regions of the inhabited Quarter: Conqueror of the Orient and the Occident with the Help of Almighty God and his Victorious Army, Possessor of the Kingdoms of the World ...

There was no possibility for compromise.[14] Charles V advised his son Philip II of Spain never to surrender any Habsburg territory: 'If your predecessors with the Grace of God held on ... you should trust that He will assist you to keep what is inherited.'[15]

In 1521, a year after he had succeeded his father, Suleiman reopened Selim's wars of conquest.[16] But instead of striking in the east he took up where his great-grandfather, Mehmed II 'the Conqueror', had failed in 1456. The young Sultan marshalled his forces outside his capital Constantinople-Istanbul and then marched north to the Danube and the White Fortress of Belgrade. This time there would be no salvation from Hungary, and on 29 August 1521 the fortress – the advance rampart of Christendom – fell to Suleiman's army. Five years later, in 1526, the Sultan slaughtered the army of Hungary on the battlefield of Mohács and in the late summer of 1529 his soldiers would stand before the walls of Vienna. The struggle between Ottoman and Habsburg continued for two and a half centuries. Its resonance lasts into the present.

PART ONE

Trying to unweave, unwind, unravel
And piece together the past and the future,
Between midnight and dawn, when the past is all deception,
The future futureless, before the morning watch
When time stops and time is never-ending;

T.S. Eliot, 'The Dry Salvages'

I

A Call to Arms

In the evening of 6 August 1682 the sultan's gardeners dug a narrow trench beside the Imperial Gate of the Topkapi Palace in Istanbul. At intervals they planted seven long crimson poles, each as thick as a man's arm; the top section was elaborately carved and gilded, and from the golden globe at the apex hung a cascade of black and coloured horses' tails. These were the *tuğ*, the ancient banners of the steppe warriors from whom the Ottoman Turks were descended.[1] Normally they were kept within the inner Treasury deep in the heart of the palace; but brought out into the light of day and planted before the palace gate, their meaning was unmistakable. Mehmed IV, the Khan of Khans, Commander of the Faithful, Padishah, the son of warriors, the father of warriors, had placed his *tuğ* before his 'tent' and was leaving on campaign. That *campaign* might mean no more than a summer's hunting, but the ritual had never lost its deeper meaning and on that evening it was a resonant call to arms.[2]

In the late summer of 1682, a very great war was intended. The decisive meeting in the small council chamber of the second court of the palace lasted most of the day. But in the end there were no dissenters: the sultan's Chief Minister, the Grand Vizier Kara Mustafa of Merzifon, had silenced all those who opposed him. The council agreed that not only would the Ottoman army march west against the Habsburgs, with their capital in Vienna, but, most significantly, it would be headed by the sultan himself. The presence of the sultan directed the whole force of the empire against their adversary. Mehmed had led the army north before and the empire had gained territory; his leadership may have been notional rather than practical but the symbolism was potent. From the moment that the *tuğ* were planted in the ground, an elaborate ceremonial of war-making began.

First the 'lord of the two continents', like his distant nomadic ancestors, established his war camp just outside the great Byzantine triple walls of Constantinople, or Istanbul as the city was also known by 1682. A small army of labourers began transforming a patch of rough grazing land, called Çirpeci Meadow and frequented only by goats and sheep, into a perfect parade ground without a single pebble or other obstruction. Soon the wagons of the Imperial Corps of Tent Pitchers and Tent Makers began to arrive, with hundreds of men to erect the imperial encampment in accordance with an exact plan. Its epicentre would be the complex of the sultan's pavilions, and close to them, the tents of the Grand Vizier, then the military commanders, and then those members of the court and lesser officials who travelled with the sultan. Finally, the tent men would string an embroidered screen (*zozak*) from poles surrounding the rust-red tents in the sultan's enclosure, symbolically cutting it off from the camp outside just as the ramparts of Topkapi kept the clamour of Istanbul at a distance.

To any westerner, a war camp suggested a dirty, disorderly collection of rudimentary bivouacs hastily erected on the line of march, peopled by raucous and dangerous ruffians. An Ottoman encampment, by contrast, was a perfect model city, but made of broadcloth, canvas, silk, brocade and embroidery rather than brick and stone. A century before, a Habsburg ambassador to Constantinople had observed wryly, 'Any one who knows the conditions which obtain in our own camps, will find difficulty in believing it, but the fact remains that everywhere [among the Turks] was complete silence and tranquillity . . . there was the utmost cleanliness, no dungheaps or rubbish, nothing to offend the eye or nose.'[3] More recently an English chaplain, Dr John Covel, described Sultan Mehmed IV's encampment set up outside the palace at Edirne in 1675. It consisted of almost sixty tents, and in the largest of them was 'a throne studded with gems and on which lay rich needlework, and on the floor – as in the other tents – were luxuriant carpets, and the interior was covered with rich fabrics. The fourth tent, entered through a corridor, was the personal tent of the sultan. Here was a bed, at the head of which stood a Qur'an stand.'⁴

The war camp so rapidly erected in 1682 looked much the same. This nomadic palace lacked none of the facilities of Topkapi itself. Every function of the court had its travelling counterpart. There was a tower-like tented Pavilion of Justice echoing the Tower of Justice at Istanbul, from which the sultan and his special guests could look down on the throng below. Close by there was a tent for ceremonial executions like the spot beside the palace gate. There were tents for latrines, for baths, or for ritual ablutions; vast tents for ceremonial events, audience chambers, withdrawing rooms, reception rooms, dressing rooms; marquees for feasting and entertainment, even a tent that could house the body of a dead sultan, as happened when Sultan Suleiman I had died campaigning in Hungary in 1566. Even the sultan's favourite horses had their own tented stables.⁵

Ottomans had a passion for the open air. Often the sultan or one of his officials would decide to hold an alfresco meal in the palace grounds, on the shores of the Bosporus or in the forests beyond the city. By the time they arrived, an array of pavilions would be ready, with food and drink prepared, and at evening the little cluster of tents would be lit by hundreds of tiny lamps and lanterns. By Mehmed IV's time, the Imperial Corps of Tent Pitchers and Tent Makers numbered almost a thousand men, who occupied a rambling former palace close to the centre of the city. In the former audience chambers and public rooms hundreds of men would sit cross-legged, sewing and embroidering new tents or repairing the old. The smaller store chambers were filled with thousands of tents, ranging in size from the vast imperial pavilions to a tiny bathing enclosure, all carefully folded and packed, labelled by size, condition, colour and purpose, each one inventoried to be available at a moment's notice.⁶

The largest tents were enormously heavy, requiring six to ten men simply to carry and then many more to erect them.⁷ All the imperial chambers had an outer layer, made of close woven canvas, usually dyed red or light green, which kept out the rain or snow, and an inner layer of much finer cloth, often embroidered or decorated. The soldiers' tents were much smaller and less elaborate, often made of wool felt, like the tents of the nomads on the Asian steppes. Within, officers cosseted themselves with carpets, embroidered hangings and furniture; but even the tents for the ordinary soldiers were well made and comfortable, much more than the crude bivouacs used by western armies. Each unit of five or ten men was supplied with shelter from the elements and a sheepskin for each soldier to sleep upon. The soldiers of the Divine Light were well cared for.

For the campaign of 1683, the imperial tent makers supplied more than 15,000 tents large and small, and every other provision was on the same scale. No possible need for an army at war was neglected. Infantrymen did not carry their weapons on the march: the muskets, spears, bows and quivers of arrows together with their rations were loaded on to camels, or stacked in carts each pulled by two bullocks. Ottoman soldiers were not forced to forage or live off the land. Fresh supplies of food were waiting at each night's encampment, while they carried with them wagons loaded with rice and flour. On the move, the army had its own flocks of sheep driven ahead of the soldiers, with the butchers ready to slaughter the livestock and prepare the meat at each night's halt.

The war camp steadily extended around the palatial imperial core. Radiating out in neat concentric circles were the tents of the infantry and the household cavalry, but in addition, as solid evidence of warlike intent, were the artillery and the engineers' lines: a sultan going hunting never took the cannon with him. Each area of the camp was different, with every detachment marking its presence by its distinctive badges and banners – painted or embroidered swords, dragons, herons, hounds, elephants – in reds, blues, black and greens. Every aspect of life in camp was regulated. Even the field latrines were dug to a prescribed pattern: surrounded by a rectangular tent, open to the sky, and with a red painted wooden seat concealing the pits beneath. Each group of seven or eight soldiers had their own cook tent, and outside each one the famous copper cauldrons used to cook the soups, rice, pilaffs or stews that provided an excellent and sustaining diet. The Habsburg ambassador Ghislain de Busbecq thought that 'the two things from which the Turks derive the greatest benefit [in war] . . . [were] rice among grains and the camel among beasts of burden, both of which are exceedingly well suited for the distant campaigns they make'.[8] Luigi Fernandino, Count Marsigli, captured and held by the Turks, was amazed at the 'excessive luxury' by western standards of the soldiers' meals served each day.[9] In Islam good order, cleanliness of body (*natheef*) and spirit were ordained by God, and enforced by the sultan, His servant.

Lined up wheel to wheel in the artillery enclosure was every size of gun from the little two-man field piece, which was carried on a single camel, to massive bronze siege guns pulled by long teams of oxen. These heavy guns were the hardest to move, and when the war was on a distant frontier the time it would take to move them by river or by land would determine the period available for campaigning. War north of the Balkans was entirely governed by weather and by the seasons. The great plain of Hungary, the Lowlands (*alföld*), was the westernmost extension of the Asian steppe, surrounded by hills and mountains on every side except the east. To the west were the Alps, running down to the Danube at Vienna; to the north, the mountainous spine of Central Europe, rising from the Czech and Slovak lands in the west, then eastwards along the Carpathian chain. South of the Danube was *balkan*, the mountain, the Turkish word that eventually gave the whole region below the great river its collective name. But between the Balkans and the foothills of the Carpathians was an endless plain, in winter a bland, empty featureless landscape, sparsely dotted with towns and villages. In early spring the dead earth became lush grassland on which the thousands of Ottoman horses could graze all the way to the boundaries of Christian Europe. But the new season had a negative aspect, for the same rivers and streams that produced the grass to feed the horses also flooded huge areas of low ground, in places creating a morass, which slowed the progress of the wagons carrying the impedimenta of the Ottoman armies to a few miles each day. The heavy guns simply became immovable, unless they could be taken north by river.

But the Ottomans had a secret weapon. Beside the guns in the camp lay the engineers' encampment, full of huge cranes, pontoons, coils of rope, baulks of timber for bridging the network of rivers that the army had to traverse, as well as all the mysterious equipment used for undermining enemy fortifications. Western fortifications were superior, but few armies in the west could equal the skill and resourcefulness of the Ottoman engineers.

What was happening in the encampment outside the great walls bespeaks a silent question. Why was the sultan and the huge array heading north-west to fight the Habsburgs for the first time in eighty-seven years? There had been great campaigns against the Habsburgs but seldom led by the sultan in person. There seemed no reason for it. The truce between the Habsburgs and the Ottomans had endured, imperfect no doubt, but nothing had happened that would have justified this massive response. Habsburg diplomats held hostage at the Ottoman court sent letter after letter of warning back to Vienna, that war really was coming, that this was no empty gesture. But they could advance no convincing reason why.

Although the Habsburgs had a strong sense of their imperial status and destiny, their material resources were more limited than their aspirations. The problem was always money, and, to a more limited extent, the fragmented nature of their domains. Leopold could not even instruct his own subjects and be sure they would obey his command. To get support from the states of the Holy Roman Empire, an Emperor had to cajole, persuade or even bribe a set of prickly, argumentative and self-interested electoral princes, local rulers and assemblies. The fundamental rift – between Catholic and Protestant – still influenced Europe's internal politics, and Protestant states felt no natural inclination to come to the aid of a Catholic Emperor. That was within the Holy Roman Empire, over which Leopold had some power. The possibility of rallying Europe as a whole – including the arch enemy France – to follow the Habsburgs' lead was infinitesimal.

Although western pundits would point to every scrap of evidence of Ottoman decline, when it came to making war the Turks' power to launch an attack was considerably greater than Europe's power to organise resistance. The Emperor Leopold had nothing like the authority of Sultan Mehmed IV to decree war, or to summon an army to rally more or less as ordered to a distant destination. In the crudest possible terms, when the sultan made a call to arms, a hundred thousand men would obey without question; when the Emperor rallied his armed might, he would be lucky if a fifth of that number arrived at the battlefront.

★   ★   ★

As the camp filled up, whole districts of the city and its suburbs, normally thronged with soldiers, were emptying. There was the great barracks besides the Şahzade Mosque, the household cavalry lines just beyond the old Byzantine walls, the arsenals where the cannon and muskets were produced at Tophane, near the Bosporus. In these military communities, traders, shops, even the mosques, all lived indirectly off the salaries paid by the sultan. Each day as detachments left to join the camp, the streets grew strangely silent. Most foreigners saw only the exotic splendour of the Ottoman host and not the elaborate system that underpinned it. Busbecq, in his day, had shrewdly observed both. He noted how the cavalrymen were 'mounted on splendid horses, excellently groomed and gorgeously attired' . . . 'Look at those marvellously handsome dresses of every kind and every colour; time would fail me to tell you how all around is glittering with gold, with silver, with purple, with silk, and with velvet; words cannot convey an adequate idea of that strange and wondrous sight: it was the most beautiful spectacle I ever saw.'[10]

They were an inspiring sight in their silks and brocades, heron's plumes and chain mail. But they were also highly effective in the right circumstances. Most of the cavalry held a fief (timar) like the medieval feudal cavalry of Western Europe or the hussars (husaria) of seventeenth-century Poland. Military service was the duty they owed for their estates, and they were summoned to join the army for a single fighting season. The elite Turkish horsemen were the six regiments of the sultan's permanent palace cavalry (alti-bölük sipahileri), all paid, trained and armed by the Ottoman state. All these heavy cavalry (sipahis) were renowned for their skill with sword, mace or war axe, but the powerful recurved bow was their most devastating weapon. From a distance, like the horsemen of the steppes, aiming and shooting at full gallop, they showered both enemy infantry and cavalry with well targeted arrows that could pierce plate armour. In a hand-to-hand mêlée with western horse, their speed and swordsmanship were deadly. So, while cavalrymen in Western Europe were abandoning their breastplates and helmets, as hand-to-hand fighting became less common, cuirassiers and dragoons facing the Turks along the eastern frontier still fought encased in steel from head to thigh, to protect them from the sipahis' arrows and sabres. In addition to the sipahis were thousands of the dowdy but effective irregular light horse (akincis) who served the sultan for the slaves and booty they might collect, and the allies, notably the horde of Tartars, superb raiders and the terror of the west, led by the Khan of the Crimea.

As remarkable, if less flamboyant than the palace cavalry, were the professional infantry, the famous (or infamous) janissaries. For many in the west, the mere name was sufficient to inspire terror. For two hundred years the corps of janissaries (*ordu*), 'the new troops' first established in the fourteenth century, had been the key to the Ottomans' extraordinary success in war. From the fourteenth century, almost all of them would have shared a common origin. The janissaries were Christian children forcibly recruited (*devshirme*) from the villages of the Balkans, then trained and converted to Islam. The janissary regiments became their family, and the sultan their father and brother. But by 1682, the ranks were filled with the sons and nephews of janissaries eager to gain the lifetime salary and pension. The janissary bore, lifelong, the marks of his status upon his body. If a Christian, circumcised upon enrolment, he became a Muslim. Once trained, the symbol and number of his detachment were tattooed on his right arm and right leg, signifying full admission to the order.[11] Their grim purpose was to identify the bodies of janissaries killed in action, but they also marked those entitled to salaries and rations. Each janissary battalion (*orta*), notionally of three hundred men, was divided into detachments of fifty to seventy janissaries living and eating together as a single unit.

The number in barracks was steadily reducing with a growing minority choosing to marry and live outside with their families. In doing so they sacrificed their claim to bonuses and promotion, but they gained the invaluable right to open businesses and engage in trade. A business run by a janissary had the power of the order standing behind it, and a natural reservoir of comrades as customers. They were becoming an economic as well as a military and political power in the city. Many janissaries prospered as the monastic exclusivity of the order lessened. Promotion was still through the ranks, and sometimes by exceptional courage in battle. There were constant complaints that the highest posts went to favourites of the court, but many ordinary janissaries also rose through talent to senior positions. Over the centuries the corps provided the empire with 79 grand viziers and 36 admirals of the fleet. The sultan himself was symbolically enrolled in the order and tattooed with the number 1.

Exactly how many janissaries and other soldiers were stationed in the capital fluctuated over time. The salary and muster rolls were often illegally enlarged, with corrupt officials living off the proceeds. Fanciful claims that the state supported 200,000 were grossly exaggerated, but probably about a tenth of that number were in and around the capital in 1682. At the heart of the main janissary barracks was a huge drill ground called Et Meydan, Meat Square. Each week, they paraded there in full equipment to practise the prescribed battlefield manoeuvres. Rushes, sudden mass attacks, sword play and archery became second nature, but they also trained with the heavy Turkish flintlock trench muskets, more like the wall-mounted guns on a fortress than lighter weapons used in western armies. Many janissaries were trained as sharpshooters: with the powerful powder charge and much greater range and killing power of their weapons, considerably more accurate than European matchlock firearms, they were a devastating weapon.

We talk of the janissary 'order' as if it were a single, uniform entity. Certainly every individual was taught to be conscious of the honour of his detachment and of the order as a whole, but in reality the strength of the janissaries (and their weakness) was that they were 'bands of brothers', of between ten and fifteen men. You trusted your brother-in-arms, tattooed like you with the emblem of your detachment. That came first; then loyalty to the battalion and its officers; ultimately there was loyalty to more distant figures, like the general (aga) of the janissaries and the sultan himself. But although janissaries would fight with extraordinary courage, they were also intractable if given orders of which they did not approve. They did not give blind, slavish obedience, as every wise janissary officer knew. Much the same could have been said of the veterans of the Roman legions more than a millennium before. Well led, the legions were capable of super-human achievements; but they would perform listlessly if they lost their centurions and decurions. Janissaries were different because they shared not only military bonds but also the exhilaration of a common faith in Islam. They were the warriors of the sultan, but also the inspired soldiers of God, their zeal and fervour encouraged by the Bektashi dervish preachers who were attached to every unit. They had to be won over and cajoled by their commanders, like wild and mettle-some horses: use some stick but also the titbits of honours, rewards and plunder. But ultimately each janissary fought and died as a warrior (gazi) of the True Faith.

Busbecq first saw the famous janissaries in Ottoman-occupied Pest. Their drab appearance came as a surprise to him:

> The dress of these men consists of a robe reaching down to the ankles, while, to cover their heads, they employ a cowl which, by their account, was originally a cloak sleeve, part of which contains the head, while the remainder hangs down and flaps against the neck. On their forehead is placed a silver gilt cone of considerable height, studded with stones of no great value . . . To tell you the truth, if I had not been told beforehand that they were Janissaries, I should, without hesitation, have taken them for members of some order of Turkish monks, or brethren of some Moslem college. Yet these are the famous Janissaries, whose approach inspires terror everywhere.[12]

Most artists, Ottoman or western, depicted the janissaries as dressed in standard, sometimes brightly coloured, uniforms. Janissary officers certainly wore long robes, with brocades and fur trimmings, but the ordinary soldiers' uniforms were the drab wools and felts that Busbecq described: 'nothing very striking in their attire'. But if their clothes were plain, their famous bonnets, with the broad white flap which served to keep the sun off a soldier's neck, were decorated with plumes and crests, 'and here they let their fancy run riot, particularly the veterans who brought up the rear. The plumes which they inserted in their frontlets give the appearance of a moving forest.'[13] But every plume, every badge or decoration, was in fact a mark of honour or long service, or, most prized of all, a distinction granted for bravery. Busbecq obviously saw battle-hardened veterans who had proved their prowess in battle.

By 6 October 1682, the huge encampment was finally complete and crammed with the janissaries and the palace cavalry. A few days later, at the end of the month of Ramadan, the sultan left the Topkapi Palace in procession, preceded by his tuğ held high for all in the streets to see, and took up residence in his war tent. This procession was the final and conclusive sign that the march to war was about to begin.[14] At every stage the elaborate ceremonial was observed and well-informed foreigners had no doubt as to what it portended. The newly arrived Habsburg envoy Count Caprara knew that war against his master, the Emperor Leopold, was being prepared. He had been sent to provide reinforcement to his luckless predecessor, Baron Georg Christoph Kunitz, who had languished in Istanbul since 1680. Kunitz and Caprara sang the same song – the Emperor wanted to prolong the twenty year truce due to expire in 1684 – but no one at the Ottoman court was willing to listen. Yet protocol meant Caprara and Kunitz had no alternative but to accompany the sultan and his army on their march north. At best they might hope to smuggle messages of warning back to Vienna. What Caprara saw and what he understood we know from the diary which his secretary, Giovanni Benaglia, kept of their journey, observing acutely what he and the ambassador saw around them. Kunitz, too, kept a graphic account of his effective captivity.[15]

Westerners often talked wonderingly about the warlike qualities of 'the Turks' and their natural bellicosity. But as the war camp made clear to all who saw it, the real power of the Turks was the serious-ness and extraordinary invention with which they approached the business of a great war. Although battle was a lottery, in Istanbul the process of making war had been reduced to a formula. Of course, no one could control events. Food and fodder would arrive late, guns would get stuck in the mud, bridge building would be delayed by bad weather, supply boats would sink on the often treacherous rivers. But the system was extraordinary in its all-embracing vision. It even calcu-lated how long a janissary's shoes would last before they needed resoling, so that there would be additional cobblers conscripted to carry out repairs when the marching column arrived. Just as the move-able palace was supported by all the trades that served the sultan in the capital, so, too, all the army's supporting services travelled with the troops, or were sent ahead to wait at each night's resting place. Not since the heyday of the Roman empire had war on the frontier been so regulated, planned and organised.[16]

Did these men live up to their fearsome reputation? They were better equipped, better supported and better fed than their future opponents. The janissaries and the palace cavalry were trained profes-sionals, but what distinguished them was how and why they fought. In the Ottoman ranks, among the janissaries (and the *sipahis*), matters were different from the armies that would confront them. Serving and living together for long periods, fiercely loyal to the emblems and badges of their units, strong and hardy fighters, nevertheless they fought as individual warriors. The tales told around the janissary soup

kettles were of heroes, past and present. In their barracks in Istanbul
old soldiers stayed close to their units, and became a living memory
for great deeds in the past. Officers seeking to rouse their men would
evoke that history. Each unit went into battle incited by the music of
the *mehter*, the band which, like the pipers of the Scottish clansmen,
stirred the bellicose spirit of men facing death. Huge kettledrums
thundered, smaller drums crashed out an insistent faster rhythm, and
over all the steady clash of cymbals announced a charge.

The charge was what they talked about in barracks, and what they
had practised on the drill ground. Each man chanted the battle cry in
unison, a single roar rising from thousands of throats growing louder
and louder as they closed with the enemy. As they rushed forward,
muskets were laid aside; bows slung for the last stages of the assault;
each man, a heavy sabre (*kiliç*) or a fearsome Janissary yataghan – a
curved short sword which could lop off a head with a flick of the
wrist – in hand, fixed his gaze upon a foe as he dashed the last few
metres into the enemy line. In those moments each janissary was an
individual bent on killing those he faced. Once launched, his charge
could not be recalled: either it succeeded or it was driven back. The
janissary style of war had evolved over two centuries, changing with
the enemies and battles that they had to fight. In the fourteenth
century, they had been the solid, disciplined heart of the Ottoman
battle line, fighting behind a screen of excitable, expendable auxil-
iaries, or a line of wagons, drawing in the enemy on to their muskets,
spears and swords. In battle they could halt the charge of armoured
knights, then run forward to shatter an enemy in disarray.

But war had changed. Between 1550 and 1600, after the Turks had
taken control of most of Hungary, war increasingly became the slow
business of besieging towns and fortresses in the borderlands between
the Habsburg and Ottoman empires, or in the Kingdom of Poland
further north.[17] The janissaries, together with the Ottoman's
artillerymen and engineers, were evolving to meet these changing
demands of war.[18] In the fifteenth and sixteenth centuries, many of
the notable encounters had been on the battlefield, but by the seventeenth century, in the western theatre of war, most of the conflicts
followed the same pattern. There were relatively few pitched battles
and increasingly each campaign would involve siege and storm of
walled towns, blockhouses called *palanka*, and even modernised

fortresses, built along Western European lines. The janissaries gradually developed some of the specialist skills necessary for this kind of
war. They became what in later centuries would be called assault
battalions, or storm troops. Extraordinary individual courage was
needed to attack over a broken wall or through a ragged breach in
the fortifications, into a hail of enemy fire. Their single task was to
attack and attack again until the objective was taken. Huge bonuses
were paid to those who braved a hail of enemy fire to secure the
breach. Similarly, those who fought underground, in the sepulchral
battles with enemy sappers burrowing into the Turkish tunnels, could
become rich men.

Carefully selected janissaries were trained in the use of hand-thrown
bombs and grenades. The men who put aside their muskets for the
final assault carried a bag of small clay or rough glass spheres filled
with gunpowder. These bombs looked very like large pomegranates –
which gave them their name in Spanish (*granata*) and French (*grenade*)
– with a short fuse protruding like the fruit's stalk. European armies
also used grenades, but they were made with an iron case and contained
less explosive; the Ottoman grenade could be thrown further and each
janissary grenadier could carry more into the mêlée.[19] In the final
moments of the desperate hand-to-hand fighting a hail of Ottoman
grenades could simply blow apart a defensive line. The grenade was
a weapon especially well suited to the janissary style of war. It could
only be used at close quarters, like swords, spears and halberds, and
it brought firepower into the final and most perilous moments of
combat. It was new, but also honourable and traditional; in later years,
grenadiers in western armies were regarded as exceptionally courageous,
simply because they were in such peril, heading an assault against the
heaviest enemy fire.

Western armies were developing in a different direction from the
Ottomans. Where the Ottomans had relied on firepower and field
fortifications to defeat the power of the armoured knights and men-
at-arms, in the west the pikeman with a three- or four-metre spear
had become the master of the infantry battlefield. The thousands of
pikemen in battle never moved above a walking pace; the key to success
was keeping formation and keeping in step. The pike was a weapon
only of use on the battlefield, as a defence against cavalry or used
offensively against other infantry. But learning to use the pike instilled

discipline. As western commanders discovered, a mob of three thousand individuals armed with spears or pikes was very different from three thousand men acting in unison.

In the west the development and spread of printing had made it possible to circulate treatises on the art of war, produced by the thousand, read by amateurs and professionals alike. With the drill book in one hand and an obedient clutch of recruits, it was possible to train adequate pikemen and even musketeers in the space of a few weeks. Teaching a janissary to use the Turkish bow could take years. The skills of the janissaries and the sultan's cavalry adapted to some extent to changing circumstances but they never changed in their essentials. Bravery and skill in arms were the most desirable qualities. In the west, by contrast, discipline and good order became prized above all else: foot soldiers were increasingly trained to manoeuvre to words of command, or drumbeats. Experienced and well-trained western infantry could change direction, unit by unit, move forward, backward, to the side; they could form dense columns or, in a few minutes, long lines.

The long reign of the pikemen with their four-metre spears had ended with the Thirty Years War in 1648 and musketeers were increasingly taking their place. Gradually, western generals had begun to develop tactics that could challenge the dominant power of the Ottomans. The sultan's splendidly arrayed palace cavalry may have been an inspiring sight, but it was less impressive to a trained eye. Like the western infantry, new weapons and equipment had appeared in western armies after 1648. Horsemen were armed with an array of different firearms: pistols, muskets, carbines designed for mounted use. Drab though the Habsburg cuirassiers and dragoons might appear in their black breastplates and open helmets, they gave western horsemen the beginnings of what the Ottomans had long possessed: firepower plus mobility. But they were still not the equal of their adversaries. The *sipahis'* sabres, designed for devastating, slashing cuts, took and kept an edge better than western weapons; *sipahis* took great pride in being able to hack off the points of enemy pikes. They made little use of firearms; some said it was because firing muskets and pistols covered their fine robes with greasy powder marks. But the new Habsburg cavalry, cuirassiers and dragoons were becoming increasingly effective against the Turks, as they took the measure of their foe. They still carried heavy swords for hand-to-hand combat, but their new power really came from the guns which they carried.

Another new device was even more effective against the Ottoman horsemen. Bayonets only came into general use in Europe at the beginning of the eighteenth century, but a rudimentary type was used by the Habsburg infantry much earlier, from the 1640s. This was a long steel shaft with a spear point hinged under the musket barrel. Extended, it would, in theory, keep Ottoman horsemen at least a sword's length away from the musketeer, although it offered much less protection than the longer pikes. But an Italian general in Habsburg service, Raimondo Montecuccoli, encouraged a further development. He turned the traditional *Schweinsfeder*, a short spear used for hunting wild boar, into a musket rest with the addition of a steel hook on which to lay the weapon. In the hands of the musketeer this doubled as a short pike for protection against cavalry as well as making musket fire more accurate. The ultimate defensive measure was the so-called 'Spanish Rider', a solid three-metre beam of timber, with sturdy mounts at each end and slotted to take the *Schweinsfeder* pointing forward at 30 and 45 degree angles. Rapidly assembled, they became a freestanding, impenetrable barrier of sharp spikes: no horse would charge such an obvious danger. For centuries archers had hammered sharpened stakes into the ground to guard themselves against a cavalry charge, but this security came at the price of complete immobility. Only the protection of the long pikes had allowed them some power of manoeuvre. Now, for the first time, musketeers could protect their flanks against an Ottoman cavalry charge by deploying these ancestors of the barbed wire entanglements which would transform the battlefield centuries later.[20]

But nothing could protect the westerners from the Turks' arrow fire. Their bows had a much longer range than any musket: the Ottoman record for an arrow shot was 800 metres. For most purposes in the 1680s, the bow was still a better weapon than any gun, but it demanded long training and constant practice to become expert. It required great strength to draw the bow string, and constant control to achieve accuracy, and cavalry bowmen had to manage their horses at full gallop by pressure of their knees alone. In western armies, raw recruits could be trained to become expert infantry musketeers in a space of a few weeks. But that was their only skill. The best of the

Ottoman infantry were astonishingly versatile. They could fight with sword, spear, yataghan, bow or musket. Each janissary would choose his favourite weapons from the common armoury: when they paraded, there was no uniformity of equipment nor did they march in step like western soldiers. The janissaries had limited skills of manoeuvre: they would rush forward in attack, but only in the time-honoured fashion.

Well led and well motivated, despite all rumours of their 'decline' the janissary corps was still formidable, in the right circumstances. But no Ottoman commander could control or direct his janissaries in the way that a western general could command his infantry. For the Ottomans as the seventeenth century was drawing towards its close the battlefield was increasingly alien and unfamiliar territory. The old verities had been overturned: the janissary hero, first into the breach, first over the wall, was still the acme, but he was becoming increasingly irrelevant in the new art of war.

★   ★   ★

A few reliable eyewitnesses provided Europe with its knowledge of the armed might of the 'dreadful or dangerous' Turk.[21] From the last quarter of the sixteenth century there was a steady flow of books, pamphlets and newsletters on the Ottomans, but most of them written by authors who worked largely from hearsay. One cannibalised another, spreading the same tales and stories, and often pictures, across territorial and linguistic borders. Works in Latin could be read everywhere by the educated, and in continental Europe were often elaborately illustrated. Thus the French antiquarian (and accomplished draughtsman) Jean-Jacques Boissard's *Lives and Portraits of the Turkish Sultans* (*Vitae et Icones Sultanorum Turcicorum*) could be found on scholars' bookshelves across Europe. It was naturally to Boissard's work that the English pedagogue Richard Knolles turned when writing his *Generall Historie of the Turkes*, published for a much wider audience (in English rather than Latin), in 1603. But Boissard in turn had based much of his book on a number of earlier authors and artists. Unreliable and frequently contradictory, these were sometimes the best sources available; and the very few eyewitness accounts were trusted even more slavishly.

In more than a century only three writers on the Ottoman east combined literary ability with an acute sense of observation, and a long acquaintance with this strange and often baffling world. All three were more than travellers passing through; their stay was measured in years not months or days. They were expatriates whose lives were changed radically by their long residence among the Turks.[22] Each of them gained renown across Europe for their writings on the Ottomans, published in many editions and translations. The longest lasting has already made an appearance: Ogier Ghislain de Busbecq, the acknowledged natural son of the Lord of Busbecq, born in Flanders in 1520 or 1521 at his father's castle close to the French border. He was his father's favourite child, but bastardy made his social position ambivalent. Busbecq escaped its constraints largely by his drive and forceful intellect. He served the Holy Roman Emperor on many minor missions, so he was a natural choice as a Habsburg imperial emissary to the court of Sultan Suleiman I. It was also a hardship post: his predecessors had been terrorised, imprisoned and threatened with a worse fate.[23]

Busbecq's *Letters of the Turkish Embassy* was a European bestseller. It appeared in Latin, French, German, Dutch and Spanish, and, notably, in English. Often other writers simply took Busbecq's observations and paraded them as their own knowledge. Three hundred years after his stay in Istanbul, his work was still in use as an accurate and contemporary source, and it remains in print to this day.[24] There is an earthy freshness to Busbecq's *Letters*, all written to Nicholas Michault, a fellow imperial diplomat and a friend from his student days in Venice. He seems to have made few changes to his original drafts when they were published but he was plainly impatient with those in the west mistaking the nature of the Ottomans; Busbecq emphasised what his fellow Christians should learn from them.

Busbecq's letters present a man of invincible curiosity who, kept under effective house arrest, filled his courtyards and stables with a menagerie, which he studied and observed. Busbecq was greedy for sensation, keen to see this new and exotic eastern world. He wrote ruefully to Michault, who had asked about what he saw in the great city: 'I do not generally do so unless I have dispatches from the Emperor for presentation to the Sultan, or instructions to protest against the ravages and malpractices of the Turkish garrisons. If I wished from time to time to take a ride through the city with my custodian, permission would probably not be refused . . . What I enjoy is the country and the fields, not the city – especially a city which is almost falling to pieces, and of whose former glory nothing remains except its splendid position.' Busbecq observed minutely, whether it was flowers and plants, scenery or human beings. His letters, in all their many editions, were unadorned by engravings and devoid of censorious comment. The plainness of his texts is odd, because he had brought with him in his ambassadorial entourage a talented young Danish artist, Melchior Lorck (Lorichs), who was able to move about freely while his master was constrained by the demands of protocol. The drawings and engravings that he produced eventually became a book, published posthumously in 1626; both echoed Busbecq's pen portraits, but also transmuted them into something more exotic. Lorck used the sights of Istanbul as he would models in a studio. He depicted a world of objects frozen in time, whether they were mosques, palaces, princes, sultans or ordinary people.[25]

Another duo had preceded Busbecq and Lorck in the city. It is almost inconceivable that Busbecq had not read Nicolas de Nicolay's depiction of the Ottoman world, published in Lyons in 1567.[26] The artist was born in the Dauphiné in south-eastern France in 1517. In 1551 the French king Henri II had sent his ambassador of ten years' standing, the Count of Aramont, back to the court of Suleiman with an enlarged retinue. In its ranks was France's official mapmaker and draughtsman, Nicolas de Nicolay.[27] From the age of twenty-five he had spent his life as a mercenary soldier-cum-traveller, journeying and warring from the Baltic in the north to Greece in the east. Eventually, it was his self-taught skill as a draughtsman that turned his career to mapmaking and took him on the embassy to the Ottoman world. Nicolay was sent, in effect, as a kind of spy. He was required to draw the ports and landmarks that they passed on the voyage out, and in particular the approaches and shore defences to Istanbul. Unofficially, he sketched everything else that came under his gaze. After his stay in the east ended in 1555 there were further journeys and more than a decade passed before, in 1567–8, he published an account of his travels to the east, complete with more than sixty engravings of costumes and some scenes from local life.

Nicolay freely admitted when his illustrations were not true to life. The images of women, like the 'great lady and wife unto the Great Turk' or a 'Gentlewoman of the Turks, being within her house' were certainly not what they seemed. He described how a palace eunuch from Ragusa, 'a man of great discretion and a lover of virtue', bought some suitable clothes from the market, dressed up two prostitutes and the artist drew his imaginary great ladies. Much of what he described was what he saw with his own eyes, like the famous wrestlers ('as I have seen them in Constantinople') but much was at second hand.[28] Some was pure imagination, like two men wearing vaguely Roman styles of dress, or pilgrims to Mecca, carrying distinctly western fringed flags.[29]

Once he described his model in detail. A delly (*deli*) was a daredevil Balkan light horseman, and Nicolay said that he saw his first *deli* 'in Adrianople, being then with the Lord of Aramont, in the house of Rustum Pasha, to whom the said Deli was retainer, who not only at my request but also in the hope of some present, did follow us to our lodging'. His appearance was remarkable: 'his doublet and his long hose . . . were of the skin of a young bear, with the hair outward. Upon his head he had a long cape after the Polish or Georgian fashion, hanging down over one of his shoulders made of leopard's skin well spotted, and over the same before the forehead for to show more fearful, was fastened a long tail of an eagle, and the two wings nailed upon the target.' Nicolay asked where he was from and the dragoman translated that he was Serbian but his grandfather was 'a descendant of the Parthians' and, although he pretended to be a Muslim, 'yet was he from his birth of heart and will a Christian, and the better to make me believe it he said in the vulgar Greek . . . the Lord's prayer, the salutation of the Angel and the symbol of the Apostle. Furthermore I asked him why he did apparel himself so strangely and with such great feathers, his answer was that it was to appear to his enemies the more furious and fearful. And as for the feathers, the custom among his people that none other was permitted to wear them as had made some memorable proof [of their valour] . . . the true ornament of a valiant man of war.'[30] This perfectly describes his 'pretty Delly'.

What was real and what was imagined in Nicolay's *Navigations*? It is very hard to be sure, and to most readers its barbaric extravagance seemed unquestionably correct. They expected nothing less. It was an instant success, and Italian, French and English translations quickly followed, with each edition using the complete set (and sometimes some additions) in Nicolay's original portfolio. The poses and types that he published to illustrate the eastern costumes of his own day became the model for many later engravings and woodcuts.[31] But Nicolay, like Melchior Lorck, was entranced with the bizarre, because to his artist's eye they produced more powerful and appealing images. Strange and unusual stories had a similar appeal, so he listened to fanciful tales about the sexual practices of the Persians, the grotesque self-mutilations of the Calenderi or the lesbian excesses aroused by the steamy heat of the Turkish bath (*hamam*). It was the same eager credulity that had caused travellers in earlier centuries to report anthropophagi, or men with heads like dogs.

The third eyewitness was very different from both Busbecq and Nicolay. Paul Rycaut was the son of a successful Huguenot merchant who had left Antwerp for London in about 1600. Peter Rycaut made a fortune in trading with Italy and the western Mediterranean, and settled on the proceeds in English society. Knighted, he supported King Charles I and made large loans to the Royalist cause during the Civil War. After the king's defeat, the new republican government forced him to leave the country. Paul, born in 1629, was the youngest of his ten sons, educated at Cambridge and at the university of Alcala de Henares in Spain, a result of his father's extensive connections with the Spanish crown. He travelled in Italy, again using the extensive Rycaut network of connections, until he joined the court of the exiled Charles II in Brussels. When the king was restored in 1660, the young Rycaut became secretary to the Earl of Winchilsea who was being sent as ambassador to Constantinople.

He was thirty-two years old when he came to the Ottoman empire and for the next forty years it remained central to his livelihood, reputation and interests.[32] In all he spent seventeen years living first in Istanbul and, from 1667, as the English consul in Smyrna, a main port for the English trade with Anatolia and the Levant. He began the book in Istanbul, and read much of it aloud, he tells us, to the ambassador. His intention was to write a scientific study, based on the best available sources, read and revised by those with expert knowledge. He tells his readers, 'I present here a true system or model of the Turkish Government and Religion; not in the same manner as certain ingenious travellers have done, who have set down their observations as they have obviously occurred in their journey; which being collected for the most part from relations [stories told to them] and discourses of such who casually intervene in the company of passengers, are consequently subject to many errors and mistakes.'[33]

Rycaut, by contrast, five years resident in 'the Imperial City', with 'constant access and practise with the Chief Ministers of State' can 'penetrate farther into the Mysteries of this Politie, which appear so strange and barbarous to us, than hasty Travellers could do, who are forced to content themselves with a superficial knowledge'. His self-promotion gained him admission to the Royal Society, and a lifelong reputation as the expert on all matters Ottoman. He did indeed, as he says, 'gain a familiarity and appearance of friendship'. He told his patron, Lord Arlington, that the Turks were 'men of the same composition with us, [who] cannot be so savage and rude as they are generally described'.[34]

And yet sometimes they *were* 'savage and rude', a mystery he could not fathom. In the end, Rycaut was baffled by the Ottoman world he had described, concluding by thanking God that his sovereign was King Charles II, and 'thanking God [to be born] in a country the most free and just in all the world; and a subject to the most indulgent, the most gracious of all the Princes of the Universe'. Like the Ottoman pashas and viziers on whom he had depended, he too had to flatter his sovereign in the hope of preferment, just as they did their sultan. And, like them, he was disappointed. Like them, he had lived in perilous times. His father's wealth had almost vanished in England's political revolution; he had wandered in exile. Like Busbecq and Nicolay before him, his account was tinged by his own memories: the illegitimate Busbecq, the soldier of fortune Nicolay, and the first-generation Englishman all gained their reputations from their encounters with the Ottomans. All found, as Rycaut suggested, a common humanity, and at the same time a fearsome and alien nation.

These three expatriates were the closest Europe in the sixteenth and seventeenth centuries came to understanding the Ottoman world. They described a state that had conquered lands that were formerly ruled by Christian sovereigns, that dominated the trade with Asia, whose corsairs even raided the coasts of Atlantic Europe, and whose savage attacks struck as far west as Linz on the borders of Germany. They looked at the military power of the Turk, weighed its strengths and weaknesses, but still saw a most dangerous enemy.

They were right, because the Ottomans challenged the whole of

Europe: as a military power, as a political force and as a competing religious faith. The last is obvious and, in the seventeenth century, all-pervasive. Only a few countries, however, faced all three challenges; some, like France and Sweden, even saw the merit of a good relationship with the Ottomans, on the principle that 'my enemy's enemy is my friend'. The French were locked in a desperate struggle with the Habsburgs that had begun in the early sixteenth century; while the Swedes were battling the Russian czars for dominance in the Baltic, supporting the Turks could be a cheap and convenient way of hurting a mortal foe. England and the Netherlands both had trading interests in the Mediterranean, which were never easy to manage with the imperious Ottoman authorities. There was no one, single, simple European response to the Turk, yet even those who were not outright enemies still regarded the Ottomans with trepidation.[35]

Looking back over three centuries to the events of 1682 and to the years that followed, it is immensely hard to understand the Ottoman state, its intentions and its motives. Its inner political life was at least as complicated as its western competitors', and the stakes were higher. Failed or unpopular statesmen would still pay with their heads for failure, as they had at the English court of Henry VIII. But this fate was not inevitable. Mehmed Köprülü came back from exile in 1656 to establish a dynasty of Grand Viziers that lasted well into the eighteenth century. The Ottoman empire regularly experienced political purges, periods of mob rule, regional revolt, military rebellion, assassinations and political murder until the very end of Ottoman monarchy in the twentieth century. There was no contemporary parallel, no state in the western world so powerful, with such a complex bureaucratic structure, governed through so ruthless and untrammelled an autocracy, and eliciting such all-pervasive fear.[36]

2

Turks and Tartars

The sultan did not stay long in the vast encampment outside Istanbul. The day after taking up residence, Mehmed IV, his court and thousands of his personal guards set out for the palace at Edirne, 150 miles north-west of the capital. The cavalcade moved slowly to take advantage of the splendid hunting available on the road into Thrace. He had neither the desire nor the need to make haste. War could not begin before the snows melted the following spring, and, in any event, the practice of war held little attraction for him. As the sultan's stately cavalcade travelled north, the main body of the janissaries, the gunners and the engineers remained behind in camp outside Istanbul, waiting for the last supplies. It was a war by timetable, but with the clock running at half-speed.

But for the chase, Mehmed IV's life was devoid of novelty and excitement. By the autumn of 1682 he was forty, and had been Sultan of Sultans, Khan of Khans, Commander of the Faithful since he was seven. Only Suleiman I 'the Lawgiver', a century before, had ruled longer. His long survival was remarkable because he had succeeded in a situation of great political turmoil. His father, Ibrahim 'the Mad', it was universally acknowledged, had been unfit to occupy the throne. Few sultans lived up to their reputation for extravagant lust that so gratified the lubricious imaginations of western writers, but Ibrahim had been an exception. Tempted by his mother, who feared he would never father a son, he was schooled into satyriasis and wild sensual fantasies. While it is hard to believe some of the stories told of the

Ottoman rulers, in Ibrahim's case many were probably true. He was deposed and then murdered, with particular brutality, in 1648. Mehmed IV succeeded him, briefly under the regency of his fearsome grandmother, and after her murder his mother Khadija Turhan Hatice Sultan became regent in her place.[1] Few could have anticipated that he would reign for almost forty years.

From early childhood, Mehmed IV was mesmerised by his heroic predecessors, foremost among them his uncle, Murad IV, whose military exploits still resonated in the popular memory. The historian Naima later described Murad as an archetypical warrior-hero, leaving the capital for the Baghdad campaign, riding 'a horse like a dragon' and wearing 'an iron helmet with over it a red turban'. A portrait showed him riding to war in the east with a jewelled dagger at his waist, his bow and quiver, and a fur mantle over his shoulders. His two great victories – the siege and capture of Erivan (1635) and Baghdad (1638) – were celebrated by two magnificent kiosks built in the gardens of the Topkapi Palace. Two years later Murad was dead, but his image lived on. His nephew had also been blessed – or cursed – with a resonant name, that of his great ancestor Mehmed II, the conqueror of Constantinople in 1453. Like Miguel de Cervantes' *Don Quijote*, 'his leisure hours, which engrossed the greatest part of the year, addicted him to the reading of books of chivalry'.[2]

The Topkapi's treasury was filled with precious books. The illustrated histories of the dynasty, produced by the imperial studio, from the reigns of Suleiman I and his son Selim II between 1520 and 1574, celebrated the achievements of the family from the founding father, Osman, and on through the centuries. Suleiman's triumphs were displayed in *The Book of Suleiman* (*Süleymanname*), from his accession to his final battle before the citadel at Szigetvár in Hungary. The succession of these great illuminated books, filled with miniatures as dazzling as those of the greatest western manuscripts, told a graphic story of Ottoman triumph. The figures of janissaries and cavalry, sieges and battles, filled the impressionable young mind of Mehmed. Not every sultan could be a Mehmed II, a Suleiman or a Murad IV; but the warrior role was considered particularly becoming to an Ottoman ruler.[3]

Constantinople or Istanbul – both names were used – is always seen as the epitome of the Ottoman identity, and the great palace of Topkapi had been built by Mehmed II 'the Conqueror' on empty waste ground behind the Byzantine Church of the Holy Wisdom, renamed as the Mosque of Aya Sofia. This point of the promontory was potentially the grandest space in the city, looking out across the Bosporus towards the Asian shore. Nowhere else in Constantinople had the sense of distant hills, trees and gardens that was so enticing at Edirne. It was called the 'new palace', designed to be used in the summer heat because the first palace Mehmed had built in the heart of the city, cramped behind high walls, was stifling and uncomfortable in both summer and winter. Topkapi was built by January 1479 and Mehmed II, in great pain from a suppurating abscess on his leg, spent his convalescence turning its innermost area into a series of secret gardens, which he designed and cultivated personally. While the outer part of the palace was a grandiose public space, the inner, private space was a park entirely separated from any sense of the city. In its innermost recess the loudest sound was birdsong, not the clamour of the city streets.[4] The sultan attempted to replicate the delights of Edirne at the heart of imperial power; he was born there in 1432 and it was his childhood home. But while Topkapi has survived, Edirne is now only a phantom. The palace of Edirne was damaged first by fire in 1745 and then by earthquake in 1751. It was then almost destroyed in a battle to prevent Russian occupation in 1878–9. All that has survived are a few grand buildings. We can now only see the Ottomans largely in terms of their urban, Istanbul, incarnation.

The brief and meteoric military career of Murad IV had been only a brief respite in the slow decay of the Ottoman political system, which westerners thought would become permanent. Palace intrigues, incapable sultans and provincial rebellions gave the impression that the empire would collapse and fragment. But the structure proved more resilient than anyone imagined. However, its revival came not from a new Suleiman I or a Mehmed the Conqueror, but through a political dynasty of Grand Viziers, the Köprülü. Unlike Japan, where the imperial family was also isolated, and rendered impotent with the installation of the Togukawa shogunate in 1603, in Istanbul the Ottoman dynasty still remained central to the political system after 1656.

An elderly pasha, Mehmed Köprülü, living quietly in effective retirement in provincial Anatolia, was unexpectedly brought back to the capital under the patronage of the Queen Mother to save her son Mehmed IV from disaster. War – the traditional rallying cry – gave the new Grand Vizier the sanction to purge his enemies. In four years the military system was revitalised, and he become adept at using the dynamic symbolism of the young sultan's persona. After the Köprülü had arranged the slaughter of a leading Anatolian rebel, Abaza Hasan, and his supporters, and the dispatch of their severed heads, skinned and stuffed solid with straw, to the capital, the triumphant Mehmed Köprülü quickly planned a slow ceremonial progress by the sultan into the rebel heartland, to the old capital of Bursa.[5] There Sultan Mehmed IV ostentatiously visited the tombs of his distant ancestors. In the evening at Bursa he sat enthroned beside the mantle of the Prophet Mohammad, brought from the treasury in the Topkapi Palace. Parties of officials and leading citizens came to pay their respects to the holy relic and to the human embodiment of the House of Osman, and its awesome authority. The message was stark. The sultan was still a minor but the power he embodied could not be challenged or defeated.[6]

However, there had to be a careful balance between debasing the currency of the sultan's august presence and making him invisible within the palace. Fazil Ahmed Köprülü, the second and most successful of the Köprülü Grand Viziers, held on to power at his father's death in 1661. He accepted Mehmed's preference for Edirne over Istanbul, for he found it useful to keep his master well away from the plots and politicking of the capital while he was on campaign. But like his father he insisted that the sultan fulfilled his emblematic duties. The sultan's participation in war could be purely symbolic: in 1663, at the age of twenty-one, Mehmed IV had 'led' his armies north, but only as far as the summer palace at Edirne, where he then commissioned Fazil Ahmed Köprulu as his field commander while he stayed to enjoy the hunting. This was fortunate because the campaign failed in all its main objectives, and the army was trounced by the small Habsburg force at the Battle of St Gotthard (1664). But this had little impact upon the sultan.

Mehmed's self-image was of a manly, energetic ruler, rarely out of the saddle. He was frenetically active, as his nickname, 'the Hunter' (Avci), indicates. This is often taken to suggest that he shamefully neglected his official duties, but the chase, among the Ottomans as in Europe, was a kind of warfare, displaying the skills of riding, marksmanship and courage. But pursuing stags, shooting wolves from horseback or even hunting bear would never earn him the epithet 'Conqueror' accorded to Sultan Murad IV for capturing Baghdad, or 'Conqueror of Eger' given (with much less reason) to the last sultan – Mehmed III – to march into Europe, in 1596.[7] Mehmed IV yearned for a great triumph on the scale of his ancestors' achievements.

In the autumn of 1665, after the new vizier's first major campaign in Hungary, he took the sultan on a second progress, with the whole court, to inspect the fortifications of the Dardanelles, built at the expense of Mehmed's mother, Turhan. This presented the eloquent symbolism of the dynasty protecting the lands and peoples of the Sublime State (*Devlet i Aliye*) against the infidel Venetians, whose fleet had blockaded the capital in 1648 and 1656, from its own pocket. It also drew attention away from the defeat of the previous year. When Mehmed IV had safely returned to Edirne, the Grand Vizier set out to embark with the army at Negroponte (Euboea) for an attack on the Venetian strongholds in Crete, while at Edirne the sultan hunted by day and in the evening listened to his court historian telling the stories of his ancestors' military triumphs.

The campaign in Crete was a success, redeeming the failure at St Gotthard. As Mehmed IV received reports of the Siege of Candia, his yearning to participate grew stronger. The campaign moved steadily towards a triumphant conclusion, and, steeling himself to a decision, in the spring of 1669 he resolved to go to the war. News of the fall of the last Venetian fortress – Iraklion – arrived just as he was about to embark.[8] Mehmed IV returned to Edirne having never set foot on Crete but the campaign was nonetheless designated as being *led by the sultan*, a convenient political fiction. Grand Vizier Fazil Ahmed Pasha came back to the capital in 1670, crowned with glory. He had ended the siege of the Venetian stronghold of Candia, which had resisted for twenty-two years, with an Ottoman triumph; within a year he was planning a new campaign, this time in the far north, beyond the River Dniester.

This time Sultan Mehmed IV was determined to participate in person. In the 1672 campaign, he travelled with the army to the battle-front, like his warrior avatars, and took his elder son, Mustafa, with him. As in Crete every objective was achieved. The walled town of Kamenets, garrisoned by the Kingdom of Poland, yielded after a short siege and bombardment of nine days. The keys of the city were surrendered to

Fazil Ahmed, and Sultan Mehmed IV entered the gates of Kamenets on the Friday after the cession, to be hailed as *gazi*, a warrior sultan, and to attend Friday prayers in the Catholic Cathedral of St Peter and St Paul, hurriedly renamed the Sultan Mehmed Cami. The parallels with Sultan Mehmed II's victory in 1453 – where 'the Conqueror' took possession of the great church of Hagia Sophia and made it into a mosque – were self-evident. The return to the south, however, showed a less glorious face of war.

A French contemporary wrote: 'The Ottoman court arrived the Eighth of December 1672 at Adrianople [Edirne] after a painful march of forty-five days whereon died a great many men and beasts, caused by the rigour of the season, the scarceness of provisions and bad ways, over which it was almost impossible to draw the cannon, in manners, that if the Poles, accustomed to the fatigue of cold and water, had been in a condition to follow those conquerors, it could not have been very difficult to have had their revenge on 'em . . .'⁹ Nevertheless it had been a victory, and Mehmed ordered a celebration in every town and city. 'All the empire was in a great joy for the news of his progress . . . commanding the governors to order a public festival of three days and three nights, to adorn and decorate the streets, the ports, and shops, the ways, and public places, to testify by their discharge of artillery and making of bonfires, a universal joy.'¹⁰

On 3 November 1676 Fazil Ahmed Pasha died suddenly and un-expectedly on the road from Istanbul to Edirne. He habitually drank excessively, and this indulgence ultimately brought on a stroke and paralysis. However, after twenty years of Köprülü family dominance, there was no question about his successor as Grand Vizier. His adopted brother Kara Mustafa was already a favourite of the sultan and the chosen candidate of all the Köprülüs. The new Grand Vizier imme-diately set out to continue the campaign Fazil Ahmed had planned against the Russians. Kara Mustafa lacked his adopted brother's sure political touch and his instinct for careful and meticulous planning. He followed his father's example – rule through fear and harsh punish-ment – to the letter, but he failed to appreciate the subtle political sense of the first Köprülü, who worked hard to build a connection that ran beyond the family. Under the command of a wiser head and a better planner, he had been a courageous and competent subordinate. But he was a poor leader. His first campaign in command did not run to plan: in 1677 he failed to achieve his objectives and retreated. But he brought the army back in the following year and this time made no mistake. The Ottomans captured the key Ukrainian town of Chyryen which the Russians had occupied. Now he began to scheme how to redeem the defeat of 1664 by the Habsburgs, the only major failure in his family's long record of success

★ ★ ★

The ceremonies of war which had began on the Çyrpeci Meadow now moved to Edirne, which was the first rallying point for war against the Christian infidel. But the sultan had already lost any appetite for the battlefield. In September 1682 he had no intention of repeating the uncomfortable experience of ten years before, preferring a winter and perhaps a spring and summer in his paradise garden.[11] Edirne had been the initial Ottoman seat of power (*Dar ul-Mulk*) in Europe, and it continued to play a special role in the Turks' European wars of conquest. The palace, built by Sultan Murad II in 1417, was the first grand structure of the Ottomans in Europe.[12] Murad's son, Mehmed II, the conqueror of Constantinople, had enlarged it as did his great-grandson Suleiman I, called 'the Magnificent' by the West. The gardens at Topkapi along the shores of the Sea of Marmara with its cool glades and garden buildings were a pale imitation of Edirne. There Busbecq saw 'a garden full of tulips on a broad meadow of fertile soil, encompassed by the River Tunca. On one side a grove, ornamented with willows, plane-trees, cypress, poplar, and elm trees, rearing their heads towards the sky ... this grove was filled to overflowing with all kinds of wild animals and birds.' Above it all, like a turret, towered the seven storeys of the Cihannüma Kasir; on the top floor an arcaded penthouse surrounding a scented pool overlooked the pleasure grounds, and beyond to the three rivers and the dark forests of the palace grounds.

Many Ottoman sultans had an ambivalent relationship with Istanbul. The city beyond the palace gates was increasingly Ottomanised, dominated by its great mosques and other state buildings. But its Byzantine setting was always evident. If the sultan rode out of the towering Gate of Salutation, to his right the great mosque of Aya Sofia, despite its Muslim appendages, was still the ancient Hagia Sophia, the Christian Church of the Holy Wisdom. Riding in procession across the ancient Hippodrome to the mosques founded by Mehmed 'the Conqueror', by Suleiman I and by Selim II, was to journey through a Roman and not a Turcic past.

Edirne spoke to a different element in their collective character.[13] It represented the essence of being Ottoman, of near limitless space, the fast-flowing rivers, the vista stretching to the distant mountains. For Mehmed IV in particular the palace at Edirne became his greatest source of pleasure. Being *Avci*, 'the Hunter', was one consuming passion that he could indulge there, but making gardens was another. The famous Ottoman traveller Evliya Çelebi, who had journeyed through Persia, North Africa, Austria and the Ottoman lands, described it in lyrical terms; he had seen nothing like it in all his wanderings: 'This shady garden was a delight to the eyes of Sultan Mehmed Han . . . words are not enough to describe it, but we have tried our poor best to portray a mere drop in the ocean of its wonders.' The gardens of Edirne Bahçesi 'cannot be equalled by any other garden on earth, not even that in the imperial city of Vienna'.

The sultan, as Evliya explained, unsurprisingly spent most of his time in Edirne, sending forth the chief commanders to conquer the land of Transylvania (Erdel), the strongly fortified castle of Uyvar (today Nové Zámky) in the Habsburg territories and Candia on the island of Crete. At his order from Edirne, eighty-one towns and fortresses in Hungary and Poland were conquered. This was precisely Mehmed's intention in 1682. He would spend the winter at Edirne, where his troops would join him; then the sultan and his ever-victorious army would advance to the Danube frontier at Belgrade, where he would hand over command in the field to the Grand Vizier, who would lead the soldiers north-west into Hungary, while Mehmed, after an interval, would move back to Edirne, which would become once again his personal command post.

There he could wage war from the pavilion and terraced garden his mother, Hatice Sultan, had built for him on a hill overlooking the river, in celebration of his twentieth birthday. On her orders rare roses had been planted on the lower terrace while the upper terrace, Dolmabahçe, was filled with white jasmine. The scent of the roses would fill the air during the day while, as dusk fell, the irresistible jasmine would perfume the air. The gift delighted Mehmed, who immediately ordered climbing jasmine to be planted to cover the walls, and pine trees brought from the nearby forests to add a more pungent note. His favourite greyhounds liveried in 'golden brocades and other costly cloths . . . their paws and tails dyed red and yellow' padded after him through the palace grounds.[14]

Everything about Edirne was contrived for his greater pleasure, both sensual and intellectual. Here he was free from the rigid formality of Topkapi; here he could indulge his impulses. On a momentary whim, he would decide to go coursing with a few companions for small game in the palace grounds, or to hunt stags in the woodland across the river. 'Here in this wonderful garden, our revered Sultan meets with ten thousand expert mounted and armed soldiers from among his private household with their warhorses for hunting or war.'[15] By 1682 Mehmed IV no longer had the same impatient energy as in his youth. When he had campaigned a decade before in person, it was on his Grand Vizier's advice. In 1682, Kara Mustafa, like any good courtier, sensed the sultan's disinclination. He made it plain that he did not expect the ruler to expose his person to the rigours of warfare. Not only was this precisely what the sultan wished to hear, but it would also give the Grand Vizier a free hand which the sultan's presence would only have held back.

In practice, very few sultans had the qualities or the stamina of an effective war leader; even fewer had much inclination for the privations of a campaign. But in 1682 Mehmed IV had agreed to do a little more than simply take up a symbolic residence for a few days in the war camp outside the city walls, and then return to the palace once his household troops had departed for the front. He would be the supreme commander as far as the Danube, and then, at the White Castle of Belgrade, the Grand Vizier would be handed authority by the sultan, in the time honoured terms and with the symbols of authority: the holy banner of the Prophet and the decree of command. All on the campaign were thereafter commanded 'to treat his [the commander's] every word as if it had issued forth in personal audience from my own [the sultan's] pearl-dispensing tongue forming part of my own auspicious utterances'.[16]

In the ceremonial of war, the Ottomans still followed the traditions of their ancestors. A supreme field commander (serasker) entrusted with the war banner could not be countermanded except by the sultan himself. Not that the battlefield commander was a completely free agent, for failure would bring disgrace, dismissal or even death. But he was, by the ruler's delegation, from that moment onwards at the apex of a military system that had delivered well-trained professional soldiers, feudal heavy cavalry, provisions, fodder, clothing and weapons to the front, and then sustained the army in the field. In the tradition of the steppe, he would exercise the power of life and death over all his subordinates, and, although supposed to plan tactics and strategy with them, could not easily be questioned or constrained. It was a cruel system, where failure often meant not merely demotion but decapitation. Yet it was not irrational.

The Ottoman system was designed around the principle of self-interest built with a well-calculated system of bonuses and promotions to provide incentives. Success in war could bring riches and honour beyond measure, rather as prize money was the foundation of many a British sea captain's fortune. Failure in war brought little or nothing. This spirit of chance ran from the very top to the bottom of the system. Sultans who failed to be generous might be deposed or murdered. A humble soldier, fighting for a feeble commander, would be lucky to return home alive. Some soldiers were motivated by religious zeal, keen to battle with the infidels, but universally they hoped to secure their own position and that of their families for the future. Most prized, therefore, were the battlefield promotions for supreme courage that provided a lifetime pension after military service was completed; the soldiers fought primarily for money and the heady elation of victory.

*   *   *

While the sultan and his entourage rode towards Edirne, and the troops remaining in the camp outside the walls prepared to follow, the invisible heart of the Ottoman system pumped steadily inside the capital. The professional troops who had assembled at Istanbul were only a fraction of the array that would ultimately confront the enemy: gathering an army sufficient for war in the west would call on resources from many parts of the empire, and beyond. Vast numbers of irregular foot soldiers and feudal cavalry would ultimately swell its ranks. Immediately after the formal decision for war was taken, teams of scribes and clerks began working at high pressure, writing orders and instructions to distant provinces to call them all to the battle. The empire was ruled through this paperwork and through the fear it inspired. Failure to comply with the sultan's command brought death; no provincial pasha would dare to act without written orders; but once the decree arrived matters would move forward with remarkable speed. The provincial governor transmitted the fear of the sultan's wrath to his subordinates, and so on down the line. Soon, in regions as far away as Syria and Baghdad, the feudal levies (timars) were summoned to gather in each district, and then they would ride en masse to the larger towns. Within weeks the roads of the Asian provinces were filled with columns of riders heading towards Istanbul, and then onward to Belgrade, although the campaign would only begin in the following spring. In the capital the Tophane gun factory geared up to increase its output, once the fresh supplies of the fuel wood and ores needed for casting arrived, as well as the labourers needed to haul and carry the half-bored barrels. Everything depended on the 'men of the pen' writing their orders.

The turbaned scribes, sitting cross-legged in long rows in the offices of the palace, were an assembly line producing the decrees that galvanised the dormant military machine into action. Soon even the sleepiest Balkan towns were roused by the arrival of the sultan's messengers delivering orders, then changing horses, and then riding hard north-west with fresh instructions to the distant Hungarian cities and fortresses which would be the base for military operations the following year. The pasha of Buda, far away up the Danube, was responsible for gathering local troops, organising depots full of food on the line of march, securing large supplies of gunpowder and employing spies to gather up-to-date intelligence of the enemy's state of readiness.[17] It was a well-tested mechanism which could deliver an army of perhaps 100,000 men to the battlefront, plus the resources to support them. In a great war this elaborate military machine gave the Ottomans many advantages over any of their opponents, but it could not guarantee success.

Like the classical Roman system of war, victory depended less on superior generalship than on following a well-tested traditional formula. Every aspect of war was governed by precedent. Ottoman siegecraft depended not on firepower but on endless teams of sturdy diggers, who would continue even under heavy fire. Ottoman infantry attacks rarely involved manoeuvre or formation, but were instead a headlong assault on an enemy reeling under a shower of arrows, musketry, archery or artillery fire. Making these simple tactics work depended on the greatest possible commitment from every individual, and here, too, there were well-tried methods of sustaining and raising morale. An Ottoman military leader needed to win and sustain the confidence of his troops. For the most part they would follow his orders, although mutiny was not unknown. But he also needed to woo and flatter them, to grease their palms with silver, to speak well of their courage and endurance. A *serasker* could command his troops into action and they would fight for him; but only a great leader could inspire them beyond the normal limits of courage and endurance.

The Grand Vizier Kara Mustafa might soon be in command, but he would never become a leader in these terms. He could not inspire or lead his men. He broke this essential rule of the Ottoman style of war: this, more than antiquated weapons, 'oriental torpor' or even stupidity, was the cause of his ultimate failure.[18] He was also incapable of taking advice from those who had fought against the Habsburgs for decades, and knew how deadly and effective western soldiers could be. The Grand Vizier had only contempt for his future enemies, whom he intended to curse and humiliate. The army would march west across the Hungarian plain against the Habsburg empire, but its task was not just to capture a few strategic fortresses.

The still-secret objective was the most cherished prize of all, taking the city of Vienna. If successful, Kara Mustafa would win the greatest triumph for Ottoman arms and transform the bastion of the Christian West into a distant buttress of the blessed Ottoman realm. Even if little territory were gained, and it would be difficult to hold the city, the political and symbolic importance would still be immense, equal to Mehmed II taking Constantinople in 1453. What more sublime act of boldness could there be, confounding the cautious advisers at court who pointed to the vast cost of the enterprise in the west, to the practical difficulties of marching almost a thousand miles and finally to the monitory example of Suleiman I who had thrice failed to take the city in his campaigns a century and a half before?

It was an ambitious strategy. Few bolder strokes would be made in the history of warfare until the armies of the Emperor Napoleon were launched against Russia in 1812 – and when Adolf Hitler followed the same path, attacking the Soviet Union in the twentieth century. In all three cases the adventure would appear insanely foolhardy if it failed; equally it would seem a military masterstroke if it succeeded.

*   *   *

The sultan's messengers carried orders north towards the Danube and then on into Europe; others crossed the Bosporus to Üsküdar and then took horse into the Asian provinces. Later, a fast galley, rowing against the strong current, carried an envoy up to the Black Sea and on to the Crimea. He did not carry peremptory commands as he would to an Ottoman pasha, but rather a honeyed invitation to a sovereign, the Khan of the Tartars in his palace at Bahçisaray, set amid the hills of the southern Crimea, at the head of a well-watered valley. Secure in the galley's after-cabin was a scroll under the sultan's personal sign (*tugra*) to his brother, seeking 'assistance for the faith of Islam', and 'and for the brotherhood of the Ottoman dynasty'; beside it, carefully wrapped in silk, were a jewelled sword, a long fur robe and a chest filled with thousands of gold coins.[19] Piled around these traditional gifts were a stack of other packages containing presents of lesser worth. This was the 'quiver price', the down payment for the Tartar riders who would join the sultan and his army.

The khan, Mehmet Giray, dominated the Crimean peninsula and the featureless plain to the north that ended only at the Ural Mountains. His Tartars sometimes raided as far north as Moscow and westwards deep into Poland, while still warring fitfully with the other steppe borderers, the Cossacks along the Russian and Polish frontiers. His power depended upon the prowess of his eighty thousand horsemen, arguably the best light cavalry in the known world. The Crimea, technically a peninsula, was effectively a large island, linked to the northern mainland only by a narrow isthmus of Perekop, which was guarded by a strongly garrisoned fortress. The Crimea's verdant and fertile southern shore was protected by Ottoman soldiers but behind that coastline a range of mountains separated the Ottoman province from the khan's domain and the Tartar nomads whom he ruled. In reality, there were three Crimeas: the rich trading ports of the south, the mountains famed for their wine and fruit, and, on their northern flank, the khan's palace, with the hills rising to the open plateau beyond. Bahçisaray was a mixture of Ottoman formality and the cruder customs of the steppes. In its courts and the streets outside officials in silks and velvets contrasted with burly warriors in rough cloth leggings, black sheepskin jerkins and drab felt bonnets. The khan was midway between a vassal of the sultan and a distant cousin, who shared a descent back to the greatest of all the leaders of the East, Genghis Khan.

The Ottoman's alliance with the Tartars, first cemented in the fifteenth century, was never easy: many ruling khans had been replaced or killed on orders from Istanbul. But the Tartar horde was the irreplaceable concomitant to the janissaries and the household cavalry. They were hardy riders who could move ten times faster than the regular troops, could swim wide and fast-flowing rivers, could fight winter and summer alike. Their stocky horses could survive on the most meagre grazing and they carried none of the impedimenta that slowed the professional army. Tartars wore no armour, shunned firearms, and few of them even used swords. But they could ride at full speed and loose four or five arrows with deadly precision in a few seconds. If the sultan's armies inspired terror in the west, it was the Tartars who evoked the deepest and most visceral fear.

In the popular mythology of the frontier, Tartars were the creatures of hell. They lived on plunder and from the sale of human flesh, taking their reward not so much in money as in slaves whom they led home, roped together in long coffles (from the Arabic word *kafila*) to the markets of the Crimea. Some of the prisoners would be ransomed at high prices, but more often they were sold on to serve in almost every part of the Ottoman empire and beyond. The Tartars took their captives mostly from the northern frontier with Russia, but prisoners from the Austrian lands and Royal Hungary were highly prized. The khan's duty to his tribesmen was to wage war from which they could profit, and if he failed to do so they would find another leader. War was their only calling; they were practised and experienced predators, never wholly to be trusted but still a most devastating weapon to deploy against an enemy. Over time the janissaries had refined their skills to a single end: as shock troops. The Tartars likewise had evolved a style of war against which their adversaries had few defences.

In battle, the Tartars were like a swarm of angry wasps, flying around and against their opponents, hundreds or thousands of horsemen seeking out a weak point or a suddenly exposed flank. For them, like western mercenaries, war was a business and false heroics had no purpose. Their boldness was legendary, but they shunned confrontation and hand-to-hand engagements, preferring to harass their enemy from a distance. Tartar raiders fought only for profit and sought out weak victims such as an undefended village or an outlying abbey. They would appear only as the night turned towards first light. Until then, before that moment when, as the Qur'an put it, 'you can tell a white thread from a black one in the light of the coming dawn', the darkness was absolute, and they were invisible.[20] But within an hour, as the buildings of the village or the abbey slowly became visible, so too did the encircling ponies and their riders. Their tactic, born of long practice on countless raids, was simple. They watched a settlement over several days, observing when the villagers left to work in the fields and when they returned. They counted the number of men, and, separately, the women and children. The defenders in an abbey were harder to gauge, but they watched patiently for a glimpse of any armed men.

Even when dawn broke, the silent riders were still blurred and indistinct figures. Their ponies were mostly black or brown, and they wore no steel breastplates that might catch the early light.[21] A few carried short lances, but without exception all had the famous Tartar bow slung across their backs, and a quiver full of arrows. Motionless and completely silent (not even the ponies shifted their feet or tossed their heads) they looked more like cast bronze than flesh and blood. For those who had met these Tartars in battle, restlessly energetic, darting and swarming, this immobility was paradoxical. Their very name in the languages of Europe – Tartar – stemmed from the Latin 'Tartarus', the bowels-of-the-Earth goddess Gaia, and by extension the deepest pit of hell.[22] Implacable in their savagery, recklessly disregarding any danger, tireless and bold, the peasants of the west named them the devil's horsemen.[23]

The Turks and Tartars were only the most recent terror that had emerged from the east. The great Hungarian plain, bounded by the Danube to the west and the Carpathian Mountains to the north, ended in a near cul-de-sac just beyond Vienna. The Wienerwald, the Vienna Woods, was a final outcrop of the Alps on the southern bank of the river, while behind the northern bank rose the Bohemian hills. But in the other direction, eastwards, there was an open plain that skirted north of the Crimea, ran south of the Urals, then north of the Aral

Sea and Lake Balkhash to the borders of Mongolia. Over the centuries, beginning with the Scythians, before the rise of Roman power, a succession of eastern nomadic steppe peoples – Sarmatians, Marcomanni, Huns, the Bulgars, Avars, Magyars, and finally the Mongols – moved westward. Some pushed along the Danube valley towards the river's source and then on into the heart of Europe. In 955, the Magyars were only definitively beaten back at the Battle of the Lechfeld, but they had penetrated as far as Augsburg, deep in southern Germany; driven back on to the plain east of Vienna, they settled and created the Kingdom of Hungary. This final assault involved only a small force – about five thousand strong – but it had penetrated deep into Western Europe without much difficulty.

Three centuries later, the victorious Mongols, usually called the Tartars, who had already destroyed the city of Kiev and defeated the combined forces of Poland and the Teutonic Knights at the Battle of Liegnitz, invaded Hungary in strength from the north in March 1241. On a single day they destroyed the King of Hungary's army at Muhi, on the banks of the River Sajó. The Hungarians outnumbered the Mongols, but they could find no means to use their numerical advantage to defeat them. Slow-moving, heavily armoured, they fought in the European style and were simply outmanoeuvred. The Mongol general Batu said they had 'closed themselves in a narrow pen, in the manner of sheep', and ordered his archers to 'slaughter them from a distance'.[24] Then he allowed the remnants to escape from the trap, only to become prey for the horsemen who harried their headlong flight. The Hungarian army was annihilated, although the king escaped, and the Mongols then moved south, storming and ransacking the town of Pest on Christmas Day 1241. An Austrian monk wrote: 'In this year the kingdom of Hungary, which had existed for 350 years, was destroyed by the army of the Tartars.' It was widely feared that the Mongols would turn west and march into Western Europe as the Magyars had done almost three centuries before. But geography and fate preserved Christendom. The towns and cities on the southern side of the Danube remained untouchable, until February 1242 when the slowly moving river froze solid on the bend north of Esztergom, and the Mongol army was able to cross en masse to the southern bank over the ice.

Hungary and the Balkans were saved when the Great Khan, Ögödey, died unexpectedly; in March Batu led his army back to Mongolia and

Europe was spared a conquest from the east. Whether the Mongols could have succeeded where the other eastern conquerors failed is questionable, but the fear that they inspired was attached to the next threat, the Crimean Tartars and the Ottomans in later centuries. The monk Matthew of Paris, writing and illustrating his *Great Chronicle* far away in England, at the Abbey of St Albans, recorded the contemporary response to the events of 1241:

> . . . All these observing from certain high places the vast army of the enemy, and abhorring the beastly cruelty of the accomplices of Antichrist, signified to the governor the hideous lamentations of his Christian subjects, who, in all the adjoining provinces, were surprised and cruelly destroyed, without any respect of rank, fortune, age, or sex. The Tartarian chieftains, and their brutishly savage followers, glutted themselves with the carcasses of the inhabitants, leaving nothing for the vultures but the bare bones; and strange to tell, the greedy and ravenous vultures disclaimed to prey on the remains left by the Tartars. Old and deformed women they gave for daily sustenance to their cannibals. The young and beautiful they devoured not, but smothered them shrieking and lamenting under their forced and unnatural ravishments; and cutting off the breasts of tender virgins to present as dainties to their leaders, they fed themselves upon their bodies.[25]

Some western travellers, like Busbecq, had been impressed by the Ottomans, but in 1682 no one considered the Tartars other than as Matthew of Paris had described them.

★　★　★

The Crimean Tartars of 1682 had all the endurance and fighting skill of their thirteenth-century forebears. They had raided and warred for more than a century, sometimes fighting against, sometimes alongside, Poles, Cossacks and Russians as well as loyally supporting their perpetual allies, the Ottomans. On the grasslands of the Crimea and across the slender isthmus of Perekop that joined the peninsula to the mainland, the tribes of Nogai Tartars raised horses. It was from among the Nogai that the khan recruited his best troops. They could ride for fifty or sixty miles a day, each man travelling with three or four horses on a leading rein behind him, as the Mongols had done centuries before. Divided into raiding parties of forty to fifty men, they would scout far ahead of the main body, usually returning every few days to the *czambul*, or fighting camp. Discipline was tight and harshly enforced, and Tartars could quickly concentrate large numbers to overwhelm even a well-armed enemy. But their success depended on speed, surprise and movement, and in mountains or wooded country where Tartars could be pinned down their advantages evaporated. Small, well-defended places, providing protection from their arrows, could fight off even the largest war bands.

On the march the warriors in a Tartar column would change their horses four or five times a day to keep them fresh and rested and would travel slowly until they reached enemy territory. Once in the zone of war, they could move very fast even over difficult ground. In one campaign a Tartar crossed 118 miles of swampy ground in less than six days.[26] Under normal conditions they could travel fifty to sixty miles in a single day. While westerners came increasingly to mock the cumbersome Ottoman style of battle, the Tartars continued to evoke both fear and admiration in equal measure. A French traveller in Russia in 1645 wrote of the Tartars' unique skills in war. '[Russian] generals retire to certain rivers and woods to prevent their passage. But the Tartar is an enemy so light and dexterous that he understands this, and amuses the Muscovite army with 20–30,000 horse, meanwhile sending a number of people to raid the land in some other way, which is done with such promptness that they have dealt their blow before the Muscovites know of it.'[27] The entire Habsburg frontier was open to the Tartars and there was nothing to prevent their raiders swarming up the river valleys into Germany, with little to contain them until they reached the Atlantic.

★   ★   ★

Ottomans and Tartars together were a potent combination. The sultan's army had sacrificed mobility as it became more sophisticated: by 1682 it was travelling at the same measured pace as the armies of the west, slowed down by its siege train and the vast quantity of baggage which accompanied every campaign. The fast moving Tartars restored the balance. Distance and the terrain always played a key part in the equation of Ottoman success. A war along the steppe frontier north by the Dniester River was more straightforward than a war in the far west because it was little more than half the distance to Vienna and involved only a few major river crossings. While the Ottomans had laboriously to bridge every river for their infantry and cavalry, the Tartars would simply swim their horses across. As the Turkish heavy cavalry, the *sipahis*, were becoming less useful in the wars against the west, the Tartars were becoming more and more valuable.

The *sipahis'* horses, like those of the western cavalry, needed good-quality food, and a huge amount of space in the Ottoman supply lines was taken up with carrying fodder for the horses. The heavy cavalry were designed to be a shock force on the battlefield and they were useless for any other purpose. Often during the increasing number of sieges, *sipahis* served as ordinary infantrymen in the trenches; but since they had little experience with muskets they could only be used either in digging trenches or as cannon fodder in an assault. Once the light horse (*akincis*) had served as scouts but they often proved unreliable or disloyal: the ranks of these irregulars contained some of the most undisciplined and disreputable elements of the whole army. By contrast, and for all their savage appearance, the Tartars operated to a clear tactical plan and under the strict control of their khan.

Their immediate loyalties were tribal, to the segment of the Nogai Tartar horde to which they belonged, which was controlled and commanded by clan princes. Calling one of the larger clans to arms might produce ten thousand men ready to fight. But tactically, like the janissaries, it was the small groups that mattered – ten men in the case of the Tartars forming the basic fighting unit. Often the men would be related. The orders were carried largely by word of mouth. In 1501, the Khan Mengli Giray sent this message to the scattered clansmen:

> As God wills, I want to mount my horse and you must all be ready to fight alongside me. There must be one cart for five men, three horses to a man . . . No man is to stay at home save he is less than 15 years old. Whoever stays behind is no servant of mine, of my sons, nor of my princes. Rob and kill such a man.

It was a simple but immensely effective military system: it took at most two to four weeks to muster a Tartar army ready for war. They took little with them: eight pounds of roasted millet was enough food for fifty days. Most would also carry a little hard mare's milk cheese and some dried or smoked meat.

War was their livelihood, and the Tartar contingent was worth more to an Ottoman commander than all his other troops except the janissaries. Once he had unloosed his Tartars against an enemy, death and destruction could strike them at any moment. Their lines of communication would be threatened with constant attack, and the civilian population stricken with a paralysing terror. Contemporaries described the panic that came from the sight of columns of smoke, as the Tartars took everything of value, enslaved or killed all the inhabitants of a village and torched all the buildings. Tartars had a sixth sense of danger. They would rarely attack groups of musketeers, but, like hyenas, 'they are content to take those infantry who are apart [from the main body of troops] and cut up others when they are setting up camp'. The Ottomans themselves were well aware that their Tartars worked through terror. Sultan Selim II, the son of Suleiman I, observed: 'I fear the Tartars most of all. They are as fast as the wind upon their enemies, for they cover five or six days' road in one day, and when they run away, they disappear as quickly. Especially important is the fact that their horses do not require shoes, nails, or fodder.[28] When they come to a river they do not wait for a boat like our troops. Their food, like their bodies, is nothing much; their strength is shown by the fact that they do not care for comfort.' But their most deadly weapon was the fear that they inspired, and this was their primary value to the Ottoman cause.

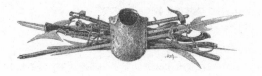

3

A Plague on the Land

On the wall of the Cathedral of Graz there is still a damaged fresco painted in 1485 by Thomas von Villach, a celebrated itinerant artist. Five years before, Styria had suffered three disasters in a single season: the hideous plague of the Black Death, which ravaged the city of Graz, locusts that swept through the fields devouring all the crops and an invasion of Turks from the south-west. The fresco was both thanks for survival and a pious hope that God the Father and the Virgin Mary would protect them from any future catastrophe. Forty years later, the Turks were back again in force. This advance, which began in 1521 and lasted until 1683, almost two hundred years, fell into three main episodes. The first spanned the entire reign of Suleiman I – beginning in the year after his accession and ending only with his death on campaign in Hungary in 1566. The second is usually known as the Long War, beginning in 1593 and ending in 1606. The third was the campaign of 1664, which led to the defeat of the full field army commanded by the Grand Vizier at the Battle of St Gotthard on the borders with Styria in southern Austria.

This was only one part of Ottoman military commitments. There were long-running wars in the Mediterranean, by sea and by land, and campaigns against the rival imperial power in the East, Persia. There were military expeditions against Poland for control of the lands around the Dniester and to control the territories of Wallachia, Moldavia and Transylvania, over which the sultan claimed authority. This meant that it was often impossible to take advantage of periods of Habsburg weakness. So while the Habsburgs were at their most vulnerable in Europe during the Thirty Years War, the Ottomans were distracted by powerful and dynamic Shah Abbas I who captured Baghdad in 1623; the ensuing war continued until 1639. The particular situation in 1682, when the Habsburgs were under great pressure from France, and desperate to renew the truce signed at Vasvár in 1664, was a moment of quite exceptional Ottoman opportunity.

Nevertheless, even when full-scale campaigns were not being fought, the little war – border raiders by land, corsairs at sea – continued ceaselessly. These may have disappeared from history but people at the time saw them as part of the same process: a continuous and unending assault on Europe that began with the fall of Constantinople in 1453. Mehmed II 'the Conqueror' set the pattern which was followed by his successors. The Ottoman empire must not suffer defeat, and a lost battle became a commitment for future generations to right the affront. The process was ineluctable.

Three years after the triumph at Constantinople, Mehmed II failed to take Belgrade. The story of the Franciscan monk John Capistrano – an impassioned preacher, the grim nemesis of the Jews, the scourge of heretics – with his horde of ragged crusaders uniting with John Hunyadi, the greatest soldier of the age, became a legend. Together, so the story went, they saved Christian Belgrade, together they fought their way into the city; together they forced the Turks back from the walls with their men dropping burning bundles of pitch-soaked branches on the solid mass of Ottoman soldiers below. Then on the day following, 22 July 1456, with the peasant crusaders on the Christian left wing, Hunyadi's veterans on the right, they marched on the Turkish camp. Capistrano gave them the battle cry: 'The Lord began it, the Lord will bring it to a good end.' After a furious hand-to-hand battle, Mehmed's army fell back in great disorder. This faraway triumph made a strong and long-lasting impression. In 1515, in distant England, the printer Wynkyn de Worde saw the market for a long metrical romance, *Capystranus*, an extremely bloody account of killing Turks. Even two centuries later, Hannah Brand's new play of 1791, *Huniades, or, The siege of Belgrade*, played to a packed house in the King's Theatre, Norwich.

Belgrade would wait for a better opportunity. But even when he was engaged in other conquests, Mehmed expected his governors and officials in the Balkans, on their own initiative, to strike north-westwards across the rivers Sava and Drava and into the rich farming country of Styria and Carinthia. Every year from 1469 until the sultan's death in 1481, mounted raiders would cross the rivers as soon as the snows had melted. At Pentecost 1471, Styria was ravaged for the first time and in the words of Mehmed's biographer, Franz Babinger: 'Everywhere churches, monasteries, and settlements went up in flames; men and cattle were carried off by the thousands; no one was sure of his life.' In the same year, thousands of mounted raiders burned the villages around Venice, with the smoke darkening the sky above the Queen of the Adriatic. Countless bags full of heads, noses and ears were sent to the sultan to demonstrate success.[1]

More than half a century before Hungary fell into Ottoman hands, the frontier from the Adriatic to the Iron Gates on the Danube was being terrorised year after year. Belgrade remained securely in Hungarian hands, but Bosnia, Croatia, Dalmatia, Styria and Carinthia all suffered from endless Turkish depredations.[2] To the east, all along the border, as far west as Klagenfurt in Carinthia, old fortified towers were strengthened to provide some defence against the invaders. In the cities like Vienna and Buda there was no sense of threat, but along the frontier there was never any real peace. Despairing of relief from their rulers, the local communities provided their own defence.

They created a network of signal fires on the hilltops, and manned them night and day. They were lit to warn of the raiders' advance. Little castles like Frondsberg, built by a twelfth-century crusader in the well wooded hills north of Graz, were strengthened to serve their original purpose of protecting the land and its people. Local lords with a handful of retainers armed with muskets were often sufficient to drive off attackers who rarely had more than a few guns. Larger strongholds like Schloss Riegersburg, unassailable on its volcanic ridge, became the base in time of war for up to five thousand armed riders and controlled the approach to Graz. Attacked several times by the Turks, it always proved impregnable.[3]

Neither Mehmed's son Bayezid II nor his grandson Selim had the opportunity to turn their attentions to the unrighted wrong – Sultan Mehmed's defeat before Belgrade. It was the Conqueror's great-grandson, the new and energetic young Sultan Suleiman I, succeeding his father Selim in 1520, who swiftly made war a terrifying reality; and this time the Turks triumphantly took possession of the great prize, only the first of Suleiman's succession of victories.[4] After winning Belgrade in 1521, he was back in 1526, advancing across the Danube into Hungary. In one great battle, at Mohács, 29 August 1526, he completely defeated the outnumbered Hungarian field army; the Hungarian king Lajos drowned in a ditch in the chaos after the battle, leaving the crown vacant and the kingdom without an heir. Much of the detail of the battle is uncertain, but at the end of the day the Ottomans were in possession of the field, and killed their two thousand prisoners. Suleiman pushed north, sacking and briefly occupying the Hungarian capital Buda. The sultan took what was left of the famous library of King Matthias Corvinus from the palace of the Hungarian kings and shipped it down the Danube to Belgrade. Today, it is in the Topkapi Palace in Istanbul.

A Hungarian nobleman, John Zápolya, an Ottoman vassal and candidate for the throne of Hungary, had occupied the capital after the Turks' departure. The Habsburg claimant to the Hungarian throne, Ferdinand II of Habsburg, then gathered his army and took Buda and a string of other fortresses from Zápolya in 1527. Suleiman's response, in 1529, was to march into Hungary with a huge army, retaking Buda and annihilating the Habsburg garrison there on 8 September; a little more than a week later the Ottomans arrived before the walls of Vienna. This was very late in the campaigning season so he began the siege with a great sense of urgency.

This first Siege of Vienna lasted almost exactly a month. The Ottomans lacked heavy artillery, but the greatest deficiency was in miners and mining equipment. The Turks began to dig trenches and excavate saps by the Carinthian Gate. But in two weeks of daily attacks, they made only minor breaches and every furious assault was repulsed. Nevertheless by early October it seemed that the city might fall unless relief arrived: only a force of experienced mercenaries led by Count Niklas Salm kept the Turks at bay. But Salm's losses were getting increasingly heavy and many believed the city could not survive. Then, in the second week in October, the torrential rain turned into early snow. On 14 October 1529 the whole Ottoman army began a hurried retreat, through deepening snowdrifts.

The shock of Mohács and the Siege of Vienna, coming so close together in time, created a sense of Ottoman invincibility. In the west, terror at their huge armies and fear of their merciless savagery was spread through books, pamphlets and news-sheets, while the printing presses produced series after series of graphic and horrifying images. In 1532, Suleiman attacked again, but by a different route. This time the Ottoman army began its march earlier, and, instead of heading north towards Buda, marched westward towards the uplands and the towns south of Vienna. En route the army had briefly invested and captured seventeen fortified towns or castles. On 5 August it arrived before the small town of Köszeg (Güns), south of Sopron and only a few miles from the Austrian border. The castle at Köszeg was an insubstantial obstacle and many stronger places had yielded without a fight. But the town's commander, Nikola Jurišić, rejected the offer to surrender on favourable terms.

For more than twenty-five days Jurišic and his garrison of eight hundred Croats, without any artillery, held out against nineteen full-scale assaults and an incessant bombardment. In the end the Ottomans struck camp and retreated: they had learned the lesson of 1529 and would not again begin a siege in late September. The defence of Köszeg stopped the advance on Vienna in 1532; in 1541, a larger town, Szigetvár, repulsed another Ottoman attack, and delayed the advance once again. In 1556, Szigetvár was attacked once more and was close to capture, but the timely arrival of a relieving force drove off the Turks. Szigetvár became a symbol of resistance. It had only an ancient castle, and was of no great inherent strength. Its only defensive advantage was being built across three connected islands in an artificial lake. Any attacking army would have to take all three, including the citadel. Its survival and resistance were an irritation and humiliation for the Ottomans, and one that the now elderly Suleiman was determined to remove.

Ten years later, old and sick, the sultan again commanded the army on its march north; he was too weak to ride and had to be carried in a palanquin. This was to be his triumphant final thrust beyond the Danube, and he was determined to obliterate this persistent obstacle, the impudent 'molehill' of Szigetvár. The governor (ban) of Croatia, Miklós Zrinyi, had garrisoned the town and citadel with 2500 men, and taunted the Ottoman army when he was summoned to surrender on 8 August 1566. The walls of the New and Old Towns, each on its separate island, were decked with bunting and flags, and guns were fired in salute (perhaps ironically) of the Turkish host from the third island, the citadel.

A baking summer had largely dried out the lake which was Szigetvár's best defence, and the Ottomans filled up the remaining pools with bundles of brushwood. On the third day of the siege the New Town on the first island was stormed and captured. But the assault cost the Turks 3000 dead, while the defenders lost almost 300. The surviving Croats and Hungarians slipped across the narrow causeway into the Old Town; that, too, suffered a wave of assaults, but it fell only after ten all-out Turkish attacks. Finally, only the citadel on the third island remained; behind its walls were the three hundred surviving soldiers of Zrinyi's command, with their wives and children. The Ottomans offered good terms for surrender which Zrinyi spurned, but it was only a matter of time before the defenders were overwhelmed.

In an open meeting all agreed that when the end was near the women and children would be killed by their own husbands and fathers, so that they should not fall alive into Turkish hands. Then, having severed their last connections on earth, the three hundred would sell their lives dearly. On the thirty-third day of the siege Zrinyi took off his battered cuirass and put on the rich clothes he had worn at his wedding, and with his father's sword in his right hand led his men to the gate of the old castle. Then the few remaining defenders, led by Zrinyi, burst out of the citadel and slaughtered the janissaries trapped on the causeway. Zrinyi was almost immediately hit by two musket balls and an arrow in the eye. Of the three hundred, all but three were killed or wounded within a few minutes of their final wild charge. The triumphant janissaries, with Zrinyi's head spiked on a lance, entered the gate and crowded into the small courtyard of the citadel. At that moment, a young woman who had hidden herself in the gunpowder store fired the explosives within it: the medieval castle was reduced to a pile of rubble, as she took three thousand janissaries with her into eternity.

The staunch defence of castles like Köszeg, Szigetvár and others like Eger created a rich vein of myth, celebrated in books, maps and prints.[5] In the nineteenth century these great victories (or even defeats) became a favourite source for vast patriotic canvases. But for the Ottomans, too, they became an epic of heroism. The Siege of Szigetvár was recorded as *The Ottoman Chronicle of the Szigetvár Campaign*, with twenty coloured painted miniatures illuminating the exquisite calligraphy and in the middle the triple islands of the city, faithfully depicted just as in the maps produced in the west.[6] Suleiman I, who died of sickness and old age in the camp before the final victory, was declared a martyr for sacrificing himself in battle against the enemy. Christians could acknowledged the bravery of their assailants, and the Ottomans frequently did the same; yet each also regarded the other as damned and accursed infidels.

★ ★ ★

War in the east was cruel. Many of the horror stories of these wars are true: the massacres and atrocities, the endless lines of newly enslaved Hungarians in Sarajevo on their road of tears to Istanbul. But it worked both ways. The Habsburg armies also flayed men alive, impaled prisoners, took slaves and raped captives. Savagery was a weapon of war and used by both sides. But so, too, were courtesy and a degree of humanity. When Suleiman took Belgrade in 1521, he did so upon the unusual terms that the lives of the defenders would be spared. At the end, after a siege of almost seventy-two days, when survivors and their families from a garrison of seven hundred opened the gates of the citadel at noon on 29 August, the sultan 'wished to see the men whose courage and perseverance he had learned to respect. As was customary, the reprieved kissed the Padishah's hand and he gave them kaftans [robes] as a present and exchanged a few words with them.' Later they were put on ships and sent across the Danube to the Hungarian side. 'Although some of the Christian chroniclers offered dramatically detailed accounts of the massacres of the withdrawing Hungarians, Suleiman seems to have kept his promise.'[7]

Suleiman's successors lacked his talent for war, and the truce agreed at Edirne with the Habsburgs in 1568 was renewed three times. This only prevented sieges and full-scale war; in effect there was an annual raiding season in the 'little war', that lasted from 1568 to 1593, and this was, if anything, more casually brutal than the large-scale campaigns.[8] Both sides denied responsibility for this unauthorised campaigning and established regular contacts to settle the constant complaints and law cases that the anarchic state of the frontier generated. However, while the Ottomans did little to improve their defences, the Habsburgs invested heavily in elaborate fixed fortifications, financed by new taxes. By the 1590s, most of the Habsburg fortresses were either newly built or expensively modernised, on the most up-to-date lines. This huge investment transformed the nature of war on the eastern frontiers. The situation was put best by Vauban, the chief engineer of Louis XIV, in about 1670. 'Since the number of strongholds has increased to the point where one can no longer enter enemy territory without encountering many fortified towns, its importance [the attack on fortresses] has increased to the point where one can say that today it alone offers the means of conquest and conservation. To be sure, winning a battle leaves the victor in control of the countryside for the time being but only the taking of fortresses will give him the entire country.'[9] Vast areas of Hungary had no fortified towns at all, but in the northern border zone west of Buda and close to the boundary between Ottoman and Habsburg territory, they dominated the terrain in the way that Vauban described a century later.

The new Habsburg strongholds were positioned *aggressively* to occupy ground that provided both a block on an Ottoman advance as well as a good base for advancing the frontier eastwards. Although the Ottomans also developed their strong places, they did so unsystematically and less effectively. The consequences of this new kind of war, already familiar in the west, became clear when the truce had broken down irreparably in 1593. Both Ottomans and Habsburgs were tired of 'the war that was no war' and were eager to try their luck on the field of battle. Both discovered that the new style of war was demanding and produced indecisive results. In the thirteen years of conflict neither side could achieve an overwhelming advantage. The future Catholic commanders in the Thirty Years War – like Albrecht von Wallenstein and Johann Tserclaes, Count Tilly – learned how war was fought in the years of the Long War, and the lessons of the war in the east were transferred into the long war in the west. Some elements of the visceral hatreds that had appeared in the eastern war were imported into the west.

After the truce in 1606 the Ottomans faced another long war in Asia against the resurgent power of Persia, while in 1618 the Habsburgs launched a counterattack against the Protestants who had taken over in Prague and throughout Bohemia. Neither the Habsburgs nor the Ottomans had any incentive to open a new front on the ground so strongly in contention after 1593. Fighting in the east had been in many respects harder than in the west, because of the great distances involved, and a harsh, inhospitable terrain. But the experience of the wars against Persia did little to equip the Ottoman armies for renewed battles on the European front, especially after the Thirty Years War transformed the whole western approach to warfare. In the Long War at the end of the sixteenth century the two antagonists had attained a kind of parity, with the Ottomans better organised but the Habsburgs benefiting from technological and tactical advances in the art of war. The Turks might not be able to match the new European styles of war, but they still outstripped their enemies in speed and mobility at a time when western war was becoming increasingly ponderous and doctrinaire.

The Habsburg commanders were more capable than any comparable Ottoman general.[10] Below them was in embryo a chain of command that in some armies ran down from the commander, to senior and junior officers, through sergeants, corporals and lance corporals to the soldiers themselves. It was this organisational structure that allowed even inexperienced soldiers to learn and then perform quite complex manoeuvres on the battlefield. The drill-book battlefield manoeuvres ordered by generals and colonels would, as far as conditions allowed, be carried out on the battlefield by soldiers who had been taught them by their junior and non-commissioned officers.

This chain of control and command did not really exist in the Ottoman ranks and it proved to be a crucial weakness. A competent Ottoman commander could do very little to manoeuvre his men. He would tell them to attack and they would attack. He could set objectives – besiege a town or fight to the death – and they would often be accomplished. But a good western general could devise a battle plan in terms (in theory) of moving the regiments or even companies around the battlefield. There were elaborate signals and battlefield communications, flags flourished to communicate with the troops. Much was obscured by the fog of war, the all-pervasive smoke that covered the battlefield in the age of firearms. But a commander would give tactical orders and by and large they would be executed. There was no real equivalent in the Ottoman ranks, despite the fact that they used the *mehter*, or military bands, both to raise morale by their stirring music and also to issue commands. Ottoman warfare depended on the professional skill and determination of the fighting units, not on the art of generalship.

There were no Ottoman equivalents of the Dutch pioneer military theorist Maurice of Nassau, or inspirational commanders like Gustavus Adolphus, or good fighting generals who were also what Thomas Barker called 'military intellectuals'. In the west, war had become a kind of philosophy; in the east, it was a complex and subtle tradition. Because of this, the Turks perfected a limited but highly effective tactical repertoire. The sultan's professional infantry – the janissaries – had better logistics and supply, more experience in siegecraft, longer-range and more deadly muskets than most European armies. With the right conditions, on the right day, they could outmatch any western foot soldiers. In the wrong circumstances, with a commander they did not trust, they could easily deteriorate into a rabble. However, the defeated army could quickly recover its spirit and sense of conviction and counterattack, with devastating consequences for an overconfident enemy.

Commanders like Raimondo Montecuccoli (the archetypal 'military intellectual'), who had fought through the Thirty Years War, found in the Turks a much faster and more deadly enemy than any that they had experienced on the battlefields of Western Europe. Montecuccoli quickly re-learned a new set of priorities. Against an enemy who used sabres, lances and arrows, armour was essential; in Western Europe it was being worn less and less. Against an elusive and highly trained Ottoman enemy, the ponderous western phalanxes of pikemen were of little value: commanders like Montecuccoli used more and more musketeers. The east quickly became an extraordinary experimental zone in the art of war, which was to produce some great commanders. There the west learned the value of hussars (light cavalry) and of mounted infantry – dragoons – armed with muskets and pistols. They also learned at great cost the need for effective firepower to negate the offensive power of the janissaries. The Ottomans learned as well. The Turks developed their considerable skill with firearms, and more and more of them were trained in musketry and sharpshooting. But despite various clever devices – such as camel-borne light guns – they failed to keep up with the west in the use of massed field artillery or in the elaborate choreography of infantry drill and manoeuvre. The Turks honed their traditional skills to ever higher standards: they trained the foot soldiers to use massed volley fire at the same time that this new technique was being developed in the west.[11] In the late seventeenth and the early eighteenth centuries their *esprit de corps*, their ideology of regimental loyalty, was an advantage which Ottoman professional soldiers possessed in abundance over the unwilling pressed men of the west.

Seventeenth-century contemporaries invariably overestimated the size of Ottoman armies. It was assumed that the Turks mustered enormous armies, often fielding as many as 200,000 men. This was a fantasy, possibly born of fear. Turkish armies were terrifying to behold, and were certainly larger than those of western states. The impression of an army so large that it filled the entire horizon was partly deliberate, made possible by hordes of feudal levies and irregulars that swelled the Ottoman ranks. These vastly outnumbered the key components – the professional infantry and cavalry – which were a relatively small element of the sultan's array. A large part of the Turkish army was of little value in battle, although it did instil fear into those who saw (and heard) it for the first time. In quality, the best of the Ottomans were at least as good as the best of the western troops, probably better, man for man. But they were expensive to maintain and there were never enough of them, despite regular increases in numbers during the seventeenth century.

Little is known about how they were commanded and managed on the battlefield, whereas we know a great deal about how western armies were commanded, from the records that were kept and the many accounts of battles and military life that were written. The Ottomans kept exceptionally good records, but the manuals of war and accounts of battles they created had to be couched in a kind of courtly hyperbole that makes it hard to extract their precise meaning. By contrast, the miniature paintings made to illustrate some of the palace histories depicted the reality of war much more successfully: they were extraordinarily exact and almost photographic in their detail.

* * *

Why did this Ottoman decline take place? None of the conventional explanations is really convincing. Was it because the Turks refused to alter a style of war sanctified by the successes of Mehmed II and Suleiman I? Was it an intransigent resistance to change? In part it was, because the Ottomans sincerely believed that their way was better, more honourable and more courageous than the alternatives. They were also unconvinced that the western way was invariably superior. They were not alone: later commentators condemned the sterility of a western style of war where increasingly armies plodded from one siege to another, and there were fewer and fewer war-winning battlefield encounters. It took the genius of Napoleon to restore mobility to the battlefield, employing cavalry in ways reminiscent of the older Turkish tradition, but much improved and systematised.[12] This fate of *relative decline* was not unique to the Ottomans. After 1791 every army in Europe, even Prussia, suffered defeat after defeat at the hands of Revolutionary France. The Turks' adversaries, the Habsburg armies, began to exhibit the same defects of military and political conservatism in the era of Revolutionary War that the Ottomans had displayed in the third phase of the Turkish War outlined above.

Already research is beginning to show that in many areas the Ottoman military were not quite the obscurantists, instinctively resisting change and progress, that they have been labelled. Where the conditions were right, the Turkish style of war was highly effective. However, the commanders of the Ottoman armies were much less in control of their men than their Habsburg counterparts. This was a fatal weakness, for Turkish commanders from 1664 onwards confronted a generation of officers who had learned their craft as young men in the Thirty Years War, who then trained a new generation of ruthless, competent fighters – the generation of Prince Eugene of Savoy. As this book moves forward I hope to show that the Habsburgs knew right up until the 1790s that on the battlefield they faced a highly dangerous, versatile and implacable foe. This was the true 'terror of the Turk'.

Fortress warfare in Hungary impeded the movement of a mass army to attack a far distant objective but it did not entirely preclude it. In the second half of the seventeenth century the Ottomans frequently showed an extraordinary capacity for *power projection*.[13] They repeatedly campaigned in the far north of their domain against Poland and Russia, and they began once again to think of attacking Vienna. The experiences described in the Ottoman campaign histories suggested that the best point for the Turks to launch an attack on the

Habsburgs was through the southern province of Styria. But the path westwards was blocked by the well-fortified capital city of Graz, dominating the land between the Mur and the Raab rivers. Beyond Graz lay the Styrian highlands, overshadowing the valleys below. But if instead the army crossed the Raab and headed north following the line of hills, it was an easy march up to Vienna and the Danube. There was only one risky point, where the fortress town of Sopron (Ödenburg) dominated the terrain. But once past Sopron, the underbelly of Vienna lay exposed. That had been Sultan Suleiman I's plan in 1532; the attack on Köszeg had been an unnecessary (and disastrous) distraction. There were many advantages to this line of attack. The army would muster at Belgrade, cross the long pontoon bridge across the fast-flowing River Drava and its surrounding marshland, and then march north-west. The commander then had two options. He could choose to loose his Tartar raiders into the Styrian valleys, or continue directly north, skirting the Styrian hills, towards Vienna.

Almost twenty years before Kara Mustafa's campaign, the Ottomans had believed that they could gain a decisive victory against the Habsburgs by exploiting strategic Habsburg vulnerabilities, which existed both north of the Danube and south on the Styrian front. In 1663, the Grand Vizier Fazil Ahmed Köprülü had led an army north into Moldavia and Wallachia, reasserted Ottoman control over the independent-minded Transylvanians and then moved west towards Vienna. His troops ravaged the towns of the prosperous province of Moravia, and the attack revealed the vulnerability of the Habsburg lands from the north-east. It was a success that emboldened the Turks and terrified the Habsburg war council. Over the winter of 1663–4, the Grand Vizier pulled his army back to Belgrade, with the aim of renewing the assault the following spring.

He learned one important lesson. The advance towards Vienna in the autumn of 1663 had been halted by the stubborn defence of one small Habsburg fortress called Neuhäusel (today Nové Zámky) on the River Nitra, which runs south into the Danube. The days spent investing and storming the castle (which the Turks called Uyvar) consumed the limited time available for campaigning in good weather. By the time the castle fell, it was too late in the year to undertake a major siege. It was an old history revisited. Köszeg in 1532, Eger in 1552, Szigetvár in 1566 and Nové Zámky in 1663 showed the huge problems posed by delay in reaching the final objective: a wise commander should seek at all costs to avoid them. So for the 1664 campaign the Grand Vizier chose not to attack along the line of the Danube, but to advance along the southern road, pushing north through the southern counties of Habsburg-ruled Royal Hungary along the line of rolling hills that ran north past Sopron towards the old town of Wiener Neustadt. This was the last substantial obstacle before Vienna.

While Fazil Ahmed had campaigned successfully north of the Danube in 1663, his Hungarian enemies had prepared to attack the Ottomans in the south. Fighting all through the winter of 1663, Count Miklós Zrinyi the Younger, grandson of the heroic defender of Szigetvár in 1566, launched attacks on the Ottoman towns and lines of communication along the Drava and Sava rivers. He raised almost thirty thousand men, with some trained soldiers, but without artillery. This weakness was also a strength. It meant they could move fast and strike hard. They first surrounded Szigetvár in the last days of January 1664, and caught the Turks completely by surprise.[14] Then, as the Ottomans slowly gathered their forces to counterattack, Zrinyi's men moved south and burned the great wooden bridge at Osijek, the main point for the Ottoman armies to cross the rivers into Hungary. With the bridge still smouldering, Zrinyi's troops marched on Ottoman occupied Pécs, burning the town, wrecking the outer fortifications but failing to take the well-defended citadel. On 6 February, they withdrew into Croatia, well satisfied at leaving the Ottoman defences in ruin, and they were ready to strike again at any weak point in the spring.[15]

In March 1664 the Turks were preparing for a new campaigning season, but most of them were encamped on the wrong side of the River Sava. Until a new pontoon bridge, carried across a line of moored boats, was ready at Osijek, all the Turkish garrisons in southern Hungary were at risk and vulnerable to Zrinyi and his men. At the end of April, the Habsburg irregulars, mostly Croat horsemen known as *pandurs*, appeared before the walled fortress town of Kaniza (Nagykaniza). It was the last major Ottoman outpost in the frontier zone. Zrinyi's men had failed to take Szigetvár and Pécs, but, if they succeeded in taking Kaniza, the Ottoman glory in capturing Nové Zámky in the previous year would be tarnished. The Grand Vizier marshalled his army, left Belgrade and crossed the River Drava into

Hungary over the pontoon bridge on 20 May 1664; it took him nine days to cover the short distance to Kaniza, slowed down by the need to construct wooden causeways over the muddy ground that would be strong enough to take the weight of their heavy artillery. The advance would have taken even longer had not the commander left all but seven of his siege guns at Osijek. They arrived just as the Hungarians and Croats were about to launch a final assault.

To secure his position in the southern borderlands, the Grand Vizier had been forced to begin his 1664 campaign far to the west of the normal line of advance, and by the time he had sacked the fortress of Count Zrinyi at Zrinvár, only two hours west of Kaniza, and ravaged his estates, another twenty-one days had passed. By early July the Ottoman army had destroyed all the Habsburg defences in the region, although the main Habsburg force led by General Raimondo Montecuccoli merely shadowed the Ottomans and hung back from an encounter. The Turks had expected them to intervene at Kaniza, then at the siege of Zrinvár, but they never appeared. As he mopped up the Habsburg strongholds one by one an enticing prospect opened before Fazil Ahmed. A few kilometres away lay the River Raab, the boundary between Royal Hungary and Styria. The Turks had not attacked in this direction for some 130 years. If Fazil Ahmed advanced along the line of the hills, he could attack Vienna from the south, or follow the high ground up to the Danube and approach from the east.

To backtrack towards Osijek and then follow the customary path north would waste still more time in a fighting season already curtailed by the campaign along the border. He decided to cross over into enemy territory, and sent out scouts both to find a good place to cross the River Raab and also to discover where Montecuccoli's army was positioned.

The scouts brought good news. Of Montecuccoli there was no sign, but they had learned he had crossed the Raab and had retreated, it was rumoured, to protect Graz. Moreover, close to the Cistercian abbey of St Gotthard, by the village of Mogersdorf, they had discovered a ford across the river, and there was very little water in the riverbed after a dry early summer. An advance party of Tartars had trotted through the shallows, and scouted for some distance along the opposite bank. This was the weak point through the enemy defences that the Ottomans had long sought. The whole army advanced rapidly through the low hills towards the river bank and set up a fortified camp. A temporary bridge was constructed across the shallow water for wagons, but most of the infantry waded impatiently across. With the army on the move the Grand Vizier called a council of war in his tent, which came to a momentous conclusion. The season was late and the army's provisions were low after two months' campaigning. While Graz would be the obvious target, the lure of Vienna was irresistible. By the afternoon most of the janissaries and the imperial cavalry plus some light guns were on the far bank while the larger part of the army – the irregulars and the cavalry from the provinces – remained on the other side of the river, awaiting the arrival of the baggage train.

The crossing point was roughly in the centre of an oxbow in the turbid river, between high banks of loose earth. On the far side was a flat, open plain, surrounded on three sides by the Raab, where the janissaries quickly dug trenches. Beyond, the land was wooded and rose towards a low ridge about half a mile from the river. Concealed in the woodland and along the high ground, the imperial army waited in silence. It was a very mixed force. The troops raised by the Emperor Leopold were under Montecuccoli's direct command but had been augmented by a contingent raised by the Rhineland states of the Holy Roman Empire and a useful if unruly force of volunteer French chevaliers. For the first time in almost a century, the Habsburgs faced the Ottomans with allies at their side. Montecuccoli, however, found managing his opinionated allies a tiresome burden, an omen of events two decades later.

Even with allies, they were heavily outnumbered. In total the little Habsburg army numbered fewer than forty thousand and with inadequate artillery.[16] But Montecuccoli had learned his fighting skills in the Thirty Years War and looking down from the crest of the ridge, he could see that roughly a third of the Ottoman army was bunched within the bend of the river. The main camp remained on the far bank, including the bulk of their cannon. They could not deploy properly, and his own artillery could fire down upon them. If he could hold them back within the oxbow, their backs to the river, disciplined musketry (as he had discovered in his earlier battles) would shatter their formations, and he could then loose his cavalry against their broken ranks.

As the Christian propagandists were later able to claim, heaven came to his aid. The Turks had begun to cross on 31 July but had delayed because it was the holy day, Friday. The remainder of the army would move across early on the morning of Saturday 1 September. But overnight, the weather broke and by morning the riverbed had filled with water streaming down in torrents off the mountains upstream and the hills nearby. The janissaries' trenches filled with water, and the cannon on the far bank could not be moved through the mud. At dawn the scarlet coats of the French squadrons and the dark armour of the imperial horsemen, interspersed with musketeers, suddenly appeared from the woods and drew up, blocking the Ottoman advance.

Montecuccoli believed in firepower and his men, ranged several ranks deep, were trained to deliver almost continuous fire. He had difficulty in controlling his eager and impetuous allies, and the German horsemen charged the Turkish mass, only to be driven off in disarray and hotly pursued. The celebrated traveller Evliya Çelebi was with the Ottoman army. He described how 'The infidels attacked first shouting "Jesus, Jesus" as the Muslim army played their great kettle drums, their little drums, and trumpets . . . The soldiers of the One God launched their assault on the infidels, shouting their battle cries, falling upon them as the wolf attacks a flock of sheep.' But subsequent Ottoman assaults in a savage battle extending over six hours were broken time and time again by the volley fire of the infantry and the deadly imperial field artillery. Evliya, excusing the defeat, reported how 'for the love of their false religion [they] attacked in seven directions with their artillery and their muskets, so that half the *sekben* and the *saridja* of the Grand Vizier found martyrdom in the first hours of the battle. The remaining Muslim soldiers, caught between the diabolical fire of the cannon and the muskets, retired from the battlefield.'

Harried by Montecuccoli's cuirassiers, whose broadswords smashed down on to the heads and exposed shoulders of their demoralised enemies, the broken Turkish regiments crowded back into the now deep waters of the Raab. Downstream, the corpses of drowned Ottoman soldiers piled up like a logjam. Only the Tartars were able to swim their horses across the river and they then returned time and again with their spare mounts to rescue as many of the trapped janissaries as possible.

The Ottomans had lost some of their best troops in the disaster on the River Raab, but the bulk of their army remained intact. The imperial army had suffered very few casualties and the triumph was greeted ecstatically in Vienna and beyond. But the success was deceptive. It was a victory secured by a skilful general leading a ramshackle and unstable coalition, who chose his ground well and had the weather on his side. There was no proper strategy to defend the frontier. Hungarians in particular suggested that this was the time to take the offensive and drive the Ottomans from their land, but Montecuccoli had neither the troops nor the resources for a major campaign. He had been lucky at St Gotthard. The Emperor Leopold wanted to stabilise his eastern frontier because he (rightly) feared Louis XIV's ambitions to advance France's border in Western Europe. A twenty-year truce was hurriedly concluded at Vasvár, not far from St Gotthard, ten days later, to the satisfaction of neither the Habsburgs nor the Ottomans, and the despairing fury of the Hungarians. It would expire in 1684.[17]

Yet the truce only meant an end to full-scale military activity. The intermittent raiding across the long frontier that ran from the mountains north of the Danube to the Adriatic in the south continued unabated, not as a matter of official policy, but from local commanders (and near-bandits) continuing a campaign of vengeance and pillage. The idea of irreconcilable conflict began to increase again, in part because a distant conflict on the borders of Hungary had an international resonance. Popular news-sheets published in Germany portrayed the 'Great Skirmish (*Haupt-Scharmützel*) between the Christian Peoples and the barbaric Turks and the great victory that came with heaven's help'. As far away as London, in 1663, Henry Marsh had published a long account of the defence of Neuhäusel and the new sense of bitterness that was growing on the frontier. The Tartars, Marsh said, were the cause of 'ruinous devastation that can hardly be represented by any pen or pencil . . . [its] nearest resemblance [is] to Doomsday; the fire flaming for twenty miles in view and laying the country in a heap of ashes, and the Tartars like so many Devils haling and dragging their captives, and chaining them together . . . as if humanity were damned and nature had expired, amid a numberless invention of torture'. Twenty thousand Tartars took several walled towns, which they burned to ashes, with all the adjacent villages, 'possessing themselves of the narrow passages between the hills, and massacring many thousands of people, putting others in chains, and in fine overbearing all in his way'.[18] These purported atrocities provoked an equal response. 'To requite the incursion of these barbarous Tartars, the counts of Serini [Zrinyi] and Budiani carried like ravagement and ruin into the Turkish provinces, where they spared nothing they could destroy and left as little of what they could carry away with them.'[19]

Over the years of the truce, the terms were breached repeatedly by both sides. Leopold had agreed to pay a substantial annual 'gift' of 200,000 gulden: it was never delivered on time. The sultan had also promised to make an annual present, and this (perhaps for reasons of prestige) was brought annually to Vienna. But these financial issues apart, both sides showed equal disregard for the provisions of the truce. The Ottomans made little attempt to control raiders from their territories, and even provided troops to support Hungarian renegades and Protestant rebels against Leopold's increasingly unpopular and oppressive rule. But, formally, peace continued, and in 1682 the Austrians opened negotiations to renew the truce. The talks made no progress and the sense of impending war grew steadily.

The preparations for war which the Austrian ambassador had witnessed in Istanbul were plainly not a ruse, but, waiting in Edirne with the sultan, the ambassador could only learn that the full army would gather at Belgrade in the spring. No one was sure whether the Ottomans would head north, as in 1663, to attack along the line of the Danube, or would drive westward as in 1664, until the defeat at St Gotthard had halted their advance. But regardless of its ultimate objective, Caprara had little confidence that the Turkish juggernaut could be halted.

Europe had hailed the victory at St Gotthard as one aided by the hand of God, a triumph on the scale of the sea battle at Lepanto in 1571, when the galleys of the Christian nations had destroyed an Ottoman fleet off the coast of Greece. But the comparison was unrealistic. At St Gotthard the allied Christian forces had been very lucky. They had, entirely by good fortune, trapped a divided Ottoman army in a position where it could neither retreat nor manoeuvre. If the entire Turkish force had made it across the Raab the result might have been very different. The Habsburgs' field artillery was hoarded in barracks close to Vienna, and lack of firepower under less favourable circumstances would have been disastrous.

The long catalogue of 'what ifs' was weighted against the Habsburgs and their allies. The Turks and Tartars together could wage a kind of war which was hard to resist. In the open field the armies of the west had the edge but most seventeenth-century wars were not like that. Rather, they were the slow erosion of an enemy's power to resist, with town after town, fortress after fortress, besieged and captured. In the past Ottoman armies had won their greatest victories by burrowing deep into the earth, demolishing the walls of towns and cities and storming through the breach. But by 1682, western siegecraft, like western infantry tactics, was surpassing the Turkish methods.

The Ottomans continued to outclass any western nation in only one particular. There was no certain defence against their Tartar horsemen except a well-defended castle, although they would rarely venture in mountainous or heavily wooded areas. For a century the Ottomans had relied on irregular horsemen gathered from all over the empire, but many of these were little better than scavengers.[20] But increasingly they came to recognise the special qualities of their Tartar allies; under the command of their tribal leaders, they still possessed the tireless energy and warrior skills of their steppe forefathers. The Tartar code of honour dealt harshly with disobedience and cowardice. Those judged guilty were staked to the ground, eviscerated with sabre slashes, and left to die with their entrails placed on their heads. In battle, consequently, they never surrendered.

The idea of Ottoman 'declination', put about by western writers since the early sixteenth century, was rhetorical. It was supposedly a decline from a high point of Ottoman expansion under Suleiman I, but even that contained an element of myth. The advance of the Ottomans in the east had been largely the work of his father, Selim I. Suleiman's march into Hungary, and especially his siege of Vienna in 1529, was a shock and surprise to the west, but it was incomplete. The greatest extension of Ottoman power in the north was to come in the seventeenth century, when the Turks pushed north of the Dniester River. The idea of decline was more complex than merely battles won or lost: it was presented as an all-encompassing moral collapse of the Ottoman state, a time when the noble austerity of Suleiman's day gave way to women in the harem dominating the state, to rebels ruling in the distant provinces and unruly janissaries, like the Praetorian Guard in ancient Rome, making emperors and destroying them.[21]

Here Paul Rycaut's influence was extraordinarily important. His view of the Ottomans, spread through many editions and translations, was predicated on the fate of imperial Rome. When he wrote 'When violence and injustice prevail there is so little distance between the most eminent height of grandeur and the lowest abyss of misery that a Prince may step in a moment from one unto the other' he italicised this sentence to indicate its particular importance.[22] The subject of Rome always preoccupied him. In 1683 he translated the life of the early Roman King Numa Pompilius for the hugely successful Dryden edition of Plutarch, which reached its seventh edition by 1716.[23]

Rycaut always presented himself as a humble but reliable chronicler of Ottoman affairs. While his early work is based on his years in the Ottoman empire, by his last version, completed in 1699, his personal experience was long in the past. By then he depended for accurate information on a large range of correspondents, not always reliable, and the same secondary sources as any other writer. But from start to finish his argument remained the same: if the Christian states could unite, they should not fear the Turk, whose strength was exaggerated. This produced a fundamental set of paradoxes. To discourage western complacency, he emphasised the power of the Turks. To stiffen the western will to resist he told his readers that the Ottoman power was waning.

In his Preface to *The History of the Decline and Fall of the Roman Empire*, Edward Gibbon, writing in 1781, described his work succinctly as the story of how a memorable series of revolutions 'destroyed the solid fabric of human greatness'. Rycaut, a century before, had a double message in his book, too, describing the threat that the Turk posed in a physical sense – a wake-up call to the west. Know your enemy, he argued: 'It hath been the happy fortune of the Turk to be accounted barbarous and ignorant; for upon this persuasion Christian princes have laid themselves open and unguarded to their greatest danger . . . whilst this puissant enemy hath made himself master of whole provinces and largely shared in the rich and present possessions of Europe.'

But he also wrote of the danger to liberty at home, in 'the country most free and just in all the world'. He was using the dangers of decay and tyranny that he saw in the Ottoman empire to warn his fellow Englishmen, who had just experienced a civil war, a murdered monarch (Rycaut was a Royalist), a royal restoration, and, by the end of his life, another (Glorious) revolution in 1688. Rycaut was not just writing a plain history but an extraordinarily powerful and complex polemic which has resonated throughout Europe and down the centuries. Yet his fundamental message had nothing to do with the Turks, whom he used as an awful warning from history as to what would happen if Englishmen failed to protect their ancient freedoms. They should 'know and prize their own Freedom, by comparison with foreign servitude, that thou mayst every day bless God and King and make thy Happiness breed thy content, without degenerating into wantonness or desire of revolution. Farewell.'[24] In the process, he made the Turk into Europe's metaphor for terror, tyranny and oppression.

4

Taking the Road to War

The coldest winter in living memory gripped the territory between Vienna and the Aegean. In the palace at Edirne, Sultan Mehmed IV and his court enjoyed good hunting over the hard, icy ground. A thousand miles to the north-west the cold offered no compensations, with the streets of Vienna almost empty as the people of the city, in effect, hibernated. One almanac had accurately predicted extraordinarily 'fierce (and prolonged) cold' for the first months of the year. Even in mid-March, the streets and squares were coated every morning with thick ice and frequent falls of snow.[1] Along the Danube between Vienna and Belgrade the foul weather continued with great floes of ice moving down the river. But eventually the snow turned into heavy and continual rain, filling the streams and rivers and transforming the low ground into a mire. Even normally solid paths and roadways became boggy and impassable by wagons and carts. Transdanubia, the vast bight formed by the Danube south of Budapest, was dotted with lowland marsh and wetlands. Towns were built on rising ground but in early spring, as the winter snows melted, many became islands in the midst of a morass. The first maps of Hungary printed in the sixteenth century ignored this seasonal inundation, but in reality it dominated every aspect of life.[2] The icy cold of the winter of 1682–3 only masked another certainty: that once spring broke the grip of winter, the Ottoman host would not be far behind.

The army that set out from Edirne for Belgrade was the Sublime State on the move. An 'Eminent Merchant in Constantinople' had written 'to a friend in London' of the sultan's departure from the capital in October 1682: 'In this sight was exposed the greatest riches of the Empire, consisting in Jewels of inestimable value, horses, clothes and furniture, the magnificence whereof is not to be expressed in writing.' Nevertheless, he did go on to write of 'a body of horsemen . . . with their bows, quivers, swords and lances; next the Bashaws [Pashas], each with his retinue of led horses, handsome pages with coats of mail richly dressed'. The Grand Vizier's procession was led by 'the Viziers Guard covered over with skins of lions, bears, tigers and leopards, every one differently habited; next came the six horse-tails, carried before the Vizier by eighteen men, on poles ten yards long; then fifty of the Vizier's pages a foot on each side of the way, between whom he rode himself. Behind him two huge camels, "the greatest to be found in the empire", the first of which carried the clothes of [the Prophet] Mahomet, which he wore in his lifetime, the latter the Alcoran as it was delivered by Mahomet to his successors.' Sultan Mehmed rode on a 'milk white horse, covered over with invaluable jewels, attended by pages dressed alike with caps of massy gold, their habit cloth of gold, reaching below their knees, girded by a girdle three inches broad, covered as thick with diamonds and other jewels as they could set together'. After these rode the prince (the heir, Mustafa) 'in a plain habit and on an ordinary horse followed by about four hundred, all the Grand Signior's pages armed with caps and coats of mail, gauntlets, swords and targets [shields] each with a quiver of gilt arrows on his right side, and a bow on his left'. The case for the bow and the quivers were set with diamonds 'and other jewels. They wore a loosely fitting garment of satin, some green, some scarlet, some blue, some yellow, and all colours, which mixed, made a delicate show.' The rear was brought up 'by about five thousand Spahis or horsemen, each carrying in his hand a pike advanced.' With them ended a parade which had lasted five or six hours.'[3] When the procession was repeated at Edirne after the snows had melted, the force had almost doubled its original size as it set out for Belgrade. The sultan was gathering his array.

The exotic spectacle of the departure represented a kind of triumph before the campaign had even begun. It would be repeated when the army left Belgrade for the final ceremonial stage, the crossing into Hungary. On the march the great cavalcade was preceded by a vanguard, Tartars and the light irregular cavalry, who rode a day or two ahead of the main force. Then came the bulk of the army, thousands upon thousands of horsemen; and behind them the mass of infantry stretching back several miles. But to the rear was an ever-growing artillery train and myriad carts which carried the powder and shot and all the army's equipment. The whole force could advance only at the pace of the ox carts and the cannon, perhaps twelve miles a day.[4] There were frequent delays. In the atrocious conditions of 1683 wheels and axles broke in the ruts and potholes of the roads, while cannon had to be manhandled through the mud. As the pace of the advance faltered, so the spirits of the troops plummeted.

As the huge mass of men began to advance through the valleys of Thrace and then under the dark mass of the Rhodope mountains, moving by stages from one temporary encampment to another, nature imposed its own ineluctable timetable. The army could only take the field when movement became possible in the spring. Until the new year's fresh grass appeared there would not be adequate grazing for the horses and oxen on the road north. One fifteenth-century account put it succinctly: 'The Turk keeps constant watch for the appearance of the first grass shoots in Spring. As soon as the grass springs from the earth he will close the gap and be upon us.'[5]

In later wars, mechanised armies would rely upon petroleum, but the Ottoman way of war depended just as much on nature's fuel for its beasts of burden. Traditionally the campaigning season began around the public festival in early May celebrating Hizir Ilyas, a Muslim saint who protected travellers and others in danger.[6] This meant that the journey north to Belgrade where the campaign was formally launched would begin in March or early April. In 1683, the sultan's war tent was put up in the palace grounds at Edirne on 15 March, signifying that the campaign would soon begin; but the artillery arrived late and it was the end of the month before the army could set out for Belgrade. It did so following an evil omen. During a great parade at the war camp, under the eyes of all his troops and foreign ambassadors, just as Sultan Mehmed IV ordered the march to begin a sudden gust of wind blew his turban off his head, and, as Caprara gleefully reported to Vienna, a shudder ran through the ranks.[7] It took nine days in torrential rain to reach their first objective, Filibe (Philippopolis), the old Roman capital of Thrace. By Filibe many of the troops were verging on mutiny, and the Grand Vizier ordered a three-day halt. Every day streams cascaded down the hillsides, swelling the rivers and often carrying away the bridges. Another week's march brought them only as far as the provincial capital Sofia, and another prolonged halt. On 24 April, the whole force reached Nish, the main garrison town of the region, and nine days later, on 3 May, the sultan and his army finally arrived at Belgrade, the point where the rivers Sava and Danube joined. The city was roughly the midpoint between Istanbul and Vienna, where the main roads from the south to the north met; the first stone *castrum* was built there by the Roman legionaries, and over time an upper and a lower town had grown up inside the walled city, Kalemegdan. The Ottomans had strengthened its defences after the city finally fell to them in 1521 and the white limestone walls and tower became the gathering point of all their expeditions into the lands beyond the Danube.

Sultan Mehmed IV and his Grand Vizier shared a secret. In the autumn of 1682 they had determined that Vienna would be the target of the 1683 campaign. Secrecy meant that if their plan proved impossible – as had happened twice to the great Suleiman I – they would avoid the humiliation of failure.[8] The sultan immersed himself in the manuscripts in the palace archives that described the conduct of earlier campaigns. The documentation was extensive, as Ottoman historians had chronicled military events thoroughly, albeit in a courtly, florid style. Nonetheless, they conveyed a great deal of information about how sieges and battles had been fought, and the lessons that could be learned. We can surmise their influence upon the sultan, but there is no manuscript diary or strategic plan that would provide any incontrovertible and decisive intent. The underlying motives behind the campaign of 1683 have never been fully considered, and the information is scanty. Yet we can see that a new war in the west was the result of burgeoning confidence inside the Topkapi Palace in Istanbul. In 1682, victory really seemed there for the taking.

Both sultan and Grand Vizier knew that a full-scale campaign would cost a fortune and would demand the investment of their political credibility. The expenditure of both demanded a worthy objective. Here the heart began to conquer the head. The campaign that the Ottoman commanders in Hungary wanted was very limited: capturing one or two of the powerful Habsburg fortresses north and south of the Danube. Seizing the star-shaped bastions of Győr or the gun emplacements of Komárno which controlled the river would have altered the strategic balance decisively and left a gaping hole in the Habsburgs' defensive line. It would have strengthened control over the Turkish-ruled lands west of Buda, and perhaps have allowed for even deeper advances into Royal Hungary. Yet the symbolic value of taking Vienna was plainly more persuasive than military logic.

The sultan yearned for renown. As we saw earlier, his uncle Murad IV was remembered as the Conqueror of Baghdad; his namesake, Mehmed II, had been the Conqueror of Constantinople. Mehmed IV had notionally 'commanded' in the capture of Candia and 'won' the city of Kamenets. But he wanted a real victory. With what we know of Mehmed IV, his extensive reading, his love of heroic literature and his sense of ancestry, to be hailed as the Conqueror of Vienna was an irresistible prospect. The motives of the Grand Vizier, Kara Mustafa, in pursuing the conquest of Vienna are less simple to divine. His object-ives are always presented as trivial and debased; he only wanted, said his critics, Ottoman and Western, money and land. He assiduously flattered his master and gratified his every whim only to advance his own ends. If the sultan wanted Vienna, who was he to contradict him? As Grand Vizier, his ambition was supposedly overweening, his corrup-tion and avarice gargantuan. So it seemed divine justice would be at work if and when his many vices ultimately brought about his downfall. But is this too much of a morality tale?

There is another possible motive: family pride and a sense of dynasty. Kara Mustafa was not born a Köprülü: he entered by adoption. The House of Köprülü's sudden accession to power and its continuing success in government was without parallel. Between 1656 and 1735 eight members of the family attained the supreme rank of Grand Vizier. Over decades, the Köprülü household developed an identifi-able ideology and ethos. Its core of interest lay not in the eastern but in the western provinces, the Mediterranean and Europe; Kara Mustafa owed everything to his adoptive father. He was an integral part of the family's heady ascent to power from its first days, going back with Mehmed Köprülü to Istanbul and his destiny in 1656. His adoptive family transformed his life: in return he became the custodian of its destiny and its honour. This relationship of clientage (*intisab*) was fundamental to the Ottoman society; it was an unbreakable bond.

For both the sultan and the Grand Vizier the conquest of Vienna represented more than just another campaign. Secretly, they were sure that Vienna would fall to them, a triumph that had eluded all Sultan Mehmed's predecessors. For the Grand Vizier, it would make him, the adopted son, the parvenu, the greatest of all the Köprülü. But all this must be surmise. Neither in 1683 nor subsequently has any unambiguous motive emerged for the decision to attack Vienna.[9] Many at the time, Ottoman and Western, rightly blamed the Grand Vizier for the ultimate failure, and conveniently and explicitly exonerated the sultan. Authors like the former English consul at Smyrna, Paul Rycaut, stressed that Kara Mustafa's success lay in gratifying his master's appetites and fancies.

But Sultan Mehmed IV was neither an incompetent nor a degenerate like his father. It is likely that he was an active partner in the plan; better read than any Ottoman ruler for several generations, he was deeply impressed with the mystique of the Ottoman dynasty and the military achievements of his greatest ancestors. In his youth, the imperial envoy, who saw him on a number of occasions, remarked on his 'solemnly quiet and melancholical nature', deeply influenced by his mother.[10] It is difficult to find any clear sense of his character, because it was so much coloured by the events of his long reign. Battle for Mehmed IV had become an adventure in the mind. He liked the image of being a warrior, and it was as a warrior that many European artists portrayed him in his mature years. With a good sense of their audience and market, they also demonised him. His slight, boyish figure was often portrayed incongruously in books and prints with captions like 'tyrant and bloodhound' or 'mad dog and savage man'. Yet concrete examples of his viciousness are notably absent. He was affectionate towards his sons: the savage tantrums that his own father, Ibrahim, had inflicted upon him were not part of his make-up.

It is harder to form an impression of Kara Mustafa. Many who met or saw him commentated on his extraordinary sense of his own importance and destiny. Unlike his half-brother and other members of the Köprülü household, he would not touch alcohol in any form, and he appeared to have a genuine contempt for Europeans and other non-Muslims. Kara Mustafa was born a Muslim, the son of a *sipahi* fief holder in the small town of Merzifon, in the mountains a little to the south of the Black Sea. In 1652, Mehmed Pasha, out of favour at court, had retired to his estate in a town called Köprü, not far from Merzifon. While the young man was in his teens, he was adopted by Mehmed, and returned with him in triumph to Istanbul when the pasha was recalled to become Grand Vizier. Within the family, the outsider quickly became a member of the clan. His friendship with Fazil Ahmed, the elder son of the family, was warm, and this relationship was cemented when he married Fazil Ahmed's sister.

He had learned a vital early lesson from his patron: a successful vizier must be feared, not loved. However, he was enough of a courtier to pay attention to the sultan, and to take an interest in the young princes, Mustafa and Ahmed; his reward was the hand of an Ottoman princess in marriage, for whom he divorced his first wife. The relationship between Sultan Mehmed IV and Kara Mustafa was different from that with all his other viziers, before or after. Kara Mustafa was the elder by about thirteen years, tall and powerfully built, with a luxuriant black beard and dark features. While the other Köprülü were all of Albanian origin, the first of them brought to Istanbul in the youth levy, Kara Mustafa was a pure Anatolian. He rose fast: in 1663 he was made admiral of the Aegean galley fleet, and battled against the ships of Venice. He fought in the Cretan campaign, and was renowned for his reckless courage. He was precisely the kind of manly figure whom, I suggest, the young sultan might admire.

So, was the attack on Vienna, rather than a plan formed in the mind of the Grand Vizier and imposed upon a dubious and unwilling sultan, perhaps hatched between them? The initiative might even have come from Mehmed IV.[11] But it seems unlikely. While the attack was being planned, the story goes that the Grand Vizier dreamed that he had put new boots on his feet, a seven-headed dragon had appeared before him, walked all over him and bitten him. And the next day he had the soothsayer interpret the dream. '[He was told] "The boots you are wearing signify departure for campaign and the dragon is the Habsburg Caesar . . . who is submissive to the command of seven kings. It is best that you withdraw from this campaign or it is certain you will regret it." '[12]

Such evil omens might have frightened Mehmed IV, a timorous character; they would certainly not have deterred Kara Mustafa. The sheer reckless boldness of the enterprise was in character. Even so, his plan was not based on some megalomanic whim. Ottoman military intelligence was robust, but provided two contradictory messages. First, it told them that the great prize of Vienna was tantalisingly out of reach, protected by the necklace of fortresses to the east. Moreover, south of the Danube the landscape pockmarked with vast marshes and swamps blocked the path to a comprehensive triumph in the west. Yet Ottoman envoys, spies and informers had also made it clear that once past these outer defences Vienna itself would not pose much of an obstacle. Its fortifications were not up to date, and it was not well defended. The symbolic value of capturing the enemy capital and citadel was immeasurably greater than capturing some border fortress even if the short-term military value of the fortress might be greater. Just as the capture of Constantinople in 1453 had been militarily insignificant but of enormous emblematic importance, so, too, the fall of Vienna would bring both glory and advantage.

We should finally consider Kara Mustafa's most personal and deep-rooted motive. Among the Köprülü the defeat at St Gotthard in 1664 remained a bitter memory, the one great failure of the family and a stain on its honour. Kara Mustafa wanted to redeem the family's reputation with the blood of its enemy: he was driven by a yearning for revenge. Sultan Mehmed IV had similar motives. For both men, the Habsburgs were more than just another Christian foe. The Ottomans regarded them with special loathing and distrust. They dealt differently with many western enemies: in the seventeenth century they negotiated successfully with the czars of Russia and the kings of Poland, always more readily than they did with the Habsburg Holy Roman Emperor. Their dislike was fundamental. The Habsburgs were despicable usurpers, who falsely used an imperial title that rightfully belonged to the Ottomans, the inheritors by conquest of Rome's imperial past.

The Ottomans had first entered both Hungary and the Habsburg lands in the fifteenth century, and began their conquest in the sixteenth. But they had not reached the limit of their ambitions. The business of conquest was incomplete, and the dictates of Islam coincided neatly with the House of Osman's deep sense of destiny. A sultan's religious duty was to extend the Domain of Peace, and reduce the Domain of War. The dynastic impulse was to make the claims of the sultan's title a reality. The *Khan of Khans*, the *Shah of Shahs*, the *Lord of Lords* should be suzerain over all other lesser rulers. The German king, who falsely called himself the Roman Emperor, ruled from the city of Vienna. In Ottoman eyes this was a lie. The real title of Roman Emperor had belonged to the Byzantine Emperor who had ruled from Constantinople. Mehmed II in conquering the city become the ruler of the Roman empire (*Rum*). The conquest of Vienna and opening a holy mosque would, in Ottoman custom, make him the veritable as well as the legal ruler of the west. Had not Suleiman I called himself 'Caesar of all the lands of Rome, master of the lands of Caesar and Alexander'?[13]

In Ottoman eyes this destiny stretched back to the beginning of time. One of the ancient Oghuz ancestors of the Ottomans had saved the entire world by killing a rabid wolf; another, by clubbing a maddened camel to death, had preserved humankind from disaster. Another legend, recorded by the historian Aşikpaşazade, told how the first chieftain of the dynasty, Osman, was staying at the house of his future father-in-law, a saintly dervish, Edebali. There he had dreamed that a moon rose from Edebali's breast and then entered his own heart. Immediately, a tree grew from Osman's navel, until its shadow covered the world. In its shadow were mountains, from which bubbling streams flowed. In the morning the dervish interpreted the dream to mean that God have given universal power and authority to Osman and his descendants.[14] These were ambiguous and slender claims to world power, but comparable Habsburg claims were not much better founded.[15] A sultan's hereditary duty and rule extended not only to the faithful, but to all humanity: he should bring all people under Ottoman rule and under the authority of Islam.

A full-scale aggressive war in the west during 1683 made good sense. The Grand Vizier and his immediate circle were very well informed about the problems of their western enemies. They knew the Habsburgs were preoccupied with defending their positions in Germany and in the Low Countries against the burgeoning power of France. In the east, they saw how extraordinarily vulnerable the Habsburgs had become, with the Emperor Leopold I's repeated mishandling of his Hungarian subjects and especially his active persecution of Hungarian Protestants. Many Hungarians were now reluctant to give any material aid to the Habsburgs. Some had even come to wonder whether the Ottomans might be no worse than – and even preferable to – the hated Austrians.

The greatest obstacles to success against the Habsburgs were time and weather. When Sultan Suleiman I had advanced in the sixteenth century he faced fewer problems than the Ottoman commanders would confront in 1683. Yet he had twice been deflected from his goal, Vienna: the first time in 1529 by a spirited defence of Vienna's old city walls and an early onset of winter; the second, in 1532, he was frustrated by the heroic (or foolhardy) resistance of an insignificant fortress. Since his day, the defences on the northern frontier had become immeasurably stronger. The Danube frontier with the Habsburgs was now dotted with new-style fortresses, some in Ottoman hands but mostly built and held by Habsburg garrisons. This new military land-scape had created a kind of stalemate in which neither side could gain an overwhelming advantage, because besieging a single fortress could take weeks. For this reason, in the Long War fought in western Hungary between 1593 and 1606 neither Ottomans nor Habsburgs had been capable of gaining a decisive advantage. More fortresses had been built in the years after 1606.

The best that Ottoman commanders could offer was the possibility that one or two fortresses might change hands, and the armies would march home. It was not enough. The Ottoman tradition of war, at least as interpreted by Kara Mustafa, demanded a better outcome. The vast cost of launching an assault that would produce only a derisory return was unacceptable. The plan to attack Vienna might be risky, but at least it offered the prospect, however slim, of a decisive success.

★   ★   ★

The summons sent out in the autumn of 1682 had ordered the array to meet the sultan in early May 1683 at the camp beside the little town of Zemun, close to the point where the Sava joined the Danube below Belgrade's castle walls. The war camp grew daily, with long lines of infantry and cavalrymen moving across the bridges that joined the old town side with the west bank of the Sava. Seen from the citadel of Kalemegdan, the neat lines of tents spreading out along the river bank and the many thousands of horses indicated the scale of the army that would march north. In the port, a procession of tubby cargo boats queued up to be loaded with the heavy guns and bulkiest siege equipment. Each day, heavily laden ships sailed upstream for Buda, or for Osijek, the river port on the Drava, a Danube tributary, where the

SELF-SACRIFICE

1. In 1859 the Hungarian artist Sándor Wagner depicted the moment of self-sacrifice at the siege of Belgrade (1521) when Titusz Dugovics threw himself and the Ottoman commander from the walls of the citadel.

HEROISM

2. The vast canvas by Austrian artist Johann Peter Krafft (1780–1856) celebrating the moment when Miklós Zrínyi and his men make their final charge to a certain death from the citadel of Szigetvár (1566).

INFELIX KARA
MAGNI TURCARUM
MINISTER
Post acceptam cladem ante
Julia Imperatoris Supremo dicti

MUSTAPHA BASSA
IMPERATORIS
PRIMARIUS;
Viennam ab Eodem obsessam.
Alba Græcæ Strangulatus et decollatus.

ERNEST
GRAVE VAN
KEYSERLYKE
EN GOUVERNEUR

RUDIGER
STERRENBERG,
VELT-MARSCHALK
DER STADT WEENEN.

THE ANTAGONISTS AT VIENNA, 1683

3.–5. (*Clockwise from top left*) Grand Vizier Kara Mustafa of Merzifon, who led the Ottoman attack; Count Rüdiger von Starhemberg, the Austrian soldier who commanded the defence; the King of Poland, John III Sobieski, who led the relieving army.

JOHANNES
REX POLONIARUM,
LITHUANIÆ

III. D. G.
MAGNUS DUX
UKRAINÆ ETC.

RECONQUEST IN THE EAST
6.–8. (*Clockwise from top left*)
Charles, Duke of Lorraine,
the conqueror of Buda; Ludwig
Wilhelm, Marquis
of Baden – the 'Türkenlouis',
hammer of the Turks;
Maximilian Emmanuel, Elector
of Bavaria, who took Belgrade
from the Ottomans.

IN THE PIT OF HELL

9. The desperate struggle for the shattered Löbl bastion, painted by Leander Russ in 1837.

THE GREAT COMMANDER

10. Napoleon called him one of the greatest generals of all time: Prince Eugene of Savoy, symbolically in battle against the Ottomans, painted by Jacob van Schuppen in 1718.

army would actually cross into Hungary. For weeks the roads leading to Belgrade had been crowded with irregular Bosnian horsemen, local landholders and their retinues, clusters of Balkan musketeers and levies, and, most significantly, with the first large contingent of Tartars from the Crimea, each rider with a string of stocky ponies behind him. From the eastern and Mediterranean provinces, a steady stream of Syrians, Anatolians and Berbers from North Africa swelled the ranks. The Grand Vizier's tent was thronged, as foreign allies, local dignitaries and officials came to pay their respects and assert their loyalty.

The foul weather that had slowed the army's advance to Belgrade was lifting, and the sodden earth finally began to dry out. From Belgrade it was 350 miles to the Habsburg frontier, 100 miles west of Budapest. It would take from the end of March until the middle of July 1683 for the Grand Vizier to lead his army to the outskirts of Vienna. Although the land between Belgrade and the Habsburg frontier was Ottoman, nothing could overcome the handicaps imposed by nature. In earlier centuries, the marshy terrain was less of an obstacle. For a seventeenth-century Ottoman army, with its huge baggage train, this water-world was a greater challenge than the enemy's forces.

Nevertheless, beyond the Danube, once across the Sava and the Drava, the second stage of the journey would be easier. Under good conditions, over solid ground, the whole force could advance at a steady speed. But even when the weather was good there were still many smaller rivers in spate now that the snow had melted. Each one had to be bridged solidly enough for the wagons and cannon to be dragged across. But often the temporary pontoon bridges broke apart under the strain and the unwieldy cannon ended in the water.

Traditionally, the campaign began when the army gathered at Belgrade. It would take anything up to six weeks for the Ottoman host to reach the northern frontier with the Habsburg lands. But every commander was acutely aware that there was limited time available for any siege on the far frontier. The army would have to begin its long march back from Vienna by the end of September at the latest, to be safe in its winter quarters before the snows fell. Nevertheless the Grand Vizier was supremely confident that they would face few difficulties in their attack against the infidel. How could it be otherwise? The land was theirs, and their enemies could not resist their advance to the war zone beyond Buda. At that point they would be

only a few days from their objective and their assault would be irresistible. Success was in the hands of God: how could they fail?

Across the river lay a land the Romans had called Pannonia and
which is better known today as Transdanubia. The region was also
under full Ottoman rule. It was distinct from both the mountainous
territory to the south, the 'Balkan' in Turkish, and from the other
highland zone, Transylvania, or Erdel in Turkish, north-east from Buda.
Transdanubia was a morass of 'marshy deserts inhabited by a steadily
and drastically declining population'. There was little agriculture and
most of the inhabitants raised livestock.[16] The Romans had cleared
the vast primeval forests, and oats and barley became the staple crops,
but in no great volume. It had always been a backward region, with
only a scattering of Roman towns and townships. The kings of
Hungary had largely ignored it. The Turks made no attempts to
colonise the countryside or to proselytise for Islam: they transformed
the towns by filling them with Muslims, razing most of the old buildings and rebuilding them in a Turkish style.[17]

In the towns and cities of the Ottoman empire, perhaps less in the
countryside, different communities lived for the most part in relative
harmony. The theory of the Ottoman state required that they should
do so, for the sake of good order. The record of religious and social
persecution and atrocity is undeniable but such occurrences were also
sporadic and circumstantial; cruelty and terror were instruments of
Ottoman policy. They did not take place at random. As in Stalin's
Russia, the needs of the state determined the uses of fear, and Istanbul
told the pashas who should be punished, hated and oppressed.

What happened in Istanbul and in the other cities was very different
from what took place elsewhere along the very edges of the Ottoman
domain. But beyond that general, cautious supposition, there were
unusual and special circumstances on the western boundaries that make
confident historical judgements risky. Or, rather, we need to know whose
history we are using. The events that unfolded in these borderlands
contained three elements. First, there had been a nation, Hungary, once
a great and powerful kingdom, which had been transformed over four
generations into a people 'ground between the millstones of great
empires'.[18] Second, Hungary became the battleground in the confrontation between two great empires, the Habsburg and the Ottoman;
both metamorphosed into world powers and thus became locked in a

primordial political struggle. Thirdly, this struggle was usually defined in religious terms, which reflected the ideological chasm dividing the two adversaries. This multiplicity of actors, the endless conflict and the bewildering array of motives, all yielded ambiguities which make the records highly partisan.[19]

Most of the long land frontiers of the Ottoman empire were lawless, shifting badlands that paid very little attention to any distant master or superior. They were like the unstable, unsettled environment described by the French cultural anthropologist Paul-Henry Chombart de Lauwe.[20] 'Badlands' lacked fixed rules of life, deeply rooted social customs, predictable ways of thought, long-established social leaders, settled patterns of religious belief, or a set of ideals conforming to some dominant social milieu.[21] The edges of the empire were in a constant state of change and flux, whether to the east of Baghdad or to the west of Buda. In the west, these borders were beyond the zone of control that radiated outward from the cities and fortresses. It was a realm of disorder stretching from the Adriatic to the peaks of the High Tatra Mountains north of the Danube.

This to-and-fro mayhem in the borderlands exasperated the pashas and their officials in Buda castle, since it reflected badly on their competence in the eyes of their superiors in Istanbul. It was their duty to keep order and every raid was a sign of failure. On the Habsburg side of the frontier wardens and castellans were similarly blamed for the Ottoman incursions. But on the western side the raids also became a literature, widely popular and spreading the notion of the cruel and ceaseless Turkish pressure far and wide. Most of them were tales from the far distant past. The story of the Bavarian Johannes Schiltberger became a minor classic. He was a page to a Bavarian nobleman and taken prisoner at the Battle of Nicopolis in 1396. He was enslaved for thirty years, and passed from master to master, traversing the east in an extraordinary set of adventures. He was slave successively to the Ottoman Sultan Bayezid after Nicopolis, made prisoner by Tamerlane's Mongols when he defeated the Ottomans, taken back by them into the steppes, traversing the Crimea, the Kipchak steppe, parts of Muscovy, the Caucasus, until he escaped in the port of Batum and eventually made his way to Istanbul. Then he walked home to Bavaria, arriving in 1427. It was an epic tale, and it was circulated widely in manuscript. When printing developed in the 1450s, it was one of the few early printed books to achieve a wide circulation, and caused a sensation with its first production in Augsburg in 1476. No fewer than eleven editions were published by 1600, and Schiltberger's tale became an archetype of all subsequent captivity memoirs.[22] The most striking element of the book was not so much Schiltberger's descriptions but the engravings inserted by the printer. This was the first presentation of the hereditary enemy (*Erbfeind*), as the Turks were routinely described, and even the illiterate could understand the brutality of the image of the sultan ordering the beheading of the survivors of Nicopolis.

A more contemporary narrative was the story of a farmer, Andreas Grein, a graphic example of the risks and fears of life in the borderland. The year 1640 was officially one of truce between the Habsburgs and the Ottomans, but nonetheless raiders still came north of the frontier. The walled village of Purbach close to Lake Neusiedl had frequently come under the threat of attack; several inhabitants had disappeared from the fields at the time of earlier raids. There were even rumours of an attack by a large Tartar band, against whom the walls would offer some protection. Nevertheless the villagers decided to abandon their homes if an attack threatened and head for the relative safety of the mountains north of the Danube, behind Pressburg.

There were many false alarms and sometimes the Tartars struck elsewhere, but in 1640 a large-scale raid was under way and approaching Purbach. Andreas Grein, whose land was about half a mile from the walls, sent his wife and family away with the other villagers; he stayed behind to care for his vines and his livestock. It was a bad decision. Unknown to Grein, the raiders were already close to the now undefended village. The Tartars ransacked Purbach, found Grein, beat him and trussed him. They moved on to the next village, dragging him at the end of a rope, but there, too, the inhabitants had all fled. After another two days, and now fearful that a column of Austrian cavalry was riding to intercept them, the war band headed back across the frontier. They roped Grein and some other unfortunates they had captured to their horses' tails, and forced them to run along behind. At the first main town the Tartars reached in the Ottoman lands, he and his companions were sold into slavery. Grein was housed in a stall with the other prisoners and they were used like a team of oxen, forced to pull a plough by day. For food he received only a handful of nuts, some millet, and water. After seven years of terrible suffering he succeeded – with the help of an Austrian woman – in escaping. In October 1647, after travelling on foot for many months, he arrived back at Purbach. There he stopped to rest on his own land, about 1000 yards from the town walls.

In the morning he went to his home where he was met by his wife, and discovered she had recently remarried. She did not recognise Grein because of his wild beard, long hair and filthy, ragged clothes. Even when he spoke to her she did not know him. He insisted that he was her husband who had come back from the dead, and after much discussion and somewhat reluctantly she finally recognised him as her husband, by his voice. Grein's story ends with her asking him for forgiveness, and they lived happily together until they died.[23] The second, less fortunate husband had to relinquish his new wife. At the place outside Purbach where he had rested upon his return, Grein erected a Holy Trinity column, inscribed with the year 1647. The marble plaque bearing his story remains to this day.

Grein's story was implausible because so few people returned home from slavery. Schiltberger and Grein would be the rare exceptions. But through the medium of the press, their stories and the pictures of their suffering spread throughout Europe, far from the badlands. The patchwork of individual raids, burnings, murders and kidnappings was woven together to produce a terrifying image. There were other such fears in western societies – of pirates at sea, robbers and murderers on the highways, of hidden Catholics in Protestant regions, of secret Protestants in Catholic areas – but the fear of the powerful and rapacious Turk knew no limitations or boundaries. English readers in 1683 were able to see an image of three Christians chained by the neck and pulling a plough, or, earlier, men being dragged behind horses by Tartars. All these things happened, but not all the time and not to everyone.[24] These real-life disasters of the eastern border were only part of life along the frontier, but they soon came to be seen as typical, quotidian and universal. It was what the Turks did (inevitably a very partial point of view), but it was also potent propaganda.

Throughout the decades of formal truce, a succession of tales of atrocity and mistreatment proliferated in the west. Schiltberger's adventures of two centuries earlier were reprinted again and again and additional survivors of the cruel and oppressive Turks wrote their own stories. The adventurer John Smith, better known for his ill-starred relationship in the North American forests with Pocahontas, published his racy memoirs in 1630. He described his capture:

> Smith, among the slaughtered bodies . . . with wounds lay groaning among the rest, till being found by the Pillagers . . . and perceiving by his armour and habit, his ransom might be better to them than his death they led him prisoner with many others; well they used him till his wounds were cured, and at Axopolis they were all sold for slaves, like beasts in the market place, where every merchant viewing their limbs and wounds, caused other slaves to struggle with them to try their strength; he fell to the share of Bashaw Bogall, who sent him forthwith to Adrianopole, so for Constantinople to his mistress for a slave. By twenty and twenty chained by the necks, they marched in file to this great city, where they were delivered to their several masters.[25]

There is an engraving of this event showing Smith, shackled in an iron collar, being dragged by the neck under the watchful eye of the pashas. The many pictures of western captives suffering in the North African Ottoman territories and Morocco were infinitely more gruesome.

There is only one comparable prisoner account from an Ottoman perspective. The son of a senior janissary at Temesvar, Osman Aga also entered the order and was taken prisoner by the Habsburg advance in 1688. After various hardships, he was taken into service and was treated as a curiosity by his employers/captors. At first he was put to work in the stables of a nobleman's house, then as a manservant, and ultimately as a pastry cook. In 1699, he at last managed to escape and finally reached home. We know from this account that others – including women – joined him in this escape. However, while the stories of western captives were printed and widely circulated, Osman Aga's remarkable account survives only in a single manuscript in the British Library.

There was an appetite for tales of eastern cruelty and sensuality, which writers, playwrights and artists were eager to satisfy. It was not so much a matter of *if* the sultan would attack, but *when* that attack would come. It was in the Turk's nature to make war, and the news that the 'Turk was on the move' in the spring of 1683 resonated not only in Vienna and the German cities but also in London, the Scandinavian capitals and as far north as Aberdeen in Scotland. For many, the attack on Vienna in 1683 was something more than a military campaign. They saw the war as yet another episode in an unending struggle between the Christian faith and the vast, malevolent, dark power of Islam.

At the time Protestant Christians, uncomfortably wedged between the theoretical threat of the infidel Turks and the immediate peril from militant Catholicism, were sometimes less committed to this view. But they were not free from it. Protestant English, Scots and Dutch writers wrote angrily about Christians enslaved on the Barbary Coast in precisely the same terms as Catholic authors. A fearful and negative view of the Turks was commonplace in virtually every Western European culture, institutionalised through teaching, words and image, oral culture, drama and folk myth. Even those most distant from the 'Turkish menace' felt threatened by it.[26]

PART TWO

OH, EAST is East, and West is West, and never the twain shall
   meet,
Till Earth and Sky stand presently at God's great Judgment Seat;
But there is neither East nor West. Border, nor Breed, nor Birth,
When two strong men stand face to face,
tho' they come from the ends of the earth!

                    Rudyard Kipling, 'The Ballad of East and West'

5

The Adversaries

In the days during which the army gathered its strength at Belgrade, Mehmed IV and Kara Mustafa had a series of meetings, both public and private.[1] The sultan would come down from the castle and cross over to the camp at Zemun. On 13 May a full-scale parade was held on the meadows along the banks of the Sava and before the entire army the Sultan, with his sons Mustafa and Ahmed sitting beside him, ceremonially handed over the command of the army to Kara Mustafa and entrusted him with one of the three banners of the Prophet that Sultan Selim I had captured in Egypt in 1517. The Grand Vizier, now *serasker*, with the untrammelled power of life and death, knelt before the Sultan and kissed the earth on which he trod.

Whatever was planned and decided in their meetings in May, the final point of decision before the army headed north is uncertain. But the appointment of Kara Mustafa put the responsibility firmly in his hands. In the Ottoman tradition the sultan would share success, as in the campaign for Crete or the conquests in the Ukraine, but would disclaim responsibility for any failure. On 20 May the sultan paid his last visit to the Grand Vizier's encampment, and watched the janissaries march off to the crossing point at Osijek. Four days later, the entire army set off in their wake, a stately four-hour march that reached the first camp at the town of Vojka, a mere fourteen miles away. By the following morning, as the horsemen and wagons set out again, heavy rain was falling. They were also heading for Osijek. The Romans first built a narrow brick bridge across the river, and, across the riparian swamps on the northern bank, a solid causeway to higher ground in the province of Pannonia beyond. Six roads converged on Osijek, five of which fanned out south-east and south-west into the Balkans. Over the centuries the river crossing and the wooden causeway beyond across the Baranja wetlands had decayed, and while ferry boats crossed back and forth between the northern and southern banks, the Drava was once more a military barrier. As Sultan Suleiman began his last campaign in Hungary in 1566, he had conscripted some 25,000 labourers to work with his engineers to build a new wooden bridge across the river and a long wooden road on piles to the village of Darda, about eight kilometres from the river.

But in 1664 Count Miklós Zrinyi, with 23,000 Croat and Hungarian mounted raiders, had captured the town, and before withdrawing had burned the bridge and causeway built by Sultan Suleiman. It was a dramatic and effective blow. The trade routes north were closed as was the supply of troops and equipment; the Ottomans quickly moored a narrow pontoon bridge beside the charred ruin, which the English traveller Edward Brown saw in September 1669. The blackened stumps of the old piles remained, 'so strongly fastened and hard that it would have cost them too great a labour to get them up. By this bridge the Turkish forces pass into Hungary.'[2] The engraving of the old bridge showed a massive structure that had carried a solid highway: without considerable strengthening a pontoon bridge could not carry the heavy guns that Kara Mustafa needed to take with him. That urgent work was still under way when the advance guard arrived.

As part of his planning for the 1683 campaign, the Grand Vizier had ordered the complete restoration of the old roadway into Hungary, so that the heavy cannon could be hauled across. But the persistent rains that had made the advance of the army from Edirne to Belgrade so difficult had virtually halted the work on the bridge and causeway. The Drava, swollen with the melted snow from far upriver in the Tyrol, battered the piles of the bridge. Across the river, many died in the swamps as they worked sometimes up to their necks in the turbid waters underneath the damaged roadway.

This ancient structure, hundreds of miles from any battlefront, was the key to the subsequent campaign. Crossing the Drava was deeply symbolic, just like the ceremonial on the Çyrpeci Meadow at Istanbul, then the parade before the palace at Edirne, and finally when Mehmed

IV formally bade farewell to the troops at Zemun; all were ceremonies of war. In his own eyes, Sultan Mehmed IV and his illustrious ancestors were Roman emperors, *sultan i-Rum*, rulers by right of conquest. He was familiar with the biographies of Caesar and of Alexander the Great. He knew the story of how Caesar (as Plutarch recounts it):

> came to the river which separates Gaul from the rest of Italy (it is called the Rubicon), and began to reflect; now that he drew nearer to the fearful step and was agitated by the magnitude of his ventures, he checked his speed. Halting in his course, he communed with himself a long time in silence ... estimating the great evils for all mankind which would follow their passage of the river, and the wide fame of it which they would leave to posterity. But finally, with a sort of passion, as if abandoning calculation and casting himself upon the future, and uttering the phrase with which men usually prelude their plunge into desperate and daring fortunes, 'Let the die be cast,' he hastened to cross the river.[3]

The river crossing at Osijek was passing the Rubicon. From that point onwards, the path to war was irrevocable and to return without victory would spell disaster. Kara Mustafa understood that the die was cast, the summit of all his hopes and ambitions. He could not fail. On 2 June 1683 the vast Ottoman host was encamped before the bridge-head of Osijek. Across the river lay Hungary and only a few weeks' march to the infidel lands. But the bridge was still not ready. For twelve days the soldiers waited impatiently in camp on the banks of the Drava while the sappers worked feverishly to complete the repairs to the causeway across the marshes to the town of Darda. Their task was formidable. Edward Brown had described the original bridge admiringly: '[It] is scarce to be paralleled by any other, built partly over the [Drava] and partly over the Fens which are often overflowed. The Bridge is at least five miles in length, having towers built upon it at the distance of every quarter of a mile: it is handsomely railed on every side, and supported by great trees, erected under it, nine or ten unto each arch.'

The *serasker* Grand Vizier Kara Mustafa put the twelve days of forced idleness to good use. Ottoman advances were always punctuated with halts and rest days, so he ordered daily drills for the janissaries and instructed that all the equipment be checked and repaired. The river port at Osijek, barely eighteen miles from the Danube, received daily cargo ships from Belgrade bringing up additional rations, ammunition and supplies. Some of the cannon left at Belgrade were shipped to Osijek, where carpenters hurriedly made carts to carry them. Kara Mustafa received a stream of spies' reports on the marshalling of the enemy forces north and south of the Danube, and surprising news of the Austrians' complete inactivity at Vienna. No work was being done on strengthening the city defences, which the Turks knew were in a poor state of repair. This news made the delay especially frustrating, since the less time their enemy had to repair the walls and bastions, the easier the Turks' task would be.

Istanbul had set the war in motion, and Vienna would stumble to respond. Both states were now linked in a series of events from which there was no certain outcome. The sultan and the Grand Vizier believed that Vienna could be taken, through a conjunction of circumstances that might never recur. The Habsburgs believed that they possessed a battle-hardened army, which, despite Montecuccoli's death in 1680, was still led by men who had learned their trade under his command. But these beliefs were superficial. These experienced (and ageing) commanders and colonels were not the answer. The Habsburg problem was more basic. There were nowhere near enough soldiers and money was perennially short, defects that could not quickly be remedied. Instead, the Emperor Leopold and his advisers reassured themselves with comfortable memories of the victory at St Gotthard. Did this not prove that heroic Habsburg paladins were more than a match for any Turkish army? They paid little attention to the Ottoman military machine about which their special envoy Caprara informed them, which could deliver 100,000 men in good order, and feed and supply them for a whole campaigning season far from home.

The differences between the two adversaries, in faith, language and society were self-evident; but much less obvious were the similarities. One contemporary English savant, Henry Neville, considered all the governments of Europe in his discourse between a *Noble Venetian*, an *English Gentleman*, and the latter's doctor. Neville observed that empires, since ancient times, were brought down by becoming enmeshed in 'ceremonious follies'.[4] He did not think much of the Habsburgs, whose neighbours 'had enough to do to defend their several liberties against the encroachments of the house of Austria'. The Turks, by contrast, he believed might have been 'the best and firmest monarchy in the world' had not the janissaries 'made the palace and the seraglio the shambles of their princes'. But Vienna and Istanbul were both courts rooted in ancient traditions of 'ceremonious follies' and they had much in common. By the late seventeenth century, both the Habsburg court in Vienna and the Ottoman court in Istanbul had become detached from the real, external world. This isolation had a considerable effect on the events of 1682–3.

Both rulers – the Emperor Leopold I and Sultan Mehmed IV – shared a number of traits. In theory they were all-powerful, but both had made themselves utterly dependent on the courtiers around them. Leading cloistered lives, both coming unexpectedly to power as minors, both devoted to books and manuscripts, they invested their time and energy in the hunting field. They were also equally reluctant to change their close advisers, who knew their masters' will and whims. No contemporary political system fostered resolute independence by any courtier but Vienna and Istanbul were exceptional in the reverence attached to the ruler. It was the duty of the courtier to preserve the tranquillity of the monarch. So, Mehmed IV never heard the advice of the local commanders on the Hungarian front, notably the pasha of Buda, who had sound reasons for opposing the Vienna adventure. Equally, Leopold never learned the dangers of his repressive policies in Hungary during the 1670s until it was too late, while all he gleaned from his advisers in 1682 was rosy optimism about the Turkish advance.

It was, of course, just an accident of fate that had produced two rulers with these curious similarities of character. But the two empires that they ruled, although hereditary enemies, also had important elements in common. By the 1680s, they were the oldest great states of Europe, excluding the spiritual power of the Popes. Habsburg and Ottoman alike had risen slowly to eminence during the fifteenth century, the Habsburgs always running a little behind the Ottomans, and with more limited resources. Both had come to maturity in the early sixteenth century, with Charles V becoming Holy Roman Emperor in 1519 and Suleiman I succeeding his father, Selim I, as sultan in 1520. Both dynasties created – and again the Habsburgs were some way behind the Ottomans – the first bureaucratic imperial systems in Europe since the Roman Empire. And both, by the 1680s, were tired and in need of renewal.

In each of the major states in Europe, a new family ruled. In France the Valois had given way to the Bourbon, in England, the Tudors to the Stuarts. In Spain, the last Spanish Habsburg ruler was perennially on the point of death, and he had no direct heir. In Sweden the native House of Vasa had given way to a German prince, a nephew of the great Gustavus Adolphus. Each change in the ruling family, in effect a new management, eventually provided a systemic shock, often a transforming change of people and policy. The Ottomans and the Habsburgs by contrast had experienced only the relentless continuity of the 'family business' for 150 years.

Continuity was not the same as stability. There were the 'perpetual revolutions' in the house of Osman, the murders, depositions and violent uprisings so gleefully recorded by European writers. But through all this long history the essential framework, the 'habitus', the complex web of custom and practice of the two states, remained unaltered; significantly, in the seventeenth century they both took increasing pride in their venerable antiquity, compared with other societies.[5] It was not as old as they believed or claimed. In the sixteenth century each had found very modern solutions to the governmental problems they confronted. They created a systematic structure of rule, centred on the ruler and his court. Both Ottomans and Habsburgs ruled, where possible, by creating precedents, by the monopoly of the records they carefully stored in their palace archives; by centralisation of power; by systematising the legal system; by creating administrative and political uniformity. In the Ottoman lands they had created a powerful military system, something that would elude the Habsburgs until the eighteenth century.[6] In each case, the key qualification is the phrase 'where possible'.

The obsessive observance of tradition was central in both the Ottoman and the Habsburg worlds. As Stephane Yerasimos observed:

As is the case in all traditional societies, among the Ottomans 'innovation' meant 'degeneration' because it was perceived as a deviation from the established order . . . Ottoman imperial processions were also an occasion on which to show off the might of the Ottoman state, to renew it, and to prove it to its own people and to everyone else. In the course of a festival foreign envoys, government officials, the heads of guilds, and men of accomplishment and talent marched before the sultan and presented him with gifts in a ceremony that implied a renewal of the whole world's allegiance to the sovereign. Indeed during the circumcision feast of 1582, the greatest of all these festivals, the fact that the procession included representations of farmers ploughing their fields, of fishermen catching fish, and of tradesmen and craftsmen of every kind plying their respective trades and crafts needs to be considered as a proof and a sign that the sovereign was the caretaker of the established order that was marching before him. Under the circumstances, we should think of Ottoman imperial processions as events staged to alleviate social tensions and also to replenish political power and authority.[7]

Habsburg processions, religious rituals, tournaments and stage productions had a similar intention.

But in the 1680s these two venerable dynasties had one profound difference. At that point, in the Ottoman world the head of state could be a cipher; in the Habsburg system he could not. Leopold's most recent biographer, John P. Spielman, described him in his youth: 'No hot-headed young ruler anxious to make history, but a perfect prince for a tradition-bound dynasty and a deeply conservative aristocratic society: modest, prudent, pious, neither a libertine nor a spoilsport, a quiet young gentleman content to let things run as they had done in the past.'[8] But the family tradition, and the expectation, was that the Emperor should be active and not relinquish all power of decision to his ministers and servants, which was quite possible in the Ottoman system. In many ways this was a hindrance to speedy and effective decisions, because Leopold was intensely cautious and a procrastinator; equally, once the Emperor had made a decision, he would not change his mind. He prayed nightly and listened devoutly to the answers he received. Symbolically, Mehmed IV had transferred the absolute power of command to Kara Mustafa at Belgrade, but none of Leopold's commanders in 1683 would have the same freedom of action.

History (written with the benefit of hindsight) has generally regarded the Ottoman confidence in victory as delusional. How could

'the Turk' possibly win, so far from home, and at the absolute extremity
of their lines of supply? What folly. But just as purblind were the Habsburg attitudes. The Emperor and his advisers were faced with an impossible conundrum: where were the military resources of the Habsburgs
best deployed? Against the menace of France in the west or against
the threat of the Ottomans to the east? The power and threat of
France was a known quantity, the Ottoman danger almost an ancient
myth. The Turk had attacked Vienna in 1529, and failed. They had
also failed to make good their subsequent attacks. On the other hand,
if there were a serious menace, then it was the responsibility of the
Holy Roman Empire to meet the challenge, with money and
manpower. Leopold and his councillors sent out envoys to the states
of the empire, and took the money eagerly offered by Pope Innocent
XI, who believed in the Holy War against the Infidel. Most creatively,
Leopold pushed for an alliance of mutual defence with John III Sobieski,
the King of Poland. Poland had already suffered Ottoman attacks north
of the Dniester River in the 1670s. All these reactions were measured,
calm and politically assured. There was no panic, but instead the
systematic response of a practised and well-oiled administration, which
then immediately passed on to other and more pressing matters: the
threat from France.

One of the best decisions that the Emperor made, on 6 May 1683,
was to appoint his brother-in-law, Charles, Duke of Lorraine, to take
the position as field commander, the role Montecuccoli had filled until
his death almost two years before. Charles of Lorraine had fought in
the French cavalcade against the Turks in the 1664 campaign, and
gained great renown in the wars against Louis XIV. In 1682 he was in
semi-retirement, representing the Emperor as the governor of Tirol, in
Innsbruck. His contemporary King John III Sobieski later described him
precisely. He had the long aquiline nose 'almost like a parrot', much
admired as a sign of good breeding. He was heavily scarred by smallpox,
and he looked like a fighting soldier. 'He wears grey, unadorned, [and]
a hat without a feather and boots which were polished two or three
months ago, with cork heels. His wig (a rotten one) is fair in colour.
His horse isn't bad, with an old saddle and trappings of worn and poor
quality leather. He is obviously little concerned about his appearance.
But he has the bearing . . . of a person of quality.'[9] Nevertheless, he
would not cut an imposing figure at the Polish or any other court.

A member of the family which had long ruled the ancient duchy of Lorraine, Charles had had a solid if not brilliant military career, but his loyalty to the Habsburgs was unquestionable; he admired and respected Leopold, whom he saw in a different light to many who knew only the Emperor rather than the man. The duke's greatest attribute as a commander was the affection and trust he inspired in his men, who knew his reputation as a courageous soldier. In battle he was used to being in the thick of the fiercest fighting. He carried the scars of many battles, and in the field wore his dark red hair cropped short, usually discarding the 'rotten wig'. But as the generalissimo, his duty was to eschew heroics and keep the army intact at all costs. It was, after all, the only line of defence for the Habsburg domains.

The ceremonial handover of the command to Lorraine was as carefully stage-managed as the equivalent Ottoman ceremony at Belgrade, when Kara Mustafa was invested with the power of *serasker*. Just as the Turkish host far to the south was making camp at Belgrade, the Emperor Leopold and his court, with all the foreign ambassadors in his train, left Vienna in a long procession of coaches for the plain of Kittsee, on the southern bank of the Danube opposite Pressburg (today Bratislava). There the army that would defend Christian Europe was drawn up in field array for inspection. There were just over 32,000 men, paraded regiment by regiment, and ranged in front of them seventy-two guns and fifteen mortars. At eight in the morning the Emperor and Empress, their fourteen-year-old daughter Maria Antonia and her newly betrothed, the Elector of Bavaria, Leopold's most significant ally, knelt before all the soldiers. The Archbishop of Gran celebrated mass, with the accompaniment of the court choristers raising their voices to heaven. The Emperor and the court received the Body of Christ from the Archbishop's own hands and then, as the field chaplains passed through the ranks administering the sacrament, each soldier and officer also received a papal indulgence to bolster them in the coming struggle against the hereditary enemy. Later, Leopold added a further inducement by promise of an additional month's pay. It was, to no one's surprise, never paid.

After the service, Leopold mounted a frisky stallion, and, followed by the imperial family and his entourage, rode on a slow tour of inspection through the ranks. For four hours, he moved from contingent to contingent, congratulating them on their fine appearance, good discipline and martial air. He admired the well-burnished cannon, spoke warmly to the regimental and company commanders and took special pains to encourage the Hungarian horsemen raised by Count Esterhazy, whose flamboyant green, red and gold uniforms contrasted with the plain white coats of the Austrian infantry and black cuirasses of the cavalry. Then, the parade over, the imperial party moved on to an elaborate banquet, while the artillerymen fired salvo after salvo in celebration, before the coaches returned to the capital. But many, especially the Hungarians, had noticed that the force was much smaller than they had anticipated.[10] At the end of day, the Emperor put his concerns about the Ottomans massing in the south to the back of his mind. His dispositions had been made and the matter was resolved.

Objectively, the political and military position of the two adversaries was unusually favourable to the Ottoman cause in 1682–3. Although in theory Christendom was uniting to resist Turkish barbarism, gaping political fissures had opened within the Christian camp. While some of the leading states of the Holy Roman Empire had pledged support in principle against any Turkish assault, it was not yet a military reality. Only his future son-in-law was ready to come to Leopold's aid. On 31 March 1683 the Emperor had signed a treaty of mutual defence with John III Sobieski, but again the realistic extent of Poland's potential assistance against any Ottoman attack was still uncertain. The worst case was that Leopold would face not only an Ottoman assault from the east, but the likelihood of an attack by the armies of France on the family's territories in the west, as well as an army marching into the Holy Roman Empire. The experienced French ambassador at Istanbul, the Comte de Guilleragues, had been in post since 1679 and developed a close contact with the Grand Vizier, based on lavish French gifts and sedulous flattery by the ambassador. A little duplicitously, Guilleragues assured Kara Mustafa that France believed it a remarkably opportune moment for the Turks to launch an attack and his master, Louis XIV, would do everything in his power to support the Ottoman state.[11]

But most beneficial to the Ottoman cause in 1683 appeared to be the hatred of Hungarians, both Protestant and Catholic, for their king, the Emperor Leopold I. The Habsburgs endlessly proclaimed the benign quality of their rule. Ruler after ruler had emphasised the kindness and 'clemency of the dynasty'. It was apparently 'inborn' and deep in their collective nature. The reality was rather different. Propagandists for Leopold declared, 'The House of Austria is as mild as honey, [and] only out of necessity it resorts to the sword and sheds the blood of the guilty.'[12] The category of 'the guilty' embraced a great many, from the powerful Magyar magnates to the ordinary people. Hungarians, of both faiths, resisted the ceaseless extension of Royal authority into the borderlands; many Protestant believers had no aversion to the House of Habsburg *per se* but suffered constant persecution for their 'heretical' beliefs.

Leopold was entitled by law and custom to enforce the Catholic religion of the state, but the manner in which it was done made him seem even more oppressive than the Sultan. By the late 1670s the government in Vienna had virtually lost control over the countryside of Royal Hungary, where increasingly tough and ferocious anti-Habsburg Protestant raiders, who called themselves 'crusaders', or *kurucok*, were creating an insurgent state. By 1680, faced with the growing threat from the Ottomans, Leopold conceded a little to his turbulent subjects; finally, in 1681, he restored the ancient rights of the Kingdom of Hungary, and the liberty of belief for Protestants. But it was too late to obliterate memories of the incessant cruelties in the previous decade.

The sapping of Protestant Hungarian loyalties could not easily be reversed. In the highlands of Transylvania and the mountains of modern Slovakia, Calvinists, Lutherans and Unitarians far outnumbered Catholics, and their numbers were swollen by refugees from persecution in the cities and the great plain. For twenty years Leopold had believed Protestants were the heart of the conspiracy against his authority in Royal Hungary and his logic was faultless. They were an affront both to his faith and to his political authority. But the persecutions in the east also undermined the Habsburgs' position in Western Europe. In the Protestant states, like England and the Netherlands, his natural allies against France, the harrying of Hungarian Calvinists in the 1670s became notorious. In 1675 forty elderly Protestant pastors were condemned to become galley slaves in the Spanish Habsburg fleet at Naples.[13] The grim fate of these 'Persecuted Martyrs' generated a flurry of books and pamphlets, calling for action against their oppressors. Eventually, the States General in The Hague dispatched the Dutch fleet under Admiral de Ruyter to Naples to secure their release. On 11 February 1676, he sent his marines on to the galleys and freed the pastors, who were taken back to Amsterdam and a hero's welcome.

The contrast between the Habsburg and the Ottoman treatment of their Protestants was stark. In a pamphlet published in London in 1676, while 'in those dominions that are under the Emperor's obedience' there was only a handful of Protestant churches, in the lands bordering the Turkish dominions there were about two hundred, but 'these are under daily and great fears', for they have been alarmed by many from the Habsburg authorities. However, in the southern part of Hungary under Turkish dominion, there were about six hundred churches and no suggestion of oppression or persecution.[14] The campaign against Hungarian Protestantism formally ended in 1681, but the hatred of Habsburg 'tyranny' persisted. Many Hungarian Catholics, after Leopold had suspended the nation's constitution in 1673, also regarded their king as a tyrant, but paradoxically still recognised him as a defender of their faith.

The most intransigent of the Protestant 'crusaders' sustained the struggle under the leadership of a young Magyar nobleman called Imre Thököly. In 1682, Mehmed IV on the Grand Vizier's advice shrewdly offered him the title of King of Upper Hungary, under Ottoman protection and subject to the payment of an annual tribute. This territory, the land to the north and east of Bratislava, included the fortresses protecting Vienna from attack on the north side of the Danube, and the Ottomans believed (wrongly, as it turned out) that Thököly could take possession of his new kingdom and so neutralise the Habsburg line of defence. In November 1682 Leopold had invited a delegation from the rebels to meet him in Vienna and in the following spring, one of them, Istvan Szirmay, now came south to make a personal report to the Ottoman court of that meeting. He had used his time and his eyes well. He told the Turks of the poor state of the city's defences. He had briefly met the Emperor in the Hofburg Palace, and he had seen for himself that the defence line close to the palace was especially weak, with the Emperor's personal quarters hard up against the outer wall.[15] One of his servants, a former monk, while waiting for his master had even managed to make some surreptitious sketches of the ravelin and bastions. Szirmay also told the sultan of the Emperor's attempt to bribe Thököly to remain neutral in any Turkish attack.

The game of bluff and double-bluff played by the Ottomans with Thököly, and by Thököly with both the Ottomans and the Habsburgs, makes it difficult to be sure of anyone's motives or intentions. But it seems likely that the sultan and the Grand Vizier hoped to use him to oversee any new territory they conquered, recognising that a long-term alien domination of Vienna would be both difficult and expensive. This form of indirect rule worked in Transylvania, Moldavia and Wallachia, and could have as easily been applied to Upper Hungary or even in the Austrian frontier lands.

★   ★   ★

The contingents from the Ottoman's distant domains in Europe, like the Christian horsemen and musketeers from Wallachia who arrived after the departure from Zemun, finally caught up with the main army. There were daily parades and inspections. In his great tent Kara Mustafa refined his plans. He held several meetings with Imre Thököly himself, who had come too late for an audience with the sultan in Belgrade. But the meetings with Kara Mustafa were more down-to-earth bargaining sessions than ceremonial encounters. The commander's secret strategy depended, at the least, on a neutralised Hungary north of the Danube. He disbelieved Thököly's wilder promises to raise the people of Royal Hungary against the Habsburgs, but it would be sufficient for his purposes if the rebels kept as many of the enemy troops occupied and far away from the main Ottoman thrust, against Vienna. The *serasker* laid out the tempting prospect of the 'kingdom' that Thököly could, with Ottoman support, win for himself, if all went well. Vienna might even be his capital, and a Hungarian would again rule in the city for the first time in centuries.

Neither man could trust the other. Thököly was secretly negotiating for an even better deal with the Emperor Leopold, while Kara Mustafa was notorious for ruthlessly ridding himself of anyone who outlived his *raison d'être*. But for the time being each suited the other's purposes. On 14 June, the construction completed, the Grand Vizier and his ally led the Ottoman host across the bridge of boats, crossing over the swamplands to the first settlement in Hungary. This was the true start of the war, the moment of commitment, for from Darda the highways fanned out northwards, and the Ottoman army was barely a month away from the frontier with the Habsburgs.[16]

As the Tartar horde moved forward, every morning many clusters of perhaps two dozen riders, each man trailing two or three horses, would detach themselves from the main body and disappear in the general direction of the enemy, some heading north-west towards Graz, others in the direction of Sopron, and many more north in the direction of the Danube. These were the commander's eyes and ears. Often they would return with prisoners, or reports on the movement of the Habsburg troops. Other little bands would come in the other direction, rejoining the main band. As the Turks moved steadily north-west, marching four or five hours a day, Kara Mustafa knew the main disposition of the Austrian cavalry and infantry, the state of readiness in the Habsburg fortresses and the state of rivers and bridges that criss-crossed the landscape. By contrast, the enemy commander, Charles, Duke of Lorraine, knew very little about *his* enemy.

The Grand Vizier had summoned the Ottoman troops in Hungary and their pashas to meet him in full force at the old Hungarian royal capital, the White Castle, which the Turks called Istolni Belgrad (today Székesfehérvár). Some sixty kilometres south-west of Buda, the ancient Hungarian capital was built on a hill rising out of the marshes. It had fallen to the Turks in 1543, was ransacked, its cathedral despoiled, and quickly repopulated with Muslims. By 1683 it looked like any Ottoman Balkan city, and only the chapel of St Anna (transmuted into a mosque) survived from the old city. The Grand Vizier's great tent was set up below the walls and on 27 June, after the midday meal, he called together his commanders for a council of war. It was an old custom, from the early days of the Ottomans, that decisions about a campaign should be made collectively by the senior commanders of the clan. Kara Mustafa suspected that the secret plan to attack Vienna and not some minor fortress would sow seeds of doubt and alarm. All knew that even the great Sultan Suleiman I 'the Lawgiver' had failed, and some might also have known the saying common among Christians that capturing Vienna, the Golden Apple of legend, would begin the decline of the Ottoman dominion.[17] Like most myths, the Golden Apple is opaque. It did not suggest that Vienna alone was the predestined symbolic goal of Turkish conquest, as Constantinople – the Red Apple – had been. Other German cities were also 'golden apples'. But it certainly suggests that conquest in the west was deeply ingrained in Ottoman political ideology, and Vienna would be a splendid, if perilous, trophy for its conqueror.

Kara Mustafa chose his war council carefully. He wanted pliant men. The pasha of Buda, the senior commander on the border, whom he knew was averse to this risky venture, was not invited. One writer records that when he announced the army's objective, as one man the war council began to chant the first sura of the Qu'ran to bring God's blessing on their enterprise, concluding: 'These are rightly guided by their Lord; these shall surely triumph.'[18] The following morning the tents were struck and the army prepared to move on Vienna.

The army which set out on the morning of 28 June 1683 stretched, one western writer said (with a little exaggeration) 'from horizon to horizon, a line six miles long, where the eye could not see its limits': it was 'in truth a new Army of Xerxes'.[19] But the sheer scale of the host with its heavy baggage limited the path it could take towards Vienna. North-west of Székesfehérvár, on a straight line to the Habsburg capital, lay the town and fortress of Györ, which the Austrians called Raab. The town was built at a strategic point where two rivers flowing from the south – the Raab (Rába) and the Rabca – met the southern branch of the Danube. The only good highway to Vienna passed close to Györ, and a powerful fortification, built in the sixteenth century and improved in the seventeeth, dominated the point where the rivers merged. This complex of bastions and ditches, with the island fortress of Komárno, twenty-five miles downstream, formed the heart of the Habsburg defensive system against invasion from the south-east. To the south and south-west, the solid ground on which Györ and neighbouring towns were built gave way to a land-scape of bog and meadow, dominated by the larger rivers. The land between the rivers was interlaced with a skein of rivulets and streams that formed a huge expanse of boggy ground.

Generations of Habsburg officers had assumed that the combin-ation of strongpoints and the marshy wilderness would blunt the edge of any Turkish assault on the capital, and would be impassable for any large army. It bred, to say the least, an attitude of complacency. The greatest threat, Austrians believed, lay along the easier ground north of the Danube and this was where their strongest defences were concentrated. These confident assumptions were not based on any real knowledge in Vienna about the lie of the land south of Györ. No one in living memory had ever inspected the wilderness, and there was no report to be found in the imperial records. But Tartar scouts had already brought detailed reports back to the Grand Vizier on his march northwards. The water level in the rivers was quite low and the scouts could either walk through them or swim across. It would not be hard to bridge them for the heavier equipment. There were already many small bridges, put up by the local peasants to allow access to their fields or for hunting game.

This was unknown to the Emperor and his advisers in Vienna, and to his commanders in the field. They discovered these unnerving facts thanks to the efforts of a twenty-five-year-old officer, an Italian nobleman from Bologna, Luigi Fernandino, Count Marsigli. He was one of the many extraordinary Italians who crossed the Alps to enter the Emperor Leopold's service. Quarrelsome, sharp-tongued as well as quick-witted, he was a cousin of Raimondo Montecuccoli, victor at St Gotthard, and of Caprara, who had unwillingly accompanied the Ottoman army on its journey north. Marsigli was constantly restless and insatiably curious. His inquisitive nature had driven him to visit Istanbul in 1680, and then to write about the waters and fierce currents of the Bosporus, learning some Turkish in the process. In the early spring of 1683 he had come to Győr because there was work for an aspirant military engineer to rebuild the defences. There he was told to visit the strange marshy world to the south of the city, which imme-diately piqued his curiosity. Marsigli's report, and a handful of his careful drawings, showed that there was a path on more or less solid ground through the marshes, but by building temporary strongpoints and defending some of the fords any enemy advance could be held up. But the frontier was definitely permeable all along the line of the River Rába, so Marsigli was told to strengthen thirty-eight vulnerable points down as far as St Gotthard, or destroy any bridges where that might hold up a Turkish advance.

As the Ottomans advanced from Osijek, the Habsburg command still had no clear strategy and no sense of Turkish intentions. They had no knowledge day by day how far their opponents had moved forward, or even the direction in which they were heading. When Kara Mustafa arrived at Székesfehérvár, they were still no wiser. Almost every senior Habsburg officer had his own opinion, each trying to enforce his own strategic view. The Ottoman commander might send his army south of the marshes, towards Sopron, as Marsigli believed he would, crossing the Rába and then wheeling his men north towards

Vienna. Or he might march straight on to Győr, the Habsburg stronghold south of the Danube, and storm it.

He might even head due north, construct a pontoon bridge of boats across the Danube, and attack the fortresses north of the great river. In reality, it was inspiration and guesswork: they had no intelligence or reports from spies: they could only guess what this huge force would do. While the Turks were well informed of the disposition of the Habsburg forces, the Emperor and his commanders enjoyed a benign ignorance. In the capital the vital improvements to the defences ordered by the renowned military engineer Georg Rimpler moved languidly forward in the unusual heat of an early summer.

When Lorraine arrived in Vienna he found a jumble of contradictory objectives and a clamour of advice. The Emperor and his inner circle believed that he should take the offensive – to demonstrate the battle readiness of the Habsburg army – and perhaps lay siege to Esztergom, a weakly defended Ottoman fortress far to the east, on the bend of the Danube above Buda. Alternatively, he could attack an Ottoman stronghold, Nové Zámky, closer to Győr, but on the northern side of the Danube, which might encourage the Poles to come more rapidly to the support of their ally. But they also made it clear that none of these enterprises should be allowed to weaken the defence of Vienna or of Styria, so some troops would need to be detached so that they could guard the southern frontier along the Rába.

Behind this chatter a serious dispute was building between the Duke of Lorraine and the President of the War Council, Hermann, Marquis of Baden. The younger son of the staunchly Catholic ruler of Baden, in southern Germany, he had, like the Emperor, been destined for the Church, the fate of many younger sons of ruling families. He was aged fifty-five in 1683, and had been promoted to succeed Montecuccoli as President of the War Council in 1680. But he resented the fact that he had not gained the other post, as the field commander, which the Emperor gave to Lorraine. A tall and strikingly imposing figure, a loyal patron but a bad enemy, most of the senior officers were dependent upon his goodwill. Unsurprisingly, they usually parroted his views, very much the best strategy for an ambitious soldier. Lorraine reluctantly set out for Esztergom with his infantry and cavalry at the end of May, only to be summoned back by the Emperor, who had changed the objective to Nové Zámky.

While the men could march back and forth, the siege artillery could not be turned around so easily. By the end of the first week in June, heavy guns and mortars were stuck in the mud, some north, some south of the Danube. On 12 June, Lorraine arrived at his objective; after ten days of desultory investment, the army headed south again. Marsigli, who had been called north to the siege, was turned around, and sent back post-haste to complete his work south of Győr. All the time, the Ottoman host was moving forward: four days after the Duke of Lorraine crossed the Danube (again) they were encamped a few days' march away from Vienna.

In those final days before the two armies came to grips, the fundamental difference between them is very evident. In the Ottoman host, despite the charade of a war council, a single man, Kara Mustafa, possessed an autocratic authority. As one senior officer, the provincial governor of the large, rich province of Damascus, was supposed to have said to the Grand Vizier: 'It is for you to command and for us to obey.' The Habsburg army was a mosaic of conflicting commands: different regiments, raised and commanded by their colonel, allies, mercenaries, and a host of private commands and, finally, the militia. All depended on a powerful, respected, and experienced battlefield commander. There was no one to equal General Raimondo Montecuccoli, but he was dead; he had no peer or successor. There was certainly a system, a military bureaucracy, which in theory worked well, if very slowly. The only truly decisive voice was the Emperor Leopold himself, but he was tremulous, uncertain and devoid of any military experience and so wisely took the advice of the expert professionals. But whose advice should he follow in these extraordinary circumstances?

Montecuccoli had been a savant, a war hero, and possessed of a steely temperament. In his youth he had been quarrelsome and febrile: by the time of St Gotthard he had calmed down a little. But in the end no one would challenge him. Dead, he had no obvious replacement. Lorraine, whom the old general had respected, was no substitute but the best available. He also possessed a quality that his old patron had lacked: charm and diplomacy. In a war that depended on quarrelsome allies, pumped up with their own sense of self-importance, Lorraine was the past master of the tactful gesture. He was no great military thinker like Montecuccoli, and, despite his status as a royal prince and a connection of the Habsburgs by marriage, he was a most unlikely courtier. But he elicited respect as an honest and courageous man, both calm and decisive.

Leopold's response to most situations was also calm, and a good deal of prayer. In the last days of June and early days of July 1683, he did what he knew best. He decreed that prayers should be said continuously day and night in the cathedral of St Stephen, while all the guilds, trades and corporations of the city were required to attend. The Emperor and the imperial family appeared on Sunday at 9.00, the Danube fishermen on Thursday at 8.00 and the violin-makers on Saturday at 3.00.[20] He also reinstituted the old custom of the Turkish peal (*Türkenglockern*), with all the church bells in Vienna and the provincial towns ringing every morning. Outwardly, he gave no indication of any difficulty or crisis. He left the military planning to his officers, and followed his daily routine without alteration. He went hunting on the imperial reserves at Perchtoldsdorf on 2 and 6 July, south-west of the city, and the only sign he gave of any crisis was an instruction that the ancient crown of St Stephen should be brought to Vienna from the church in Bratislava where it was always kept for the installation of the Kings of Hungary. He returned to the city on the evening of 6 July, in good humour after an excellent day's hunting, although the blistering heat of the summer was now felt everywhere.

On the next day, Saturday 7 July, the Emperor heard mass in the early morning as normal, and proceeded impassively with his usual routine. But from about midday, a stream of messengers brought worsening reports from the Hungarian border. The news was catastrophic. The huge Ottoman army was on the move, spreading like a tidal wave westwards from Györ. The Tartars were across the marshes, moving fast, burning villages and setting fire to woodland and cornfields. But Kara Mustafa and the Turkish host were also on the march, moving very fast towards Vienna, creating a huge dust storm made by thousands of horses and marching men. They were heading towards the point opposite Bratislava where a line of hills on the southern bank of the river matched the hills on the northern side. It was the last position before Vienna it which the army could make a stand and still hope to stop the Ottomans in their tracks. It was where Lorraine was basing the army, ironically, close to Kittsee where the Habsburg army had gathered for the great parade on 6 May, two months before. Beyond this high ground, at the village of Berg, the terrain became easier with the road open to the capital.

As Lorraine had ridden out to review the position early in the morning, an officer galloped up from the east to tell him that the Turks had reached the town of Moson, where the River Leitha, the traditional boundary between Hungary and Austria, flowed into the Danube. As the duke looked to the east, he could see a huge reddish cloud of dust rising into the air in the distance. Then, as they spoke, he noticed that there were numerous columns of smoke behind him, between the army and Vienna, indicating that the Turks' advance guard was already between him and the capital. Throughout the shadow campaign, in June and July, the Habsburg army had consistently underestimated the capabilities of the Ottoman army. Many had assumed that it had become torpid and ineffective, that it would never even reach the frontier. Such intelligence as they had received appeared to confirm that judgement. Informers had suggested that the Grand Vizier was weak, undermined by rivalry and dissension among his commanders, and the host had relatively few good soldiers and a vast baggage train. Now Lorraine saw the enemy could outflank and overwhelm him. A soldier all his adult life, he knew he now had three tasks. Firstly, to regroup his troops, strung out in positions on both sides of the Danube. He had to keep the army intact. Secondly, to slow the Ottoman advance to allow the capital a few days to ready its defences. And, thirdly, to recognise that with the weak forces at his disposal he could do nothing to prevent the siege and possible capture of Vienna.

This scenario of imminent catastrophe played out a few hours later in the Emperor's rooms in the Hofburg. There was a swelling chorus of Rumour.[21] First Count Auersperg, sent by Lorraine, to report that the Turks had broken out from Győr; then came General Enio Caprara, brother of the ill-omened special envoy to Istanbul, who brought news that the Turks were across the Leitha; within the hour, Colonel Montecuccoli (son of the victor of St Gotthard) arrived to say that the Tartars were harrying Lorraine's retreating troops and (wrongly) that they had already seized the bridge across the River Fischa, the last natural barrier before the capital itself. Leopold listened to this growing tumult of alarm and gave orders that the imperial family and the War Council should prepare to leave immediately for the supposed safety of Linz, 135 miles away, far up the Danube. The court carriages and baggage wagons were gathered and prepared; the treasury, the court archives and Leopold's prized library were stripped of the most valuable and important items.

The news of the feverish preparations in the Hofburg spread quickly through the city, and many of the leading families made their own arrangements to run. At 6.00 p.m. the Emperor formally announced that he and the court would depart that evening, leaving behind him a shadow war government to manage the defence of the city against Turkish savagery.[22] At that point there were only about a thousand trained soldiers available to man the walls, and his chosen commander, Rüdiger von Starhemberg, a tough and battle-hardened soldier, was still with the army on the far side of the Danube, and not in the city. The decision to flee the city was regarded by many as a craven act of cowardice, but in Habsburg eyes it had an absolute logic. Leopold had two sons, Joseph, aged five, and a sickly infant, Leopold Joseph, barely a year old, both with him in the city. He had no brothers, nor any living uncles. If he and his sons were killed or captured by the Turks, the dynasty would in effect come to an end. The closest male heir would then be Carlos II, King of Spain, wrongly held by many to be an imbecile, but not expected to live long. He had no male heir. In Leopold's eyes Vienna might be taken but it could be recaptured or rebuilt; but with the loss of the ruler and his heirs, the last of the Habsburgs, the dynasty could never be restored.

At about eight in the evening a long procession of carriages and carts with Leopold, his children and his pregnant third wife, plus a large armed retinue, left the Palace Gate, travelling eastwards along the line of walls towards the sluggish and half-empty tributary of the Danube that separated the eastern rampart from the newly developed area called Leopoldstadt. It crossed the bridge on to the flat island, driving on across the bridges that linked one island to another until the caravan reached the northern shore of the river. It was not the best or the easiest route, but there was a terror that bands of Tartars were already roaming the Vienna Woods to the west of the city. Cuirassiers and dragoons were waiting on the river bank to form a protective shield against attack. Meanwhile, Leopold's stepmother, with a strong troop of horsemen, set out from the palace to follow the shorter direct route on the southern bank, towards the fortified abbey of Klosterneuburg, a tempting but diversionary target for raiders;

the two parties planned to meet upstream at the abbey of Melk, on its promontory high above the river.

Leaving Vienna was not easy for Leopold I.[23] Part of the Habsburgs' mythology was the courageous behaviour of his grandfather, Ferdinand II, who in 1619 had been surrounded in the Hofburg by Protestant rebels from Bohemia. Ferdinand rejected their demands, and put his fate into the hands of God. It became one of the key episodes in the panegyric *The Virtues of Ferdinand* by his confessor, Lamormaini. Ferdinand, elected King of Bohemia, still to be elected Emperor and rejected by his Bohemian subjects, had shown no doubt or fear. As the enemy fired their muskets directly into his rooms, he was steadfast. This was the model for a Habsburg to follow, and his grandson had been found wanting. Nonetheless, Leopold had made the right political judgement. His duty lay in rallying the Empire to provide the army that could, even if the city were lost, save Christendom from the infidel. Almost as soon as the imperial family reached the town of Linz, a legend of the Emperor's heroic determination was already being written, although it could not entirely replace the evidence of a panic-stricken flight from danger.

In reality, the Emperor, like the people of Vienna, had been infected by the madness of the crowd. It was said that almost sixty thousand people fled from the city in the days following the Emperor's departure, with their places taken by refugees from the countryside seeking the protection of its walls. There was one week between the flight from the city to the arrival of the Turks and the beginning of an epic siege. In that time, the city had to be made ready for a fight to the finish.

6

'Rise Up, Rise Up, Ye Christians'[1]

The straggling imperial cavalcade left the city on the evening of Wednesday 7 July; twenty-four hours later, the new military commander of the city, Count Rüdiger von Starhemberg, returned to Vienna. Before the power and speed of the Ottoman advance became evident, Lorraine had split his cavalry regiments from his infantry, sending the foot soldiers across the Danube under Starhemberg's command, until the Turks' objective was unmistakeable. Many in the Austrian command still believed that the Ottoman plan was to cross the great river and smash the defensive line of Habsburg fortresses. But once it was all too clear that their target was Vienna itself, Lorraine ordered Starhemberg and his regiments back to the capital as fast as they could march. He told him to ride ahead as rapidly as possible, using the pontoon bridges over the Danube at either Bratislava or Vienna itself, whichever would cause the least delay.

On the southern bank, Lorraine, now fearful of being outflanked and attacked on several sides by the faster moving Ottoman horsemen, had fallen back before the *sipahis*, leaving the infantry on the northern bank to make the best speed they could. The swiftness of the Turks' advance was evident from the dust clouds that swirled ever closer to Lorraine's outnumbered cuirassiers and dragoons. Riding hard, they managed to put some distance between themselves and the Ottoman host, largely because the Turks had slowed their pace. Finally, riding at a brisk trot through the eastern outskirts, they arrived before Vienna. Hailed as the city's saviours, Lorraine's horsemen rode around the city walls, entering on the southern side, and paraded through the streets to the sound of trumpets and the steady beat of their drums, as if celebrating a victory. Their confident arrival began to halt the growing sense of imminent disaster after the more prominent families had fled the city in the wake of the Emperor and the imperial family.[2] Rumour now ran riot, with most of the refugees pouring in through the city gates never having seen a Turk, but telling hysterical stories that spread and magnified with each repetition. But now the city was under military command and a harsh discipline was imposed on civilians and soldiers alike.

On 9 July the remaining citizens and the thousands of refugees were quickly put to work repairing the walls and bastions, dragging the artillery into position and hammering long timbers into the earth to make a continuous palisade along the crumbling outer line of defence. This, in the printed panoramas of the city, appears as a strong wooden wall, but in reality in many places it had fallen over or rotted in the ground. In other places, holes had been made so that the Viennese could find an easier route to the world outside, rather than use the gates. This was the city's first line of defence, and, although it seemed flimsy, held with determination it was a major obstacle. These timbers were as thick as ships' masts, evenly spaced and buried deep into the ground. The height above ground varied, never less than six foot tall, sometimes more than eight. Only a direct hit from a cannon-ball would obliterate them, although gunfire could splinter and shred the new bulwarks. Yet even their battered stumps, used as shelter by musketeers, could halt an assault. Most palisading was done on the southern side of the city, opposite the Hofburg, where the outer earth rampart was higher, with a parapet and narrow roadway running along its length. As some working parties strengthened the steep slope running down into the moat with logs and beams, others laid smooth planks side by side on the outer face to make a slippery surface, sometimes interspersed with sharpened stakes.

As they worked with an energy fuelled by fear, the guild of carpenters built a strongly roofed passage out of planks, logs and wicker baskets called gabions (from the Italian word *gabbia*, cage) filled with earth or sand and stones. This would protect those defending the earth rampart, while a set of strongpoints was made where the defenders could fire down into the dry moat below, and on any enemy approaching up the outer slope. Work began just before dawn, continued on through the intense heat of the day and into the night by the light of flares and torches. The whole population was mobilised, and even the hundreds of monks and priests laboured with the laity. The sense of crisis comes out in the diary kept by Johann Vaelckeren (Valcaren), a military judge-advocate who lived through the siege in the city. 'No time was lost nor labour spared by all sorts of men, and sexes, young and old, both laity and clergy, as well in digging and removing the earth as plaining [levelling] the ditches and making them deeper, that the enemy might find the passage more difficult.'³

As they worked, it became clear that Vienna was woefully unprepared for a siege. The city, in military terms, was a thirteenth-century walled town, to which, through the sixteenth and seventeenth centuries, more effective and modern fortifications had been added piecemeal to the older defences. The people of England had indirectly financed those first walls. The great crusader King Richard the Lionheart had fallen out with his rival and fellow crusader Leopold V of Babenberg, Duke of Austria; on returning from the Third Crusade, Richard made the mistake of travelling (in disguise) through the duke's lands on his way home. Captured, imprisoned, accused of murder, he was freed only on payment of a huge ransom, approximately twice the entire annual revenues of England. The reputed 'six hundred buckets of silver' paid for the grand new walls for Leopold of Babenberg's capital, Vienna, and for his pet project, the new frontier town of Wiener Neustadt to the south. The splendid ramparts and towers were completed by his son, Leopold VI 'the Glorious', and Josef Mathias Trenkwald's romantic painting of 1872 depicted the day in 1221 that he first rode ceremoniously into the city.⁴

When the walls were first put up open spaces and vegetable gardens interspersed the streets and houses, but by the early sixteenth century these open spaces had mostly been built over.⁵ By the time Sultan Suleiman I had laid siege to the city in 1529, Vienna, still shut in the same medieval walls and gates, had almost outgrown its vital resources of water and housing. Then the city had survived the siege largely by good luck, because the Turkish miners took longer than anticipated to breach the walls near the Carinthian Gate, and an early onset of winter forced the Ottoman army to retreat. But after that terrifying experience, from the late 1530s onwards a new ring of defences was slowly constructed just beyond the old perimeter. These new strong-points – massive bastions – extended out from the ancient walls, while the walls themselves were lowered, strengthened, buttressed and rebuilt becoming the outer wall, or enceinte, for the new defence line. Inside the city, as noblemen, churchmen and merchants had created new grand residences during the sixteenth and the early seventeenth centuries, Vienna within the walls became ever more crowded and oppressive. Inevitably, as the Habsburgs became secure in their 'imperial' status, Vienna grew prodigiously, but it had to be upwards more than outwards, until eventually the city spilled out beyond the new defence line.

In 1529, the only visually dominant building had been the Cathedral of St Stephen.[6] By 1680 there were tall buildings everywhere, with the medieval streets in the heart of the old city transformed into deep, narrow canyons into which the sun sometimes penetrated for only an hour or two each day. Late in the seventeenth century, for all the new palaces and small pleasure gardens, it appeared irredeemably not a grand capital, but a fortified city, with the inescapable presence of the hereditary Ottoman enemy within a few days' hard riding to the east. Every year Turks would raid into the villages just a few miles from Vienna, carrying off villagers into slavery. The people of Vienna now had cause to be grateful for money lavished on the defences about which they had grumbled perennially. Decayed though the walls and bastions might be, they still presented a daunting challenge to any attacker.

The transformation of Vienna's defences had taken place in stages over more than a hundred years. The cost was enormous and decades often passed without further building; but once completed, the new fortifications looked very different from the old. The ancient ramparts were now encircled with a girdle of squat, solid, angular blocks, shaped like broad arrowheads and mostly surfaced with brick rather than stone. Their sharply angled points thrust outward towards an enemy. The outside edges were crowned with a parapet behind which marksmen could shelter, and where cannon could be emplaced. Already by 1547, a bird's-eye view showed the city entirely surrounded by a wide moat, fed from the Danube, with bastions at intervals around the walls, jutting out into the river.[7] Inevitably, this moat leaked into the basements and cellars within the walls, making Vienna's buildings closest to the walls dank and unpleasant. The Emperor's palace, the Hofburg, was particularly damp. But the defences proved their worth. Through the seventeenth century 'improvements' were added to the older bastions; in front of the sixteenth-century defences a line of massive detached triangular firing platforms (ravelins), more than twenty foot high, were like the prows of a great warship bristling with cannon, filling the empty spaces in front of the enceinte.

In the 1670s these ravelins were connected by a complex of walkways or trenches to the bastions and to the city wall. The moat was a constant problem. In the many paintings and prints of the city it looks imposing but it was never of much practical use. As well as leaking in hot weather the water evaporated leaving only a sluggish stream in the section by the Hofburg; even this rivulet dried up completely every summer.[8] As a result the idea of a moat was abandoned and it was replaced by a broad, steep-sided, dry ditch with a raised earthen rampart on its outer edge. Beyond the rampart was the open space called the glacis, a killing ground swept by cannon fire in which an attacking force would find no cover. The word glacis derived from the icy slope of a glacier, and was intended to be just as unwelcoming. Travellers entered the city over the glacis, through narrow and well-defended gates in the outer earthen wall, then over a causeway across the ditch and finally through a second gatehouse into the city itself. The Carinthian Gate, the focus of the Ottoman attack in 1529, was especially well protected; the newer entry, the Burgtor, close to the Hofburg, much less so.

For the traveller, the first sight of Vienna from the south and west was now unprepossessing: a steep earthen bank surmounted by a wooden fence of stout timbers and pierced by narrow entrances. The indefatigable Edward Brown walked around the city in 1677 and noted in his journal: 'There are two walls, the one old and inward, little considerable at the moment . . . the other outward of a great breadth made of earth, and faced with Brick, edged with Freestone, so well built, as to render this city one of the most considerable fortified places in Europe. The esplanade gently descendeth from the town for three hundred paces; there are very few outworks.'[9]

This new system of defence, of which Vienna was by the 1680s an old-fashioned example, had originated in Italy almost two hundred years earlier. It was at first known as *alla moderna*, the new method; by the mid-sixteenth century most Italian cities had defences in this style, and Italian architects and engineers soon exported the design throughout Europe. Functionally, it was designed to answer the problem posed by artillery which meant that even the strongest walls of stone fortresses could be smashed by bombardment. The great Roman walls of Constantinople, which had protected the city for almost a thousand years, had been breached by the huge siege cannon of Sultan Mehmed II in 1453. Under constant bombardment stone fortresses would, in effect, auto-destruct, brought down by the basic laws of physics. Their strength lay in their weight and mass, one stone block resting heavily on those below. The repeated impact of cannon-balls gradually dislodged the blocks until, with their stability shattered, they tumbled down through force of gravity. Concentrated gunfire knocked the layers apart. In the past tall buildings had been the best defence; the great medieval castles towering over the land were invulnerable to those far below. But in artillery warfare, the tallest buildings were especially at risk, providing the best targets, and were the easiest to knock down.

The new fortresses exposed themselves as little as possible to gunfire. Often the ground around them was artificially raised to make it impossible for artillery to fire directly at close range against walls or strongpoints. In this new era, the best defences were those that could absorb the shock of gunfire and would not be destroyed by it. Packed earth, held in place by brick or even timber, was all but impervious to cannonballs.

This new military architecture bred its own theories, fads and philosophies. The conceptual geometrical symmetries of the new science of fortification attracted artists and designers as much as military men. Dürer, Michelangelo and many others applied their sense of line and design to the arts of war. This 'modern' art of military architecture united the natural resources of the earth with gunpowder weapons: the two were inseparable. Bonding human artifice to the forces of nature was pioneered by architects deeply infused with the holistic concepts of the Renaissance. In his book *The Universal Idea of Architecture*, Vincenzo Scamozzi wrote: 'For a powerful and well-designed fortress, you must dispose and arrange the elements in the same way that Nature, the true teacher of all things, has ordered . . .'[10] They looked to nature in all its aspects for the answer: what terrain was best for building fortresses; what natural animal was strongest and best defended and could resist much more powerful beasts? The answer was familiar and close at hand. Not the noble lion or even the heavily armoured rhinoceros, but the *istrice*, or porcupine, an animal very familiar to Italians. Pacific in temperament, it had no natural enemies, because once roused it was almost impossible to overcome without the aggressor receiving savage wounds. If attacked it would raise an almost impenetrable array of strong sharp quills. King Louis XII of France (1462–1515) chose the porcupine as his emblem, coupled with the motto 'From near and afar, I can defend myself'.[11] Symbolically, it resembled the mass of pikemen, the Spanish *tercio*, which was the key innovation of sixteenth-century warfare. The *tercio*'s pikemen were supported by detachments of musketeers, who could indeed 'defend from afar'. The motif of strong defence was applied both to military architecture and to strong formations like the *tercio*, that were vulnerable only to gunfire. The great military thinker the Habsburg general Raimondo Montecuccoli described the pikemen en masse as the 'castles of the battlefield'.[12]

The new fortresses exemplified this emblematic theme. Bristling on every side like a porcupine, they left no obvious gap or point of weakness for an enemy attack. With low earth ramparts, solid bastions and detached strongpoints, they provided a meagre target for artillery fire. Military architects and engineers designed a space close to the walls and bastions, where an attacker could neither move nor take shelter, but was showered with deadly gunfire from above, from the flanks and from the front. Firearms were the *sine qua non* of these new 'natural' defences. Cram a rampart or an arrowhead bastion with cannon, and, with men firing muskets or harquebuses, these defenders could scythe down attackers long before they came within striking distance of the walls. It was an epic struggle, as the modern historian of siege warfare Christopher Duffy put it, 'of fire *and* stone'. With the confidence born of defending a secure position ('stone'), the defenders could hold the attack at a safe distance.

But if the elaborate defences were once breached this neat equation of power would be reversed. Then the advantage would return to the assailants. The skill of the engineer was to prevent this happening. The complex of bastions – joined by a strongly built curtain wall, with the outworks that Brown mentioned – generated a whole new specialist idiom and a new form of geometry. In their drawings, architects sketched in the lines of fire, showing how the walls, bastions and outer ramparts created an unconquerable system of defence. But the Ottomans had already shown on Crete, with the capture of Candia in 1669, that even the new defences could be overwhelmed, but not by cannon fire or a head-on assault. They had pioneered the arts of tunnelling beneath walls and bastions, and then demolishing them from below by exploding gunpowder mines.[13]

It was rare by the 1680s that a well-defended fortress could be overwhelmed by a frontal assault, although the Swedish armies of Gustavus Adolphus had done so with success in the early stages of the Thirty Years War. The dangers and difficulties were obvious. Attackers had to cross a succession of obstacles, clambering over low ramparts, wading or swimming across moats or scaling the walls of deep ditches, then battling across an open killing ground, all the time under fire. At close quarters, from the ditch, the massive new defences towered over the attackers below like gigantic buttes or huge boulders, the parapet crammed with infantrymen armed with matchlocks, wheel locks or, latterly, flintlocks, interspersed with artillery pieces that could blast the attackers' formations advancing en masse.

As the art of fortification developed military architects began to design fortresses to cope with every type of assault, including mining. But the best defences could only be made when they had a new site, a *tabula rasa*, chosen with a view to defence. Some of the best were isolated fortresses protected by deep water, like Komárno and Győr; some of the worst were large walled towns, with a sizeable area to defend. Vienna posed insuperable difficulties for even the most inspired engineer. Rivers ran past two sides of the city. To the east, one of the many branches of the Danube had been turned into a sluggish channel or canal, which followed the line of the city walls on the northern and eastern sides, before bending back to join the main line of the river. This was Vienna's port and at one time it also provided the water for the ill-starred moat that ran around the line of defences. Nevertheless, water remained the most effective barrier against mining, but by 1683 the moat no longer served its original purpose. On the canal side to the east of the city a century of erosion and the constant dumping of rubbish had made the channel shallower. Where it had dried out in summer, holes and cracks appeared in the banks through which the water would drain away.

On the south-western side of the city a narrow river called the Wien ran down from the high ground of the Vienna Woods to join the Danube; but it too was often dry during the summer. However, after only a few days' heavy summer rain, it could turn into a torrent, overflowing its banks almost up to the city walls close to where it joined the Danube canal. The two rivers – the Danube canal and the River Wien – made it impossible to build a strong, modern defence in depth. The weakest point in the city's perimeter was undoubtedly the eastern flank facing the Leopoldstadt island, which was surrounded by the Danube on all sides, both by the canal and by the main stream of the river. There was no space to build proper bastions and ravelins between the old city wall and the river bank, and in a bird's-eye map produced by Heinrich Schmitt the quays and wharfs looked like a gaping hole in a solid line of protection, secured only by a massive wooden palisade and the old medieval walls.[14] This weak point was well known to the Habsburg War Council, and some of the most recent rebuilding of the defence system had been carried out there in the 1670s. But there was little that could be done to strengthen it without demolishing a large part of the old city.

Yet this tantalising vulnerability also posed great problems for any attacking force. A general would have to move a large body of men and equipment on to the Leopoldstadt island, where there was little room for manoeuvre, and where, in effect, they could easily be trapped. Although the Danube was often low enough to wade across, sudden rain could increase the flow in a matter of a few hours. This indeed happened during the siege of 1683. Moreover, the Ottomans remembered the flash flood which had trapped their army at St Gotthard in 1664.[15] Most dangerous of all for an attacking army, with the river so close to the walls it gave no opportunity for any kind of mining: the palisade and then the city wall could only be taken by heavy bombardment and then by storm. Even if the defences were feeble, the new bastions, the Gonzaga and the Little Gonzaga, known colloquially as The Spike, had been designed to provide as much crossfire as possible on any troops wading through the muddy waters of the Danube canal. An assault would be very bloody, and with no guarantee of success.

The walls facing the River Wien were another obvious weak point.

When the riverbed was dry, an attacker could begin to dig trenches from a point very close to the walls. On the south-eastern corner, there were orchards and many buildings between the river bend and the bastions, providing even better cover for an attacking force. The bastions in this area were small and did not provide much space for either men or cannon. Yet although they lacked the sophistication of more up-to-date work, and were in a poor state of repair, their basic design was good. Ahead of each bastion was a new ravelin whose cannon and musketeers would have to be overwhelmed before the bastions and the walls could be assailed.

The land to the south-west sloped gently down towards the city, and apart from a few streams was dry and flat. To the north it sloped up more steeply towards the walls. For these reasons, the main expansion of Vienna beyond the walls had spread outward on this southern flank, an area of villas, some industry and the occasional nobleman's palace. Here it was possible to build on a much grander scale than within the cramped, narrow streets of the walled city. Some rich men had a town palace and also a summer palace in these new suburbs. All the theories of military architecture decreed that the space in front of a fortification should be kept completely clear of any buildings or obstructions for several hundred yards, since these could provide shelter for an attacker's artillery, and would allow mining to begin from a point close to the walls.

There had been plans since the mid-sixteenth century to extend the defences to enclose these new districts, to the west and on the Leopoldstadt island to the east, or alternatively to demolish the new buildings; but the expansion of these suburbs proved irresistible, and, despite many edicts to remove them, nothing was done. Eventually, in 1704, some twenty years after the Ottoman attack in 1683 and faced with a new crop of marauders from Hungary, a new protective earth rampart – the Linienwall – and a deep ditch were constructed in a huge arc around the city and its suburbs. Traces of these defence lines remain to this day: the Ringstrasse essentially follows the inner line of the old city defences, while the Gürtel, or 'girdle', has taken the place of the Linienwall.

By 1683, Vienna would have been in a splendid state to resist the first Ottoman siege that it had suffered in 1529. Then, Sultan Suleiman I's engineers had dug their trenches towards one end of this south-western approach, by the Carinthian Gate; although now much more heavily defended, this front, heading north-west from the Carinthian Gate to the Scottish Gate (Schottentor) still offered the best opportunity for attack. Here the moat was only a dry ditch. Close to the Hofburg Palace there had been a curious mismatch during the different phases in building the new fortification. They did not align properly with the structures on either side, and there was too long a line of exposed curtain wall that joined the two nearby fortifications, the small Löbl and the larger Burg bastions. This section was constructed in the 1540s and should have been built further out from the old city wall. In later construction, instead of simply following the old rampart, it should have been realigned with correctly spaced ravelins and a succession of ditches – not a single barrier – projecting out still further in front of the bastions. The essential symmetry of the line had been lost, and the defensive positions could not fully support their neighbours on either side with gunfire, as the theories of military architecture demanded. At this point the line had been distorted, as on the Danube front on the opposite side of the city, and there was a point close to the palace where it would be difficult to bring the full weight of fire from the bastions on to an attacking force. None of the strongpoints was connected very well, so it was hard to move men from one section to another.

This section was like the face and neck of the porcupine, the only parts of the animal's body where the sharp quills did not threaten an assailant. Immediately behind this weak sector was a complex of buildings that made up the imperial palace and, beyond it, the maze of city streets, with one long straight avenue, the Herrengasse, flanked by noble palaces.[16] Once an enemy had broken through at that point there was little space to build emergency defences behind any breaches in the curtain wall: a determined assault would be hard to stop. The inherent weakness was heightened by a circumstantial flaw: the very close proximity of the suburbs, notably the garden and its buildings attached to the grand summer palace of Count Trautson. These extended to within a few hundred yards of the outer city defences. The open space, or glacis, had been dug up and carefully cultivated to provide pleasure gardens and productive vegetable plots and this well-tilled earth would make it very easy going for the Turkish sappers digging towards the walls.

All this was well known to those responsible for the defence of the

city. In 1682, at the insistence of Hermann, Marquis of Baden, the
President of the War Council, Georg Rimpler, one of the best fortress
engineers in Europe, had been employed at an enormous salary to
improve the protection of the Habsburg lands and Vienna against an
attack from the east. He had first advised strengthening the outer
line of fortresses, especially Győr, and then turned his critical eye on
Vienna itself. Rimpler had been present at the Ottoman siege of the
Venetian fortress of Candia, and in 1671 and 1674 he had published two
important studies on the use of artillery and on fortification. The two
treatises revealed how deeply that experience in Candia had affected
him.[17] He brought with him to Vienna a team of experienced engineers,
two of whom, a fellow Saxon, Daniel Suttinger, and an Italian, Leander
Anguissola, later produced detailed studies of the siege. Together they
looked systematically at the flaws in the defences and what could be
done to remedy them.

Rimpler understood the Turkish style of siege warfare, and knew
that he needed to blunt the power of the Ottoman assaults. Nothing
could be done to remedy the fundamental defects of the fixed fortifications except to repair the collapsing walls of the moat and the
heavily eroded brickwork of some of the bastions. But beyond that
he could achieve a great deal by improvisation. In siege warfare an
assault was like a strong jet of water directed against the defences, its
thrust and pressure remorselessly scouring all the weak points in the
perimeter. Once these lay open and exposed, infantry and grenadiers
could rush forward and overwhelm the defenders. But find some
means to obstruct, divert or even delay this impetuous human mass,
and the attack would waste its force and energy. Rimpler saw Vienna
in these essentially practical terms. In the few days that he had available before the Turks arrived, the main task was to repair the first line
of defence, the palisade. Then he worked ceaselessly, designing new
strongpoints closer to the city walls. He ordered new entrenchments
and new firing points on top of the bastions and the ravelins; he
designed simple obstructions, dug trenches and erected temporary
strongpoints that would shelter musketeers and gunners protecting the
floor of the dry ditch. Held with determination, they could seriously
delay the enemy's advance.

The raw materials Rimpler needed were to hand: stout baulks of
timber or even tree trunks, sharpened at both ends, ready to be

hammered into the earth. Roped together, or strengthened with wooden cross-members, buttressed with more timbers behind, they could be used to make an open wooden wall. A thin man could turn sideways and slip between the staves, but an attacking mass of men would be brought to a halt.

The Ottomans themselves were expert in using *palanka*, solid blockhouses, made of logs and earth, and Rimpler was constructing something very similar.[18] Using wooden barrels or gabions he created a line of blockhouses along the timber-covered way that ran along the top of the steep inner wall (counterscarp). The defenders could then fire down on any Turks who penetrated the old moat. Each one was a little fort, and the Turks would have to eliminate them one by one. In the moat itself, he ordered the digging of entrenchments at the base of the ravelins, constructed bunkers and blockhouses, and on the bastions, each one to be crowded with musketeers, who could hinder the enemy advance across the moat towards the walls and ravelin. He cut gaps in the parapet (embrasures) so that the bastion guns could fire down into the ditch on to the attackers below. These modifications were designed to cover the blind spots in the dry ditch that were otherwise out of sight of the defenders on the wall. But these desperate last-minute measures were still being completed as the Turks began their assault.

Rimpler could do nothing to counter the most deadly form of attack. As at the Siege of Candia, the mortal blow would come not from bombardment but from the steady advance of the well-protected enemy tunnels (saps) underground. As they dug, the Ottomans roofed over their advancing excavations with stout beams covered with earth that protected them from gunfire. Sometimes they would dig deeper – fifteen or twenty feet underground – and buttress their tunnels like mineshafts. Here they were invulnerable, except to a counter-mine dug by the defenders. During the siege a battle often raged underground as Ottoman and Austrian miners met and struggled in the dark. Vienna was ill defended against attacks from below. It was not built on an impenetrable rocky outcrop, but on stony river soil, hard going for a miner but no serious impediment. In 1529 the Turks had shown how deep they could dig and how far they could advance. Their approach in 1683 would be no different. They would burrow into the outer earth rampart (escarpment), dig through the wall of the old moat and cut their way onwards to the ravelins and the curtain wall. These old fortifications had no protection against enemy mines, and an explosion could reduce a solid fortification to a mound of stones and loose earth in an instant.[19]

It was certain that the Ottoman saps would inevitably dig through the earth rampart, but the best Rimpler could hope was that the men stationed on either side of any breach could direct a withering fire into the flanks of an Ottoman assault. He was right. In the end, by an enormous effort, the attackers had to level a huge tranche of the outer wall to give them free access to the ditch behind, to protect their assault troops from the Habsburg musketeers still emplaced in the blockhouses on the covered way, now at the Turks' backs.

That all these defences were crude and makeshift was unimportant, for they would only have to last at most for a few weeks before either the enemy retreated or Vienna was destroyed. This would be a siege unlike most others in recent memory. In most sieges in the west, it was not a matter of importance that a fortress was impregnable, merely that it could be defended until the attacking army rather than the defending force gave up the attempt. Buying time was what mattered. In Western Europe, the mere completion of the preparations for the first entrenchments, the cutting off of the city from the outside world, was a point at which most cities sought honourable terms. The Ottoman engineers, Rimpler knew, were entirely capable of breaching the inadequate defences of Vienna, but unless the city surrendered (which seemed unlikely) it would have to be taken by storm. Candia had finally surrendered on good terms in 1669 before the final assault, but for Vienna that option seemed out of the question. Christian Vienna would be annihilated, ransacked and ravaged according to the customs of war that operated in both east and west.

Rimpler's ingenious improvised defences were all designed to wear down the enemy, to negate his vast numerical advantage. And, if all else failed, he had planned to stretch heavy iron chains across the streets and then to turn every house into a little citadel. The chains were ready and waiting in the arsenal. These blocked streets would stop the Ottomans bringing their artillery into the city, and force them to fight hand-to-hand for every few yards. Later generations of military writers would describe Vienna as the Ottomans' Stalingrad, and that anachronism is wholly apt. Starhemberg was determined that the city would only be conquered block by block, and the Turkish infidels would be left in possession of a vast pile of shattered masonry and burning timbers. The last redoubt would be St Stephen's Cathedral, and the people of Vienna would fight to the death by the walls of the cathedral, their *Steffl*.

*   *   *

History would play up Starhemberg's heroic credentials but he was an unremarkable soldier. His family had been barons in Upper Austria since the days of the first Habsburg emperor, Rudolf, in the thirteenth century. Ernst Rüdiger von Starhemberg was in his forty-sixth year in 1683. He had fought with Charles of Lorraine beside Montecuccoli, against the Turks at St Gotthard and against French armies in Germany. None of his portraits, at the time or subsequently, gives a true impression of the man. Contemporary portraitists softened his face with a cascading wig, and later generations turned him into a crypto-saint. But in the National Museum of Art in Budapest there is a bronze statuette, one of a series by Alexy Károly of Habsburg generals. Starhemberg, his arm resting on a parapet, his cuirass strapped tight over a heavy buff coat, looks as though he himself were made of tanned leather. Resilient yet impenetrable, a long thin nose like an eagle's beak, tall and wiry, Károly's little statue presents the man described by his contemporaries as endlessly active, for whom attack and not defence was an instinctive response. But Starhemberg was no *beau sabreur*, throwing himself recklessly into the mêlée. He calculated, planned and then led the defenders into daily acts of impossible courage. He was not a great general, but he possessed exactly the qualities of mind and spirit to inspire a resistance without previous or subsequent parallel.

In the week between the Emperor's flight and the arrival of the Turks, the work under Starhemberg's orders was hectic but purposeful. Some preparations had been made already, and the city's two arsenals were well stocked with gunpowder, shot and musket balls. More was brought in before the Turks closed their grip around the city. This unusual plenitude, filling the Viennese arsenals to bursting point, was because the city was designated as the supply base for the army as it battled with the advancing Turks in Royal Hungary. On the first day of the siege, a rumour that Turkish saboteurs had set fire to the arsenal, stacked to the ceilings with gunpowder, caused panic. 'A youth of sixteen years found in woman's apparel . . . had flung some fires into the straw or litter lying near the stables of the Scotch abbey which presently consumed the best and largest monastery of the town . . . the flame also making its way till it came to the arsenal where a great quantity of powder and other ammunition lay in store; the very door where the powder was kept taking fire.' The inside of the room was doused with water, and 'the arsenal was saved, as if by a miracle'.[20]

The boy, an actor or transvestite, or perhaps a groom from the stables, suffered a terrible death. The crowd caught him and he was hacked and ripped into pieces, leaving only a naked trunk, disembowelled, the head, arms and legs carried off, from which great handfuls of flesh were torn, as if a wild beast had savaged him. This was only the first of many acts of savagery in a city now subsumed with rage and panic.

The capital was exceptionally well supplied with artillery pieces, also held in store for action in Hungary. When the siege began there were 317 guns on the walls, half as many again as the Ottomans would deploy against them. What Vienna still lacked was a garrison: little more than a thousand soldiers (plus the city militia) was its normal strength. A thousand more men of Keiserstein's Regiment had arrived from Prague, but these two thousand were nowhere near enough to man the four miles of walls which had to be defended. But more infantry were on their way. The regiments commanded by Starhemberg had been stationed by Lorraine north of the Danube, to prevent a sudden advance by the Turks and their allies towards the fortress city of Bratislava. Others had been detailed to protect the fortresses of Upper Hungary. Now, summoned urgently to return to Vienna, their commander, Lieutenant General Schultz, drove the remaining infantry plus some cavalry, seven thousand men, a mixture of Polish mercenaries and Austrian regulars, on a long march, from dawn to dusk.[21] Good fortune ensured that they arrived the day before the Ottoman host rather than the day after. On 13 July they wearily trudged the last few miles across the pontoon bridges joining the islands in the Danube close to the city, arriving at midnight at Lorraine's cantonment on the Leopoldstadt. All were exhausted and many retching from the rampant diseases that were spreading rapidly in the summer heat. They brought with them the red flux, a mixture of blood and faeces, caused by an infection they had picked up as they marched through the marshlands north of the great river.

On the same day a cloud of dust announced that the remaining infantry and the field artillery were close at hand. The skilled artillerymen were the key to the defence. Until they arrived, the city had plenty of guns but no one to man them. They were still standing in neat rows in the arsenal. Now they were pulled into place, massed in batteries at key points along the walls, set up to rake the ground outside. Within a day of pitching camp outside the capital, Lorraine ordered that all the infantry and artillerymen and some heavy cavalry at his disposal should man the city defences while he would eventually take the remaining cavalry across the wooden bridges over the Danube to the north bank, guarding against any thrust from Thököly's insurgents and the Ottoman garrisons in Upper Hungary. But it was evening on 14 July before the main Ottoman host arrived before the city, by which time Tartars and *delis* were already roaming unopposed in sight of the city walls. The last of the soldiers arrived from the east a few hours before the Turks, with many sick and wounded. They were taken into Vienna, and then the main gates were bricked up and the bridges over the dry ditch and Danube demolished. Only a single gate, the Red Tower Gate (Rotenturmtor) on the eastern side, still remained open for any stragglers, and the strongly defended outer Carinthian Gate, which passed through a ravelin, was kept open for attacks on the Turkish lines.

Starhemberg's garrison now comprised seventy-two companies of infantry and the cuirassiers, plus the local Vienna City Guard, the city militia and watchmen, and the gamekeepers from outlying estates (who proved to be expert snipers). They numbered at most about 15,000 men-in-arms, but many of these were walking wounded and, in reality, perhaps only ten thousand were fit and well. What, then, were the city's prospects of survival? Not good. Roughly two hundred years before, the Ottomans under Sultan Mehmed II had besieged and captured Constantinople in one of the great catastrophes of Christendom. The long, straggling Byzantine walls could be neither manned nor defended, and eventually the attackers broke through in many places to overwhelm the defenders. Vienna, for all the deficiencies in its fortifications, was a tougher prospect. Yet the Ottoman army was also a more dangerous opponent. It may have lacked some of the passion and raw courage of those who attacked Constantinople in 1453, but it had much more experience and training in the art of taking fortified cities. More to the point, it had the lessons of the failed attempt to take Vienna in 1529, as well as many successes against modern fortresses. Most cities eventually succumbed to siege; some were saved by a relieving army. That was Vienna's situation in 1683. Every day that the city could resist made the prospect of relief more likely, and that resistance depended largely on the willpower of those sheltering behind the walls. Constantinople fell because its small garrison lost the will to resist. Vienna was defended by battle hardened soldiers who knew the consequences of a failure in morale.

On the day after the Emperor had fled there had been a mass exodus from the city of the fearful and timorous. An eyewitness described it: 'So great a terror [that] no man was willing to stay behind; all the horses and carts that could be found were immediately hired, and the wagons and carts filled with ladies of the greatest quality and their children, who deserting their houses and rich furniture, and leaving all their provisions behind them took only what was most valuable that would lie in the least room. Nothing but cries and lamentation were heard in every place, as though the Turks were already the masters of Vienna.'[22] Their departure made the defence easier. The few leading figures who remained had determined to live or die in their city. There were, inevitably, crises of morale, doubts and fears as the siege tightened, but there was also a strong sense of common adversity. There was no 'enemy within', no group willing to compromise. An implacable sense of resistance united the soldiers, the citizens who remained and the many thousands from the countryside who had taken refuge in the capital city.

The Ottoman host had advanced steadily but slowly from their first encounter with Lorraine's men on 8 July. There were streams and rivulets flowing down towards the great river which impeded their advance. Each one of them had to be bridged. Nevertheless, there was a sense of exaltation as they came, on 11 July, to the walled town of Hainburg, the easternmost town in Austria, on the banks of the Danube. The city had resisted Tartar attacks for more than a week, for the horsemen had no means of getting past the walls. Before dusk, the janissaries and artillery arrived and surrounded the town. Two guns battered the walls and the town was stormed. As the sun fell, the first living prisoners and sacks of severed heads from Hainburg were brought in triumph to the Grand Vizier and laid out before him. After the town was sacked, all the leading citizens who had resisted the summons to surrender, as the account of the Ottoman Master of Ceremonies recorded in his diary, 'came under the blade'.[23] The remainder of the population were enslaved. On the following day, as the army moved forward along the Danube, after morning prayers Kara Mustafa received a fresh offering of two hundred severed heads from Hainburg, plus ten prisoners. Those who brought these welcome gifts received the traditional robes of honour and generous presents. Then the Grand Vizier set out with his commanders to visit the scene of their triumph, returning to his camp by nightfall. By midday on 13 July the Ottoman host had crossed the River Fischa and was encamped at Schwechat, only seven miles from the walls of Vienna. At the riverside town of Fischamend, which the inhabitants had wisely abandoned, Kara Mustafa ordered the destruction of everything in the town, creating a fire that lit up the night sky.

If the inhabitants of Vienna had had any expectations of relief or salvation before, they now evaporated. The Turks would bring only death or fire, and there was no prospect of any relieving army. Only the King of Poland was committed by treaty and no state of the Holy Roman Empire had offered any military support. It would be 6 August before the Bavarian Elector offered his army against the Turks, and he was effectively a member of the House of Habsburg. On 14 July, the Ottoman Master of Ceremonies began his diary entry, 'The camp in front of Vienna. Today, beginning at sunrise, led by the horsetails of the Grand Vizier, and continuing throughout the day, the entire host moved ahead to their new camp.' They advanced past the deserted village of Simmering 'slowly past the fortress of Vienna, with meas- ured pace', in plain view of the garrison lining the walls. Inside Vienna, Johann Peter Vaelckeren kept a vivid and accurate diary, subsequently published in numerous editions and several languages, including, by the command of King Charles II, in English.

On the 14th of July, the whole army of the Turks, with an incredible number of horses, wagons, buffalos and camels, appeared moving towards Vienna over the hill by St Mark's Church, their main body marching on the side of the hill from whence they could not be so well discovered from the walls of the town . . . they immediately spread themselves from the banks of the Danube throughout which circuit they continued encamping themselves till late at night, when they were observed to begin their works before the Emperor's Gate [Burgtor], where our men that were posted upon the counterscarp, fired upon them continually from behind our palisades to hinder the approaches which they had already begun in such a manner that we soon found ourselves formally besieged.[24]

The Ottoman encirclement of the city was speedy and decisive. It showed they had very good intelligence about the weak points of Vienna. A tent city quickly appeared: at dawn on 16 July a mass of Ottoman *sipahis* splashed through the shallow waters of the canal on to the islands that contained the Leopoldstadt suburbs and the bridges across to the northern shore of the Danube. They drove back the three squadrons of Austrian dragoons and the Polish mercenaries – armoured horsemen – commanded by Prince Lubomirski, still guarding the bridgehead. Some of the cavalry defended the tower on the open meadow, until they were overwhelmed. But the delay gave the remaining horsemen time to retreat across the bridges to the north bank under constant attack from the Ottoman *sipahis*. The speed and ferocity of their enemies' attack, their reckless boldness and skilful horsemanship, deeply impressed Lubomirski's men, themselves considered near-savages by their Habsburg allies. In two days the situation had been transformed. The whole eastern face of the city, through which traffic had continued to enter the Rotenturmtor, was under attack, dominated by newly made Ottoman batteries in huge new earth emplacements made amid the burned ruins of Leopoldstadt. The heart of the city was soon under heavy bombardment, with church spires making excellent targets. Similarly, the speed with which the Turkish entrenchments advanced on the other side of the city was just as alarming. In two days of digging, at first in the soft earth of the suburb's garden, but then in the stony soil of the glacis, the Turkish engineers had dug trenches up to six feet in depth to within fifty yards of the defenders' outer palisade.

This easy success developed into overconfidence. Kara Mustafa did not have a high opinion of his opponents, who had fled before him towards the capital and ignored his formal demand that they surrender and convert to Islam. The Turkish tents blocked off the city from contact with the outside world to the west. But unlike an experienced western general, the Grand Vizier made no attempt to protect his own camp against attack from a westerly direction, nor even to guard the high ground – the Vienna Woods – above the city. Although his Tartars roamed across a huge area westward from Vienna, he seems to have done nothing to gain information from them about the enemy's movements, as he had on the march north through western Hungary. All that interested the *serasker* was the city lying before him.

Kara Mustafa knew war at first hand and he was a bold leader. But his previous experience had been limited to battles against very much weaker opponents: two campaigns in the Ukraine and a minor part in the war for Crete. His current opponents might in his eyes seem negligible, but they were battle-hardened. Lorraine had fought at St Gotthard, and spent years campaigning against Louis XIV's armies.[25] He still walked with a limp from a leg broken at the siege of Philippsburg in 1676; Rüdiger von Starhemberg had learned his craft under Montecuccoli, fought in the Dutch wars, was wounded and had served under Lorraine at Philippsburg. The other commanders in the city were a cross-section of the international freemasonry of soldiers who had gravitated to Habsburg service. The Leslies of Balquhain and Fetternear were reputed to be the most successful Scottish mercenaries of the seventeenth century. They had served the Habsburgs loyally through the Thirty Years War and Walter Leslie had ended an imperial count and owner of vast estates in Styria and Bohemia. His two nephews, James and Alexander Leslie, both fought in defence of the city. Prince Ferdinand Charles of Wirtenberg led his own regiment, as did Colonel Charles de Souches, who had inherited it from his father. These were men in the Zrinyi tradition, who would prefer death to dishonour. In Vienna, they fought along-side their men on the walls and in the old moat, and many of the regimental commanders were among the dead and wounded.

But for the *serasker* those opposing him were no more significant than the humble folk – some eight hundred according to the Ottoman record – captured in the villages around the capital, who were either beheaded or enslaved at the whim of their captors. In Ottoman eyes the western infidels had scattered before their advance like so many sheep. Kara Mustafa was sure that his miners would demolish the walls before them and the prize would be his. Contemporaries later suggested he was half-hearted in his attack on the city, because he wanted to seize it intact, greedily taking possession of its great riches. But this was just their moralistic (or opportunistic) perspective of the Grand Vizier as a supremely vicious and greedy man. Apart from his failure to guard his sprawling camp, his plan of attack made sense, concentrating his best troops where they would do most good. Kara Mustafa may have commanded the largest army ever seen in Europe, but the number of skilled musketeers and trained assault troops, of artillerymen and engineers, was limited. The huge arc of tents, extending over fifteen miles around the city, was for the most part filled with men doing nothing much, apart from occasionally patrolling the space before the ditch and palisade. Or they were half-hearted, like the Christian levies from Moldavia and Wallachia who had reluctantly joined the campaign under threat. The provincial cavalry were not even capable of firing a musket, although they later proved as zealous in attack on foot as they had on horseback.

For the Grand Vizier, taking Vienna was like opening a walnut, that familiar staple of Ottoman cuisine. Crack the walnut's hard and impenetrable shell at the right point and the soft kernel would be exposed. The point of fracture, all accepted (even the defenders), would be the zone by Leopold's palace. Kara Mustafa pitched his palatial tent before this flank, looking down on the city. Further forward, in the still-smouldering ruins of the suburbs, which Starhemberg had torched only two days before the Turks arrived, he ordered that an elaborate and luxurious *palanka*-like structure should be built as his forward command post only some 450 yards from Vienna's palisade, well within cannon shot. This was a more luxurious version of the traditional Ottoman wooden-walled fortification. Evliya described these as 'wooden walls filled with mortar' and Luigi Marsigli drew its likeness precisely. Two solid lines of stout poles were hammered into the ground with a gap of at least two feet between each line. That gap was filled with compacted earth, and the structure strengthened with wooden ties and braces.[26]

Covered with canvas outside and silk inside, the solidity of the structure would have been completely hidden. It would withstand a fire from small arms, and even a direct hit from a heavy cannonball. From here Kara Mustafa would watch the advance of the Ottoman trenches and, from a distance, command the repeated assaults. From this vantage point he could see and hear the constant activity behind the city lines. Now that the thrust of the main enemy attack was clear to Rimpler and Starhemberg, all the defenders' activity concentrated on the south-western side. Throughout the day there was constant hammering as the palisade was further buttressed and strengthened, while up on the bastions and ravelins the cannon were quickly moved into place.

Late seventeenth-century warfare was becoming a kind of choreography. The advance of the Turkish trenches and the laggardly hardening of the defences appeared almost synchronised, taking place simultaneously. Three days after they started digging, the heads of the Ottoman saps had snaked forward until they were only thirty yards from the outer defensive earthen rampart crowned by its wooden line of stakes, and, behind it, the ranks of musketeers ready behind the parapet. At intervals there were broader platforms, mostly mounted with light wall guns charged with shot, stones and old nails, and with silent ranks of grenadiers, each man carrying a haversack stuffed with bombs.

The elaborate drill for throwing them was complex and risky. A grenadier carried a slow match, and after blowing the smoking end to a red glow, he would light the grenade's fuse. Then making sure it was burning well, he would stand erect and hurl the bomb with a circular overarm movement into the enemy trenches or into a mass of Turks struggling up towards the palisade. The explosion of a grenade was devastating – and a skilled grenadier could hurl one bomb after another in the space of less than a minute. On both sides the grenade became the master weapon of the siege. The grenadiers could move quickly to the point of any Ottoman attack, and lay down a devastating barrage of close-quarters support for the musketeers. A strong man could hurl a grenade for twenty or thirty yards. Their casualty rates were high, because they were very exposed at the moment of throwing their bombs. Nor were the fuses entirely reliable, and a bomb exploding prematurely could cause mayhem in the defenders' ranks. But they were ideal for the hand-to-hand battle that soon became a daily occurrence by the palisades, killing or maiming the enemy, scouring and scarring the stout wooden staves set into the earth but leaving them fundamentally undamaged.

The solid mound of earth stretching around the city, capped by its line of evenly spaced stakes, was unimpressive in comparison to the massive ravelins and bastions behind, but it turned out to be Vienna's best defence. As the Turkish saps advanced towards the walls, they sprouted lines of trenches on either side, parallel to the outer rampart. In some places these parallels were widened so that Ottoman gunners could bring their light cannon forward, and, protected from gunfire by gabions and bales of cotton roped together, they would support the janissary assaults. The forward trenches were filled with the shock troops. The attacks in the first week of the siege were made by janissary musketeers laying aside their long weapons, rushing across the short distance of open ground, up the steep slope to the palisade and attempting to climb over. Before them rank after rank of Habsburg musketeers would rise, steady their weapons against the stakes and fire down into the mass of attackers. Then they would move back and a new firing line would take their place as they reloaded. Turks who reached the barrier would thrust through the gaps at their enemies with spears, swords and yataghans. The defenders would fight back with swords, cut-down pikes and boar spears, and, once the line of attack was clear, the guns on the neighbouring gun platforms would retarget the assault and grenadiers would move quickly to the point of attack.

Contemporary accounts suggest the savagery of these attacks. They talk of how the defenders fixed long hooks on poles to drag the Ottomans in to their deaths on Christian spears and daggers, and how the flayed skins of Turkish soldiers would be nailed to the palisade in view of their comrades. But these details are incidental not reportage, and it remains hard to imagine the frenzied attacks and the response to them only from the stories that have come down to us. Still less do they explain how little defensive walls and ramparts played their part in allowing a small force of defenders to repel a much larger attacking force.[27]

So what happened at Vienna? Why was the earthen rampart with its palisade so significant? In the first place, it was well defended. Starhemberg stripped the garrison inside the city to man the outer defence line and the ditch behind. In the second, it was the sudden steep incline up to the fence, and then the strength of the fence itself. These were new timbers hammered deep into the earth and strongly buttressed by cross-beams. Ottoman artillery might blow away a section, but it could be quickly repaired and replaced. By the time the charging janissaries reached the fence, their impetus was slowing in the last few yards. There was no flat ground where they could place scaling ladders, no space for their men to mass before the wooden rampart. Reports of those first assaults and the evidence of his own eyes made the Grand Vizier realise that this bank of earth and line of stakes was as formidable an obstacle as the great walls of the main defences of the city, almost forty feet in height. The palisade was too strongly defended to be rushed; it would have to be besieged and undermined section by section, like the city behind it.

All this would take time. The Ottoman lines reached the palisade on 16 July; ten days later it had still not been overwhelmed. After the first assaults were driven back with huge losses, the Ottoman engineers began the slower task of digging under the fence and exploding great mines below the palisade in an attempt to break through. But still the assault failed. The mines exploded creating a huge mound of soft earth and a great pit, but the Ottoman infantry were driven off yet again by 'Count Sereni (Serenyi) and St Croy Lieutenant Colonel of the Regiment of Dupigni coming to [our men's] Succour, with a Hundred fresh Men armed with Granadoes; soon they got the better of the Turks and cutting off many of their Heads, fixed them on the Stakes and Palisadoes on the counterscarp in sight of the Enemy'.[28] Three weeks after the beginning of the first attack, in the first week of August, the Ottomans were still desperately seeking to break through the outer line. By 5 August, they had built earth mounds on either side of their assault saps so that they were higher than the palisade. From these elevated positions they could now shoot down on to the musketeers defending it; then the Turks moved their artillery forward in a concentrated bombardment of the palisade, and, for the first time, waves of janissaries also armed with grenades managed to push across through the open space in the wooden rampart to the edge of the ditch sixteen feet below.

And so, on 7 August, the twenty-fifth day of the siege, Kara Mustafa's men had broken through the first obstacle. As the first Turks entrenched themselves in the floor of the ditch, they stared up at the main defences of the city that now towered above them, bristling with guns. To each side as far as they could see there were massive brick walls; in the ditch before them there were trenches filled with musketeers, and behind them, at the foot of the bastion and the curtain wall, strongpoints with light artillery pieces that covered the dead zones where the guns above could not. In this narrow quadrangle, pock-marked with trenches, excavations and deep craters made by bombs dropped from the ramparts above, the two armies duelled for the survival of Christendom's bulwark.

7

The Pit of Hell

For thirty-seven days ten thousand men battled over the narrow strip of ground separating the Löbl and the Burg bastions. From early August the old moat, now an empty ditch between the outer and inner lines of defence, was the key to the city's survival. Day by day the soldiers on the wall looked down on the spider's web of Ottoman diggings, and watched as the earth itself seemed to move inexorably forward. Piles of loose soil, like vast worm casts, continued to rise on each side of the half-hidden entrenchments. Soon these mounds towered above the sheer walls of the ravelin, so that Ottoman gunners and musketeers could fire down into the shallow trenches dug by defenders atop the battered fortification. As the Turkish bombardment intensified, the Habsburg infantry dug deeper, throwing up their own earthen ramparts for protection against the continual gunfire. This grim battle was waged with spade and shovel.

Rüdiger von Starhemberg, wearing a cavalryman's buff leather coat after he had been wounded by flying splinters of bricks and stone, spent much of each day on the walls above this battleground. Racked by repeated bouts of the bloody flux, dysentery, so that he could only walk a few steps unaided, he would be carried in a chair to a vantage point from which he could see the battle below. His letters smuggled out of the city make a powerful impact. Some were published as the battle raged, describing the state of the city to the generalissimo, fretting on the other side of the Danube. Sometimes Charles of Lorraine was himself close enough to the city to hear the sound of the bombardment, but usually he was far to the west, anxiously awaiting an attack along the northern bank of the Danube.[1]

The Ottoman cannon, grouped in three large clusters in a single huge battery opposite the bastions, fired with a steady rhythm into the city, and the defenders' batteries riposted. No target was too insignificant. As one diary records for 20 August: 'This day a gunner from the ravelin between the Gate of Carinthia and the Bastion of the Waterworks [on the south side of the city], observing a Turk watering two horses at the Vienna river fired upon him and broke his legs with a shot, killing him instantly.'[2]

The individual marksmen on each side waited for targets, or fired in the hope of doing some damage; the irregular crackle of gunfire lasted all day. Soon the Christians learned which were the Turks' most deadly weapons. At various points the city walls were edged with dressed stone, and when hit by a heavy cannonball these copings would shatter into sharp fragments, which caused terrible flesh wounds. Some of the Turkish mortars lobbed bombs high into the sky, which exploded like huge grenades when they hit the ground.[3] Dozens of men could be killed or mortally wounded by these silent angels of death. Both sides had expert snipers, the Balkan musketeers the most expert in the Ottoman ranks, while the parties of *Jäger* (gamekeepers) from the noble estates around Vienna, stationed at key points on the walls, were deadly with their long muskets. The Turkish weapons fired huge, heavy, lead balls, which would smash through armour or helmets. The Austrian hunting rifles were less powerful but precise and accurate, as Turks who imprudently exposed themselves discovered to their cost.

Once night fell a different kind of battle began. The Habsburg troops on the ravelin and in the trenches at the bottom of the ditch used the cover of darkness to take in new supplies of food, men and ammunition, and sometimes to send their wounded back into the city. But both sides mounted sudden raids on the enemy trenches, so that most nights were punctuated by the sounds of musket fire, the explosion of grenades or the screams of the dying. Some expeditions were more bizarre, as the Christians employed a long file of men, each one with a wheelbarrow, to trundle away the loose earth from the base of the tallest mounds so that little landslips would occur, thus exposing the Ottoman guns above. Like most sallies, these ended in disaster as the Turks were roused and showered those below with arrows and grenades.

Just to the south of the ferocious struggle at the Burg and Löbl bastions was the main entry to the city, the Carinthian Gate, protected by its own ravelin, two sets of great gates on the outer rampart and a protected way back to the city wall. Raiding parties would mass under cover out of sight of the Turks and at dusk or in deepest night the outer gates would swing open and the horsemen and musketeers charge towards the Ottoman camp. The gunfire from the walls would suddenly stop and they would rush the complex of Turkish trenches hurling grenades at the men huddled below. At other times they would head for the line of Ottoman tents beyond, and return to the gate driving cattle or sheep before them. Occasionally they would capture unwary sentries and bring them back for interrogation, and, in the later stages, a gruesome death.

The morale in both camps waned as each week passed. Starhemberg and his senior officers launched raids in an effort to keep up the spirits of both civilians and soldiers. At first these offensives had been very successful. A strong counterattack led by Count Sereni (Serenyi) and Count Scherffenberg killed all the Ottoman sappers pressing hard on the Löbl bastion, setting fires that spread rapidly. They succeeded in destroying the stores of cotton-filled gabions and the timbers used to construct the attack trenches, setting back the Turkish advance in that sector by about twelve days. But the human cost was very heavy. One hundred men died in this sally, and these offensives called for the best and the most spirited members of garrison. The remorseless pressure of the Ottoman bombardment and the ceaseless tunnelling fostered wild fears. Rumours were rife. Where once in the early days there had been talk of relief, now there was none. They would die, but in a good cause, and God was with them. The city churches were thronged, even though these were points of particular danger. The Ottoman artillery on the Leopoldstadt island naturally used the spires and towers as targets because they offered the only clear targets within the walls.

On 1 August a cannon shot had burst through the tall lancet windows of St Stephen's Cathedral and crashed against a pillar, showering the congregation with stone splinters and fragments of metal. But as the citizens and garrison soon learned, through God's mercy only one man had suffered serious injury: his legs were smashed to a pulp. On the next day the Ottoman batteries on the south-western side took up the bombardment. 'Being a Holy day, the Turks very early in the morning shot many bombs at the Church of the Capuchins whereby they gave great disturbance to the people in their devotions . . . a bomb falling with horrid noise on the top of the church and stopping on the great arch, while the people were within at their prayers, it occasioned so great fright amongst them, that they all ran out of the church, but afterwards returned to their devotions when they saw no hurt was done.'[4] Every glimmer of hope was magnified. On the same day as the miracle at the Capuchin church, 'at about eight in the evening, we sprang a mine that was carried from the Lebel [Löbl] bastion to the enemy's works, with so great success that many of them [Turks] were blown up and torn in pieces, we perceiving from the walls several arms and legs in the air, mingled with the smoke and the rubbish'.[5] But this hopeful enthusiasm was wishful thinking. Starhemberg's engineers might have the occasional success but they could not prevent the Turkish advance. It progressed more slowly than the Grand Vizier demanded, but the Ottoman sappers and the janissary assault troops in the trenches steadily overcame every obstacle in their path: the outer rampart, the palisade, the ditch, the ravelin. The attack was remorseless, with the city being bombarded constantly through the day, and often at night as well. Below ground, the Turkish miners and the Habsburgs' counterminers worked ceaselessly, shift after shift. On one or two occasions they even came face to face in the loose earth, pick suddenly striking pick. As the war diary recorded: 'On this occasion it may be worthy of notice that whilst the Turks were working continually . . . and our men were digging from above to countermine them, it happened that their pickaxes met together, the ground being opened between them. But the Turks being as unwilling to make their way upwards as our men were to go down, the conflict soon ended.'[6] Neither group wanted to be suffocated in the falling soil if their tunnels collapsed. In the Turkish trenches and on the walls of the city the smaller guns were rarely silent, each barrage engendering a riposte from the enemy's guns. Indeed, when the artillery ceased fire, it was usually only the prelude to the explosion of a mine and a new assault from the Ottoman lines.

★   ★   ★

The diaries written during and after the siege all point insistently to the defenders' courage and to their minor successes. They speak less of the overwhelming power of their enemy; subsequent history has also forgotten the grim reality of the siege. The scale and intensity of Vienna's struggle had no equal, not even in a Europe that had been constantly at war for thirty years until peace was made in 1648. But even the most sanguineous events of the Thirty Years War were dwarfed by the potential catastrophe in the east. The bloodiest siege earlier in the century had been the capture of the Lutheran city of Magdeburg in 1631 by the army of the Catholic League. An old walled city on the banks of the Elbe, and, like Vienna, with medieval defences, Magdeburg had been reinforced with modern bastions and strong-points. The Siege of Magdeburg had begun on 3 April 1631, and on 20 May all its outer defences were taken. The city was stormed simul-taneously from six directions and captured in a single day. By night-fall, it had been sacked, and twenty thousand Magdeburgers slaughtered. But even in this catastrophe there was nothing to equal the daily yard-by-yard struggle in the ditch before Vienna, nor the deaths and enslavement that would have followed any conquest.

At Vienna the zone of the most intense conflict was almost at the ceremonial heart of the Habsburg capital. It was precisely the point where theatrical extravaganzas had once been performed. In the final hectic days before the Ottomans arrived, Starhemberg had ordered the demolition of the wooden Court Theatre which had been built in the narrow space between the walls and the palace. It was the Emperor Leopold's delight and he had himself written numerous dramas and musical spectaculars for its stage. The equestrian ballet of 1667, *La Contesa dell'aria e dell'acqua*, included fleets of ships afloat on artificial lakes, parades of horses and carriages, some seeming to fly through the air, and fireworks discharged from plaster and stucco recreations of Mount Etna and Mount Parnassus.[7] Now the drama that was taking place close to where the theatre had once stood was infinitely more compelling.

Looking down from the city wall into the hellish pit below revealed a scene of continuous struggle from dawn to dusk. On one side of this arena the Turks dominated the huge mound of earth that had once been the outer rampart, and every night hundreds of Ottoman infantrymen and engineers shovelled soft earth into the ditch below. Underground hundreds of diggers laboured in tunnels shored up with wooden staves and props as they moved forward, laying thick timbers on the top, under a layer of soil. In these wooden tunnels, the Turks dug steadily forward, more or less impervious to the fire, grenades and bombs that rained down from above. On the other side the defenders of Vienna, high on the bastions and the walls a few yards away, battered at the enemy lines with constant gunfire, hoping for an exposed target. Almost every day they had small successes, but nothing stopped the Turks' progress. Hundreds of janissaries and sappers might be killed in the sudden attacks from within the walls, or in a successful countermine, but they were instantly replaced. One or two Turkish mines were exploded every day, the pits and craters moving closer and closer to the ravelin and the two bastions.

Most land battles of the period occupied at most a day of intense conflict, interspersed with intervals and pauses. War at sea was more intense and more visceral, with men hacking at each other on deck and below deck as ships battered each other with gunfire, and then fighting crews boarded a crippled enemy. Nothing until the battle for Stalingrad in 1942 equalled the relentless struggle in the ditch before Vienna. In both battles men fought over the mountains of debris, shattered buildings and a landscape of utter desolation.

From the tower of St Stephen's it was possible to see everything that happened on the north bank of the Danube. Often scouting parties of the Duke of Lorraine's army came into view, sometimes parties of Tartars swimming the river to raid towards the west. Starhemberg would send out messengers to carry news of the city to the duke and, eventually, to get back news of the slow progress of a relieving force. Occasionally, in the far distance, columns of black smoke would show that yet another village or farmhouse had been fired by Turkish raiding parties. Slowly, day by day, within Vienna the sense of impending catastrophe deepened, as the raiding parties became less productive and there was no good news of imminent relief. More deadly than gunfire, and worse than the lack of food, was the relentless spread of disease. All the cats (sardonically nicknamed 'roof rabbits') had been eaten and some Viennese trapped and ate rats. Even in times of peace, Vienna was a sump of infection and contagion. Plague had ravaged the capital in 1679, with new outbreaks in the early 1680s, causing more than 76,000 deaths in the city and the outlying countryside. The outbreak had begun in the Ottoman lands far to the east, spreading west through the Balkans; other cities suffered worse than Vienna –

81,000 died in Prague in 1681. Miraculously there was no fresh outbreak during the siege. Perhaps the killing and eating of the rats reduced the sources of infection. But although the citizens and the garrison evaded the plague, many other diseases laid them low. Wounds quickly became infected, and repeated bouts of dysentery ravaged the defenders on the walls. One recognised cause of sickness was the mounds of stinking waste that began to fill the streets, discarded by 'the soldiers and market people who throw the blood of slaughtered cattle into the gutters, causing great odour and illness'. The same source, from a commission of the city's doctors alluded to the psychological pressure upon those imprisoned within the city walls: 'great fear, worry and mental affliction'.[8]

The conditions in the Ottoman camp were not much better. As the siege was prolonged, the discipline which normally ruled gradually broke down. The sanitary arrangements that governed the preparation of food and the disposal of waste were less and less observed. Even the use and cleaning of latrines that had seemed a marvel to western observers – Luigi Fernandino, Count Marsigli, at the time a prisoner of the Grand Vizier, drew a touching little sketch of the latrine in use – gradually disappeared. In Kara Mustafa's enclosure, the traditional standards still applied, but elsewhere the camp came to resemble (and smell like) a cesspit. The number of casualties was huge, and they were frequently afflicted by gaping wounds that festered almost immediately thanks to the vast swarms of flies in the heat of high summer. Food supplies were erratic, but those in the Ottoman camp ate better and more regularly than those within the city. Early in the siege, city women would creep through the palisade on the northern wall of Vienna, set up an informal food market close to the Scottish Gate and trade bread with the Turks for fresh vegetables. But when that loophole was closed the Ottoman army was reduced to a diet of soup and rice.

As the fortieth day of the siege passed – it fell on 23 August, in the traditional period of combat for the janissaries and the cavalry – Kara Mustafa had to look to the morale of his own troops. Feared rather than respected, he lacked the skill to deal with his own men. Successful Ottoman commanders met constantly with their soldiers, offered them rewards for their courage, spoke to them of the great prospects that victory offered them, of the richness of the prize that lay before them;

they even instructed the preachers attached to each unit to remind them of their duty before God. Parades, reviews, awards for bravery in the face of the enemy were both expected and valued by the key troops. But the *serasker* seems to have been better at chastising than encouraging. He handled his commanders badly; each one assigned a different sector on the battle front received only peremptory commands to push their men harder and make more progress. There was a single-mindedness to his approach that brooked neither argument nor discussion. His strategy was fixed immutably in the first days: Vienna would fall in accordance with the plan that he had decreed.

Kara Mustafa would not listen to those more experienced commanders who suggested that he should not underestimate the enemy. It was less that the Ottomans had no intelligence from the Tartars sweeping far to the west, rather that their leader was not interested in hearing it. It seemed that only the city interested him and the actions of the pitiful infidels were of no importance. Nor was he concerned that the vast Ottoman camp was losing all the order and discipline that westerners had so long admired. Dead animals were swelling and rotting under the heat of the sun, and even human corpses, buried in shallow graves, distended with the gases of corruption, began to push up through the loose soil above them.

His subordinates who had fought along the Hungarian frontier for a decade or more were less contemptuous of their enemy than their commander. They knew that the Habsburg cavalry would fight doggedly rather than flee, and their infantry could smash a cavalry charge with its measured volleys of musket fire, protected from a flank attack by a variety of spikes, stakes, or the clusters of boar spears known as *cheveaux de frise*. Their collective memory of battle was the Long War of the 1590s, when armies had fought bloody and largely inconclusive battles until, from sheer exhaustion and battle weariness, both sides had agreed a peace. But Kara Mustafa would not listen to his pashas, and rarely moved beyond his well-protected blockhouse before the walls.

Yet was he wrong? By following his tactics, the sultan's army was moving steadily forward and when the walls were broken and the city theirs, the *serasker* believed he would be remembered as the greatest conqueror in the history of the empire, the most successful of the Köprülü, whose victory would be on a par with those of the past under triumphant sultans like Mehmed II 'the Conqueror', Suleiman I 'the Lawgiver' and Murad IV 'the Cruel'.

In the city, as the Turkish excavations advanced closer and closer to the old walls, there were fears that the enemy was already burrowing beneath their feet. There were no deep foundations to the walls, just large, flat slabs of stone buried deep into the ground and the walls built up above them. On the city side there were damp and musty cellars and storerooms, which in the area of the imperial palace housed the Emperor's wine. In some places the walls were buttressed and supported, but in others they stood by their own mass and weight. It was rumoured that in addition to the daily explosions of mines against the ravelin and the bastions, the Turks were digging even deeper, under the walls themselves, below the wine cellars, providing a secret passage into the city. Such was the feeling of suppressed panic that Starhemberg ordered all the cellars to be watched and guarded, and citizens were admonished to listen for noises of picks and shovels below the streets. Every day he and his civil commander, Count Caplirs, received reports of the Ottoman advance, yet there was little that they could do to impede its relentless progress.

On 25 August, Starhemberg met in the early morning with his senior officers on the Löbl bastion which was being undermined from below and battered constantly by the Turks' heaviest guns. They agreed that they had to slow the pace and power of the attack. Throughout the morning they gathered two detachments of picked men and at four in the afternoon the large body of infantry rushed out from the sally ports close to the main point of attack. They pushed along the ditch, attacking the Turks with musket fire, swords and spears, with those behind hurling grenades down into the trenches. The guns on the walls blazed away at the Ottoman batteries to prevent them from responding to this unexpected attack. From the largest sally port by the Carinthian Gate another attacking party charged towards an advanced Ottoman battery that had done great damage to the defenders. The Prince of Hirtenberg with a few men killed the gunners but they had brought nothing with which to spike the guns, so they retreated, pursued by enraged Turks.

This escapade cost the lives of four officers and two hundred ordinary soldiers, and achieved nothing. On the following day two more mines exploded under the battered ravelin, one in the morning and one at nine in the evening. Both sides were now locked into a fixed pattern of action and response. A mine would explode, shaking the ground. The Ottoman horse-tail banners would be lifted in the trenches, and a mass of men rise behind them, charging towards the pit left by the blast and the prolapsed flank of the ravelin. From above, the garrison would batter the attackers below with gunfire, boiling water, stones and grenades, while the heavier guns, quickly realigned, blasted the janissaries from the adjacent bastions. Each attack failed, but every time a little more of the ravelin was destroyed and the defenders had an ever smaller terrain from which to fire on the enemy. Day by day the Turks were advancing and the Christians were being forced back. On 26 August it was the defenders' turn. Three hundred musketeers of Dupigny's regiment and thirty cavalry led by their colonel sallied out into the ditch, racing forward to the enemy trenches, killing all the sappers at their work, and blowing in the tunnels with grenades and charges of gunpowder. But the Turks were now wise to these sudden assaults and special troops were stationed to guard the excavations: this time a furious and bloody battle ensued, which lasted for more than an hour, until the musketeers retreated, carrying the body of their colonel. On the day of Dupigny's death and the destruction of the forward Ottoman saps, two more large mines exploded, one shattering more of the ravelin, the other uncomfortably close to the Burg bastion. Clearly, once the ravelin had been overwhelmed, this would become the main target.

With the ravelin gone, the garrison's capacity to resist would be decisively impaired. In better designed fortifications, layer upon layer of mutually supportive defences would guard the inner heart of the city. Fire from one would protect another, and if one were taken another could assume this protective role. But at Vienna the bastions and ravelin were like a three-legged stool: take away one leg and nothing could stop it toppling over. Matters were made worse because on the Burg bastion a solid bunker filled up much of the surface space, impeding men and guns from moving speedily on or off the platform, while the Löbl was shoddily built. The stronger emplacements to left and right, the Mölker bastion, which still survives in part, and the Carinthian Gate, could not provide supporting fire. So the Ottoman plan of attack had pinpointed the city's weakest spot.[9] Destroy the ravelin, attack the Burg and the Löbl bastions more or less at the same time, and then breach the curtain wall in between the two. It was impossible to move in men or guns fast enough to reinforce the two bastions in the case of an all-out attack and Starhemberg could never know precisely where the fatal blow would fall. Similarly, he could not drain the other sectors of men lest the Ottomans launch the long-feared assault on some other part of the city. Even though the ravelin now existed only as a mound of earth with a few square yards of solid ground on the top, it could still provide supporting fire for the two bastions. But for how long?

It was coming down to a matter of time for both sides. Supplies were now running short in the Ottoman camp, so that they slaughtered their Christian prisoners rather than feed them. In the city soldiers caught deserting were summarily hanged in the market place, evidence that morale was slipping. Venturing out beyond the protection of the walls, as the Turks had now sighted their guns on the sally ports, was like a sentence of death. There were fewer and fewer volunteers for these heroics, and anyway Starhemberg knew he could not afford to lose his men so pointlessly. The daily losses were mounting. One lucky shot fired from a heavy Turkish musket went through a file of five men, killing them all instantly. Gradually, the hellish quality of the battle came to fulfil the eschatological expectations of both sides. Both expected something like a last battle between Good and Evil: their priests and preachers had told them so. Christians knew how the Book of Revelation had described it: 'And when the thousand years are expired, Satan shall be loosed out of his prison, And shall go out to deceive the nations which are in the four quarters of the earth, Gog and Magog, to gather them together to battle: the number of whom is as the sand of the sea.'[10] For Muslims there was the reminder in the Qu'ran: 'It is ordained that no nation we have destroyed shall ever rise again. But when Gog and Magog rush headlong down every hill, when the true promise nears its fulfilments, the unbelievers shall stare in amazement crying, "Woe to us! Of this we have been heedless. We have done wrong."'[11]

On 28 August, the weather broke with a ferocious summer storm, which silenced the guns because the powder could not be kept dry. But as the rain ceased in the afternoon another mine was exploded at the side of the ravelin. The janissaries rose to attack, the few defenders on the top fired down and the guns on the side of the Burg and Löbl bastions scoured the faces of the ruined ravelin with canister shot, filled with nails and musket balls. But the Turks were now so close to the defenders that it was difficult to shoot accurately enough to avoid killing their own men. Then, on the following morning, between 'nine and ten [the Turks] sprung a mine under the remaining part of the ravelin, which utterly destroyed it, after it had been torn in pieces by so many mines, no firm ground being left for us or the enemy to fight upon; our men keeping only a very small retrenchment in the middle of the ravelin that had escaped the last assault of the enemy. This they maintained very obstinately, beset as it was on every side by the enemy.'[12] From that point onwards, the ravelin was no more than a symbol of the city's defiance because it could no longer provide any flanking fire in support of the two bastions.

Starhemberg sent soldiers from his own regiment under a Captain Heisterman to garrison this forlorn hope. The captain, previously Starhemberg's adjutant, was already a hero among the defenders. On one of the many sallies against the Ottoman camp, he had grappled with a powerful janissary, wrestled him to the ground, wrenched his yataghan from his enemy's hand, and, like David conquering Goliath, severed the Turk's head 'with his own Scimitar'. He carried both head and sword back within the walls, spiking the former on a spear and presenting the latter to his commander.[13] Starhemberg had told him that if the Turks pressed too hard, he was to retreat under cover of darkness and abandon the little scrap of ground still in Christian hands. He had no intention of retreating: 'having posted himself upon the ravelin with fifty men, [he] would not retreat notwithstanding the fierce attacks of the enemy who had set fire to the palisades and traverses of wood that was the only defence our men had remaining'. Twenty soldiers were killed in the night, including his second-in-command, Lieutenant Sommervogel, leaving a garrison of thirty against hundreds of Turks pressing up from below. On the next morning, 3 September, a relief party was driven back by a shower of Turkish arrows, and Starhemberg sent direct orders by word of mouth that Heisterman was to set fire to the remaining defences and take his men back as best he could under covering fire to the curtain wall. This he did at midnight, 'so that the Turks were that day being the third of September being possessed of that ravelin that had cost them so much blood'.

On the evening of 27 August a small party of artillerymen commanded by Count Kielmansegg had carried a bundle of signal rockets to the tower of St Stephen's Cathedral and fired forty of them into the night sky. They were a 'signal to the Duke [of Lorraine] that we expected a speedy relief'. This *relief* was a chimera, but those in the city believed salvation was at hand. In fact there had been a devastating silence about the military communications smuggled into the city. We might speculate whether Starhemberg, that most grimly realistic of soldiers, actually believed it was coming, or, if coming, whether it would arrive in time. Nevertheless, every evening thereafter the rocket party made the same journey up the tower, even though there was no hint of any relieving army.

Charles of Lorraine on the far side of the Danube had at first doubted that the city's days were numbered. All through the siege he had received gloomy messages and dispatches from Starhemberg. But now he knew that with the final loss of the ravelin, the Turks would redouble their efforts and the city could not hold out for much more than two weeks at the most. The heightened intensity of Ottoman assaults began immediately. On the day after they had finally occupied the ravelin, the most powerful mine to date, which the Turkish sappers had long been preparing, was exploded under the northern face of the Burg bastion. This rendered most of the artillery pieces facing the Ottoman assault trenches unusable. Thirty feet of the bastion collapsed completely and more than a thousand janissaries surged from the trenches, clambering over loose earth, bricks and stone blocks, up the near-vertical slope towards the platform atop the bastion. The explosion came at precisely 2.00 p.m., when the watch was changed among the defenders, so that both the old and the new watch were crowded on the bastion. Some were killed and wounded in the massive explosion, but once they had recovered and re-formed, their available firepower was almost doubled.

As the smoke and dust cleared, the defenders saw a solid mass of Turks climbing up towards them, as Ottoman arrows and musket fire played remorselessly upon them. 'Whilst the cannon, mortar pieces, and small shot played furiously from all parts, there appeared on the top of the ditch about a thousand Turks, who on the sudden let themselves down one by one through certain holes and galleries that conveyed them into the very bottom of the ditch, and running from thence towards that part of the bastion which had been thrown down by the mine. They found a way by digging and removing the loose earth to shelter themselves in the hollow parts of the ruins, making also rooms for greater numbers.' More and more attackers were fed up to the front through the communication trenches, with a forest of horse-tail banners converging on the breach. The first line, some janissaries with badges denoting valour, some irregulars, *serdengeçti*, seeking to make a name by their berserk courage, were only a few yards away, and the defenders hurled loose timbers, palisade poles, bricks and stones down to keep them at a distance. Behind this first attack line were thousands of Turks, eager to clamber over the piles of rubble to engage with the infidel.

The situation was desperate. If the Ottomans gained a toe-hold at the top of the cavernous gap in the wall they would be impossible to dislodge. The officers and sergeants quickly rallied their men, setting some to make an improvised redoubt, out of 'great beams and sacks filled with sand and earth, while in front stood three files of men standing shoulder to shoulder, who fired down, then turned off to each side to reload and then enter the firing line again'. They managed to keep up a near-continuous barrage of fire, possible only because so many musketeers were on hand. *Cheveaux de frise* were hurriedly assembled and pushed to the edge of the breach, creating an emergency field fortification. Some were also pushed down into the breach; several Turks were impaled on the spear points as they tried to scramble over them.

Smaller cannon were hurriedly manhandled on to the bastion and propped up so that they could fire down with canister shot on the enemy massed below. Hundreds of grenades were passed out, fuses lit, and then sent cascading down on to the Turks' heads; inevitably, some exploded prematurely, wreaking havoc in the defenders' lines. The whole platform of the bastion was filled with fighting men, struggling to repel the Turks' onslaught, which seemed to swell from almost every direction. The defenders were so tightly packed that the bodies of the dead were held up by the crush around them. 'While I was holding a soldier by his scarf, his head was knocked off by a cannonball. Blood and brains were splattered on to my nose and right into my mouth, which was open because of the day's great heat . . . This incident caused me great suffering afterward, above all violent palpitations and vomiting.'[14]

The battle raged ferociously for more than two hours. Starhemberg
and all his commanders rushed to the scene, to stiffen their troops in
the crisis. Hundreds of the defenders were killed in this narrow battleground as the Ottoman mortars and artillery rained down fire on to
the bastion, regardless of any damage to their own men. After nightfall, hundreds of palisade posts were hammered into the ground around
the bastion platform: there were fears of another huge blast. There
now remained only 40 per cent of the original garrison, who still had
to man sixty-four defence points. There were no more trained soldiers
in reserve. On 6 September three mines exploded under the Löbl
bastion, destroying most of the retaining wall facing the Burg bastion.
A diary recorded: 'What we feared came to pass. About one in the
afternoon the enemy springing several mines . . . made such a breach
that a great part of the bastion, at least twenty feet thick, being of
brick and stone, was quite thrown down from the top to the very
bottom leaving a gap of thirty-six feet broad, and our men quite un-
covered. Whereupon the enemy made a furious assault but soon retired
by reason of the difficulty of the passage occasioned by the heaps and
pieces of the ruins that lay in their way.'[15]

In the explosions, all bar a few of the defenders' artillery pieces on
the left side of the Löbl bastion were destroyed or immobilised. The
remaining defenders rushed down to stand shoulder to shoulder in
the breach, armed with swords, spears, long hooks and even scythes,
as they were raked with cannon fire and Turkish arrows. Leander
Russ's dramatic oil painting of 1837 could not fully capture the savagery
of the fighting. Again the *cheveaux de frise* – the seventeenth-century
equivalent of barbed wire – were eventually pushed into place to
provide some barrier against the janissaries and the dismounted cavalry,
which charged in, wave after wave. The hand-to-hand fighting lasted
all day, ending only as night fell. Overnight the defenders had no rest,
as they prepared new redoubts, erected a palisade and several wooden
palanka behind the bastions, and as others dragged artillery pieces into
position to make new batteries. The curtain wall was reinforced, with
more men and wall pieces (light artillery), as well as bombs and even
coping stones from the parapet that could be dropped on to the enemy
below; plainly, Starhemberg realised that this, the last line of his
defences, would soon be under heavy attack.

The capacity of the two bastions to support each other was by now drastically reduced, and, as the Turks saw them badly damaged by each exploding mine, their spirits rose; the smell of rotting corpses, brick dust and burned powder now became the sweet scent of imminent victory. Masses of volunteers pushed forward into the ditch to wait for the next assault. There was activity all along the now narrowed front. While the two bastions were under attack the Ottoman sappers dug three deep galleries, pushing steadily towards the curtain wall where it joined the corner of the Löbl bastion. The soldiers on the walls began to drop bombs to the base of the curtain wall to crater the ground and make it harder to tunnel underneath the ramparts: it made no difference, as the Ottoman sappers simply dug deeper. Starhemberg and his officers now began to make preparations for such resistance as they could mount once the walls had been breached. Well-planned but improvised defences might be just as effective as brick and stone.

The centrepiece of this second line of resistance was a section of the medieval fortified wall close to the palace, left intact when the Burg bastion had been built. It had long been a nuisance for carriages drivers leaving the palace for the nearby gate, the Burgtor. It made for an awkward turn between the curtain wall and the new palace range built by the Emperor Leopold. It was the full height of the outer wall and made of solid, undressed stone. Heavy artillery could knock it apart in a couple of days, yet it would still be a major obstacle for infantry. This would become the bulwark of the final line of resistance. It was surrounded by entrenchments and low walls of timber, carts, sandbags and gabions. The towering new palace behind would provide innumerable firing points for musketeers, while the gunners and musketeers on the curtain wall could turn their weapons around and fire down into the space behind them once it filled with Turks. Behind the Löbl bastion there were fewer points for defence. There was an old blockhouse above and behind the bastion, but, once past that, the Turks could fan out through the open streets of the city.

The main problem for the defenders was the seemingly endless supply of Ottoman manpower. The city was still surrounded, and there were Turks ready and eager to attack at any point. If the other parts of the walls were denuded of troops to plug the gaps on the palace front, the rest of the city would be exposed. Every large building was made ready as a centre of resistance. Churches, hospitals, tracts of housing were filled with weapons, and baulks of timber hammered in place to block doors and windows. The city watch and men young and old were made responsible for defending their homes and neighbourhoods. Every street and square would be turned into a killing ground, while the great iron chains, long prepared, were, at Starhemberg's order, finally slung across the streets.

The Ottoman troops were also making their preparations for the final assault. The reserve troops from Buda had been called in, and with them a stream of carts filled with fresh supplies of powder, weapons and food. Once the janissaries, *sipahis* and the huge number of irregulars had entered the city, the Grand Vizier and his officers concluded that they would quickly overcome any remaining resistance, although the Ottoman war histories were full of stories of infidels fighting to the last, men and women alike. They had also heard rumours that a relieving army had been massing to the west, on both sides of the Danube; yet they had no idea as to its size or its current position. The paramount task, they all agreed, was to take the city, their predestined prize. If they captured Vienna they would gain immortal fame throughout the whole world of Islam. But a darker thought filled their minds. Their camp had turned into a cesspit of filth and human carcasses, quite unlike the traditional model of Ottoman good order and discipline. The commanders closer to the troops than Kara Mustafa sensed a rising tide of mutiny. No one dared voice what all of them feared: what would happen if they could not take the city in this final surge?

8

'A Flood of Black Pitch'

On Wednesday 8 September Vienna celebrated the nativity of the Blessed Virgin Mary. The Emperor Leopold's grandfather, Ferdinand II, had declared that Mary, the Mother of God, was the *generalissima sacrale* who commanded the Habsburg armies in their struggles against heretic Protestants and infidel Turks alike. In the cathedral and throughout the city, the day was celebrated with special fervour, and priests, served by altar boys and thurifers, brought the Host to the men on the walls. At the masses held through the day, soldiers and civilians alike prayed for their supreme commander and patroness to save them in this, their hour of desperate need. There was a hint that a miracle might indeed unfold before their eyes. The nightly procession to St Stephen's, to launch the signal rockets from the roof, had become a vain ritual, but on the night of 8 September there was the long-hoped-for response. As the rockets soared into the sky, flared and died away, the little party prepared to descend the narrow stairway into the cathedral. Then they noticed, high on the Kahlenberg Hill to the west of the city, 'five rockets as a signal that our expected succours were at hand . . . answered by us in the same manner'.

But on the following day, from the walls they saw only the Grand Vizier massing his men far back out of cannon shot. It was clear that there was intense activity all along the battlefront, signs of renewed Turkish mining, men moving into the trenches. During that day, there was less gunfire, often an ominous prelude to the explosion of a mine. At two in the afternoon, a mine brought down more of the wall of the Löbl bastion, and Starhemberg's men now knew where the assault was likely to come. Men stood side by side in reserve behind both bastions, while others dug trenches and built redoubts in the space between the new defences and the old city wall. Many of the guns on the bastions and the wall were now firing canister shot instead of cannonballs, canvas sacks filled with scraps of iron, old nails and slivers of flint and sharp stones, while only a few pieces waged an artillery duel with the Ottoman guns dug into the trench lines farther away. Two Turkish assaults were made on the new breaches on the bastion, but were driven back, with heavy losses. All the while, 'Count Starhemberg applied his utmost care towards making retrenchments and traverses, repairing the ramparts, reproving the breaches upon the bastions . . . fortifying the streets and houses near the ramparts and bastions, with iron chains and barricadoes, that in every place and on every event the enemy might find all resistance imaginable.'[1]

This stalwart resistance was likely to prove fruitless. Savage hand-to-hand fighting was at the heart of the Ottoman art of war. It had by 1683 become common to talk about the Turks' decline, about how the janissaries had gone soft, how they had lost the military *virtù* of their predecessors. This was not how the soldiers who faced them in the breaches at Vienna or in battles afterwards saw it. They faced an enemy in a state of spiritual exaltation, brimming with confidence, courage and daring. One janissary wrote: 'We are the believers since the beginning of the world. Since that time we have recognized the unity of Allah – we will sacrifice our heads for this belief . . . We have been the intoxicated ones from all eternity – we are the butterflies of the Divine Light – we are in this world a legion forever in ecstasy before the grandeur of Allah.' And the defenders saw before them the truth of the final lines of this manifesto: 'We are so numerous that we cannot be counted upon the fingers – our spring is inexhaustible.'[2] Habsburg soldiers knew their enemy's spirit.

The English ambassador Sir Robert Sutton later wrote of a battle on the River Pruth in 1711: 'A janissary coming before the vizier's tent, crying out, "Shall we lie here to die of sickness and misery? Let all true Musselmen follow me to attack the infidels", he snatched up one of the colours [*tuğ*] that stood before the tents and went forwards. He was immediately followed by other janissaries, the hand-picked assault troops [*serdengeçti*] and the desperados [*deli*] gathered together and with their usual cries moved towards the enemy. They were repulsed three times with a loss of about 8000 men . . .'³ These were the 'heaven-selected warriors' and, once inside the walls, they would be impossible to dislodge. A century after the Siege of Vienna a Habsburg general writing of the Turks defending a city declared: 'It is beyond the human powers of comprehension to grasp . . . just how obstinately the Turks defend themselves. As soon as one fortification is demolished, they simply dig themselves another one. It is easier to deal with any conventional fortress and with any other army than with the Turks when they are defending a stronghold.'⁴

On 8 September it looked certain that the Ottomans would take the city. It was also likely that – once in possession, with all the defenders slaughtered and the city depopulated – they would not be easily dislodged.⁵ Although the defenders hoped that relief was at hand, the Turks displayed no signs of alarm or panic: 'they continued working on their mines, as if they feared nothing from abroad . . .' Day by day the strength of the Turks' assaults grew, despite the increasingly obvious presence of a large Christian force in the hills above the city.

★   ★   ★

From early in July the only sizeable Habsburg force beyond the walls of Vienna had been Lorraine's battle-scarred cavalry, dragoons and cuirassiers, plus a few precious musketeers on foot. They had blocked every advance by the Turks and Hungarians along the northern bank of the Danube, throwing back every Ottoman column probing westward. Now, two months later, they prepared to join with an army of relief that had gathered to the west of Vienna, fully equipped and ready for action. These were not Leopold's own men, but contingents drawn from the states and cities of the Holy Roman Empire and a cavalry army led by his ally the King of Poland. The empire had many critics and few defenders. The pre-eminent political philosopher Samuel Pufendorf wrote in 1667 of 'a body that conforms to no rule and resembles a monster'.⁶ Europe's primordial savant, Voltaire, later apostrophised it as follows: 'This body, which was called and which still calls itself the Holy Roman Empire, was neither holy, nor Roman, nor an empire.'⁷ As a body it was indeed enfeebled, but its individual limbs were extremely powerful. The new armies of Brandenburg,

Bavaria and Saxony, the quintessence of three decades of war up to 1648, were second to none. Some of the smaller states had smaller forces but of high quality. The Empire after the end of the Thirty Years War had been regarded as a fossil, seemingly incapable of any coherent action whatsoever. Yet this moribund Empire had produced both infantry and cavalry, about forty thousand men from both Catholic and Protestant states, for the salvation of Vienna.[8]

What brought the German soldiers was a mixture of political, economic and psychological motives, but the most powerful was fear. They also benefited considerably from subsidies and other payments made from the funds flowing from the Vatican into Leopold's treasury. The German states that contributed most to the relief force were those that would be next in line if the Ottoman army, triumphant at Vienna, moved further west. Bavaria would be among the first victims; so too would the duchies and principalities of Swabia and Franconia. If the Turks pushed northwards, the electorate of Saxony would be in their line of march. Their support for the Habsburgs in 1683 was directly related to the sense of threat from the east. With the exception of Hanover, which sent the heir to the duchy, George (later to succeed as King George I of England), with a token contribution of six hundred cavalry, the powerful states of northern Germany, like Brandenburg, eventually chose not to send troops to join the alliance.[9] The direct Ottoman threat to them was negligible.

The Emperor Leopold could call for support from the entire Empire, but he and his diplomats had sensibly concentrated their efforts on those with the strongest interest in saving Vienna.[10] First to move was his future son-in-law, Max Emmanuel, the Elector of Bavaria. On 6 August, he committed himself to sending more than 11,000 men, including five infantry regiments. In fact, his troops were already on the move. They passed Passau, under the approving eye of the Emperor, at the end of July, and marched east along the Danube to set up camp beside the Traisen River on the northern bank, less than fifty miles from Vienna.[11] The states of Franconia and Swabia, after some hard bargaining with the Emperor, provided 6000 infantry and 2000 cavalry; they were at Passau on 21 August and encamped at Linz on 30 August. The final and perhaps most valuable contingent was the Saxon troops led by the Elector of Saxony, John George, in person. His force of 7000 musketeers, 2000 horsemen and some of the best light field artillery in Europe, moved slowly south-east through Bohemia to the town of Maissau. By the end of August, there were more than 20,000 infantry in bivouacs on the plain north of the Danube.

It was not an overwhelming force, but with the addition of its major component (numerically speaking) – the Polish cavalry – then still moving south, it could certainly challenge the Ottomans. Most important, it was fresh, eager to do battle and well financed. The miracle that might save Vienna was not just the men gathering north of the river bridges across the Danube but the torrent of money pouring from the Vatican into the Emperor's treasury, and hypothecated exclusively for the war against the Turk. The contingents from the Empire (with the exception of Bavaria) required to be paid handsomely for their services, and all their expenses had to be met. By August 1683 Leopold was near-bankrupt: he had exhausted almost all his financial resources. Nor could he borrow money. The extravagantly rich Archbishop of Salzburg rejected a pleading personal letter from the Emperor out of hand. But Benedetto Odescalchi, elected as Pope in 1676, and taking the resonant name of Innocent XI, was obsessed with the Ottoman threat. He was also preoccupied with the menace of Louis XIV's France, which occupied the papal territory of Avignon, undermined the Pope's authority within the Catholic Church and pursued a foreign policy diametrically opposed to Innocent's plans and wishes. Thus, supporting Leopold, a faithful and pious son of the Church, and afflicted by the French in the west and the Ottomans in the east, would advance Innocent's political as well as his ethical ends.

The Pope believed, like his predecessor Pius V a century before, that he had an extraordinary opportunity to halt the advance of Islam, if only the united forces of Christendom could be marshalled. The answer was a coalition led by the Pope, a Holy League, like that which under Pius V's patronage had produced the stunning victory at Lepanto in 1571. Even if the Pope had no military sanction he could deploy both economic and ideological power. Only he could unlock the vast resources at the disposal of the Church. Only he could authorise taxes on ecclesiastical lands, collections to be levied on the surpluses generated within the richer dioceses, or offer valuable spiritual benefits to the laity in exchange for voluntary contributions to the great cause. Few secular states could raise money with such ease, certainly not Leopold.

Innocent had worked hard from the beginning of his pontificate to curb waste and extravagance, and to improve the financial structures of the Holy See. As a result, the Vatican had money to spend on his great project. The Pope bankrolled the 'army of liberation' for Vienna, as he had King John III Sobieski in Poland.

On 31 August the long-awaited Polish host appeared after a long journey to the Danube. Charles of Lorraine rode to greet the King of Poland, riding at the head of about 3000 light horsemen. The bulk of the Poles followed behind, led by two thousand of the *husaria*, the fabled noble 'winged horsemen', and 10,000 other cavalry plus a few foot soldiers. The Polish hussars were a unique elite shock force, heavily armoured in plate armour and chain mail, resplendent in leopard skins and plumed helmets. They rode with a lance (*kopia*) of about sixteen foot in length, two swords and a brace or more of pistols. The role of the *husaria*, striking en masse at full gallop with lowered lances, was to crack open any enemy formation, while the lighter horsemen armed with sabres, maces and hand axes chased behind, slaughtering the disordered foe. The Polish hussars were heavy cavalry par excellence, and they had no equivalent in seventeenth-century Europe. In effect a hold-over from the great age of medieval chivalry, man and horse together were a missile, with their lance or wielding their long spear-like triangular swords (*koncerz*) more than four foot long – they existed only for the charge.[12] Facing the disciplined volley fire of western armies, they had largely become a liability, but against the janissary infantry of the Ottomans or the loose-flowing formations of the *sipahis*, they could be as devastating as artillery fire.

As the new army of Christendom assembled, Lorraine met all the commanders and gained the confidence of each in turn. He won over the suspicious and thin-skinned Polish king with a respectful but also comradely tone: he, a duke of Lorraine, implicitly acknowledged the king's superior status, but also appealed to him, soldier to soldier, as a comrade-in-arms. The Polish king, actually fourteen years older than the duke, often appeared the more vigorous man, and certainly much grander in poise and appearance. Two months in the field made Lorraine look even more dowdy than his customary lack of style. The danger was a chaotic assembly of ill-coordinated soldiers, each section led towards glory by a self-obsessed commander. Lorraine managed his fellow commanders with the greatest skill. The problem was not new to him. The Habsburg corps of officers had for more than seventy years been a hotchpotch of Italians, Germans, Scots, Irish, English and French. Charles of Lorraine, himself a distant descendant of the ancient Kings of Lotharingia, a Prince of the Empire and a son-in-law of the Emperor, had long before learned the art of winning the confidence of those with whom he served.[13] He also had the knack of winning over almost everyone he met, from bluff, self-opinionated fighting soldiers to conniving courtiers. He had no great ambitions, but he wanted to succeed against the Turks; above all he was determined to save Vienna. Yet time was short.

Charles of Lorraine's fellow commanders had only the haziest notion of the true situation, and the power of the Ottoman advance. He alone had recently come to grips with the Turks – smashing a powerful Ottoman advance along the northern bank of the river late in July; only he had watched the city under assault, week by week, and knew how close Starhemberg was to being overwhelmed. Yet Charles of Lorraine did not command the largest part of the relief army, and he ranked well below the King of Poland and John George, the Elector of Saxony. Lorraine recognised that this was a temporary alliance, with each leader having his own ambitions as well as subscribing to the great overall objective. So he could not command them, but he had to persuade them that his plan was the best of the limited number of alternatives.

Lorraine had a disarming charm and an easy manner and appeared to all as a simple battlefield soldier. He challenged nobody: John Sobieski commented negatively only on his poor clothes and spoke warmly of his courage and soldierly bearing. Gathered at the castle of Stetteldorf owned by Count Hardegg, almost in sight of the Danube close to the town of Stockerau, all the main players planned the decisive battle that would settle the fate of Vienna. The duke represented the Habsburg forces and the Emperor; General Hannibal von Degenfeld took the place of his master, Max Emmanuel, the Elector of Bavaria. Degenfeld was a fine organiser, but also an adventurer who made his career successively in the armies of Saxony, Bavaria and the Republic of Venice. He was following a family tradition: his father had fought in the Thirty Years War, with the imperials under Tilly and Wallenstein, then with the Swedes, finally with the French, and ended his days in the comfortable service of Venice. The third professional soldier was the Field Marshal of the Holy Roman Empire, Count Karl von Waldeck. Battle-scarred like Lorraine, he had fought for Brandenburg, for the Swedes in Poland, with Montecuccoli and Lorraine at St Gotthard, and would finally end his career as General Field Marshal to William III in the Netherlands.

Between them they quickly agreed a plan of attack, along the lines that Lorraine proposed. The Emperor, whom Waldeck had openly suggested showed cowardice in abandoning his capital, had wanted a more cautious advance, following the easier ground and approaching Vienna from the south. Lorraine, knowing that every day counted, proposed that they should take the shortest route, due east across the long mountainous outcrop of the Wienerwald, the Vienna Woods. They ignored Leopold's implicit command, and concentrated on the more daring and risky direct route. All the contingents north of the river would rendezvous towards the Danube crossing points on 5 September. The Saxons would cross to the southern bank across the old bridge of Stein near Krems, and with the Bavarians advance to make camp before the town of Tulln.

On the northern bank of the river opposite Tulln the land was a riparian bog known colloquially as the Danube meadows. Over ten days Lorraine's men had hacked out a rough road through these marshlands and built two pontoon bridges across to Tulln. On the southern side, Lorraine's engineers, under his Scots aide Leslie, protected the southern bank with a wooden palisade against the Tartars who still made attacks in the plain. The first of the sustained autumn rains raised the height and flow of the river, and the pressure of water broke the frail bridge apart several times. On 6 September the rain stopped and the following day the Polish horsemen began to cross, followed by Lorraine's men, all except three battalions of cavalry and a few foot soldiers left behind to protect the river traverse.

Crossing a river was one of the most risky manoeuvres in seventeenth-century warfare, and there were real fears that the Tartars would try to disrupt it; on the north bank there were still large numbers of Ottoman regulars and their Hungarian allies, their exact location unknown, even after Lorraine's crushing victory over them ten days before. The Poles had to leave all their supply wagons behind because the temporary bridge was not solid enough to take so much weight. After it was strengthened and the flow diminished a little, they were able to take them across one at a time; by 9 September only half the baggage train was across the river, by which time the army had already set out for Vienna.

Supplies had to be sent downriver from Linz by barge: the combined army that gathered on the plain before Tulln was issued with enough bread to last them a week, and they were expected to be in the hills above Vienna within three or four days. But soon thereafter they would run out of food and supplies, and there was none to be gleaned from the ravaged countryside as they approached Vienna. This was to be no promenade. On 8 September, the birthday of the Blessed Virgin Mary, all the troops drew up for a review on the flat ground before the palisade at Tulln. There were three ruling princes – John III Sobieski, King of Poland, John George, the Elector of Saxony, and the young Max Emmanuel, Elector of Bavaria, who had now joined his men; the professional commanders, and a large group of young nobles who had flocked to join the crusade to save Vienna. One of them, attached to the bodyguard of Charles of Lorraine, was the slightly built young Prince of the House of Savoy, Eugene, in his first experience of war. As Prince Eugene, he was to become, in the opinion of Napoleon Bonaparte, one of the greatest commanders of all time. Earlier, Lorraine had dispatched six hundred dragoons under a Colonel Heissler to ride hard towards Vienna, scout the Turkish positions, and if possible take up a defensible position on the Kahlenberg, or Bleak Mountain. It was Heissler who would fire the signal rockets that told Vienna's defenders that relief was on its way.

From Tulln to Vienna was little more than twenty miles, but there was only a single high road winding up through the Wienerwald. To either side in the forest there were myriad pathways through the hills and deep valleys, and a better road that followed the Danube. The final plan was agreed. The Duke of Lorraine would be in overall command of the left wing, closest to the Danube, with all imperial infantry and cavalry and the Saxon contingent; the Elector of Saxony would have direct authority over his own troops. The centre was made up of the Franconian and Bavarian infantry under the command of Count Waldeck, and then to their right the Bavarian and Franconian cavalry with Max Emmanuel riding with his own men, but the overall command of the wing given to Julius Francis, Duke of Sachsen Lauenberg, one of the few north German rulers to come to the aid

of Vienna. The traditional place of honour, on the right wing, was
held by the Poles under their king, John Sobieski. In simple terms,
the infantry was concentrated on the left and the bulk of the cavalry
on the right, with the army intending to descend the hills in a huge
arc, stretching from the Danube to beyond the Wien River, attacking
the whole western face of the vast Ottoman camp encircling the city.

At dawn on 9 September, the Habsburg and the German forces
struck their tents on the plain of Tulln and began their march east.
The thousands of Polish horsemen remained behind, no doubt because
they would move faster than the infantry; they began to move out in
the mid-afternoon. The commanders had unanimously agreed to
follow Lorraine's advice and attack the city across the Wienerwald. It
did not seem too great an obstacle from the maps that he had shown
them and none of the commanders had much detailed knowledge of
their route. Nor did Lorraine until he personally scouted some
approaches to the ridge of the Wienerwald after the advance began.
In 1683 the whole area was a wilderness, unmapped, and, since 1493,
when the Emperor Maximilian had banned further settlement within
it, mostly uninhabited except for a few hunters and woodcutters.
Stretching like a narrow peninsula of high ground from the eastern
Alps to the Danube elbow west of Vienna, it was a huge, established
forest of beech and oak, with scrubland on the steep slopes on the
Vienna side. It had long provided the Viennese with firewood and a
constant supply of game; the Habsburgs claimed rights over it as hunting
domain, but since it had no palace or hunting lodge it had gradually
lost favour. Leopold certainly preferred the greater convenience of
hunting grounds artificially stocked with game and with a fully
equipped palace close at hand.

On the Vienna side of the forest there was an easy slope upwards
which was covered with vineyards and small villages; higher up the
slope became much steeper and was fissured with streams and little
valleys. Along the ridge which ran from the Danube to the south-
west, the woods were dense and where there were no trees the undergrowth grew profusely. There were a few buildings on the highest
knoll, with an old monastery, by 1683 falling into ruin. When it rained
the numerous brooks filled with water, pouring down the hillsides in
white torrents.

Just before the Danube, studded at intervals along a ridge about six miles long, was a set of named high points, landmarks, from the Rosskopf, farthest away to the south-west, to the highest, the Hermannskogel, at a little over 1700 feet, running along to the last, the Kahlenberg, about 1300 feet, towering over the Danube below. Next to the Kahlenberg was another hilltop rather prosaically known as the Sauberg, or Sow Mountain, from the herds of wild pigs that roamed there, living off the acorns from the oak trees. This peak was bought in 1628 by the Emperor Ferdinand II from the monks of Klosterneuburg; he promptly renamed it the Josephsberg, and built a small monastery dedicated to the saint.[14]

Lorraine discovered from Colonel Heissler that a few Turks had occupied the two high points at the end of the ridge but only as observation posts. They had recently dug some ditches and might be about to strengthen the position further. It was fortunate that the Ottomans had not occupied the ridge and built field fortifications: even a few musketeers well entrenched there would have wrought havoc. By dusk the infantry and German cavalry had encamped by the little town of St Andra on the western edge of the Wienerwald and the Polish force, arriving late in the day, bivouacked a few miles to the west. The commanders met and agreed their final plan for attack. They drew up the battle plans: how each unit would relate to its neighbours, how they would manoeuvre in the assault, even where the artillery would be placed. They agreed that the relief army should occupy the whole six-mile front from the Kahlenberg south-westwards to the Rosskopf.

Most European battles were then fought on flat or rolling countryside and the problems of manoeuvring so many men through a forest, up steep slopes, over so long a front were barely understood. The ridges were not especially high and there were pathways to the summit, but none was suitable for many thousands of men. Perhaps the caution of Leopold and his military advisers in Passau had not been as foolish as it had seemed to Lorraine and the other commanders? The entire army had to struggle up one long slope covered with scrub and small trees, descend into the valley beyond and then climb the other side of the valley to the top of the line of hills on the next, and then, finally, fight a battle.

The huge Polish cavalry force suffered most. Psychologically, they would be the key component in the battle. As they toiled up the long slope of the mountain, at first riding their horses, and, after they dismounted, stumbling on the loose stony ground, the mass of men thinned out and the lines grew longer and longer. As they advanced out of the valley of the Hagen River, only two miles from where they had started, the terrain became even worse, with huge boulders and shale on the ground and, later, narrow clefts in the rock through which only one or two horses could pass at a time.

It was well after nightfall before the advance guard arrived at the agreed mustering point, with an additional demanding climb the following day. As the whole army gathered beyond the first line of foothills in the deep valley cut by the Weidling River, a small group of volunteer Savoyard mountain troops (with the young Prince Eugene) and some musketeers were sent ahead on the evening of 10 September. Their task, guided by local hunters, was to find their way up the maze of forest pathways to the summit of the Kahlenberg ridge. Once it was dark they were to capture the Turkish outposts on the Kahlenberg in a sudden night attack. By dawn on Saturday 11 September they had surprised the small Ottoman outpost and slaughtered all the Turks they could find. But some of the Ottoman force slipped away in the dark, returning to the main Turkish camp on the plain below, bearing news of the impending attack. By eleven in the morning the main body of the Austrian and German troops had arrived along the ridge. They made camp on the slopes of the three peaks – the Kahlenberg, the Vogelsangberg, and the Hermannskogel, company by company, in accordance with the field orders. Closest to the Danube on the Kahlenberg were the Austrian troops of Charles of Lorraine; next to them below the summit of the Vogelsangberg were the contingents from the Holy Roman Empire under Waldeck, and then the Saxons under the direct command of Julius Francis, Duke of Lauenberg covering the lower slopes of the Hermannskogel. When the Poles arrived on the ridge, they took up position on the slopes below the last three hilltops, farthest from the river – the Dreimarkstein, the Gränberg and the Rosskopf. All this activity could be seen by the observers in the cathedral tower in the city below, and by the Turks in their camp.

The camps along the ridge were laid out in lines, corresponding to the plan of attack. But when Charles of Lorraine and King John Sobieski rode up to the vantage point on the Kahlenberg, it became clear that the maps they had used and the reality of the terrain were very different. The maps had presented a set of flat, open, rectangular fields below the hills, even showing the neat lines of the plough. What they saw below them was a much riskier prospect. There was not a slope running smoothly down towards the city, but a pockmarked, rocky landscape enfolded into a succession of clefts and ridges. There were little villages clustered amid the fields. The fields were not flat, but steeply sloping, and often bounded by stone walls, thick hedgerows or dense scrub. Worst of all the descent was precipitous. Most of the crops were not grain but grapevines, growing rampantly entangled, heavily laden with swollen fruit. It was only a few weeks before they would be picked. Most were strung on long hurdles woven from withies, but where the land was pitted with fissures they often snaked along the ground. Through the fields were little gulches with fast-flowing streams, tumbling down towards the Danube after the rains; and larger, deeper ravines cut by small rivers, also heading towards the Danube. Below the fields were a string of villages, which survived on the wine that they produced.

It was difficult ground for infantry, but for cavalry it might be murderous. Tall on their horses, Sobieski's *husaria*, slowly picking their way downhill, would be perfect targets for Ottoman marksmen. They could be wiped out long before they were in a position to launch a charge. The only hope was strong support from musketeers who could exchange fire with the Ottomans, and Sobieski had few of these. He demanded that some of the best German infantry should reinforce his men, and Lorraine immediately agreed. As they looked at the ground, both men realised that this would not be the battle that they had antici-pated. They might outnumber the enemy, they were fresh and they had been spiritually and psychologically reinforced by the sermons of their preachers and the Body of Christ, but the ground favoured the Ottoman defenders, who could set up a succession of ambushes and close encounters. Here a flight of arrows could be as deadly as a musket volley, and the lighter Turkish horses were better adapted to the rough terrain than the sturdier German or Polish chargers.

In tactical terms, then, it threatened disaster. Neither pikemen nor musketeers could advance in line, weapons at the ready, as the commanders' plan proposed. At best, groups of men could scramble down, over rocks and other obstacles, halt, re-form and move on again. There was no possibility of sophisticated manoeuvre. Then each village beyond the vine-laden fields could be made into a strongpoint by the

Turks; field fortifications or trenches could join one village to the next. Ottoman musketeers or gunners could pick off the relief army as it stumbled down the hill, with little in the way of effective cover. It was also exceptionally and insufferably hot, and the sudden storms did little to break the oppressive, sultry atmosphere.

The generals might command and throw 'the dice of war' but the reality of the forthcoming battle would be controlled entirely by the company officers and the sergeants.[15] Yet the objective was clear – the city below them, and the sea of Ottoman tents surrounding it. With a telescope, the spider's web of trenches leading to the walls and the damage inflicted on the defences were clearly visible. They could also watch, as the morning wore on, the Ottoman response to the unexpected presence of the relieving army. Prisoners taken by Ottoman patrols revealed that an army was assembling north of the Danube; and on 9 September Kara Mustafa learned that they had crossed the river and had camped on the plain before Tulln. The size of this army was rumoured to be huge, with most of the infidel world contributing to it.[16] A council of war had been summoned to the Grand Vizier's tent for the morning of 10 September. It was decided that the siege should continue but that the bulk of the cavalry still waiting idly in camp around the city should move to face the new challenge. Meanwhile, the Grand Vizier had summoned reserves from Hungary, both infantry and cavalry and fresh supplies, which arrived as the meeting was taking place.

The enemy was coming and the assault on the Kahlenberg outpost confirmed that this would be the line of attack: none of the Tartar scouts reported any movement to the south. Kara Mustafa rode out with his commanders and began a slow sweep across the whole front below the Dreimarkstein peak to the Danube, close to the Kahlenberg. To all of them it seemed most likely that the attack would centre on the area close to the Danube, where the road approached from the great abbey of Klosterneuburg, and then push down through the villages of Nussdorf, Heiligenstadt, Unterdöbling and Oberdöbling. The plan was simple and logical. Their main defensive position would be on the ridge above the village of Oberdöbling, with the ground above the villages of Weinhaus and Gersthof strengthened with field fortifications. An advance detachment of 5400 under an experienced commander, Kara Mehmed, pasha of Diyarbakir, moved quickly uphill and turned Nussdorf into a strongpoint. Further to the Ottoman left a smaller force covered the less likely line of approach from the heights below the Rosskopf peak. The front was so extended that Kara Mustafa could not defend in equal strength all along the line, and he relied on Tartars encamped on the far left of his positions to provide emergency cover.

Each of the strongpoints was equipped with artillery, some sixty cannon in all, stripped out of the batteries facing Vienna. Those in the city began to notice a lightening in the bombardment. Nowhere did the Turks attempt to construct any kind of defensive wall, even if made only from gabions and rough timber. Marsigli, watching the events take place, was mystified. He wrote admiringly of the way in which the Ottomans had managed their siege of the city, but wondered why with all those skills they made no attempt to provide protection for the infantry and cavalry as the relief army approached. A few *palanka* were quickly thrown together from materials to hand; at Nussdorf, entrenchments on the high ground between the villages, even an impromptu palisade of sharpened stakes, would have strengthened the Ottoman position immeasurably. Nonetheless, Kara Mustafa reinforced the cavalry holding the new positions by drawing off janissaries from the trenches before the city as well as the new arrivals from Hungary under the command of the eighty-year-old Ibrahim, pasha of Buda. The Grand Vizier, whose experience of war had been largely restricted to sieges, had little of the elderly pasha's military instincts, gained in a career spent fighting and raiding in the hilly country of the Hungarian borderlands. But Kara Mustafa regarded Ibrahim with deep mistrust, and, although he had placed him in command of this key flank, allowed him little discretion as to how he blocked the enemy advance.

In theory, the Ottoman defence was very sound: a succession of strongpoints, from the summit of the Nussberg hill below the heights of Kahlenberg, then the strongly defended village of Nussdorf on the reverse side of the slope. If the enemy took Nussdorf, the Danube lay ahead so the Christian army would have to veer to the right, and into the little gorge cut by the Schreiberbach. All this time it would be under fire from the occupied village to Heiligenstadt ahead, and beyond was the defended ridge above the two villages of Unterdöbling and Oberdöbling packed with cannon and musketeers, where the bulk of the Turks were marshalled. Before the ridge lay another stream, the

Erbsenbach, with steep sides and more than ten feet deep at some points. The Habsburg and German infantry would have to fight all the way down, over fields, vineyards and rough ground, over all the rivers and many streams flowing down the slope towards the Danube and across the line of advance. The steep slope of the land made it difficult for the relief army to manoeuvre to left or right, and at each point channelled it back on to the Ottoman defences. It was a sequence of fire zones constructed by nature and strengthened by man's malign artifice.

Away to the west there were fewer watercourses and more open ground, and there Kara Mustafa relied on his superiority in cavalry. Moreover, there was no sign of any activity in the hills to the west of the city. There was, indeed, nothing to see, for the Poles did not arrive on the crest, after a terrible struggle uphill, until after nightfall on 11 September. As Kara Mustafa watched the ant-like activity of the Christian army on the Kahlenberg, the emplacement of gun batteries and signs of movement, he was certain that this was where the attack would come, and rejoiced. He pushed more and more men into the positions facing the expected assault. He sent some of his personal forces to take up position above the village of Gersthof, on the steep bluff still known as the Türkenschanz (the Turk's Redoubt).

5.00 a.m.

Dawn on the Kahlenberg. Charles of Lorraine had been out in the early hours of Sunday 12 September, 'without eating and without sleeping', as the Emperor's closest confidant and the Chaplain to the Army Father Marco d'Aviano wrote to the Emperor Leopold.[17] The Ottoman advance guard commanded by Kara Mehmed had taken possession of Nussdorf, and the pasha had sent small groups of musketeers further up the hill during 11 September, in plain sight of those on the Kahlenberg. Lorraine told the gunners to target Nussdorf, but at about 5.00 a.m., the Turkish skirmishers who had crept very close in the night opened fire sporadically from behind a small rise of ground, and with more success from behind a sturdy fence further down the slope. The heavy Turkish muskets outranged the lighter Austrian weapons, and it was easier to shoot accurately uphill than down. Men began dropping, dead or wounded; the Habsburg troops hurriedly formed their two battalions into two lines, one behind the other, and began to advance down the hill towards their tormentors.

In the front rank they bore a huge white flag emblazoned with a scarlet cross, clearly visible in the bright dawn from the walls of Vienna, and most of them had taken communion very early in the day. This was the avenging army of Christ Crucified. They quickly overwhelmed the skirmishers and carried on moving slowly forward. Behind and away to their right, the contingents from the Empire saw what was happening but stood firm; then the Saxons closer to the Habsburg contingent formed up and began to descend the slope. In the space of an hour, the left flank of the relief army had begun to move down-hill. Far above them on the high point of the Kahlenberg, Lorraine was alarmed as he saw them move off: this was not his plan. He had to act decisively if he were to regain control of the action.

At 8.00 a.m. he ordered his dragoons and a final Saxon regiment to move quickly down to block any Turkish attack up from Nussdorf along the Danube side of the battle, with the hope of outflanking the Habsburg troops. Simultaneously he dispatched a series of gallopers with orders to slow the advance of the Habsburg infantry, also sending the last of his foot – the Bavarians and the remaining imperial contin-gents – to move down to support them. Eventually, at about 10.00 a.m., the advance paused on the lower slopes of the Nussberg hill, and began to take heavy enemy fire. The entire hillside was alive with men. The Ottoman Master of Ceremonies later wrote in his diary for the early morning of 12 September that a huge army of 'the *Giours*' (Christians) was advancing upon the Ottoman camp. 'It looked as if a flood of black pitch was pouring downhill, crushing and burning everything that opposed it.' Thus they attacked 'in the vain hope of encircling the fighters of Islam from both sides'.[18]

10.00 a.m.

It was 'a vain hope' because the impetuous advance followed the course that the Turkish commanders had anticipated. The Turks were outnumbered by the army moving steadily down the hill, but they had cannon and well-chosen positions. Still the battle did not go as the Ottomans anticipated. Soon the Saxons' light guns were pulled down the hillside by their gunners, and the army before Nussdorf soon had cannon positioned in support. After a hard fight and taking casualties, the Christian forces stormed the crown of the Nussberg, and directed their artillery fire down into the Ottoman-occupied village. The Ottomans, more used to facing Christians who broke and ran before them, were now confronted by men who fought like demons, constantly pushing forward, sometimes firing in unison, sometimes picking their individual targets. The Ottomans despised those who lacked the courage to fight like them, but these were soldiers who would close with them, driven it seemed by a divine anger, shouting and screaming the words of the day 'Jesus, Maria' against the Ottoman cries of 'Allah, Allah'.

Watching from a distance, and certain that this was the decisive moment, Kara Mustafa ordered his strategic reserve forward, and he himself moved with all his remaining bodyguard and household troops to the prepared positions on the Türkenschanz. There he set up the Standard of the Prophet in front of a scarlet tent as a rallying point. By 11.00 in the morning, five hours after the battle had began, Lorraine succeeded in keeping his various units in line and together, a near-impossible task with the rivers and streams running in deep crevasses, making it impossible to move forward with anything more than an appearance of synchronicity. Any mistake made, any gap that opened in the line, was immediately attacked by the Ottomans with speed and fierce élan. The Turks were now committed to the ferocious battle with the Habsburg and imperial forces on a line from Wahring village to a position close to the channel of the Danube that led down to Vienna. Kara Mustafa had literally turned his back to the inactive front close to his great tented enclosure, and in front of it the trenches attacking the city walls.

No general had given the order to start the battle, but it had begun nonetheless. If it was to be won, then all the commanders needed to keep control of the action on the ground. Once Lorraine had set the army in motion, he rode off at speed to meet the King of Poland. The Poles had arrived under cover of darkness, and had assembled in battle order covering the ground below the Dreimarkstein and the Rosskopf peaks. Both parts of the relief army were in position. They had, as far as was possible under the conditions, decided on a common plan, which reflected the reality on the ground. Sobieski would command the attack of the right wing, while Lorraine would push his men forward to a decisive encounter with the Grand Vizier, positioned around the standard of the Prophet. In contrast, Kara Mustafa had abandoned any attempt to coordinate his pashas in front of the Ottoman camp or the Tartars in their camp to the south-west. No field fortifications were created or any kind of defensive lines established. The great war camp was completely open to attack from the Wienerwald.

Before Noon

The Habsburg advance steadily converged on the newly fortified village of Nussdorf, while the Saxons pushed down the little Muckenthal valley towards the strongly defended village of Heiligenstadt. The Ottomans immediately counterattacked, with Kara Mustafa's household troops swelling their ranks, and there was savage hand-to-hand fighting all along the line, with the more numerous Ottoman cavalry pressing hard into any gap. Lorraine's cuirassiers and the Saxon cavalry under John George, the Elector of Saxony, held back behind the line of infantry, then surged forward to join the fight, striking the *sipahis* at a fast trot. Nussberg finally fell to the Christians after a house-to-house battle, but then the Saxons were driven back. They regrouped and charged down again to take the second Ottoman strongpoint. With both Nussdorf and Heiligenstadt securely in his hands, and the Turks concentrated in their redoubt above the two villages of upper and lower Döbling, Lorraine called a halt at some time after noon. The sun was blazing down, the men had had nothing to eat and little water since dawn, and an uneasy stillness descended on the battlefront. The battle cries of both sides had ceased; there was considerable movement atop the Ottoman strongpoint but no cannon fire. The relief army had taken all the villages – Neustift, Sievering, Grinzing and nearly down to the Türkenschanz, where the Grand Vizier had planted his flag. But the Ottoman defence line still blocked any closer advance on the city, which might fall at any moment.

As the two front lines grew silent, the Christian soldiers in Nussdorf and Heiligenstadt were watching movements on the hills above them to the south-west. A cloud of dust from horses' hooves appeared above the ridge: the movement of nearly twenty thousand cavalry was impossible to conceal. The Polish host was drawn up in three divisions: on the far right was Stanislaw Jablonowski, one of the most renowned soldiers in the Polish host. He had fought the Swedes, Cossacks, Russians, Turks and Tartars and his support had ensured Sobieski's election as King of Poland in 1674. Next came the king himself, with his troops grouped on the slopes of the Gränberg; to Sobieski's left, with his men lined up on the Rosskopf, Nicolas Hieronymus Sieniawski, who had fought at Sobieski's side in earlier wars. These were all men whom the king could trust. In front of the horse were lines of Polish infantry, stiffened by the German musketeers and pikemen sent by Lorraine. Beside them were the twenty-eight Polish cannon so laboriously dragged up the hill. Some were mounted at the foot of the Gränberg, to cover the advance of the army down the hill. Other field guns, on wheeled carriages, followed the horsemen down the hill, and were placed to give close supporting fire. They were charged with case shot, designed to obliterate any infantry or cavalry that came within range.

At about 1.00 p.m. King John III Sobieski led the army slowly downhill over the rough ground, to be followed by Jablonowski and Sieniawski with their columns, each taking a different route through the ravines and rough ground. Once Sobieski's men reached the Michaelerberg directly below them, at about 2.00 p.m., the Polish cavalry turned from a dust cloud into lines of armed men, visible to the Ottomans and the Habsburg and imperial forces alike. From afar it looked like a stately progress, but in reality the horses stumbled, a few broke their legs and the gun carriages often lost their wheels. The three columns moved slowly downhill, until the whole Polish army was lined up on flat and easy ground for cavalry.

2.00 p.m.

The king was prepared to take a day or even two to secure a solid position from which to launch his attack. Ottoman *sipahis* and some infantry made vain attempts to impede their advance, and eventually, by about 4.00 p.m., Sobieski and Sieniaowski's columns were drawn up in a long line stretching westwards from the village of Gersthof, past all the hills and foothills that led up to the Wienerwald.

The Grand Vizier on his velvet chair on the Türkenschanz now watched a possible disaster unfolding before him. He faced the classic military dilemma: a double assault, with his defences penetrated simultaneously from in front and behind. The huge Polish army could burst through behind him and cut him off both from Vienna and his line of retreat to Hungary. In front he faced an implacable enemy who had demolished every line of defence his commanders had erected. His whole plan was void. His instinct was correct – to attack and disrupt both enemies – but he was not competent to carry out the complex manoeuvres that it required. Nor was he at first aware that the third Polish column, led by Jablonowski, was still descending from the hills. His aim was to build a new front to the west of his current position but he needed time to put it in place. It was a last, vain hope.

However, at that point both Lorraine and Sobieski were faced with the same decision. Both had moved forward faster and farther than they had ever anticipated in the early morning. All their doubts and fears about the rugged terrain had proved unfounded. Now they had to decide whether they should go for the kill, to shatter the Turks in one final blow, or rest and deliver the final onslaught on the following day. Legends abound about the fateful decision. One has it that Lorraine assembled his weary officers and asked them which choice he should make. At first there was silence, and then an old Saxon general, von der Goltz, said that God was giving them this victory and they should fight on to accomplish what He had ordained for them. And, besides, he added, he was an old man and fancied a comfortable bed in Vienna that night. This was the kind of soldierly bravado that appealed to Lorraine, so, saying 'We march on', he ordered the battle to be continued.[19] On the other side of the battle line, quite independently, Sobieski had also decided that this was the moment to finish the enemy.

Mid-afternoon

Both Lorraine and Sobieski's decisions were characteristic. It was the middle of the afternoon, but if they could not finish off the Turks by the time night fell (and there was no moon to speak of) the enemy might slip away or regroup; worse still, the besiegers might take the city, from which they had no news, other than the earlier report that they were expecting the worst. The Grand Vizier's entire strategy had been based on capturing Vienna. If his troops still attacking the city succeeded in breaking through at this last moment, he might pull his army back, and, below the walls of his prize, fight out the denoue-ment before a city over which the crescent of Islam had at last been raised on the great tower of the *Steffl*. Prudence might dictate that the allies should wait, but the fear that a complete victory might be denied them weighed heavily. Just before 3.30 p.m., the Habsburg and Saxon assault started again all along the Ottoman defence line, which at first responded with great vigour. The Bavarian and imperial troops, mostly from Franconia, began to bombard the Türkenschanz. By 5.00 the Döbling villages had fallen and Lorraine ordered the victorious soldiers, who had slaughtered every Turk they found, to concentrate on the Türkenschanz from the northern side.

As they attacked more than a mile away, but in clear view, the Poles began to launch a series of cavalry charges on the heart of the vast Ottoman encampment. Here the defenders had massed their cannon and a large force of *sipahis*. The Polish tactic was to launch a trial charge, with a detachment of *husaria* and retainers (*choragiew*) to test the enemy's mettle and firepower. At about 4.00 p.m., the king ordered a charge by the *husaria* company, some 120 men, named after his infant son Alexander. They trotted off in the direction of the enemy, their black and gold pennant visible above the dust kicked up by the Ottoman gunfire and the horses' hooves. The charge itself was as Rakowski's *Reveille to worthy sons* had put it in 1670: 'Over the horse's head lower your lance; charge forward, stroking the flying beast beneath you with the spur, and aim at the enemy's navel.' The historian Vespasian Kochowski was present at the battle for Vienna, and published his *Commentary* on the great victory in 1684. He described how:

No sooner does the hussar lower his lance
Than a Turk is impaled upon its spike
Which not only disorders, but terrifies the foe
That blow that cannot be defended against or deflected . . .
Oft transfixing two persons at a time, others flee in eager haste from
    such a sight
Like flies in a frenzy.[20]

Just before impact on the solid mass of the Turks before them, each
man dropped his lance point, to make sure that it would bury itself
in the entrails or the chest of the front rank before them. As the
'forlorn hope' struck home, the sharp crack of the doomed horsemen's
lances splintering could be heard over the noise of battle. Very few
of the *husaria* rode out again. But the king deemed the trial a great
success and he prepared a full advance of all three columns into the
heart of the Ottoman camp.

By now, the Grand Vizier had already abandoned his position on
the Türkenschanz and ridden to his great tent in the main encampment, carrying the Standard of the Prophet with him. The Turks left
behind watched his departure, then abandoned their own positions
on the bluff and began to flee. Soon thousands of Turks were riding
or running back, not into the battle between the Poles and the
Ottomans for possession of the camp, but past the line of tents and
beyond the struggle, towards the high road into Hungary.

6.00 p.m.

The Poles prepared to launch their final attack just before 6.00 p.m.
King John Sobieski had at his disposal almost three thousand *husars*,
and probably double that number of other horsemen, some of their
riders in chain mail and others less heavily armoured. They were
grouped close together in solid squares, *husars* with their retinue and
supporters massed behind them. It is often said that this mass charge
had little effect, and was more a grand, valorous display than an effective tactic. But on 12 September 1683, the Poles did not face western
pikemen or well-disciplined musketeers. Before them was a huge mass
of Ottoman cavalry and some infantry, demoralised and with no space
left in which to manoeuvre. All this was apparent to the Grand Vizier
in his tented enclosure. He had seen and heard the first assault by the
Poles, and he watched as their squadrons in three great columns
stopped, and then moved laterally, slowly spreading across the flat
ground. They formed up into the traditional pattern of a Polish army
just before the charge. Every company was a compact block, every
husar in the front line a little more than a sword's length from his
neighbour, his lance held vertical. Behind them was the mass of his

retainers, their sabres drawn, or some preferring the long straight Polish *koncerz*, more lance than sword. On each side of the company ranks of musketeers flanked the horsemen. It was a terrifying sight for the Turks expecting their charge.

The Poles' power and weight were devastating against men in the open field – cavalry or infantry. They were much less effective against an enemy entrenched behind field fortifications, with cannon in support. The Turks' best hope was to tempt the Poles to attack a defended position. Anything would do: wagons yoked together, a line of spiked palisades with muskets and artillery behind. This was the tactic that had destroyed the Hungarian chivalry at the Battle of Mohács in 1526 – the chivalry of Hungary was shot to pieces by the janissaries and the Turkish guns, protected by sharpened stakes from Hungarian swords and lances. But in the heat of the day on 12 September ('for never was there a hotter day known than this') no preparations had been made. The camp before Vienna was full of beams, gabions, wooden stakes and the like; yet none were put to use. This oversight, indolence or mere carelessness, cost the Turks dearly. They faced the Polish host out in the open, lined up before their tents.

These Polish horsemen in their burnished steel breastplates moved more like well-drilled automata, terrifying in their appearance. They took up their positions on command, and halted; they moved forward and waited. On Sobieski's order, perhaps between 5000 and 9000 horsemen, with the *husaria* in front, made ready to charge the Turkish host. But about that moment, the final and most dramatic of Polish chivalry, contemporaries are silent as to the detail. Dalerac in his *Secret History* says: 'Everything happened as he supposed: the hussars of Prince Alexander fell upon the main body of the Grand Vizier, routed them, and in that instant, the whole army of the enemy retreated without making any resistance.'[22]. The mere threat of this vast mounted army seemed to break the spirit of the Ottomans before them. The mettle of the *husaria*, their forlorn hope of little more than a hundred men charging recklessly into the much larger body of Ottoman horse and janissaries, was a display of courage that immensely impressed the Turks; in the same way that Miklós Zrinyi's storming out of Szigetvár to his death in 1566 had become legendary among the sultan's trained regiments.

Thus, when Sobieski's cavalry army, stretching almost as far as the eye could see, and many times larger than the little detachment of hussars who had driven into the heart of the Ottoman host, began to stir and make ready to charge, the Turks believed the battle lost. They abandoned the camp, and fled. Some Ottomans blundered into the flank of Jablonowski's *husars*, and attacked them fiercely; but soon they broke off the engagement to resume their flight. 'The great victory, so complete and so happy cost but very few men . . . the second lines were no more than spectators, because the enemy fled before they were come up: so that none but only the dragoons, the infantry and the Husars, bore the fire and engaged the enemy.'[23]

As he heard the small group of *husars* charge home, Kara Mustafa left his tent to rejoin the fight, charging into the flank of Jablonowski's column. Most of his bodyguard was killed, and he had been told that if he were captured the sacred standard entrusted to him by the sultan would fall into infidel hands. He returned to his tent for the last time, wrapped the standard in its cover, took his private treasure chest and rode off with a few *sipahis* towards the safety of Hungary. His final official act was to order the troops besieging Vienna to leave their posts, destroying anything that might be useful to the enemy, and to slaughter all captives. All three orders were carried out as far as was possible in the final chaotic hour.

The Polish hussars, many abandoning their clumsy lances for their sabres hanging from their wrists, plunged forward as the enemy began to flee. Their discipline allowed them to wreak enormous havoc on a disorganised and dispirited enemy. They slashed at the backs of the retreating *sipahis*, sometimes having to fight hard against those Turks who turned and fought back with desperate zeal; but most of the Ottoman troops simply wanted to escape. The Poles harried them for a short distance, but, seeing that they were not going to return to the fight, let them continue and moved back to take control of the vast camp.

Thus, twelve hours after the battle had begun in confusion it ended in chaos, with complete victory for the relief army. Lorraine, now on the Türkenschanz, sent a messenger to the city with the news which was already obvious from the city walls: Vienna had been relieved. Starhemberg and all the dignitaries of the city plus a huge crowd of the citizens and refugees received him at the Scottish Gate. The first part of the army to enter the city was led by Ludwig Wilhelm, Margrave of Baden-Baden, and his dragoons, riding to 'the happy tune of kettle drums and trumpets'. Von der Goltz had to spend another night under canvas, the Poles and other parts of the relief army stayed awake in case the Turks returned – an old trick – but by 10.00 p.m. it was clear they had gone for good. Vienna and Christendom had been saved.

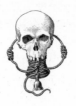

9

A Holy War?

When dawn broke on Monday 13 September 1683 the Turkish host had already vanished. A few unfortunate miners stumbling up from the underground workings before the walls, oblivious of time and the transformation of events, were taken prisoner and quickly slaughtered. The Ottomans had left behind a ghost city of tents, a vast camp that was pillaged and re-pillaged. Overnight the Polish cavalry had taken the first cut, and then in the morning the Habsburg and imperial forces took what was left as their share. The Viennese swarmed out from the foetid city and snatched what remained. A half-truth was that they found bags of small beans – coffee – that were used to establish the first of Vienna's coffee houses. Rumour had it that Georg Franz Kolschitzky, whose exploits carrying messages through the Turkish lines had made him a hero of the siege, knew what these nondescript goods were, and secured the right to establish the first coffee shop in the city. This was a fiction, put about by Kolschitzky, who wanted a new monopoly for his own coffee house. It now seems that an Armenian, Johannes Diodato, is a more likely candidate, but the men had something in common. Both spoke Ottoman Turkish, both moved freely and easily between the cultures of West and East.

The coffee house legend illustrates a facet of Vienna obscured in the exultation of triumph. The city, like almost any frontier town, had commercial connections across the notional border, usually carried out by intermediaries.[1] Many of those expelled from the city or killed at the beginning of the siege were 'Turks', outsiders from the lands east of Royal Hungary, but Christians or Jews and not Muslims. Vienna had been the bastion of the West against the Ottoman East for centuries, but it was also a point of contact with the East. Certainly a long history of fear and hostility dominated popular attitudes. The old tale of Ottoman captivity written by Johannes Schiltberger was one of the most successful medieval texts to be printed in German, and was still widely read in the seventeenth century.[2] Schiltberger told a graphic story of the crusade of Nicopolis, and the battle in which he had been captured. It was fought in September 1396 and afterwards the Ottoman sultan had watched as the defeated chivalry of Europe were decapitated one by one, in revenge for the Turks killed when the crusaders had taken Nicopolis. The story of Hans, lord of Greif, made him a hero for future generations.

I saw the lord Greif, who was a noble of [Bavaria], and four others, bound with the same cord. When he saw the great revenge that was taking place, he cried with a loud voice and consoled the horsemen and foot soldiers who were standing there to die. 'Stand firm,' he said. 'When our blood this day is spilt for the Christian faith, we by God's help shall become the children of heaven.' When he said this he knelt, and was beheaded together with his companions. Blood was spilled from morning until vespers, and when the [Turkish] king's counsellors saw that so much blood was spilled and that still it would not stop, they rose and fell upon their knees before the king, and entreated him for the sake of God that he would forget his rage, that he might not draw down upon himself the vengeance of God, as enough blood was already spilled. He consented, and ordered that they should stop.[3]

Nicopolis was not the humiliating last episode in the medieval crusades which had begun in 1099 with the capture of Jerusalem. It was the beginning of a new cycle of war, centred in Europe and the Mediterranean rather than the Holy Land, the first confrontation with a new enemy even more deadly than Christendom's earlier foes. The Kurdish Sultan Saladin had taken Jerusalem from the crusaders in 1186; a Mamluk slave from Egypt, Sultan Baybars, had driven the last of them from Palestine in 1268. But the Ottoman Sultan Bayezid had dealt an even more crushing blow, annihilating the new crusaders within sight of the Danube. The horror of Nicopolis was not forgotten.

Many of the old crusading narratives were printed and republished. Europe itself was now in the front line, and after the abortive siege of Vienna in 1529 the city became known as the 'Forward Bulwark' of the Christian world. The fear that one day this bulwark would fall, and Europe with it, became a serious if latent fear.

Now the feared Ottoman host had been trounced, and there was a widespread call for a renewed crusade that could conquer the lands lost to the Turks since 1453. At last a Reconquest seemed a real possibility. This hope was not just an outcome of the adventitious circumstances of 1683, but the fulfilment of a deep desire in the western Catholic world. For almost three centuries a succession of impassioned scholars had written and preached the message of holy war, usually, however, to deaf ears. Occasionally there were successes, as at Lepanto, but normally the rulers of Europe failed to combine in the great common goal. Crusading was a collective endeavour, and it depended upon the strong and active leadership of the papacy. Very few Popes considered it much more than a theoretical obligation, for they had more substantial fish to fry. But short-lived 'Holy Leagues' had been created under papal guidance. Not all were victorious: the league formed in 1538 was demolished by the decisive Ottoman naval victory over its ships off Preveza in north-west Greece. A second league created in 1570–71 was more successful, leading to an equally emphatic Christian victory at Lepanto. But these encounters had little effect in the long run, and no one attempted the far harder task of uniting Christendom for a land war against the Turks. In the seventeenth century the emergencies of 1664 and of 1683 revived the idea of a holy war on land. It was perhaps the last act of a temporarily united Christendom, for both Catholics and Protestants felt threatened and participated actively against the common enemy. It was papal money that provided the essential lubricant of these occasional alliances, and Pope Innocent XI was prepared to lavish huge amounts on the war to expel Islam from formerly Christian-ruled lands.[4]

The Emperor Leopold was sedulously devoted to the cult of his ancestors and in the days after this sudden triumph before Vienna he began to feel that destiny had settled upon his shoulders. He was being called to fulfil a God-given mission: to complete the recovery of Christian lands which his ancestors had begun a century before in Spain.[5] Leopold I was not an impulsive man, but on every side he heard the same seductive siren voices. He read voraciously and in his court library were books like the popular work of a Capuchin monk, Michel Febure, *L'état présent de la Turquie*, published in 1675. This was written in Italian, and translated into French, Spanish and German. Febure's line was that 'All empires fall into decadence and this is Turkey's moment'. In 1675 he followed with a second book, *Théâtre de la Turquie*, shamelessly dedicated to the French minister of war, Louvois, in the hope of his patronage and support. His equally impassioned contemporary Father Jean Coppin, born about 1615, served as a cavalry officer under Louis XIII and was then successively a traveller in Egypt and North Africa, soldier of fortune, and finally the French consul at Damietta from 1644. After he returned to France in 1647, he became a Catholic priest and an impassioned advocate of the idea of a holy war. None of the clergy, or Louvois, showed the remotest interest in his project.

Coppin retired to his parish at Le Puy and gave up hope of the great struggle. The victory at Vienna roused him to publish his old proposal, *Le Bouclier de l'Europe et la Guerre sainte . . .* (The Shield of Europe and the Holy War). It first appeared in his home town, and was picked up by an enterprising printer in Lyons and then republished in Paris in 1686. Copies spread rapidly across Europe.[6] As a former soldier, Coppin illustrated his book with sketches of the sort of military formations and tactics that could defeat the Turk, as well as a lengthy account of his travels and experiences in the eastern world forty years before.

His argument was simple: 'The Turk has in these last two years received very considerable losses, as never before since the establishment of their tyranny . . . the occasion for attacking this infidels people might never be more favourable.' Unquestionably, this was Pope Innocent XI's firm view, and he promised to finance the crusade on the same scale that he had supported the relief of Vienna. But regardless of the costs of a war of Reconquest, Leopold was faced with a pragmatic dilemma. He was the Emperor of the German Nation, and the Empire was faced with a real and deadly threat from the Most Christian King of France. France was intent on achieving a dramatic realignment of its border from the Channel to the Danube, encroaching both on the states and free cities of Germany, and on the rich Habsburg territories in the Low Countries. In terms of power and money, the Habsburg dynasty had more to lose by neglecting its western lands than it could possibly gain in the vast Hungarian void, which it had never previously occupied.

After the relief of Vienna, two options lay before the Emperor. One supposed that the Ottomans had suffered such losses before Vienna in 1683 that it might be another century and a half before they tried their luck again, if indeed, they ever advanced so far. The other offered a forward policy in the east, the 'God-given' option. This debate, between those who would later be called 'the Westerners', who favoured abandoning conquest in the east, and 'the Easterners', who wanted to advance into Hungary and beyond, was eventually decided by Leopold in favour of the eastern (God-given) strategy. There is little doubt that piety played a large part in his decision, but even stronger was his sense of his own heritage.

His ancestor the Emperor Charles V had confronted Islam in person with his campaign against Tunis, celebrated in a series of vast tapestries now in Vienna's Kunsthistorisches Museum. The Emperor Leopold was conscious of the Catholic kings' completion of the Reconquest in Spain, and now he was offered the chance to recover land from Islam on a vaster scale than had ever before been offered to his family. It was not wholly impossible that Constantinople itself might be recovered. The old universal Roman empire might be restored anew. While campaigning in the west might bring political gain, it did not offer the sublime benefits of honour and reputation that a victorious campaign in the east might deliver. The Emperor Leopold was an ardent true believer but he was not a fanatic, and although the call to a holy war held an emotional attraction, his ultimate decision would be political and pragmatic.

On the day after the victory at Vienna, King John Sobieski entered the city and mounted an impromptu procession, with the Grand Vizier's horse led behind him, and the Turkish *tuğ* and the Ottoman banners carried aloft as in a Roman triumph. As the cavalcade passed the main churches of the city, crowds roared their approbation and gratitude. Later in the day he wrote to his wife, 'Cry's and Acclamations reach the sky, of "Long live the King of Poland".'[7] At the dinner Starhemberg gave for the king later in the day, the all-pervasive stench of the rotting bodies in the streets overlaid the more subtle tastes of the food and wine, and the Polish party retired early to the Grand Vizier's tent outside the walls, where Sobieski wrote letters announcing the triumph to the other rulers of Europe, beginning each one with a phrase echoing Julius Caesar, 'We came, we saw', and ending piously 'God conquered'. He sent a large embroidered Ottoman banner which he believed was the flag of the Prophet Mohammad by the hands of his secretary to the Pope in Rome. Then, on the following morning, overpowered by the filth and flies in the Ottoman encampment, the Poles decamped to the outlying village of Schwechat.[8]

In the days after battle, sickness and epidemic disease began to spread through the victorious army. Even princes and generals were overcome by the effects of dysentery and by other myriad 'fluxes', and took to their beds. The Prince of Waldeck was struck down, 'indisposed' by a sudden gastric effusion, while waiting for an audience with the Emperor. Leopold arrived on the day following Sobieski's victory march after sailing down the Danube; met by Starhemberg, he had inspected the empty Ottoman camp and then the damage to the city. His palace was in ruins with almost every room devastated by Turkish gunfire, so that the imperial party was forced to bed down in the Stallburg, the grandiose imperial stable block behind the Hofburg. There the Emperor received his commanders and guests, held a banquet, and then rode out on the following morning, 15 September, to greet the Polish king at his new encampment. He was formal and unemotional towards Sobieski and his son, which some of the Poles read as a lack of gratitude and a snub for all their efforts. The king certainly believed it, as he angrily wrote to his wife that evening.[9]

In the intoxication of victory no one anticipated a war of conquest that would last for sixteen years, still less a succession of wars that would not be ended for more than a hundred years. In the heady days following the relief of Vienna there was little planning and no sober thinking about what a Reconquest might demand. The lure of a vast empire in the east first gripped the previously level-headed Lorraine, and then the King of Poland. Both had convinced themselves that after saving the capital, the Ottoman lands were there for the taking, Hungary certainly, perhaps the entire Balkans. On 17 September, chafing at the Emperor's reluctance to order an advance, the Poles broke camp and began to march east. Sobieski had a wild idea of heading straight for Buda, while Lorraine's contingents followed reluctantly in their wake. Around Vienna, the Bavarians and the German troops were still uncommitted, and some detachments, like the Saxons, were already heading home.

The first thought was hot pursuit, chasing the fleeing Ottoman army, only a few days away and in almost total chaos. This was also the easiest option, for nearly all the Christian troops were on the southern side of the Danube. But the most tempting targets were north of the river. Here were rich lands where the allied armies might find winter quarters while, on the southern side of the Danube, most villages had been stripped bare of any morsel of food, and most of the houses burned. North of the river were the Turkish fortresses like Nové Zámky, which still threatened the defensive line protecting Vienna. So Sobieski and Lorraine decided to move north. They halted opposite Bratislava, and impatiently waited for the engineers to assemble the bridge of boats that would allow them and their hussars, cuirassiers and dragoons to cross the Danube. But the pontoons and the skilled engineers were still far upriver at Tulln, exactly at the point where the advancing army had left them before the relief of Vienna. It took ten days for the little flotilla to sail down the river to Bratislava and two more days for the barges to be lashed together, and planked over to link the northern to the southern shore. On 27 September Lorraine's cavalry and the Polish horse clattered across into Upper Hungary, and, giving the marshy lands by the Danube a wide berth, trotted off north-eastwards.

At every stage in the Reconquest of Hungary during the seventeenth and eighteenth centuries, the narrative at some point returns to rivers and marshland. This image of a land dominated and divided by water first emerged in the ancient mythology of Hungary, as the first tribes had travelled from Scythia in the distant east to the Atilköz, the land of the great river.[10] They were led by Álmos, the Magyar Adam, who acquired his name because in a vision his mother had seen the Turul, a gigantic bird of prey, which 'descended from heaven on her and made her fertile. A great spring welled forth from her womb and began flowing westward. It grew and grew until it became a torrent which swept over the snow-covered mountains into the beautiful lowlands on the other side. There the waters stopped and from the water grew a wondrous tree with golden branches. She imagined famed kings were to be born from her descendants, who shall rule not here in their present lands but over that distant land in her dreams, surrounded with tall mountains.'[11]

The pen of Luigi Fernandino, Count Marsigli, transmuted this myth of Hungary's origins into science. In the autumn of 1683 he was, though, still a slave, being carried back with the retreating Ottomans, making notes on their hectic retreat.[12] But in later years Marsigli, whose life had been dominated, as soldier, engineer and scholar, with the idea of Hungary, presented the whole of this watery world in six vast volumes, from the fish that swam in its waters, to the birds that lived in the surrounding marshes, and the ancient peoples who had dwelt along its banks and tributaries.[13]

Hungary was different in almost every way from the lands to the west, and the war of conquest was similarly different from any campaign fought by a western army. The Austrians and the Poles might be used to skirmishing along their frontiers with the Ottoman lands, but neither had any real notion of what it would be like to fight in the vast Hungarian hinterland. On the northern side of the Danube, beyond the well-defended Habsburg fortress of Komárno, lay a no-man's land.[14] There was only one bridge across the Danube before the capital, Buda, built on the great bend of the Danube that turned the river's flow sharply southwards towards Belgrade. This bridge joined the well-garrisoned Ottoman *palanka* of Barkan on the northern bank and the ancient Hungarian city of Esztergom (Gran) on the southern side. Esztergom's citadel was built upon the massive rock above the walled town below: Ottomans and Habsburgs had struggled for posses-sion ever since the city was first conquered by Sultan Suleiman I in 1543, although it took him two years of bitter fighting to take the fortress. Once across the river, Buda was little more than thirty miles away, only a few days' easy march.[15] Sobieski and Lorraine were secretly preparing a lightning strike towards Buda, where they would take the Turks by surprise and deliver the heart of Hungary from the yoke of Islam. All that stood in their way was the onset of winter, but for once the weather was on their side.

The King of Poland set the pace, with Lorraine following behind. 'The King of Poland impatient of delay, contrary to expectation imme-diately mounted on horseback and sent to advise the Duke of Lorraine that he was marching towards [Barkan].'[16] Leaving his infantry to follow, Lorraine hurried with his cuirassiers and dragoons to catch up with the Poles. As Sobieski blundered forward, without sending scouts ahead, the Turks prepared an ambush. Their Tartars watched every move of the advancing Poles, counted their numbers and observed their ragged formation. The commander in Esztergom dispatched thousands of reinforcements sent from Buda across the Esztergom bridge. By the time the Poles neared the Barkan *palanka*, more than seven thousand Ottomans were concealed on the reverse side of the hillside. All that Sobieski saw were a few Turkish and Tartar horse in front of the wooden fortress and he ordered a full attack to over-whelm this thin line of defence.

As soon as the Polish hussars were committed irrevocably to the charge, led by the king himself, the Ottoman commander sprung his trap. It was a classic Turkish manoeuvre. Fast-moving *sipahis* swarmed on all sides, racing forward to cut off the Poles' retreat. Lorraine's liaison officer, riding with the king, saw the looming catastrophe and hurriedly sent a galloper back to the duke, telling him that the Poles were being overwhelmed, and more and more Ottomans were pouring into the attack. Lorraine immediately took his leading dragoons and cuirassiers forward through the scrubland at a fast trot, until he reached the edge of the plain before Barkan. He dismounted the dragoons and drew them up in formation like musketeers (*bataglia*), but protected by the cuirassier squadrons. As the Poles fled from the battlefield, with the bulky figure of Sobieski the target for every Turk, they passed through Lorraine's lines, and many of the Turks racing forward in pursuit were brought down by the dragoons' firepower.

At dusk the battered and bedraggled Ottoman *sipahis* withdrew below the walls of Barkan while Lorraine and Sobieski pulled back to wait for their infantry and field guns to arrive. After dark the Ottoman commander in Esztergom sent thousands more men across the narrow bridge to reinforce his troops on the northern bank. But as dawn came the Turks saw before them sixteen thousand Poles and imperial troops drawn up in battle formation: almost the whole army had arrived from the west. At about nine o'clock, Turks and Chris-tians began to move slowly forward towards each other, when the Ottoman cavalry made a sudden, mass assault on the Polish wing. In a moment, the whole body of the Ottomans began to converge on Sobieski's banners. As the Turks locked in hand-to-hand combat with the hussars and the Polish footmen behind, Lorraine charged at the head of his cuirassiers and dragoons, smashing into the *sipahis'* flank. In one instant the confident Ottoman horsemen were slaughtering the Poles; in the next they were being attacked on both sides, crushed by the heavier and larger western horse, and without any space to manoeuvre. Trapped, without the heavy armour of their adversaries, they managed finally to cut a passage back towards the fort. As they fled, smashing volleys of musket fire from the Habsburg infantry under Starhemberg's command broke up their ranks while Prince Ludwig Wilhelm of Baden was blooded for the first time in battle against the Turk. Soon to be nicknamed 'Türkenlouis', a scarlet poppy was later named after him, recalling the fountains of enemy blood he had spilt. It perhaps referred as well to the vast quantity of Ottoman booty (*Türkenbeute*) that he had carried back to decorate his great (unfinished) palace, Schloss Rastatt.[17] A kinsman of Eugene, he had the same spirit of daring and adaptability as his younger cousin and in a few minutes he turned the confident Ottoman assault into a rout, as they raced back to the *palanka*, then across the bridge to the fortress of Esztergom.

What happened in the two days of battle before Barken was to be repeated many times in the years that followed. The speed of an Ottoman attack was a constant terror for the westerners. In a few seconds the Turks and Tartars would appear as if from nowhere, slashing with their swords and cutting down men and horses alike. If the western line broke, either under pressure from the swarms of *sipahi* horsemen or crushed by the irresistible rush of the janissaries, ululating and bellowing their battle cries, then the Turks would gain the day. But if the solid western lines could hold, their discipline intact, if they could push forward field fortifications like the spiked *chevaux de frises*, and keep up a steady rate of fire, it would be the Turks who would break and flee from the field in chaos and panic. At Barkan, they fled back into the *palanka*, so many of them that they completely filled the small enclosure, leaving hundreds exposed outside, clamouring to enter. Ludwig Wilhelm of Baden brought up three cannon and also lined up his dragoons to fire at close range into the seething Ottoman mass. The wooden walls of the *palanka* caught fire, and 'the Slaughter that was there made by fire and sword was very cruel and bloody'.[18] Of the thousands who crowded into the small courtyard, only some seven or eight hundred survived, relatively safe in the fort, until they could surrender.

Worse still was the fate of those who tried to cross the Danube by the wooden bridge. When this broke apart under the weight of the men pressing to cross, thousands were thrown into the water. 'Some endeavoured to save themselves by swimming, others by their horses, hanging on their manes and tails, others on planks and boards of the broken bridge . . . the greatest part perished in the waters; as appeared by the bodies of men and horses, together with their garments, which covered the surface of the river.'[19] As he watched the Ottomans perish in the river, a driving compulsion gripped Charles of Lorraine. He would lead the army securely across the Danube, besiege and take the strategic city of Esztergom, and thus crown the year with a final triumph. The fortress had been fought over six times since the Ottoman conquest in 1543, with possession shifting back and forth between Turk and Habsburg. The Ottomans had held it securely for almost eighty years, and gradually obliterated the last vestiges of its Hungarian identity. If Lorraine could not take Buda, as he had hoped, Esztergom was a good alternative. The guns of its citadel controlled all traffic up and down the Danube, and, until it was taken, it would be impossible to ship the siege artillery necessary for taking Buda down the river.

The last of Lorraine's troops had finally caught up with the hard-riding cavalry, and the Bavarian infantry were rested and keen to engage the enemy. The Poles were not: morale was at a low ebb in the Polish camp after the initial humiliation at Barkan and beginning a long siege was not the way to restore it. The hussars and their retinues wanted revenge against the Ottoman cavalry, not frustrating inaction in the trenches before a well-defended city. King John Sobieski was reluctant to expose his men to what might be a long siege. There were insistent murmurings that he was seeking to drag them into a protracted war in Hungary, which seemed unnecessary, and even against Poland's interests. While Lorraine and his staff found a point downstream out of range of the Ottoman artillery where the river could be bridged, the Poles sulked in their tents. On 20 October the new bridge was completed, and the Habsburg and allied infantry began to file across, followed, one by one, by the siege guns. Within a day, in driving rain, they created batteries which could reach every part of the city; on the 24th, the rain slackened and the guns began to bombard the walled town and the citadel.[20] Before the assault began, the Grand Vizier had sent reinforcements and supplies to Esztergom, believing that the attackers would be destroyed by a long siege, the same fate he had suffered before Vienna. If that happened the defeat at Barkan could be justified to the sultan, and Kara Mustafa could then rout his enemies at court, while presenting a plausible strategy to redeem Ottoman losses in the following year.

Unfortunately for his plan, six days after the guns began to fire on Esztergom the Turkish garrison surrendered on exceptionally favourable terms.[21] The Grand Vizier had left Buda before the attack started, and arriving in Belgrade to find that the sultan had already returned to his palace at Edirne, he began to wreak vengeance on his enemies. But he could not prevent news of these fresh disasters reaching the ears of Mehmed IV on 14 December, and from that moment he was doomed. Esztergom, first captured by Suleiman I, then defended with great valour by its garrison in 1595, had fallen in less than a week. The sultan felt dishonoured, and traditionally those responsible for such a loss paid with their lives. Two senior court officials were sent north to Belgrade and on 25 December they came to the Grand Vizier at the time of the midday prayer. They showed him the warrant from the sultan demanding return of the Seal, the Holy Standard of the Prophet and the Key to the Kaaba in Mecca, emblems of his office. Then they told him that he was to suffer death.

Kara Mustafa met his death with stoic Ottoman calm, as befitted a Köprülü. First he removed his rich fur-trimmed robe, then his turban, and handed them to a servant. Next he asked that the carpet on which he had been kneeling be removed so that his body would fall to the earth, symbolising that he died as a warrior and so his entry into Paradise would be assured. Two executioners with the silken cord stepped forward and stood silently behind him. The Grand Vizier knelt again, this time in the dust of the floor, raising his long beard with his hands, so that his neck was exposed. Then, with practised ease, his executioners flipped the soft cord over his head and tightened it around his neck, pulling steadily with all their strength. He died quickly with barely a visible tremor, a corpse held up by the stranglers' noose. They lowered his body into the dirt, and one swiftly severed the head from the corpse, exactly in accordance with the sultan's orders. Then, between them, they stripped the skull of its skin and stuffed it with dry straw, making a grisly but recognisable trophy. The head and the trunk, wrapped together in a white grave cloth, were taken to a nearby mosque and buried just outside the enclosure. Mission accomplished, the little party, with the stuffed head wrapped in a silk cloth and placed in a saddlebag, set out for Edirne. So ended the long and controversial career of Kara Mustafa of Merzifon.[22]

10

Storming Buda

While Europeans regarded Sultan Mehmed IV with a mixture of disdain and distaste, Kara Mustafa was the Enemy Incarnate. The attack on Vienna was seen, with reason, as his personal malign intention, conceived from his deep hatred of the west in all its works. I have argued that there were good political motives for the Ottoman assault in 1683, and it failed largely because of the Grand Vizier's military ineptitude. He was experienced, but in the wrong kind of war. Kara Mustafa's failure, ignominious retreat and condign punishment were greeted with glee in Western Europe. There were images of the wounded vizier, hunched over a half-starved horse, in flight from Vienna. The popular French novelist Jean de Préchac found an international market with his life of the Grand Vizier; the frontispiece depicted his end, and, as his English translator observed, showed how the vizier, who had killed so many, 'was paid with his own coin'.[1] The lesson for English readers was very simple: 'English men cannot be very sensible of their happiness, when they see . . . the most tyrannical government of the Turkish Empire. They cannot, I say, but praise God . . . when they consider how unhappy is the condition of subjects that live under a monarch who makes the law the only rule of his government, in comparison to that of those that groan under the heavy yoke of a Prince who follows no other rule but his own will.' The rise and fall of Kara Mustafa became a moral fable, epitomising the inexorable decline of the Ottomans. Sir Paul Rycaut in his great history of the Turkish empire published in 1700 declared *ex cathedra*, with his unquestionable authority, that the defeat before Vienna was 'so fatal to them that they never recovered their courage and spirits again'.[2]

At this point fact and fiction became entirely and irretrievably intermingled. Rycaut was simply wrong: the Ottomans did recover their spirits. The allies were happy to believe otherwise, for they were organising the Reconquest of Hungary. The shock of success at Vienna, the hopeful wish-fulfilment typified by Rycaut, stimulated vast ambitions to throw Islam back into Asia. In France, the elderly Father Coppin, putting the finishing touches to his manuscript, observed, 'What I am seeking today will be incomparably more than a crusade.' He proposed a unified attack on the Ottomans, by sea in the Mediterranean and the Adriatic, by land in Hungary, with the Christian states acting together to destroy their hereditary enemy. For once this aspiration was being transformed into something like reality.

Early in February 1684 Sultan Mehmed IV at Edirne received an alarming report from Belgrade. The commander in Hungary had heard that the Christian states were joining together against the Turks, determined to win the 'Battle for Europe'. The Ottoman empire would be assailed on every side. In the spring the Russians would attack the Tartars in the Crimea, while the Poles would advance along the River Dniester and then push south into Ottoman-dominated Wallachia. Venice would attack Bosnia, seek to regain Crete and ravage the Aegean. All were engaged in this great encircling action: Sweden, France, Spain, England, the United Provinces of the Netherlands, Genoa and the Papacy.[3] Although this vast combined attack was exaggerated, in essence the threat was real. On 5 March 1684 the King of Poland, the Emperor Leopold and the Doge of Venice signed an agreement to wage war on the Ottomans and not to make peace unless all three parties agreed. Even after any future peace was signed, they were still to remain committed to a permanent mutual defensive alliance against any future Ottoman attack.

Behind the agreement stood Pope Innocent XI: all the Christian nations were invited to join in this assault on the common enemy. And not merely Christian nations. The Emperor Leopold even commissioned a Catholic archbishop, Sebastian Knab, already in Persia, to see if the Shah could be drawn into an alliance against the common

Turkish enemy. But the course of events was not as Rycaut described it. The Ottomans displayed an extraordinary resilience and fortitude which the west put down to their innate bellicosity; but what it revealed was their capacity to raise and support armies in the field year after year. The capital Istanbul might seethe with discontent, the court might be riven with faction, but the sultan's decree could still set the entire military and logistical system in motion once again.

Through the winter of 1683–4 the Habsburg administration worked feverishly to reassemble an army for the conquest of the east. It was much easier than the task which had confronted them a year before. This new war in the east would still be a war of Good against Evil, but it also promised booty and glory, if the perquisites of victory from the Ottoman camp at Vienna were any precedent.[4] There was intense competition for the supreme command, the office formerly occupied by King John Sobieski. The challengers included the young Elector Max Emmanuel of Bavaria, who demanded his own independent command; after his marriage in July 1685, he would be a member of Habsburg dynasty. But Charles of Lorraine was already part of the imperial circle, and insisted that he should be supreme commander, and, if not, he might take no further part in the campaign. A new and fresh contender was Ludwig Wilhelm, the ruling Margrave of Baden-Baden, who had the influential support of his uncle Hermann, Marquis of Baden, President of the Habsburg War Council.

Another powerful participant in the offensive would be the Calvinist ruler of Brandenburg, Friedrich Wilhelm. The Great Elector had been one of the more successful generals in the Thirty Years War, but in 1683 he had resisted all appeals to help the Emperor Leopold: now he volunteered his superbly trained troops for the new war. Too old to take command in person, he demanded a sweetener, in the form of Habsburg territory in Silesia, as recompense for his trouble. But it was April 1686 before the agreement could be signed and only then did eight thousand well-trained Prussian infantry and cavalry join the war in Hungary.

In the Habsburg court there was strong pressure, led by Lorraine and the Emperor's spiritual adviser, Marco d'Aviano, for immediate action: under pressure the Emperor gave the order to attack the weakened Ottoman army in 1684, before this lengthy process of assembling the allied army could be completed.[5] The troops gathered at the town

of Scalia on the River Waag (Váh) with about 43,000 men dedicated
to the conquest of Buda. On 20 May they began marching in separate columns along the northern bank of the Danube past Barkan and
along the southern bank heading for the hilltop Ottoman fortress of
Visegrád, which lay a few miles away at the narrowest part of the
sharp bend of the Danube. This was the last strongpoint on the
southern bank before Buda, some thirty miles away. On 15 June,
Lorraine emplaced his guns before Visegrád and began the bombardment. Two days later, with the garrison still resisting, he sent them
an ultimatum. If they opened the gates and yielded the citadel, they
would be set free. If they continued to resist, 'the whole garrison
should be impaled'.[6] On the following day, the 'garrison of Visegrad
marched away bag and baggage' and so avoided the awful and humiliating death that had been threatened. Now the path was completely
clear as far as Buda.

The allies' mood was confident because they had heard that 'the
garrison of Pest and Buda consisted of only 8000 men and that near
Buda there were only two or three thousand Tartars'. Count Florimond
von Mercy, a young Lorrainer, who had only entered Habsburg service
in 1682, led the scouts in the 1684 campaign. He brought direct
confirmation – the entire Turkish force in Hungary between the
Danube in the north and the Drava River in the south was no more
than 17,000 men and there was no sign of any more marching north.[7]
But as the army marched on towards Buda, Ottoman resistance
increased. As the infantry pressed forward, protected by cuirassiers
in their black helmets and armour, they were suddenly opposed by
a huge body of Turkish cavalry in the traditional crescent-moon
formation. General Halliweil, leading the cavalry squadrons, was
nearly overwhelmed, and, as they retreated, he fell from his horse,
pierced by 'a dart in the breast and an arrow in the face'.[8] More
heavy cavalry galloped into the mêlée to support the hard-pressed
cuirassiers, and drove off the *sipahis*, who retired carrying Austrian
prisoners away with them.

The idea that the Turks had no will or capacity to resist quickly
vanished as more of these swift and unexpected attacks dogged the
advance through hilly country. When they came upon the Ottoman
field army at Weizen [Vác], close to Pest, it was more than 18,000
strong, with cannon and infantry. The Ottomans immediately attacked,

and 'fell upon our left wing with very great noise and fury'. Each time they were beaten back but charged again and again. Only when the allies' field artillery was brought forward and fired repeated salvos into the mass of Turkish troops were they driven off. More than a thousand Turks, men and officers, were killed and about the same number taken prisoner. The body of one pasha attracted much attention 'because of his prodigious corpulence'; many wondered how he could ride a horse at all, let alone into battle.[9]

This would not be a straightforward campaign. Much of the cavalry's time was spent in searching for fodder for the horses, as the Habsburg supply system was less effective than the Ottoman. Moreover, Tartars could live simply off the country and could survive on whatever was available. These foraging parties were easy prey for Turkish raiders. In each encounter, once they could bring their firepower and superior discipline into play, the allies would drive their enemy from the field, but there could never be any sense of security. The Tartars and *sipahis* would be back the following day or even the same evening, hacking at the fringes of the advancing army. The Turkish infantry could also move at great speed and the contemporary accounts tell time and again of detachments caught unawares, cut down by a mass of Turks, who quickly retreated ('fled the field') when reinforcements came up. 'The Turks having rallied, were immediately at their heels, and putting themselves into some order, fell barbarously on our right wing.'[10]

In the summer of 1684 Lorraine took a very sanguine view of his chances of taking Buda. He was still waiting for the arrival of the Bavarians who would greatly strengthen his infantry and artillery, but even without them he decided to begin the siege. He now had an open supply line along the Danube to Vienna and his engineers quickly reinstated the floating bridges across the Danube between Pest and Buda, which the retreating Ottomans had tried to destroy. Most important of all, he had the entire summer to complete the siege and still be back in winter quarters before the weather broke. On 14 June the army crossed the newly restored pontoon bridges and finally gathered before Buda. The broad river divided the walled town of Pest, on the northern bank of the Danube, from the separate fortress city of Buda.

The two settlements could not have been more different. While

Pest was low-lying, on the river bank and surrounded by a medieval stone wall, the castle of Buda dominated all the land below. It was built on steeply rising rocky ground and ringed by hills. The huge fortified palace occupied the high plateau above the Danube, separated by near-vertical escarpments from the land below, heavily defended by entrenchments, concentric walls (*zwingers*) and redoubts. It was shaped rather like a club or cudgel, with the narrow handle at the southern end, closest to the river. But Buda was not impregnable, for Suleiman I had occupied it briefly in 1526, and taken its moveable treasures.[11] It was occupied permanently in 1541 when, as Budin, it became the capital of Ottoman Hungary. In 1603 the Habsburgs had briefly put it under siege but failed to capture the fortress on the plateau.

Among Lorraine's commanders was Rüdiger von Starhemberg, who had defended Vienna against the Grand Vizier the previous summer. He ensured that none of the mistakes the Turks had made in 1683 were repeated at the Habsburgs' siege of Buda in 1684. Batteries were set up to bombard the city from every side, while mines and saps were prepared against different faces of the city. But Buda was quite unlike Vienna. it was more like a mountain fastness. The Ottomans allowed the royal palace of the Hungarian kings to fall into ruin, but had spent extensively on its defences, and on factories to produce gunpowder, cannonballs and artillery. In 1684 there were 684 metric tons of powder stored within its walls.[12] Moreover, it had defence in depth, unlike Vienna, and, as the siege progressed, the garrison were able to build strong new defences inside the lines of the older fortifications. But the greatest problem facing the Habsburgs and their allies was the strength and mettle of the garrison. At Vienna, the garrison was one-fifth (at best) of the attacking force. At Buda, it was almost half the size of the besieging force, and the allied army had always to fear the strong Ottoman field army, which could attack them at any moment. The war of conquest had been based on a fundamental miscalculation: the Turks had not fled from Hungary, nor had they lost their courage and confidence.

The expression *éminence grise* was first coined to reflect the power of a grey-robed Capuchin confessor over Cardinal Richelieu of France early in the seventeenth century. But the grey-robed Father Marco d'Aviano was an even more powerful influence over the throne of the

Emperor Leopold. D'Aviano had devoted much of his life to confront-
ing the Turk. At the age of sixteen, he had attempted (and failed) to
take ship to Crete, intending to seek martyrdom at the hands of the
Turks besieging the fortress of Candia. Frustrated in his individual
crusade, he joined the Capuchin order and over the decades became
renowned for his preaching and sanctity. In 1680 he became the spiritual
adviser to the Emperor, who, until d'Aviano's death in 1699, consulted
him about the many problems, political as well as spiritual, which
confronted him. He became Leopold's most trusted adviser, and often
his eyes and ears. The grey robe and tonsured head of Father d'Aviano
was very visible in the lines and trenches before Buda. He was
fearless, exposing himself constantly to enemy fire; his invulnera-
bility and sangfroid made him a legend among the soldiers. Now
he wrote to Leopold from the camp that a great blow could be
struck against the Turks at Buda, 'throwing them into the greatest
consternation'.[13]

He knew something about war, as he was present at the battle to
relieve Vienna in 1683; later he would be with the army through the
first years of the Reconquest of Hungary. Even on his deathbed, he
was still telling Leopold how he could continue the holy war to a satis-
factory conclusion. The letters they exchanged give perhaps the
sharpest insight into the Emperor's complex and convoluted thinking.
It was to Marco d'Aviano that he had unburdened his feelings of unease
at leaving Vienna to its fate in July 1683.[14] It was d'Aviano who wrote
to the Emperor in triumph about the ending of the siege of Vienna,
and who would give him the news of victory in Hungary in 1686, on
an ill-written and barely legible scrap of paper: 'Glory be to God and
to Maria. Buda is taken by storm . . . a true miracle from God.'[15]

But, despite d'Aviano's perennial optimism, there was to be no
miracle in the long summer and autumn of 1684. Below the towering
citadel of Buda was the lower town and, despite constant bombardment, mining and frontal assaults, Lorraine's forces never gained a
completely secure hold on this, their first objective. Soon most of the
buildings were in ruins, burned-out shells, an impossible area to defend.
By night it was a no-man's-land, with parties from the citadel infil-
trating and sometimes taking over the westerners' trenches. There
were steady losses, and the roll-call of officers, even colonels and
generals, killed or wounded rose by the week. But yard by yard the

siege did make progress, and gradually some sections of the citadel's outer defences were battered into ruin. The reports from the field to Vienna retained an air of optimism, but they could not attempt to conceal the lack of real progress.

Lorraine was a bold and fearless commander, but he had little notion or experience of how to organise the supply of food and ammunition for a prolonged siege. The most pressing problem was to keep the cavalry regiments active and their horses well fed, because roaming in the land to the west and south of the city was the Ottoman field army. This meant that daily patrols had to be sent out to find if an attack threatened, and, when it did, the cuirassiers and dragoons had to be fit and ready for battle. The supply chain back up the Danube to Vienna had a string of barges shuttling up and down the river, sometimes protected by galleys, and carrying (mostly) powder and shot. But there was simply not enough river transport to keep the army properly supplied. Near the roads to the west, north and south of the city, there were Ottoman strongholds, from which Tartar and *sipahi* raiders roamed to attack any supply caravan coming east, and only those that were well protected by soldiers had any real hope of a secure passage.

As the siege advanced, the essential difference between Ottoman and western sapping skills became clear. On Wednesday 9 August, the besiegers exploded a mine beside a small tower, but, as the diary says, 'it returned upon us, though without much hurt; which the Turks perceiving, sallied out in great numbers and horrible noise through a breach in the old wall. There was now on both sides great confusion shown, firing both great and small shot [musket fire] and Granadoes, but the enemy was at last forced to retreat with a considerable loss.' Putting the best gloss possible on this event, the diarist concluded, 'The Mine though ill-placed had nevertheless made holes convenient enough to lodge in, which we were resolved to defend.' By the end of the day, no progress had been made, and on the Thursday and Friday the troops rested. On Saturday, the council of war decided to launch a frontal attack on the weakened but not broken section of the tower. 'It was concluded to attack the breaches. Our infantry fired bravely, but the enemy coming in great numbers opposed us, throwing stones, hand-Granadoes, and bombs down from the tower with great fury upon us; so that our men, after above two hours resolute fight, were forced to retire.'

On the same day, in an adjacent section of the perimeter, another mine exploded under the defences 'at a corner of the town, upon the springing of which a general assault was to be given; but it having no effect otherwise than throwing up a small part of the wall, it flew back on us. This unhappy accident hindered the prosecution of our designs at that time. It is generally agreed that some of our Deserters had given the enemy notice of our intentions, though but yesterday we hanged a horseman for endeavouring to leave us.'[16]

Here, for the first time, after a month of daily attacks, there is mention of deserters and of two successive futile assaults. The Ottomans were actually strengthening their defences under fire, building redoubts and new earthworks behind the old fortified lines of the upper town. After more than six weeks of encirclement and bombardment, the allied army had made virtually no impression on the Ottoman defence. In the diary, the catalogue of misfortune continued. On 17 August, the Turks launched a surprise attack on the siege line, and then at night exploded two mines with devastating effect. We do not have Rüdiger von Starhemberg's thoughts as he watched the lack of progress in the Siege of Buda, but he must have remembered the ineffective Habsburg mines and the relentless and well-placed Ottoman saps destroying the defences of Vienna the year before. Perhaps he also recalled the effect of the Turks' tireless energy upon his men.

On 9 September the Bavarians finally arrived in full force and morale rose. But within a few minutes of the Elector Max Emmanuel coming into the lines there was a horrific incident that showed the dangers of the siege to officers and common soldiers alike. He had just dismounted from his horse and moved aside to greet some of his fellow commanders. His groom was holding the horse by its reins, when an Ottoman cannon shot blasted the back legs off the animal, splattering blood, bone and guts over the nearby tent of Ludwig Wilhelm of Baden and the Duke of Salms.[17] This was very different from Max Emmanuel's experience in the heroic victory before Vienna. He celebrated the anniversary by ordering his fresh and eager troops to make a major assault. It failed. But on the following day he sent a Turkish-speaking corporal up the hill under a flag of truce, with a Turk captured in an earlier encounter as a token of his good intentions. The corporal carried 'a summons in Turkish and Latin, in his

Imperial Majesty's name. He was brought before the Pasha of Buda, who listened silently to the reading of the summons to surrender, and then told the corporal that he had no reason to surrender the town, that he had plentiful supplies of food, shot and powder, that he had no need of the captive Turk, and gave the corporal fifteen ducats for his trouble in climbing the hill.'[18]

That same night a scout brought news into the camp that a fresh army of Turks had crossed the bridge at Osijek on the River Drava and was marching north, and might arrive in a few days. The night was filled with feverish preparations to meet this new threat, although a further report reduced the force from 40,000 to 15,000. The Bavarians continued to batter furiously at Buda's defences while, in the imperial trenches, 'there was little action'. But as September advanced the weather broke and incessant rain filled the trenches around the city. The infamous 'morbus hungaricus', a deadly fever common in all the marshy and low-lying ground, began to spread and incapacitated large numbers of men, with hundreds dying each day. Even the Bavarians lost their martial zeal, and the war diary increasingly noted 'Saturday 7 October: nothing happened worthy of remark', or the laconic 'Wednesday the 11th: nothing happened'. By Friday 20 October, the diarist could only report 'nothing happened', until a few days later he wrote, 'an Ague [vomiting sickness] seized me' but he recorded the gist of what happened for the rest of October. 'The Turks showed themselves daily before the camp in small parties and also made diverse sallies, in one of which they took from us an Imperial mine at the entrance into the town but otherwise they did no great harm.'[19]

Plainly, this was a disaster in the making, and it is unclear how much news of it had reached Vienna. Thousands of men were dead or dying from sickness.[20] Half the army that had set out in June 1684 was either dead, wounded or incapacitated by disease, and the city was no nearer capture than it had been in the early summer. Although the allied forces had defeated the Ottoman field army whenever they had met in battle, the numbers were changing to Lorraine's disadvantage. If morale continued to decline and the daily losses from sickness continued, there was always the danger that the allies could be trapped by worsening weather in their siege lines through the winter, between the Turkish field army and the defenders of the upper town of Buda. Then there might be a catastrophe on the scale of the Ottoman flight from Vienna the year before, or else the allies would simply starve.

In the end the matter was taken out of Lorraine's hands. He wanted to continue the siege, stubbornly resisting the reality of his situation. But early in November the chief of the Habsburg War Council (Hofkriegsrat), Hermann of Baden, arrived in the camp ostensibly to take up Starhemberg's command (the saviour of Vienna was in poor health). In fact, Hermann had been sent by the Emperor to see the true state of affairs for himself. A series of acrimonious councils of war followed until Hermann concluded the discussions with the blunt determination that the army must withdraw.[21] The siege works were demolished and the artillery pulled back to the northern bank of the Danube. A fleet of ships loaded the guns and sailed upriver on 29 November, and on 30 November the whole army began the march westward towards Esztergom. The Ottomans harassed their withdrawal in a half-hearted fashion.

It is not known who had alerted the Emperor or the War Council, but the prime candidates must be Ludwig Wilhelm of Baden or Maximilian Emmanuel, who had no reason to protect their rival, Lorraine. But it is possible that the most potent voice was that of Marco d'Aviano. There is no letter or other document, except a very long report he sent to the Emperor on 24 November outlining in detail (much of it showing considerable military expertise) how the next campaign should be carried through. The failures of 1684 could be put down to arrogance and complacency. Many remembered the popular engraving of Kara Mustafa fleeing from Vienna, and the easy capture of Esztergom and the rout at Barkan confirmed the feeling that the Ottomans were finished as a military power. The failed siege of Buda had taught them otherwise. Even the setpiece battles around the city, always ending in the allied army driving off the Turks with heavy losses, were desperately hard-fought. Lorraine, fortified by d'Aviano's ardent zeal, wanted complete victory in the holy war. But by pushing on to Buda, he had left powerful and unconquered strongholds like Nové Zámky north of the Danube and there was a string of well-defended Ottoman cities south of the river. As the weakened army moved slowly westwards, it was self-evident that everything would need to change before they attacked Buda again.

The soldiers were left in winter quarters north of the Danube and the commanders returned to Vienna. There was a series of private and official meetings before and after Christmas. Some commanders wanted to return to attack Buda before the damage done to the defences could be repaired. Others believed that the attack had been hurried and ill prepared, without enough men to make success certain. There were pragmatic voices that suggested it would be better to regain the initiative by taking some smaller Turkish fortresses, by siege or by storm, and then there was also the question of the rebels in Transylvania who were still a serious potential threat. This latter fear was not fanciful. Twenty years later, in 1704, it would not be an Ottoman army that menaced Vienna but the *kuruc* raiders of Prince Francis II Rákóczi of Transylvania. Those attacks and the constant public fear that the Ottomans might return prompted Prince Eugene, then head of the Habsburg War Council, to order construction (at vast cost) of a twelve-foot-high outer fortification – the Linienwall – designed by the court mathematician Johann Jakob Marinoni.

Made of stone, earth and wooden palisades, and built with the experience of 1683 in mind, it ran in a huge sweep protecting both city and suburbs. This continuing fear of a menace from the east did not end with the victory in 1683. As the Habsburg government planned how to reconquer Hungary, it was rebuilding and restoring the city's old fortifications damaged in 1683 as fast as possible, realigning and strengthening the bastions, learning the lessons of the siege. By 1710 Vienna was better fortified against any new Turkish assault than ever before. Nor was this simply a matter, common to most armies, of preparing to win the war they had just fought. The public mood remained jittery and fearful, overlaid with a consistent official propa-ganda of triumph. This froth of persistent governmental optimism masked a popular feeling of fear and doubt beneath the surface. These popular fears had to be assuaged, and the Habsburgs' salient role in the holy war against the Turk sustained. So the conquest of the east became not a matter of strategic choice but a necessity.

The new strategy created in the winter of 1684–5 would extend across two campaigning seasons. A realistic understanding of the diffi-culty in overcoming the Ottomans had replaced the reckless over-confidence of 1684. The scale of forces needed to take Buda could not be assembled before 1686, especially since the negotiations necessary to cajole a number of the key German states into sending troops seemed interminable. The strategy finally agreed for 1685 was much more prudent than the overconfident surge of the previous year.[22] The army would gather near Barkan and systematically clear the northern bank of the Danube of the Ottoman-garrisoned fortresses that breached the line of protection for Vienna. Then, once there was no chance of a surprise attack westward into Austria, the full force of the allies could gather before Buda in 1686. After the loss of Barkan at the end of 1683 the Ottomans still held three major strongholds north of the Danube. The most menacing was Nové Zámky sitting in a bend of the Nitra River, north of the Habsburg citadel of Komárno on the Danube. Farther east were castles of the Novohrád region and the most easterly of all, the fortress of Eger.[23]

Charles of Lorraine arrived at Nové Zámky with the army on 13 June 1685, where a limited siege was already under way.[24] This fortress was built by the Habsburgs in 1571, to the best Western European standards, to be the strongest forward defence for Vienna. It resisted numerous Ottoman attacks, but surrendered in 1663 after a bitter and sustained siege.[25] The Ottoman capture of Nové Zámky had been widely reported throughout northern Europe, as a warning sign that Turkish power was rising again.[26] The recapture of this fortress would be a signal of renewed Habsburg power, revenging a signal defeat still in living memory. The Ottomans took exactly the same view: the commander in Hungary was ordered by the sultan to hold the fortress to the last man. It was rare in sieges that they would be fought out to the last extremity, with the killing of the entire garrison. In the siege of 1663 after a most stubborn defence, with cruelties on both sides, the Habsburg garrison eventually asked for terms of surrender. 'They sent to the Grand Vizier, demanding honourable conditions.' He answered that 'they should set down their own terms, leaving only the great guns in the fort'.[27] In 1684, the Duke of Lorraine had allowed terms just as generous to the Ottoman garrison of Esztergom, allowing them to sail down the Danube to Buda.

The siege and capture of Nové Zámky marked a sudden hardening of attitudes. Not all wars between Christian and Muslim were necessarily battles to the death. The holy war on the borders of Christendom had often been gentler than the wars of Sunni Muslim against Shia Muslim or Catholic Christian against Protestant Christian; but no more.[28] The besiegers became enraged by the atrocities they witnessed.

On 16 July they watched as a Christian slave 'with chains on his legs' stumbled out of the Ottoman lines which were being battered by the allied artillery. 'But three Turks pursued him and cut off his head in full view of the besiegers' trenches.' Yet, the account suggests, God's vengeance fell speedily upon his murderers: before they could return to their lines, 'two of them were killed by the shot of the Imperials'. On the following day, the Turks impaled the severed heads of three or four hundred Christians on the sharpened points of the wooden palisade. These were all gestures of bravado: in 1683 the defenders of Vienna had flayed Turkish prisoners and hung their bloody skins over the city wall. Symbolic savagery signalled that the battle would be fought to the very end. On 22 July Christian slaves were brought out in chains to repair the bastions damaged by the imperial artillery, and the Duke of Lorraine wrote 'a letter to the Pasha, letting him understand that if he misused those slaves, he would not give any quarter to the garrison if the place were taken: to which no answer was received'.[29] On 30 July, a large part of the besieging force broke camp and moved south to meet a threat by the Ottoman field army near Esztergom. The garrison of Nové Zámky, thinking they were abandoning the siege, demanded unrealistic terms for yielding the city and fortress. Lorraine spurned the offer: he would take the city by storm and there would be no quarter.

Before daybreak on 19 August, reinforced by two thousand Hungarians recruited by Count Esterhazy, the allied army surged over the ruined bastions into the city. There was little resistance and soon white flags were flying from houses and from the undamaged fortifications. But the call for mercy was refused, and as the contemporary account puts it, 'the Turks endeavoured to save themselves within their houses, but all that were met in the first heat were put to the sword'. All, in this context, would have meant old and young alike, women as well as men. One group attempted to defend a bastion, and, as the allies closed on them, they threw themselves into the water below, 'where they were either drowned or put to the sword'. The laconic conclusion: 'Neuhäusel recovered, which cost the Turks so dear in taking.'[30]

Meanwhile, the cavalry led by Lorraine had smashed the Ottoman field army under the walls of Esztergom, while to the north of the Danube, Ottoman garrisons learning of Nové Zámky's grim fate simply

THE SIEGE OF VIENNA: A BIRD'S EYE VIEW

11. Daniel Suttinger, a well-known military engineer, was in Vienna throughout the siege.
His plan of the Ottoman attack, based on his own observations, was remarkably accurate and
published throughout Europe.

IMAGING THE SIEGE OF VIENNA, 1683

Romeyn de Hooghe (1645–1708), a celebrated Dutch artist, prepared a series of eleven engravings of the siege of Vienna, from drawings made by Jacob Peeters.

The engravings were published within a month of the siege: more imaginative than documentary they nonetheless became the defining image of Vienna in 1683.

12. Conquering Tabor Island on the outskirts of Leopoldstadt.

13. The Turkish trenches

14. The submission of the Hungarians.

15. Entry of Emperor Leopold into the abandoned tent of the Grand Vizier.

STORMING BUDA

16. Bertalan Székely (1835–1910) labored for more than ten years working on his vast panorama of the storming of Buda in 1686. The heroic Pasha of Buda lies dead as the triumphant Charles of Lorraine and his officers ride slowly past their fallen adversary. Two hundred years after the event Székely makes Charles of Lorraine and Ali Pasha both paladins, but even in 1686 the Christian and the Muslim were celebrated as men of honour.

Wer suecht / der findt.

Deß Türckischen Groß-Vizirs Cara Mustapha Bassa Zuruck-Marsch / von Wienn nacher Constantinopel.

CHI CERCA ACCATTA

Mustafa Carra Gran Vizir, che ritorna dall'assedio di Vienna a Constantinopoli.

Nÿmort f.   Lerch exc.

A. Groß-Vizir.

ACh weh mir armen Tropff! jetzt muß ich billich klagen!
Mir lage stäts im Kopff / die Christenheit zu plagen /
Ich bildete mir ein / Wienn hätte ich gewiß /
Ey ja wol hintersich / es wurd ein anders G'biß
Davor mir eingelegt / es ist nit außzusprechen /
Wie ich hab eingebüst / das Hertz möcht mir zerbrechen:
Ich andern Grueben grueb / und fiele selbst hinein /
Das Land ich zwar verderbt / und gienge blind darein /
Kunnt meinen Fall nicht sehn / es blieb nicht ungerochen /
Der tapffre Stahrenberg / hat mir den Stahren gstochen /
Nun hab ichs übersehn / daß Machomet erbarm!
Die Christliche Armee die machte mir erst warm /
Daß ich alls ließ im Stich / ich brachte kaum zu decken /
Den Kotzen noch darvon / ach weh mir Alten Gecken /
Wienn lachet mein auß / welchs ich vor mein geschätzt /
Daß es so tapffer mich hat auff den Esel gesetzt.

B. Deß Vizirs Weib / sambt ihren Freunden und Kindern.

Ach was bedeutet diß / was nuest ich da ansehen /
Ist diß mein lieber Mann / wie muß ihm seyn geschehen ?
Wo ist die Beuth von Wienn? So er uns mitgebracht /
Ey schöner Groß-Vizir / wo bleibt die grosse Pracht?
Den du vorhin geführt / wo seynd die schönen Kleyder ?
Wo ist dein stoltzes Roß? ach ach ich sihe leyder /
Den dürren Esel nur / und förcht bey dieser Sach /
Daß endtlich mich der Strick / noch gar zur Wittib mach:

Ich mueß vor Hertzen-Leyd / mir alle Haar außrauffen /
Ihr Freund und Kinder secht mit Jammer an! den Hauffen /
Den er mit sich geführt / wie seynd sie zugericht /
Dieser ist Krumb und Lahmb / und jener nichts mehr sicht /
Ist diß die Tapfferkeit / der starcken Muselmannen /
Daß sie lauffen darvon / verlassen Stuck und Fahnen /
Gezelt und Proviant: ich kan nicht reden mehr /
Vor lauter Schaam und Spott / es jammert mich zu sehr.

C. Die gesambte Rott der Türckischen Soldaten.

Ey daß der Teuffel hätt / wie seynd wir doch betrogen /
Wie hat der alte Schelm uns dißmahl vorgelogen;
Es hiesse täglich nur / frischauff ihr Janitscharn /
Wienn ist uns schon gewiß / aber es fehlt dem Narrn:
Wir hofften reiche Beuth / dafür wir Stösse kriegen /
Die Köpffe / Füß und Händ vor Wienn wir liessen ligen /
Die Helfft kombt kaum zuruck / wir seynd gantz ruinirt /
Der Teuffel hole den / der uns so angeführt.

D. Mufti.

Das hab ich vorgesagt / es werde so ergehen /
Wie ich mir bildet ein / so ist es auch geschehen /
Ich rathet treulich dir / laß doch die Wienn-Statt seyn /
Weil du dann nicht gefolgt / so bleibt die Schand auch dein.
Nimb nur damit verlieb / dem Sultan fall zu Füssen /
Damit dein alter Halß / nicht mög' am Strange büssen /
Diß wär der rechte Lohn / auff solche tapffre That /
Dieweil du nicht gefolgt / dem treugemeinten Rath.

OTTOMAN DISASTER

17. The flight of Kara Mustafa from the defeat at Vienna in 1683 and his later strangulation were gleefully portrayed by western engravers. This widely-circulated broadsheet appeared shortly after the relief of the city in September 1683.

abandoned their posts. Far to the south, General Leslie stormed the bridgehead at Osijek, while in the hills in Transylvania, General Schultz and General Caprara ravaged the land and disposed of the threat from the Turks' ineffectual Christian allies, led by the unfortunate Count Thököly, who had to watch his own independent future and that of Transylvania vanish.[31] The Ottomans were pressed on every side, with the Venetians active in the eastern Mediterranean and the Poles and Cossacks along the Dniester river. The logic of the Holy League – to press the Turkish enemy on every side – was becoming a reality.[32]

But the final push to take Buda remained for the following year. The most optimistic believed that at some point the Turks would simply abandon the struggle and withdraw, leaving the 'Christian lands' for ever. Perhaps even the elusive prize of Constantinople might be regained, with the Christian cross implanted on the Church of the Holy Wisdom. These were the thoughts circulating in Vienna and Rome rather than among those who had actually met the Ottomans on the battlefield. In the winter of 1685–6 the end certainly seemed in sight. The Emperor's diplomats finally concluded terms for a treaty with the Elector of Brandenburg, which would put his superbly trained troops into the line against the Ottomans. This agreement, finally sealed only in the early spring of 1686, was hard-fought, but eventually eight thousand infantry and cavalry marched south-east to the assembly point for the 1686 campaign.[33]

This contribution was probably a key factor in the ultimate success of the assault on Buda.[34] But the Habsburgs' Austrian troops were now better trained and equipped than they had been in the immediate aftermath of the Siege of Vienna. More men had bayonets for their muskets and had been taught to use them. Moreover, the bristling spikes of the *cheveaux de frise*, which had provided such effective protection against the Ottoman cavalry, were now issued generally to the Habsburg infantry.[35] Even the supply and commissariat system, which had failed so badly in 1684, was much improved. However, the underlying problem of who actually controlled this ramshackle coalition remained unresolved. In the contemporary histories, writers talked of 'the Duke of Lorraine's Side', 'The Bavarians' or 'the Auxiliary Forces of Brandenburg', each under its own generals and officers. A council of war, which met regularly, was supposed to settle policy and implement an agreed strategy. But with everyone yearning for glory, honour and, ultimately, plunder, national and personal interests often prevailed.

Before the 1686 campaigning season began, the Emperor Leopold sent his chancellor to the war camp close to Barkan. On 10 June, Count Strattmann told all the generals in a full council of war that their objective was not only Buda, but 'the Ruin of the Ottoman Empire'. If the capital fell, then they could take the rest of Hungary from the Turk forever. There were to be no diversions from this great aim; victory at the citadel of Buda 'would revenge their comrades which had laid their bones in the trenches of the former siege'.[36] On 12 June the army set out in two long columns, led by the cavalry, on either side of the Danube. A constant stream of boats moved past them down the river, filled with 'the great guns, ammunition, hay, and other necessary provisions for subsistence'. Lighter craft were packed with thousands of wicker gabions to be filled with earth in front of the Ottoman lines. There were also tents, medical supplies, food and fodder in abundance, entrenching tools, all the impedimenta of war that had been lacking in 1684. As they marched steadily forward there was no sign of the enemy, although one or two Turks captured by scouts said that all the garrisons for miles around had moved back to Buda. By the 16th the army had halted a few hours from Buda while the engineers assembled a bridge of boats to link the northern to the southern bank, the infantry being put to work filling the gabions with earth. For two days, they moved slowly forward, digging trenches, placing the gabions and building strongpoints in a line all around the city so that (in theory) Buda would be entirely cut off from contact with the outside world.

The fortress of Buda had two connected parts. The high town – the castle – was a flat, rocky outcrop, raised almost 200 feet above the river level. This was where the royal palace of the kings of Hungary had been built, but these old buildings had mostly fallen into decay and were now used as depots and firing points. At its easternmost end, the escarpment was nearly vertical and it only sloped down a little to the western extremity. The natural strength of the place was reinforced by an elaborate set of defences in depth, with strong redoubts set behind stone and earthen walls. The lower town – 'the water town' – was built on the rising ground between the river bank and the escarpment, protecting the gates and sally ports of the citadel, and containing the homes of many of the garrison officials and their families. Here the walls had been hastily repaired after the siege of 1684, but these were old-fashioned fortifications, vulnerable to bombardment. The defenders had guns, powder and shot in plenty, as well as abundant food and water.

As the allies slowly established their line of trenches around the upper and lower towns, there was the occasional salvo from the lower town or the citadel, and parties of *sipahis* dashed out from the town gates, only to be chased back by the allied cavalry. A captured janissary told his interrogators of the speech the pasha of Buda had made to all his troops. He had told them he had orders [from the sultan] to defend Buda 'to the last drop of his blood, which he was resolved to do . . . the Janissaries and Saphis replied that they were ready to sacrifice their lives in the service of His Highness and defence of their law.' But they did so on strict conditions. He must make an immediate payment to each one of them; he must set all prisoners free from the city jails, whatever their crime; and, most important of all, 'that he would not hold out until the last extremity, lest the same misfortune befall them as befell the garrison of Neuhäusel'. This referred to the massacre of 1685, which had surprised and horrified the Ottomans.[37] All this he promised. This accord meant that they would fight both for the money they had received and for their honour, for as long as the siege might last. They would not give in until all hope of relief was lost.

The allied batteries began to fire in earnest on the walls of the lower town on 21 June. The fire was accurate and concentrated: two days later they had made the first breach in the outer wall. There was not much return fire, and for two days they methodically enlarged the hole in the wall with the heaviest guns. On the evening of 24 June, the Bavarians launched an assault on the wall, and met little resistance. Pushing through into the town beyond, they found it empty, for all the Ottoman troops had concentrated in the city above. The early success elated the troops, and the skill of coordination in attack was much more effective than two years before. Moreover, troops were moved regularly in and out of the attack line, to ensure that they were always fresh; nor did they succumb so easily to the disease which had previously killed many men in the trenches. A party of irregulars captured boats containing some ninety women and their children, including the pasha's family and a great deal of bullion, sailing under cover of darkness downriver towards Belgrade.[38]

The siege which began in earnest on 21 June would last seventy-four days, longer than the Siege of Vienna three years before, and it was harder and more bitterly fought. The allied army in 1686 was better organised and commanded than the vast array led by Kara Mustafa. At Buda the Ottomans had fewer men than Starhemberg commanded in Vienna, and they faced attacks on every side of the long limestone escarpment – Castle Hill – and the lower town. The siege was both more systematic and professional: the allies battered the lower and upper towns of Buda relentlessly on every side. Lorraine had many heavy guns at his disposal and from 24 June, once the Bavarians had occupied the high ground of St Gellert's Hill overlooking the upper town, they could direct an accurate and devastating mortar fire on to the castle below.[39] But despite assault after assault, the allies made little impression on the Ottoman positions. It was often said that the Turks were exceptionally tenacious in defence, and at Buda they adapted their traditional battle tactics to the rocky terrain leading to the upper town.

The allies attacked somewhere on the perimeter almost every day, and the Turks would quickly reinforce the area under pressure. Behind the existing positions, they would put up new lines of palisades or field fortifications. Once these were ready, the Ottoman front line in contact with the enemy would fall back; the triumphant westerners would then push forward only to meet a withering and well-aimed fire from the new defence line. Often, well-trained janissaries would then launch a counterattack into the allied trench lines behind the attackers.[40] In hand-to-hand fighting, the Ottoman style of war proved more useful than the formal tactics of the westerners. A contemporary account tried to put the best face upon this situation. 'We could not force the palisadoed retrenchment of the besieged behind the breach . . . and our chief officers were all either wounded or killed by the continual firing of the enemy, it was thought convenient [for our] assailants to retreat, though they had fought like lions.'[41] Even the compact, fast-firing Turkish bow proved a better weapon than the musket. Prince Eugene was shot through the hand with a Turkish arrow, Rüdiger von Starhemberg's cousin, Guido, had a musket ball in his foot and a grenade splinter in his shoulder; there was a long list of other officers, from all over Europe, who were hacked about with sabres or yataghans in the daily hand-to-hand fighting.

It became clear after several weeks of fighting that, unless the Ottomans could be persuaded to surrender, the best hope of victory was to take the upper town by storm. The only plausible way up the slope was through the strongest point, the great gateway at the northern end of Castle Hill, protected by a huge arc of fortifications called the roundel.[42] There was little chance of undermining it as the Turks had done so proficiently with the bastions and ravelins of Vienna. The allied artillery did some damage but not enough to destroy it. But it was the only key that could unlock the Ottoman defences. So, just as Kara Mustafa had poured all his resources into the attack on the two bastions by the Emperor's palace in Vienna, so, too, increasingly the weight of the allies' assault at Buda was concentrated on a single point, the city gate.

On 24 July a lucky mortar shell from a Bavarian battery exploded a powder magazine within the city, killing as many as a thousand Turks; but still there was no decisive advance, and the allied casualties were mounting daily. On the day after the magazine exploded, the Duke of Lorraine sent an emissary under flag of truce to the pasha with a summons to surrender. Two hours later he returned with a letter in a red velvet purse. Abdurrahman Abdi Pasha, the Ottoman commander, declared that 'he could not dream of such a vile piece of cowardice; that he fought for the glory of his Prophet and the honour of the Musselmen; that he and his garrison were resolved to hold out to the utmost extremity; and defend it to the last gasp of breath: that the place being entrusted to his care by the Grand Signior [Sultan Mehmed IV], he would preserve it or lose his life. Let the Duke come and wrest it from him,' he said; 'he should find him upon the breach ready to dispute his entrance.'

The duke received the letter calmly and simply ordered the batteries to redouble their fire. It seems that he regarded the pasha as a soldier, a worthy opponent; it was, after all, the kind of defiance that he or Rüdiger von Starhemberg would have shown in similar circumstances. Although the fighting had been fierce and constant since the day it began, there were none of the symbolic atrocities – flayed captives, heads spiked on palisades – that both sides had performed in the Siege of Vienna, or at Nové Zámky. Nothing worse had happened than

Lorraine's troops bringing him sixty Turkish heads from the dead janissaries in the trenches after a fierce assault on the allied lines had been repelled with great slaughter.

By the last days of July 1686, the siege had arrived at the point of stasis. Rumours abounded: a huge Ottoman army had supposedly crossed the Drava at Osijek, and was marching north to relieve Buda. Lorraine began to conserve his own troops, using Hungarian volunteers as cannon fodder in the daily attacks.[43] A massive assault launched on 27 July produced immense heroism, especially from the eager Brandenburgers, but little progress and a casualty list of more than three thousand men, dead and wounded.[44] On 30 July, Lorraine held another council of war because he had heard whispers that there was dissension among the Ottomans, and that many were willing to surrender. Another emissary was sent up the hill. The pasha received his message and said he needed to consult his officers. The answer he sent to Lorraine was more temporising than the former letter. 'He neither could nor would surrender the city which was "the Key to the Ottoman Empire", but if he would make a general peace, they would surrender into our hands some other equivalent town.'

There was a sense that both sides wanted an honourable way out of the impasse. Allied officers were well received by the Ottomans in the upper town, while Ottoman officers sent as hostages for their safe return were well treated in the Bavarian lines. The pasha made it clear that he felt trapped in the city, that the promised relief had not arrived, but to surrender Buda without proper terms would cost him his life at the hands of the Grand Vizier. Lorraine's envoy, a Baron Creux, answered through the interpreter that he had no power to negotiate. But it was a fact that if there were another costly assault, then 'the power of the generals to repress the fury of the soldiers [was uncertain] ... This siege might become no less tragical than that of Neuhäusel.' That is, the entire garrison and all the people would be slaughtered or enslaved.

It is impossible to know how sincere these discussions might have been, but it was normal to try and seek some accommodation once the capture of the city had become a foregone conclusion. Within hours, hostilities had resumed. August began with no more progress. Lorraine sent for reinforcements; there were stronger rumours of the advance of a huge Ottoman relieving force; and the daily artillery duel continued. The Turks apparently had no shortage of munitions despite the explosion of the powder store. By 13 August the rumours about the Ottoman relief force were confirmed: there were about forty thousand men moving north. The plan was that reinforcements would fight their way through into the upper town while eight thousand Tartars would ravage the country for miles around, raiding the allies' supply lines. Some of the Tartars had already been sighted on the hills close to the city. On the next day the Duke of Lorraine took all his cavalry and a few infantry out of the city, stripping the siege lines of most of his men, and set out to confront the relieving force. It was a high-risk strategy, because, if his enemy evaded him and managed to reinforce Buda, then the siege, as in 1684, would end in complete failure.

However, the reverse happened. Lorraine's cuirassiers caught part of the Ottoman cavalry and pinned it down, while a larger number of *sipahis* and Tartars caught the Hungarian irregular cavalry, who immediately feigned flight, using an old Ottoman trick. As they set out in pursuit, the Ottomans were caught by an overwhelming flank attack with the full force of Lorraine's remaining squadrons. With the cavalry in disorder, the Ottoman infantry were mercilessly cut down by the allies. As the siege diary records, the Turks were 'massacred like wild beasts that fall into the hunter's net'. Three thousand Turkish dead lay on the battlefield, and the rest were in full retreat. These were 'for the most part janissaries and choice men . . . who had sworn to get into the city or perish'.[45] This was a heaven-sent victory, and Lorraine was able to send 'the young Count Palffy to carry the news to the Emperor, and lay at his feet 28 colours and standards won from the enemy during the fight'.

The other trophies from the battle Lorraine displayed on sections of the fortifications taken by the allies, so that the Ottomans above should be in no doubt that their long-expected relief would never arrive. But the depleted garrison fought back with ever greater fury and by 19 August the duke realised that they 'were resolved to hold out to the last gasp'.[46] The Grand Vizier did make a more energetic attempt to relieve the city, so that a small group of Turks successfully fought through the allied lines and managed to enter the city. These few hundred men were insufficient to affect the course of the siege, but the defenders' spirits were raised and they hung red banners of victory over the walls. But this was not a stratagem that could work twice, and later attempts were driven off with heavy loss of life.

Almost every day the allies intercepted messengers carrying letters from Buda to the Ottoman army lurking outside the city. Lorraine was fully informed of the fragile morale within the upper town, and the pasha's refrain that the next assault would overwhelm his defence. But there was no sign of any slackening of resistance, and every attack gained little fresh advantage. Desperate measures were tried. The Austrian engineers put together a wonder weapon, a type of covered wooden bridge made of planks, mounted on wheels. The infantry were to push this contraption forward to the enemy palisade, then drop it down on to the wooden poles, smashing and splintering them, while the best assault troops would rush over the covered bridge into the Turkish lines. The engineers covered it with sheets of tin to prevent this medieval-style war engine catching fire. But the first time it was used the Turks doused it with inflammable liquids – 'pitch, tar, sulphur, and other combustible materials' – from the walls and trenches, so that it was in flames from end to end and quickly reduced to ashes. On 30 August the long-awaited allied reinforcements arrived, five infantry regiments – 'all lusty men and well disciplined' – and twenty-five squadrons of cavalry. This was a decisive moment.

On the evening that the new troops appeared Lorraine met the Elector Max Emmanuel and all the other generals and they agreed that their best chance was to storm the castle within the next few days. But some thought they should obtain sanction from Vienna, which would delay matters. By an extraordinary coincidence, Chancellor Strattmann arrived on the same day with secret orders from the Emperor. Leopold demanded a decisive outcome: now all were in accord. The commanders agreed that the city could be taken; the reinforcements of fresh and eager men now gave them an advantage. But they thought surprise was the key to success, so a rumour was put around the camp that the army would march against the Grand Vizier in full strength, apparently leaving the lines of circumvallation nearly empty. On the morning of 2 September there were great signs of movement in the allied lines. The cavalry horses were saddled and made ready for battle; the infantry were paraded and all the generals and field officers gathered at the head of their detachments. All this urgent activity was in full view of the Ottomans above. But as they prepared to march away towards the Grand Vizier's army, there was a sudden order to 'about face'. In a few moments the army began to move en masse in three columns ('attacks') towards the roundel and the city gate behind. At the same time all the guns began a barrage against the city.

The first attack was launched against the forward Turkish lines and was driven back; a second was pushed forward almost immediately. That, too, was driven back, but by now the soldiers were roused and they returned to the assault maddened with rage and hatred for the enemy. This time all three assault columns overwhelmed the dogged but outnumbered defenders. They pushed on uphill towards the city. No quarter was given and the attackers hacked and stabbed at any Turk living or dead. About a thousand men defended themselves in a small fort, and hung out white flags, seeking mercy. A mob of allied soldiers burst in and began to slaughter the unresisting Turks, until the Duke of Lorraine and the Elector of Bavaria sent direct orders for the killing to stop, the enemy to be disarmed and the troops, now gripped by a bloodlust, to fight their way through the gate into the upper town.

There the Governor Pasha met his fate. He 'died bravely upon the breach where he defended himself valiantly with his scimitar in his hand, scorning to retreat or demand quarter'. He had sworn 'either to preserve the town or gloriously end his days'.[47] Many died with him: there were in all no more than 2000 survivors of the 13,000 who had initially defended the city. Rycaut wrote: 'The garrison retreating from house to house, from wall to wall, firing from windows and holes, and all parts, being resolved to sell their habitations and lives at the dearest rate . . . The imperialists being now masters of the town, made a most direful slaughter of all they met, and being in the heat of their fury, put women and children to the sword.' We can see the results. A little oil painting, made for the Duke of Lorraine, and now in the Hofburg in Innsbruck, shows the main square of the upper town. It is dated 6 September 1686. The ground is littered with bodies, men and women, some alive, and others dead. One woman's body shields her child, another tries to cover her genitals as a soldier roughly pulls the clothes off her. Other Turks look on in horror, hold their hands to their mouths, while platoons of soldiers march disarmed janissaries away into captivity and slavery. There is no senior officer in view. This small painting was later used as the source for a much larger tapestry, part of a series which celebrated the military triumphs of the duke, commissioned by his dutiful son. But in this version, the naked and abused women have vanished, to be replaced by Lorraine and his commanders gravely surveying the scene.

The implications of the victory were obvious to contemporaries. It was significant that Buda had been reconquered on exactly the same day – 2 September – that Suleiman I had occupied it in 1541. Other coincidences came to the surface. Constantinople had been conquered by Mehmed II in 1453. Now an ancient Turkish proverb was 'discovered': that 'it will be retaken when another Mehmed rules'.[48] The miracle of victory, first at Vienna, now at Buda, meant that nothing was impossible. As the writer of the siege diary concluded: 'We [now] have reasons to hope for conquests far more glorious and more considerable for the advancement of the Cause of God, advancement for the Austrian Family, and consolation of so great a number of Christian souls as groaned under the tyrannous yoke of Infidels.' But that was only the beginning: the whole world might be conquered for Christ: Islam itself would fall, and soon there would be the 'recovery of an infinite number of barbarians into the bosom of the true Church of God'.[49] The double miracle – the salvation of Vienna and the recovery of Buda – might usher in, at the hands of the most holy House of Habsburg, a greater outcome than any previous holy war had ever contemplated. Total victory.

PART THREE

The moment of the rose and the moment of the yew-tree
Are of equal duration. A people without history
Is not redeemed from time, for history is a pattern
Of timeless moments.

T. S. Eliot, 'Little Gidding'

II

The Age of Heroes[1]

Behind the grand Baroque façade of Number Sixteen, Herrengasse in the city of Graz is the city armoury, the Landeszeughaus. Built between 1642 and 1644, it was an emblem of Styria's central role in the war against the Turks, crammed with more than 85,000 spears, swords, suits of armour, harnesses, pistols, muskets and cannon.[2] In times of danger the men of Graz and its vicinity would line up to collect their weapons; a few might be experienced former soldiers or mercenaries but mostly they were citizens and farm boys, performing their civic duty to protect their homes and the *Land*. This pattern was repeated on a smaller scale in many places.[3] The Habsburg domains never had much of a military tradition, relying instead on local institutions, employing mercenaries, or encouraging individuals to recruit (and pay for) their own bands of irregulars. In stark contrast to the military state created by the Ottomans, it was a makeshift arrangement. The Landeszeughaus demonstrated the power of the rich city, but it also showed the basic amateurism that marked Austria's war-making. The Austrian historian Michael Hochedlinger, describing this 'belated great power', put it rather neatly: a 'splendid baroque surface, it perhaps had more of a *trompe l'oeil* and resembled a colossus on feet of clay, whose fate was always hanging by a thread'.[4]

These two ideas – the deception of surface and the deceit of *trompe l'oeil* – were characteristic of the Habsburgs. These qualities were inherent in the tradition of purposefully muddling through (*weiter-wursteln*) which, many critics averred, was the Habsburg version of progress.[5] Sometimes, however, external circumstances galvanised this somnolent system. The triple shock – the Siege of Vienna, the miraculous rescue of the city and the God-given reconquest of Buda – was one of them. For just over thirty years, the Habsburg system surged with the adrenalin of victory and success, until the dynamism slackened.

Real victories were unfamiliar to the Habsburgs: more often than not, from the early sixteenth century, their skill had been to turn defeat into victory by artful propaganda. The endless and inconclusive Long War between the Ottomans and the Habsburgs from 1593 to 1606 was made to look like a triumph, in which the failures were glossed over and the successes magnified. But in the second Long War, from 1683 to 1699, followed by a short reprise from 1716 to 1718, there were real triumphs on an unparalleled scale. There was a triumphant Reconquest of Hungary, taking back all the lands won by Suleiman I for Islam. Over sixteen years the armies of Leopold I and then of his sons Joseph I (1705–11) and Charles VI (1711–39) redeemed almost every Ottoman success since 1521. Only Belgrade remained in contention – oscillating to and fro from Ottoman to Habsburg hands. There had been a whole series of triumphs for Habsburg arms in the War of the Spanish Succession from 1704 to 1713, when the allied generals, the Duke of Marlborough and the imperial commander, Prince Eugene of Savoy, humbled the armies of France, the greatest military power in Europe.[6]

The battles with the Turk were not just a success for the Habsburgs but for much of Christian Europe, aside from France.[7] On 5 March 1684, Pope Innocent XI had sponsored a new and highly effective Holy League for a war that was to last until final victory, and no party was to make a separate peace with the Ottomans. Even the Czar of Muscovy was invited to join. This alliance was to produce immediate, concerted action – the Habsburgs in Hungary, the Poles in lands north of the Dniester and the Venetians in the Adriatic, the Mediterranean, and in Greece.[8] The strategic concept – squeezing the Ottomans on every side – put decisive pressure on the Turks. The decade of active campaigning seasons after the occupation of Buda was marked by a series of extraordinary victories in the field. The common name now given to this period of war in Austrian history is the 'Age of Heroes' (*Heldenzeitalter*): the heroes included Charles of Lorraine, 'Türkenlouis'

– Ludwig Wilhelm of Baden, Guido von Starhemberg (cousin of Rüdiger), Florimond de Mercy, and many others who had made their names in the east, but later also fought with equal success against the armies of France in Western Europe during the War of the Spanish Succession. Thereafter, with the exception of the spare figure of Prince Eugene of Savoy, the greatest hero of all, they grew old and fat, died or retired, and Austria stultified. There had been a string of six miraculous victories, which people could recite like a litany. The first, of course, was the salvation of Vienna by King John Sobieski of Poland. The second was Charles of Lorraine storming Buda in 1686 with the old pasha lying dead by the gate. The third was the Battle of Nagyhársany in 1687, often called 'the second Mohács', the capstone to Charles of Lorraine's triumphs; the memory of Suleiman I destroying the old Kingdom of Hungary at Mohács in 1526 had finally been redeemed. The fourth victory was the Elector Max Emmanuel of Bavaria's who captured Belgrade, the city of battles, in 1688; the Turks recaptured it the following year. 'Türkenlouis' destroyed the Turkish army at the Battle of Slankamen in 1691. In the sixth battle at Zenta in 1697 Prince Eugene of Savoy humiliated the Sultan Mustafa, who fled from the battlefield in panic, leaving the River Tisza filled with the Ottoman dead. Fourteen campaigning seasons finally brought a settlement, and in a little pavilion by the town of Karlowitz near Belgrade peace was signed in 1699.

These victories were the more remarkable because they were gained with limited resources. The renewal of war in the west against France meant that the Habsburgs, like the Ottomans, were now fighting two enemies at once. So at Slankamen, forty miles north of Belgrade, on 19 August 1691 Ludwig Wilhelm of Baden had only twenty thousand men against a much larger Ottoman army, led by another vigorous Köprülü, Fazil Mustafa Pasha. 'Türkenlouis' won, in part because the Ottomans lacked the vital Tartar component of their army, which was still travelling south, and partly because his small but battle-hardened regiments could respond precisely and effectively to his command. But perhaps most important of all was a lucky chance of war. A stray bullet killed the Ottoman commander and his army immediately disintegrated, abandoned all its artillery and even the army war chest, and fled back towards the safety of Belgrade. Had the reverse happened, and 'Türkenlouis' ended his days on the battlefield, his

small force would not have fallen apart. Another senior officer would
have assumed command and carried on the battle, while planning the
withdrawal. This fragility was inherent in the Ottoman system: an
Ottoman army without its head was no more than a rabble. But as
the Habsburg army dwindled in numbers (mostly through sickness)
and lacked men, food and money, it was soon just as demoralised.
One Englishman said that the army protecting the bridge at Osijek
'look generally like dead men'. [9]

When the Habsburgs' war against France ended in 1697, Vienna
slowly released more resources for the east, and, most important of
all, the Imperial War Council allowed Prince Eugene, the only
commander of genius in Habsburg history, to return to the Hungarian
front. Typically, the Emperor Leopold appointed him with the advice
that 'he should act with extreme caution . . . forgo all risks and avoid
engaging the enemy unless he has overwhelming strength and is prac-
tically certain of being completely victorious'. [10] At the end of July 1697
Eugene arrived at the new Habsburg marshalling point, the old fortress
of Peterwardein (now Petrovaradin) on the Danube, upriver from
Belgrade. His army consisted (notionally) of thirty thousand Austrian,
Saxon and Brandenburg infantry and cavalry, but many were unfit for
duty. Within a month he had prepared plans for ranging across a huge
area east of the Danube, and as far north as Transylvania, and galvanised
the morale and the physical situation of his men. He had threatened
there would be catastrophe if the men were not paid, and he borrowed
money to pay them. He demanded that ammunition, rations and
equipment be brought up to the level of an army of fifty thousand.
He sent the fittest men north to deal with Hungarian rebels and concentrated on rebuilding the remainder of the army. Soon ships were
shuttling back and forth from Vienna and Buda, filled with supplies.
It was only just in time.

On 18 August the Sultan Mustafa III led a re-energised Ottoman
army from Belgrade, about eighty thousand men, crossed the Danube
and marched north towards the river Tisza, the last main river barrier
before Transylvania, and from there, to the west, the road to Bratislava,
and ultimately Vienna. Eugene's military intelligence was excellent,
and his scouts shadowed the Ottoman advance. As the sultan moved
slowly north, Eugene marched his men south from Petrovaradin,
crossed the Tisza and headed upriver along the east bank. He had

THE AGE OF HEROES

recalled his men from the north, and meeting on the Tisza his force numbered about fifty thousand. The Ottomans had no notion of where the enemy was, and probably assumed that Eugene had moved away to escape their relentless advance.

River crossings continued to be a dangerous manoeuvre for any army, especially when half of it was on one bank and half on the other. In many of the Ottomans' most devastating defeats, rivers played a part, as at St Gotthard in 1664. But when they reached Zenta on the Tisza, the sultan ordered precautions to protect the troops. Unusually, as the pontoon bridge was being built, the janissaries dug trenches to protect the crossing point and even erected palisades and chained carts together make a field fortification. As the cavalry and the artillery began to move early on 11 September 1691, the Ottoman infantry were in position, at the ready, behind their field fortifications, looking warily for the enemy. It was a textbook defence of a river crossing, and an indication that the Ottomans were capable of learning from their earlier defeats. Had Eugene followed his instructions to behave cautiously, especially against a larger enemy force, the Turks would have crossed in safety. But, once they did so, there was no guarantee that he could stop their advance.

He adopted an extraordinarily high-risk approach. In the early morning of 11 September Eugene's hussars had captured an Ottoman pasha. The general told his captive that he had a choice: either tell him where the sultan and his army were or he would have him hacked to death. The pasha hesitated, and Eugene ordered his Croats to draw their swords and cut the Turk to pieces. As they moved on him, the pasha told Eugene what he wanted to know. The sultan was at Zenta, his artillery and baggage were on the far bank, but most of the infantry had still to cross. Eugene immediately rode ahead at full speed with his hussars, while the infantry and field guns made a forced march to rendezvous at Zenta. The prince and the light cavalry arrived in the mid-afternoon, the main body a few hours later. There were less than three hours of daylight left, but the river transit was still incomplete. The enemy were still vulnerable.

The Habsburg army's sudden and unanticipated arrival surprised and shocked the Ottomans. Who was in command? The sultan was on one bank and the Grand Vizier on the other. They were even more surprised when, instead of the slow positional manoeuvring that they associated with western armies, he adopted a typically Ottoman tactic. As the light was beginning to fail, the entire Habsburg force, with the cavalry on each wing and the infantry in the centre, launched an immediate all-out assault on the protected bridgehead, enveloping it on all sides. There were no reserves, because Eugene relied on his capacity to move his men about the battlefield in the heat of combat. Soon, weaknesses began to appear in the defensive perimeter, and in some places the janissaries began to pull out of the line and back towards the bridge. Eugene withdrew some of his cuirassiers and dragoons out of the line in turn, a few men here and a few there, recombined them into a tactical mass and pushed them against the Turkish defences at the points where they were beginning to crack. In most places the janissaries were defending with amazing tenacity: in such a case, Eugene ordered his men simply to pin them down. But, inexorably, pressure was applied to the points of fracture. The ferocious battle went on through the twilight, with Eugene, his messengers around him, close to the combat in the centre of the Ottoman line, observing the ebb and flow of the fighting through the deepening gloom.

As dusk fell, the Turks' defensive circle broke. The Habsburg cavalry hacked away at the thousands of panic-stricken Ottomans milling around the bridge, while the dragoons and infantry picked them off one by one until it was too dark to see a target. They then fired volleys into the heaving mass of bodies. The artillery, arriving after the main action was over, bombarded the bridge and any surviving Turks. On the following morning, it resembled a charnel house: Turkish bodies on the river bank, dead from sabre cuts or blown apart by musketry or artillery fire, were beginning to rot. The river, at a low ebb and slow moving, was filled from bank to bank with dead Turks, some entangled with the debris from the pontoons, others knotted together in little clumps where the slight current had taken them. It was said that 20,000 had been slaughtered on the bank and perhaps 10,000 had drowned in the river. Eugene's army had lost 300 dead, and when they finally crossed to the far bank they found the sultan and the cavalry had fled towards Temesvar (now Timişoara), leaving 9000 baggage carts, 6000 camels and 15,000 oxen. In addition there was the abandoned Ottoman war chest, containing three million piastres.[11]

After Zenta Eugene mounted a raid with six thousand cavalry and some light guns south into Bosnia, sacked Sarajevo and returned north of the River Sava with 'a great quantity of Turkish cloth, with many Turkish women . . .'[12] In 1698 both sides wanted peace and eventually, after endless delays and diplomatic intrigues, a settlement rather than a truce was concluded at Karlowitz, not far from Belgrade. A good deal was made of how much the Ottomans had been forced to concede – which they had – but by the terms of the treaty they held Belgrade, which they had recovered from the Habsburgs in 1689.

The real end of the Reconquest came only after one final war waged between 1716 and 1718. In 1715 the Ottomans had begun a successful campaign to recover the territory they had lost in Greece to the Venetians during the heyday of the Holy Alliance. The Habsburgs came to the aid of their Venetian allies, and in July 1716, puffed up with overconfidence, the Grand Vizier, Silahdar Ali Pasha, once again marshalled an army at Belgrade to attack the Habsburgs. Any memories of the Zenta disaster were put aside, and the consequences were dire. The Turks crossed the Danube close to Karlowitz, in sight of the place where the treaty was signed in 1699, and moved rapidly north towards Petrovaradin, where they began to lay siege to the newly rebuilt fortress. The general who faced them was, once again, Prince Eugene, fighting on ground that he knew well and the Turks did not. On 5 August 1716, he trapped the Grand Vizier's huge army against the anvil of the fiercely defended fortress that loomed above the flat landscape along the Danube and in the network of streams and rivers around it. Had he not been close at hand, it is likely that the fortress would have fallen because the janissaries had already taken the outer defences. But, as at Zenta, the Ottomans had no clear idea where he was, and the attack came as a surprise.

The Grand Vizier was in an untenable position, attacked on one side by the garrison of Petrovaradin and on the other by Eugene's vengeful army. At Zenta he had forced them into the river to drown, now he destroyed them with waves of cavalry, remorseless artillery and musket fire. Silahdar Ali was found after the battle under a mountainous pile of Ottoman dead. Those who fought in the battle remembered the sudden summer snowstorm that turned the land and the soldiers white. In the Austrian ranks it was whispered that the Virgin Mary herself had thrown her protection over them. A pilgrimage church was built afterwards at Tekije to house the shrine of Our Lady of the Snows, and the victory is still remembered every 5 August. Again the river waters were filled with human carcasses.

Yet neither this string of victories in the field nor the Peace of Karlowitz in 1699, nor the Treaty of Passarowitz in 1718, after Prince Eugene had recaptured Belgrade in 1717, brought the Battle for Europe to a final and definitive conclusion. After the Peace of Passarowitz the boundary between Ottomans and Habsburgs was now set not a few days' march from Vienna but on the Danube and Sava rivers, close to the Balkan heartland of Turkey-in-Europe. Belgrade now sat neatly in the borderland. Whereas in 1683 the Habsburgs had the most to fear, now the position was reversed: the Ottomans were deeply threatened by the strengthening of the border fortresses. But it was the Habsburgs who manifested the greater anxiety. At times they saw the Ottomans as a feeble enemy, beaten time after time, and offering no real obstacle to their grandiose plans for further conquest, which still surfaced now and then, for a Habsburg empire that would extend as far as Istanbul. On other occasions they considered the Turks a deadly menace, forever ready to overrun Hungary and even penetrate into the provinces of Austria. No one seriously expected another Siege of Vienna but a new Tartar terror was entirely possible.

As a result, the government in Vienna spent vast sums of money on creating in the southern part of Hungary and along the frontier through Croatia one of the most elaborately defended frontiers in Europe. The War Council saw matters in simplistic terms: unless there was defence in depth, a garrisoned frontier and plentiful reserves, there was no guarantee that 1683 might not be repeated, in some form. Already, by 1699, the Habsburgs were building a fortress much more substantial than the citadel of Belgrade, fifty miles downstream on the Danube. The key to their defensive system would be the old fort of Petrovaradin, captured by the allied army in 1687 and then the base for both of Prince Eugene's great victories. Work began on the vast new fortress complex in 1692 and it was only completed in 1760. This fortress, nicknamed 'Gibraltar on the Danube', strongly suggests that the Habsburgs anticipated a major threat from the Ottoman in the south, against common sense and all the evidence.

It was not just Petrovaradin blocking one route north, but a line of new fortresses between the Sava and the Drava, built between 1712 and

1721, Brod, completed by the 1770s, and Karlovac, close to the Adriatic coast.[13] These massive fortifications along the southern frontier
cost a fortune, haemorrhaging money from the military budget. Behind
this grandiose programme lay a paradox. By mid-century, all Austria's
serious enemies were now in the west: yet there was no money left
to build fortifications where they might have been valuable against
the predatory French or Frederick II and his Prussian armies. Michael
Hochedlinger points to an unanswerable question: 'Through the
second half of the eighteenth century Prussia remained Austria's main
enemy. Following the loss of Silesia it became increasingly important
to protect Bohemia.' But relatively little was done, except strengthening Olomouc in Moravia. But at the same time the fortress building
in the south continued with heightened urgency. 'It was considered
necessary to strengthen the bigger fortresses on the frontier with the
Ottoman empire.'[14]

So, why was it 'necessary' to create these elaborate defences against
Austria's least pressing danger? The reason is that, while the threat
may not have been real, it was certainly there in people's minds. Like
the Maginot Line between the two world wars of the twentieth century,
Petrovaradin provided a sense of reassurance, protection against a
nightmare. After the Siege of Vienna, Austrians feared the Turks more,
if that were possible, than they had before. The Austrian provinces
had been ravaged by Tartars almost as far as Steyr – some estimates
say that as many as 100,000 had been killed or taken into slavery. One
of the maps made at the time graphically showed villages in flames:
the landscape was covered with these little symbols. The whole fabric
of social life had been destroyed, with most of the parish and land
records burned in the wholesale Tartar pillage. Three generations on,
the memories of that time were still vivid and personal. Further south,
in Styria and in the borderland with Croatia, the Turks were actually
still very close.

By the conclusion of the Peace of Passarowitz, the Habsburg army
had perfected its response to the eastern style of war. In the east,
simple survival made it essential that infantry and cavalry work in
close harmony: the narrowest gap, a momentary inattention, and the
Turks would move at lightning speed to exploit that weakness. The
slow, measured, ponderous style of western war would not work. But
the new Habsburg army had to meet the demands of fighting both

in the east and in the west, two quite different kinds of conflict in utterly different terrain. A senior officer serving in the 1680s had summed up war fighting in the east:

> This tactic of fighting [the enemy] he says, is superb because, lined up tightly and with firm attention, the imperial army faces the Turks like an iron wall. This method of fighting was invented by the general Montecuccoli who through this tactic kept the upper hand over the Turks, which heavily outnumbered them. In a valuable manuscript he bequeathed to the Emperor his thoughts about this way of waging a war resulting from experience and thoughtful consideration. His successor, the Duke of Lorraine, has picked up these ideas and applies them with great success and in doing so has remained victorious in many confrontations with the Turks.
>
> In a tight line the [cuirassier] squadrons slowly advance. No shots are allowed unless in close vicinity [of the enemy]. The Turks who are unable to break the close line of the squadrons cannot make use of their sharp sabres, which would mean immediate death and destruction from all sides should a line break up. But since they crash against the impenetrable steadfastness of the imperial troops they retreat and consider themselves the losers. In this way 10,000 men of the imperial troupes [sic] can withstand 20,000 Turks. This may sound improbable but has none the less been proven during more than just one encounter.[15]

War in the west was predictable; war in the east was not. Austrian infantry facing the janissaries were eventually told to keep up a continuous aimed fire, rather than the volley that was becoming the rule in the west, because any pause in the barrage of fire would allow the Ottomans to close with them: hand to hand, the Turks had an insuperable advantage. Similarly, scouting ahead of the army, knowing where the elusive Ottoman enemy could be found, became a prime task of the hussars and other light cavalry. Gradually this new way of fighting, built up from decades of experience, sometimes written down by officers and passed hand to hand in manuscript, created the nucleus of a new style of war.

Christopher Duffy, historian of eighteenth-century war, and especially of the Habsburg empire and Russia, described this as 'war on the wilder fringes'.[16] Western war in the seventeenth and eighteenth centuries may have pretended to a degree of gentility, but there was nothing of that on the eastern frontier. Flaying, impalement, endless casual brutalities on both sides were commonplace: all were done for a purpose, to frighten or infuriate the enemy. They sometimes succeeded in both respects, but usually only invited tit-for-tat retaliation. The pace and savagery of war on the wilder fringes bred a different attitude to fighting, more like that of the 'special forces' in the twenty-first century than the rule-bound tactics of the conventional military.

Duffy describes the lesson that the twenty-one-year-old Maurice de Saxe, later a supremely talented general, learned during Eugene's battle for Belgrade on 16 August 1717. Saxe was watching two Austrian infantry battalions deployed in isolation on a hill not far away: 'I saw the two battalions level their muskets, take aim and make a general discharge at a range of twenty paces at a mass of Turks which was coming to attack them. The volley and the ensuing mêlée were almost simultaneous. There was no time for the two battalions to flee, and all the men were cut down by the sword on a stretch of ground measuring thirty or forty paces deep.'[17] He saw the terrifying reality of an Ottoman attack for the first time. He counted how many janissaries had been killed by the volley: there were only thirty Turkish corpses, but a mass of Austrian dead. For anyone who fought in the east, these were risks they faced daily. These were foes more dangerous, swifter and more lethal than any European enemy. To face a howling tide of janissaries racing towards you, to watch the heads and limbs of your companions spin off the sharp edge of a *sipahi* sabre required exceptional courage.

The annals of the Reconquest of Hungary were filled with many such casual acts of heroism and brutality. 'I mounted the breach. A Janissary cleft my helmet with a blow of his sabre, I ran him through the body; the Elector, who had received a musket ball in his hand the previous campaign, was also wounded by an arrow in the right cheek. Nothing could be more glorious or more bloody. How singularly are the terrible and the ridiculous grouped together.'[18] For subsequent generations these tough men seemed to embody a model of military courage, the hard-fighting 'pure and noble knight', exemplified by Prince Eugene. There was a popular ballad, published in Leipzig in 1719, called 'Prince Eugene, the noble knight'. It told the story, in Latin and German, of his capture of Belgrade in 1717.[19] It was the kind of bravery that the dynasty wanted to honour, celebrate and reward, the *military virtue* that the Habsburgs believed to be the special inheritance of their army, derived from its heroic origins in battle with the Turk.

★   ★   ★

Had the Turkish wars ended conveniently with the Habsburgs' apogee at the Peace of Passarowitz in 1718, then the conventional assumptions about Ottoman decay and decline would have been triumphantly vindicated. But they did not end then. There were two more wars which destroyed the euphoric confidence generated by the victories won by the generation of heroes. The aggressive war fought against the Ottomans between 1737 and 1739, and the defensive war between 1788 and 1791, were probably the most pointless and inept campaigns in the annals of Habsburg warfare. In hindsight, both were ill considered, created solely to meet diplomatic expedients, by Habsburg officials with scant understanding of the military realities. Nevertheless, in 1737 the war began with huge optimism and a grand flourish.

> On July 14 a great procession including representatives of the religious orders, judges, ministers, the court and the emperor himself wound its way from the Hofburg to St Stephen's Cathedral to announce to the citizens of Vienna that war had broken out. Gathered before the great door of the church all heard the declaration of war and an edict proclaiming that the bells of the city churches would ring every morning at 7.00 and each individual was to fall to his knees wherever they were and whatever they were doing and pray for the blessing of the Almighty upon the army of the emperor.[20]

This was the only part of the war that passed off according to plan.[21]

All along the long frontier there were inadequate supplies, not enough troops, and, by late August 1737, no evidence of a plan of campaign. The Austrians were dilatory in attacking the Turkish fortress of Vidin, which would have fallen to a swift attack, while a thrust into Bosnia to take the town of Banjaluka ran into a large Ottoman force and had to retire rapidly on the far side of the River Sava, leaving 922 men and 66 officers dead on the battlefield. The final failure of the year was truly humiliating. The only real success of the campaign had been taking the strategic town of Nish, on the road south to Istanbul. The pasha there had surrendered as soon as the Austrian army had appeared. In Vienna the seizure of such a famous town as Nish had been taken as a great victory, and confirmation that the Ottomans had indeed lost their old fighting spirit.

But in October 1737 a mass of Turkish *sipahis* arrived before the city and sent a message to the commander that the Grand Vizier, Ahmed Köprülü, was on his way with his entire army. General Doxat calculated that supplies were low and he had no hope of relief: when Köprülü arrived, Doxat offered to surrender the city in exchange for a safe conduct to Austrian lines for his men and himself. This appeared to be precisely the kind of craven conduct that the Turks had shown when they had given up the city in July 1737. There was popular outrage in Vienna at this cowardice: after a swift court-martial, Doxat, who had designed and built the massive new fortifications protecting Belgrade, was beheaded.

Doxat was not the last officer to be punished. By the end of the war in 1738, every senior commander had been cashiered, suspended from duty or lampooned in the press. Public outrage in Vienna grew as rabble-rousers asked: 'Where is the new Eugene?' The old prince had died barely two years before. He had no obvious replacement. The field commander, Field Marshal Seckendorf, was recalled and placed under house arrest to await court martial. He was a Protestant, and Father Peikhart preached from the pulpit of St Stephen's that 'a heretical general at the head of a Catholic army could only insult the Almighty and turn his benediction away from the army of his Imperial and Catholic Majesty'. For reassurance that the dynasty's Catholic credentials were still paramount, the Emperor appointed his son-in-law, Francis Stephen of Lorraine, to the titular command for the 1738 campaign season, and he left for the southern frontier. This failed 'to win the people' until it was reported that young Lorraine had 'issued orders calmly under fire': at this point the court hailed him both as a second Eugene (unlikely) and as a true grandson of Charles V, Duke of Lorraine, who had saved Vienna in 1683.

Soon Seckendorf's replacement, Count Königsegg, also suffered a loss of nerve and ordered a strategic withdrawal away from contact with the Ottomans; his junior officers protested, demanding he should pursue the enemy as Prince Eugene would have done. The Emperor decided that his inexperienced son-in-law possessed better credentials to lead the army to victory and gave him full command. Francis Stephen wisely fell sick and returned to Vienna, so the duty devolved back on Königsegg, while Francis Stephen and his wife, Maria Theresa, were rusticated to their duchy of Tuscany, to their delight. Meanwhile, the Emperor was 'in the middle of the general discontent . . . violently agitated and in the agony of his mind exclaimed "Is the fortune of my empire departed with Eugene?"' He continued to look for a commander with some spark of daring.[22] Running out of plausible candidates, he eventually chose Field Marshal George Oliver Wallis, of an old Jacobite family with a long record of service to the Habsburgs. Wallis had fought under Eugene at Zenta in 1697, at Petrovaradin, in the capture of Timişoara, and at the occupation of Belgrade in 1717–18. He had been passed over before because he was not an easy subordinate: difficult, overbearing and hot-headed. His first instinct was to attack, although he had learned a degree of prudence in his later career. If Charles VI wanted a new Eugene, then the elderly Wallis was probably his best option.

By mid-July 1739 he had joined his new command of thirty thousand men encamped at Belgrade, and scouts brought him news that the Grand Vizier's army was marching towards him from the east: their advance party was at the small town of Grocka on the Danube, a few hours' march away. The events that followed were graphically described by a Scots officer in the British army on secondment to the Austrian command. The young Scottish nobleman, John Lindsay, 20th Earl of Crawford, had fought as a volunteer with Prince Eugene on his last western campaign in 1735, and joined the eastern army for the war in 1737. He left a remarkable manuscript account of the savage fighting.[23] As Crawford relates, part of Wallis' army was still north of the Danube with General Neipperg, and the advice was that he should wait for the additional 15,000 men to reach him. Wallis sent a messenger to Neipperg to meet him on the road to Grocka and began to march his men overnight to seize the village from the few Turks that supposedly held it. Then he could await the Grand Vizier on ground he had chosen. It was a good road from Belgrade through low hills, and it began to rise towards a line of higher ground behind Grocka.

Just before the village, the track narrowed and entered a gully that then opened out on to the plain before reaching the riverside town. It then came out in a southerly direction, heading towards higher ground. Wallis knew that speed was essential so he pushed forward with the cavalry – mostly cuirassiers and dragoons, with some hussars – sending them through the gully to take possession of the land below, driving away any Turks occupying the ground. Led by Count Pálffy's cuirassiers, they burst out of the gully and began to trot down into the more open ground in front of Grocka. It was first light, and they dimly saw a large body of men below them and then there was a sudden cacophony of fire from the front and from each side of the road. They still had the advantage of the higher ground, but it was clear that this was not just an Ottoman advance party. In fact the entire Ottoman force had taken up position on the hills and in the valley below, with a complete command of the road in front of the Austrian horsemen. Many had been killed or wounded in the first salvo of Turkish fire, and the ground was littered with dead or dying men and horses.

One of the wounded was the Earl of Crawford. He survived the battle, but was seriously injured by a musket ball in the groin, a painful, suppurating wound that would kill him ten years later. In the interval he managed to write his vivid account of the battle and what followed.[25]

From dawn to mid-morning they kept the janissaries at bay, by constant carbine fire and support from the troops behind. At midday the infantry arrived, and eighteen companies of grenadiers pushed through the gap and heavy fire to relieve them. Through the morning the Grand Vizier had ordered men to move forward up the slope to the crown of the hills on either side of the Austrian cavalry so that they could envelop them, unleashing musket fire from directly above their makeshift positions. On the other side of the gully, Field Marshal Hildburghausen, in command of the infantry, ordered his men to storm the heights and throw the Turks back. Field guns were pulled up the slope and began to duel with the Ottoman artillery on the hillside opposite. The battle lasted the whole day, with more and more of the Austrians pushing through the gully while the Ottomans kept up a murderous fire. As night fell, the Grand Vizier pulled his men back in good order and, apart from the cries of the wounded, a stillness fell over the battlefield. The carnage was horrifying: in a single day from dawn to dusk, 2222 Austrians were dead and 2492 wounded. This was more than 10 per cent of Wallis' entire force. The Pálffy cuirassiers had lost almost half their number, including the majority of their officers. Even a year later, it was still like a charnel house. A traveller described how 'Today one cannot go ten steps without stepping on human corpses piled on top of another, all only half decomposed, many still in uniforms. Lying about are maimed bodies, hats, saddles, cartridge belts, boots, cleaning utensils, and other cavalry equipment. Everything is embedded in undergrowth. In the surrounding countryside, peasants use skulls as scarecrows: many wear hats, and one even wears a wig.'[25] Some of Wallis' senior officers suggested a hot pursuit, but he rightly feared another ambush: he did not want to face the Ottomans, now in the hills, again from positions designed to entrap him, as they had done so successfully at Grocka.

So a third campaigning season degenerated into a fearful torpor, only to be crowned by the ultimate misfortune. Belgrade, taken in 1717, had been turned into a fine town, but only for German speakers; it had been brilliantly fortified by the luckless Doxat. In the chaos of the campaign, it was surrendered by mistake to the Turks. The Grand Vizier, negotiating in his camp with Neipperg, managed to persuade him that the Ottomans were bound to capture the city, and, to save lives, it should be surrendered to him immediately. Neipperg eventually agreed, extracting a single concession. The fortifications built since the Treaty of Passarowitz, paid for by the Pope and Catholics throughout Europe, would be demolished so they did not fall into infidel hands. The vizier readily agreed, provided his janissaries should first occupy the gates and walls of the citadel.

After this agreement, which Neipperg had plenipotentiary power to negotiate, the court in Vienna redoubled its quest for scapegoats. Both men were recalled and imprisoned, while a court of enquiry eventually drew up forty-nine charges against Wallis and thirty-one against Neipperg. The latter, by signing away Belgrade, had committed a crime with 'no precedent in history'. Both men looked likely to suffer the same fate as Doxat, but they were saved by the unexpected death of Emperor Charles VI in October 1740. His twenty-three-year-old daughter, the Archduchess of Austria, Maria Theresa, wanted to bring an end to the whole catastrophe, so she closed down all the investigations and pardoned those who had been punished. She restored their ranks and privileges, and even made up their lost pay.

The credibility of the dynasty – and, indeed, its very existence – was now tied to its newly minted heroic tradition and to success on the battlefield. It could not risk a new humiliation in a contest with its weakest enemy. There was an absolute determination not to make the same mistakes again, neatly chronicled in Johann Georg Brown's five manuscript volumes in the Kriegsarchiv. So when war with the Ottomans resumed (for one final round) in 1788, the Emperor Joseph II took the field against *the infidel* in person, the first Habsburg ruler to do so since Charles V at Tunis in 1535. Unfortunately, it repeated many of the errors of the war half a century before and even improvised some new mistakes. In a sense this was inevitable, because the fundamental difficulties remained. There was not enough young talent in the army: too many officers who just yearned for the Maria Theresa Order for purblind heroics on the battlefield and not enough planners, strategists and engineers. The army sent south in 1788 was perhaps the best-equipped and best-trained that the Habsburgs had ever sent into action against the Turks, but men still died from disease in their thousands before they ever saw a Turk.

This was not how the war was presented to the public. It was carefully sanitised before it got to them. During the war, the hugely popular Viennese artist Johann Hieronymus Löschenkohl published a series of etchings, an illustrated variant on the well-known publication *The War, Day by Day* (*Kriegskalender*). In one series he satirised the ineptitude of the Turks, who were shown as completely incapable of absorbing the European art of war, and in another he showed the decay of the Ottoman army, which he suggested consisted mostly of decrepit greybeards. The artist made his name and fortune by catering to popular tastes, and this was plainly what the Viennese wanted to hear. Austrians had been brought up on the stories of triumph in the 'Age of Heroes', when Christian courage, enterprise and skill had always defeated the eastern hordes. Luckily, history redeemed the artist's fiction.

Although nothing went to plan, nonetheless there was still a triumphant coda: Field Marshal Laudon recaptured Belgrade in September 1789. He addressed his army before the bombardment almost as an echo of Prince Eugene: 'Here is the place we must be victorious or die. I will not withdraw.'[26] The city surrendered after the most powerful bombardment used in warfare up that point. Laudon's artillery commander, the Prince de Ligne, delivered a continuous barrage for sixteen hours, a bombardment of such power and ferocity that the Turks were stunned into submission. The Ottoman commander, Osman Pasha, wrote to Laudon, 'My Lord, your name is terrible to our people; your fire cleaves the rocks in two; your cannon shot carries away my soldiers in the streets. I must yield to the pleas of my despairing garrison.'[27] This final battle was fought exactly in Eugene's style: remorselessly, until victory. But it proved irrelevant. When peace was finally signed at the town of Sistova, on the Danube, near Nicopolis, Belgrade was handed back to Sultan Selim II as part of the settlement. Joseph II did not live to see peace, which was hastily concluded by his brother, the new Emperor Leopold II. Like their mother, Maria Theresa, he quickly distanced himself from the follies of the dead emperor.

12

Myth Displacing History

The 'Age of Heroes' was an invented tradition, started in the 1690s and initially manufactured by the heroes themselves.[1] Charles of Lorraine and Prince Eugene were the core figures; we can see ways in which their myth was created, how it spread and how it survived. Lorraine was a less potent role model than his younger protégé, but he created the prototype. Lorraine, when he began his Hungarian campaign, had a war artist (we do not know his name) in his entourage. In this he was simply following the Emperor Charles V, who had a painter, Jan Vermeulen, with him on the military expedition to Tunis in 1535; Vermeulen painted to order and the events of the siege he reproduced eventually became a magnificent series of tapestries, now in the Kunsthistorisches Museum in Vienna. In the following century Louis XIV of France had further developed tapestry as a powerful means of cultural propaganda through the establishment of the Gobelins factory; he presented the Emperor Leopold I with a magnificent set entitled *The Conquests of Alexander the Great* in 1699. The intention behind the prestigious gift was unsubtle.

We do not know if Charles of Lorraine had planned this style of cele-brating his achievement, but his dutiful son Leopold, Duke of Lorraine, commissioned and paid for a sequence of nineteen tapestries, made in Nancy between 1709 and 1718.[2] The tapestries present a panorama of his military career beginning with the liberation of Bratislava, captured by the Hungarian rebels and the Ottomans before the allied army gathered to save Vienna. Four were devoted to the salvation of Vienna, eight to the triumphant campaign that led to the capture of Buda. The last was of Lorraine returning Transylvania to the Emperor Leopold. These tapestries were based on images approved by the duke, and derived from the small group of paintings which he had personally commissioned. But there were significant changes between the tapestries and the oil paintings. While the paintings provided the raw materials, the results of observation, the tapestries were a much more elaborate visual narrative. The Duke of Lorraine was invariably put centre stage in every scene, even if he had not been there in the paintings.

The commander of an army might keep a war diary, and suitable information was sometimes passed from it to be written up and published by various authors and printers.[3] In effect, this was the official war history, from which any writer or artist departed at his peril. Authors and publishers avidly exploited the genre.[4] *The Duke of Lorraine's Political and Military Observations* was assembled from fragments left by Lorraine and the book was actually compiled by Chancellor Strattmann. His sole experience of the Reconquest had been the journeys in 1684 and 1686 that he had made to the War Council at Barkan and Buda, carrying the Emperor's personal message to his generals. The first hundred or so pages read differently from the last section, or the 'military observations'. Perhaps Strattmann gave it a more dignified air by adding something beyond the crude details of managing a campaign? It was translated and regularly reprinted; the last edition appeared seventy years after Lorraine's death, in 1760. When the first was published in 1699, there were no printed manuals for the Habsburg army: Lorraine's military observations filled the gap.

Lorraine and Prince Eugene often gave much the same advice. The older man sounded like the prince when he wrote: 'The character of a soldier is that he have courage as to dare to look danger in the face, one who is armed with resolution, either to vanquish or die.'[5] Lorraine's military observations ring true for all ages, not merely his own. A captain, he writes, should be stern when necessary, but never become a martinet: 'Small faults [in his men] need not be observed – but he must be fair to all.' Lorraine likens him to a father: 'a parent, who though he may have a secret tendency for some of his children above the rest, yet he wisely conceals it – encourages all and disobliges none'.[6] A field marshal, a role he knew well, 'is exposed to envy and censure, so it is a station of more honour and care than satisfaction'.[7]

Of the common enemy, the Turk, 'who loved to mangle, murder and wallow in the blood of innocents', he observed, 'Know an enemy before you despise him . . . He that feareth not an enemy knows not what war is.' Predictably, Lorraine, the impetuous cavalry general, who led his men from the front, really comes to life when he talks of war on horseback: 'By the horse it is that the country is ravaged and harassed by incursions. There is not an enterprise of hazard or difficulty where the horse is not concerned.' It is the man on horseback that brings fear to the enemy.[8] The man on horseback the Turks really came to fear was the tiny figure of Prince Eugene.

Charles V, Duke of Lorraine, died at the age of forty-seven. He did not have the opportunity enjoyed by Eugene, who lived into his seventies with both time and enormous riches to refine his image for posterity. Like Lorraine, Eugene employed an artist. His name was Jan Huchtenburg, who accompanied him on campaign in 1708 and 1709. Among other work, he finally produced a set of eleven paintings, all of identical size, that satisfied Eugene as being properly representative of his military career. They included both the great battles against the Turks and his victories in the west, during the War of the Spanish Succession.[9] Huchtenburg was painting for an imperious and determined client and these images must have represented Eugene's wishes.[10]

Books were Eugene's greatest passion; his entire library was bound in red leather with his crest in gold.[11] He decided to turn the artist's work into a book of high quality. He authorised the engraving of Huchtenburg's paintings for a work under his own patronage and under the authorship of a French writer, Jean Dumont. Together, Dumont and Huchtenburg produced a masterpiece of effective hagiography, and we know that Eugene himself had a hand in its construction, at least at the level of planning the structure, the choice of additional material, maps and plans for the most part. But since Eugene left no papers, the degree of his involvement will remain forever uncertain, like so much of his private life.[12]

Dumont and Huchtenburg prepared a text of 132 pages and then Huchtenburg engraved all the plates himself. The book was published as a folio volume in The Hague in 1725 under the title *The Battles won by the Most Serene Prince Eugene of Savoy over the Enemies of the Faith,*

*over the Enemies of the Emperor and the Empire, in Hungary, Italy, Germany.
And the Low Countries.*[13] It is a very strange publication and certainly
seemed so at the time. Prince Eugene also made sure that his civic
and cultural status was publicised. He commissioned the young artist
Salomon Kleiner to engrave plates of the Belvedere Palace and his
zoo. These are designs of the palace, but side by side with them is
the life lived within it: a hound running down the grand staircase as
a coach arrives in the *porte cochère*, grand and not so grand visitors
awaiting an audience and servants bustling about.[14] Occasionally the
prince himself can be seen. He is there, a slight figure wearing the
collar of the Golden Fleece, the highly prized order of chivalry personally awarded by the Habsburgs, receiving an Ottoman embassy – pashas
and janissaries – in the Audience Chamber.[15] He stands alone, rather
formally, in his library, or caught unawares in his private picture gallery.[16]

But absent or present, his personality is stamped on every print. The
prince made this place, Vienna's Versailles, grander by far than any of
the Emperor's palaces. He is, as Salomon Kleiner describes his patron
on the title page, 'The Incomparable Hero of our Century'.[17] Kleiner
proudly tells us that everything was *'levé et désigné'* within the palace.
In his delicious short volume of folio images of the Prince's menagerie
– the Prince loved his animals – he subtly suggests in his engravings
that, as the human society passed through the Belvedere, so, too, the
whole of nature has been brought within Eugene's orbit, from parrots,
apes and monkeys, through wildcats and African foxes, a stern-looking
lion and stalwart bison, eagles from Sicily, India and Hungary, to a
remarkable collection of sheep and goats. All are displayed roaming
among or clambering over the sculptures and plants that filled the
gardens of the Belvedere. These volumes were published in Augsburg
in 1731–4, and were reprinted after his death. Eugene even intended that
Huchtenburg's engravings should be used to create a set of tapestries,
like the ten Victory tapestries woven for the Duke of Marlborough and
still hanging on the walls of Blenheim Palace. For some unknown reason,
Eugene's victories were never immortalised in this fashion.

Through Dumont and Huchtenburg's work, the image of Prince
Eugene was repackaged, translated and widely disseminated around
Europe through the eighteenth and nineteenth centuries. There were
editions in French, English and German, special editions which
embraced other great European commanders. A partner, Rousset, went

on publishing new editions after the death of Dumont, and ensured that Eugene became a multipurpose European hero. In the Habsburg lands, from the eighteenth to the twentieth century he remained the great national hero, the unifying emblem of the nation.

The 'Age of Heroes' cast a powerful influence over the whole subsequent history of the Habsburg empire. It exalted heroism, the spirit of attack, over the more sober and boring military arts; Prince Eugene's indifferent generalship in the War of the Polish Succession (1733–8) was put down to old age and ill health. But he was still, as the song went, 'The Noble Knight', the embodiment of dash and heroism. When the Habsburg empire was attacked by Prussia in 1740, and was overwhelmed by the genius of Frederick II and his extraordinary military machine, the diagnosis at every level of society was that the Habsburg empire needed new heroes, a new Eugene.

This yearning for heroism was officially sanctioned when, in 1757, Maria Theresa, Archduchess of Austria, Queen of Hungary, ordered the creation of a new order of military chivalry, to commemorate the unexpected Austrian victory at Kolin over the invading Prussians, explicitly to promote the Austrian tradition of courage exemplified in the 'Age of Heroes'.[18] The victor at Kolin had been Field Marshal Leopold von Daun, who epitomised the Austrian tradition of duty and service. Three generations of Dauns had served successively as field marshals in the service of the Habsburgs; he had trounced the hitherto invincible Frederick II, Austria's new mortal enemy, redeeming a string of Habsburg defeats. Daun became the first Grand Cross of the Order of Maria Theresa. Only a holder of the Habsburgs' personal Order of the Golden Fleece ranked higher in honour. The Military Order of Maria Theresa, designed to reward men of exceptional daring, was given only for acts of conspicuous heroism. Winning the Order transformed an officer's life and future prospects, opening the door into higher echelons of Austrian society. It placed so great a premium on heroism that young officers thought of little else.[19]

But whom should they emulate? In 1809, at the time that Napoleon threatened the very existence of the Austrian empire, the people of the empire were reminded of their national hero. *The Life of Prince Eugene: from his Own Manuscript* became a bestseller when it was first published in 1809–10. It had a very strange history. Eugene had left no memoirs, no personal letters, no details at all about his personal life.

His friends and admirers proved impossibly taciturn and died with the prince's secrets unrevealed. All of which proved a great challenge to the Habsburg Field Marshal Charles-Joseph, Prince de Ligne, who worshipped Eugene, as soldier and hero. He decided to write the auto-biography that Eugene had so tiresomely neglected to provide. The Prince's short Life – less than a hundred pages – was first published in Weimar in 1809. The mystery of its rediscovery was intriguing but no one initially questioned its authenticity.

The book was immensely successful, printed in Germany, France, in England in both French and English versions, and in the United States, going through many impressions. Suddenly, Prince Eugene was seen afresh, as a masterful, irreverent, clever and recklessly brave man. But why had de Ligne written it? He had idolised Eugene, he said, since he was a small boy. His own military career had ended – he was seventy-four when *The Life* was published. In the last decade of his life de Ligne had watched the Austrian army stumble from one defeat to another, and saw the hard-won lessons of the 'noble knight' being ignored or forgotten, in the old Austrian tradition of 'muddling through'. So he brought his hero back to life. The Prince of Savoy became like one of the Sleeping Heroes of German mythology, Charle-magne and Frederick Barbarossa, waiting patiently century after century to save the nation in its hour of need. De Ligne reawakened his dead hero, to save the Habsburgs.[20].

We can follow the twists and turns of Eugene's emblematic iden-tity down the centuries. In the eighteenth and the nineteenth century, he was a loyal Habsburg, an imperial patriot. Ultimately he became a monument. In 1878, the empty space between the Leopoldine wing of the Hofburg – so badly battered by Ottoman fire during the siege – and the new Ringstrasse atop the old fortifications was designated by the Emperor Franz Joseph I as the Heldenplatz, Heroes Square. It was designed around two huge bronze equestrian statues that had already been in store for a decade. Around the plinth upon which Eugene controls his plunging stallion are inscribed the names of his victories. They are not arranged in a strictly chronological order. Place of honour on the front of the plinth is given to victories over the Turks, not to his achievements in the wars against France.[21] Eugene as the Prince of Victory also served as a splendid emblem for Austro-fascists in the early 1930s and was then expropriated by the Nazis after 1938. He survived this enslavement in the service of malign ideals, and in the post-war *Book of Austria* of 1948 he was the universal hero for a *new* Austria:[22]

> And at last it was there. Victory! If ever in the world's history had there been a true victory, then this was it. It cannot be dismissed with mere accounts of the expeditions of Prince Eugen of Savoy, of the Peace Treaties of Karlowitz (1699) and Passarowitz (1718) which made Austria a great western power extending far into the Balkans.[23]

The link was now to the benign Austrian mission, a 'sweet miracle', not 'the sorrow and echoes of wars' but what the people longed for:

> Their dream was of hearts and minds flung open for the fullness of life, the ready and joyous acceptance of all things good, lovely and strong, – yes, and of contrasting elements from East and West, North and South, making up the harmony of contrasts.

Did anyone take this seriously? By the 1950s, primary school children in Austria were having great fun making up a ribald version of the old and famous song about Prinz Eugen:

> *Prinz Eugenius, der edle Ritter*
> *sitzt am scherbm und spielt die Zither . . .*

This roughly translates as:

> Prince Eugene, the noble knight,
> sat on the potty and played the zither.

That's the kind of thing that children do everywhere; part of the way they begin to use language. But it might just be that they were sick of hearing about him and his exemplary character. We have no way of knowing.

★   ★   ★

Prince Eugene died in 1736 after an evening playing cards with the dark-eyed beauty Countess Batthyany, his muse. He was in his seventy-third year. Even his death became mythologised: the story spread that on the same morning he was found dead in bed the great lion in his menagerie was also discovered dead in its den. The Emperor Charles VI peevishly recorded in his diary, 'Now, see, everything will be better organised'; but after the disasters of the Turkish war in 1739, he changed his tune: 'Has then our lucky star completely disappeared with Eugene?'[24] Within a few years the prince's niece, the last surviving heir, whom he had never met, sold off the palaces, the country estates, the art collection, the books bound in red morocco of a man who had become one of the wealthiest in Europe. For a young refugee who arrived in Vienna with empty pockets, who had depended on the charity of friends and relatives, it was a story of extraordinary success. But he left nothing behind him except a well-earned reputation and a proliferating mythology. By contrast, his English partner in the wars against France, John Churchill, Duke of Marlborough, also ended his days as a wealthy landowner, in his great house at Blenheim, near Oxford, but established a dynasty, which still lives in a grand style in the palace that he built.

So Prince Eugene's possessions have passed into other hands. His Winter Palace in the old city is now occupied by clerks and bureaucrats. The Belvedere is a museum, Schlosshof and his other country retreats have been neglected. Yet we can still gain an impression of that world through the eyes of the Venetian artist Bernardo Bellotto, better known as Canaletto. He painted the city panorama from the prince's Belvedere; he painted the country palace of Schlosshof lyrically, from its grand façade to its long garden avenues. Those canvasses now reveal an illusion, of deceiving and constraining the eye through the painterly arts, like those grandiose churches where the soaring marble columns are in reality nothing more permanent than painted plaster. Eugene worked hard to create his own posterity. Had he married and created his own dynasty, they would have had an extraordinary patrimony, like the Dukes of Marlborough. Had his brothers been more fecund, and less frail, his line could have continued.

Instead, rather like Alexander the Great, the prince became a heroic myth. A *New York Times* headline written in the last week of the First World War, as the Habsburg empire crumbled, summed it up with tombstone brevity: ***AUSTRIA'S WARS IN 300 YEARS***. *Defeated except when Prince Eugene of Savoy commanded.*[25] Myths like Eugene's are founded on reality, but memories of that reality erode and decay over time. The myths described here – the 'Age of Heroes', the battle for

Europe and the fear of the Turk – all began with real triumphs and real fears. But over time that history has dwindled to nothing while the myths and legends have survived and flourished.[26]

The long history of conflict described in these pages had ended with all the traditional formalities: Ottoman and Habsburg negotiators made peace on 4 August 1791, in the sweltering torpor of the Danube port town of Sistova. Their decision was quickly ratified in Istanbul and in Vienna. Sistova was a reprise of all the peace settlements of the previous ninety years: at Karlowitz in 1699, at Passarowitz in 1718 and at Belgrade in 1739. The first two were hailed by contemporaries (and almost universally by subsequent historians) as conclusive evidence of the final and irrevocable collapse of the Ottomans. We should be more questioning: diplomacy, treaties and political settlements provide convenient markers, but at best they are only a snapshot of the state of play, advantage or disadvantage, at a particular moment.

So, 'the Turkish Wars' as contemporaries then called them, ended. 'After that, nothing happened' – this was merely a convenient historical assumption that one period of the past was over and a new one had begun. In reality, things went on, but not in the same way as before.[27] They had reached their *terminus ad quem*, the definitive final point, and history speedily moved on to something more interesting and important. Just a year after the negotiators thankfully escaped from the torrid humidity of the Danube, something had happened so that, in Goethe's words, 'from this day forth, commences a new era in the world's history'. On 19 September 1792, the incomparable Prussian army (the most powerful element of a European coalition against the French Revolution) was marching from the Rhine to reverse the events of 1789. The Prussian regiments had brushed aside the feeble attempts of the Revolutionary government to oppose their advance; the frontier fortresses of Verdun and Longwy rapidly surrendered so that only a makeshift army stood between the best-trained infantry in Europe and Paris. Close to the village of Valmy on the edge of the Argonne mountains and the deep woodland of northwestern France, the mass of French soldiers were drawn up on rising ground. With them were thirty-four field guns, expertly handled by trained artillerymen: it was the gunners' carefully directed rapid fire that smashed the measured advance of the Prussians.

After suffering only 184 casualities to his 35,000 strong force, the

Prussian commander, the Duke of Brunswick, withdrew his men and marched away. This was not a great battle, but the 'cannonade of Valmy' on 20 September stopped the march on Paris, saved the Revolution and made possible the Napoleonic transformation of Europe, including the abolition of the Holy Roman Empire and the occupation of Vienna by his armies. In 1809 the Austrian Emperor, Francis I, had to yield his sister in marriage to the French ogre; as the Prince de Ligne crudely but realistically put it: 'Better that an archduchess should be *foutue* [fucked] than the monarchy.'[28]

When Napoleon had finally been defeated in 1815 and the old order had been 'restored', it was plain that the restoration could not simply put the clock back: too much had altered irrevocably. The fantasy of 'restoration' was perfectly summed up in a small gouache by an artist from Dessau named Heinrich Olivier. The dominating figure of the restoration was the Russian Czar, Alexander I, who had decreed a 'Holy Alliance' of Russia, Austria and Prussia against godless revolution. Olivier set his painting in an imaginary Gothic cathedral, and depicted the three rulers as paladins of virtue, crusader knights. All were clad from head to foot in glimmering plate armour; in the centre stood Francis I of Austria, gilded from head to toe, where they were merely silvered. The Holy Roman Empire had been abolished by Napoleon in 1806 so Francis no longer had his ancient and prized title. The King of Prussia and the Czar stood on either side of the Emperor, clasping him fraternally by the hand. But he was much smaller than these two strapping rulers and their hearty handshakes make him look like a puppet held between them. Intentionally or not, this image represented the political reality of the new age.

In 1789, the Habsburgs had stood in the first rank of European states; in 1815 they remained there primarily as a necessary symbol of traditionalist solidarity. The struggle with Napoleonic France had shifted the balance of power among the leading European powers: the dominant forces in 1815 were Russia, Prussia, and Britain, as the world power. France was temporarily eclipsed but would recover; the also-rans included Spain and some of the larger German states. The Habsburg monarchy, seemingly at its apogee, as the host of Europe's rulers at the (ruinously expensive) Congress of Vienna, was in reality dwindling in significance. Outside the framework of Europe was the Ottoman empire, also in reduced circumstances.

The Habsburgs and the Ottomans were soon fixed in an ambiguous position, below the major powers but above the also-rans. They had effectively been relegated: both aspired to rise again in status, but it was a futile hope. These old hereditary enemies began to discover mutual interests, with an unspoken commonality that began to unite them. In 1828, the pragmatic Austrian chancellor Metternich could write with every indication of sincerity: 'We look on the Ottoman Empire as the best of our neighbours: since she is scrupulously true to her word, we regard contact with her as equivalent to contact with a natural frontier which never claims our attention or dissipates our energies.'[29] What he avoided saying was that they both shared a border with the same truculent and aggressive neighbour. Russia may have been the solid buttress of Metternichean autocracy, but it was also a difficult and overbearing partner. By comparison, Austria had no fears of the Ottomans on their southern frontier.

This rebalancing was part of the process that Christopher Bayly has described as 'Passages from the Old Regimes to Modernity'.[30] In fact, neither the Ottoman nor the Habsburg dynasties would ever fully make the passage to modernity, although many of their subjects did so enthusiastically. The dynasts saw no reason to change. Emperor Franz Joseph I of Austria, who came to the throne in 1848 and lived until 1916, described himself with pride as 'the last European monarch of the Old School'. Sultan Abdul Hamid II, the last Ottoman autocrat, partially rebuilt the internal authority of the Ottoman dynasty by emphasising its ancient and traditional role as the guardian of Islam. Both the Habsburg monarchy and the Ottoman empire turned their attention inwards. France, Britain, Germany and Russia could anticipate a grand imperial future; the two second-rank European states had only one good option: making the forlorn grandeur of their past the central principle of their present and future status.

They painstakingly created a new political culture based on commemoration, an innovation for which there was no existing model. In the past both Habsburgs and Ottomans had evolved elaborate and often deliberately arcane ceremonials. Instinctively, they now began to celebrate and commemorate the triumphs of the past for public consumption. In the Austrian case, the 'Age of Heroes' had perhaps shown the way forward, but from the second half of the nineteenth century these two antique dynasties independently invented the concept of *the heritage* roughly a century before it was rediscovered in Europe during the 1970s. Both Habsburgs and Ottomans consciously edited and remade their history, putting together a selective version of their past. Today, we might call it articulating the brand image. None of the mythological edifices they created could stand up to serious historical scrutiny, but this was not the point. They successfully enhanced the mystique and popular appeal of the dynasty and for nearly seven decades their programmes functioned well as cultural and political ideologies. These *heritage* campaigns effectively defined what it meant to be a loyal (*kaisertreu*) Habsburg subject or a loyal Ottoman citizen.

If this language sounds anachronistic, so, too, were these concepts that were well in advance of their time.[31] The Habsburgs and Ottomans created a system that could rewrite reality and even triumph over humiliation. The Habsburgs, once the leading power in Germany, excluded entirely from the new German empire after 1870, wrote themselves a new role, as the visionary creators of a moral empire of service. A few years later the Ottoman sultan, after suffering the humiliation in 1878 of a victorious Russian army camped in sight of Istanbul, began to turn his attention to his dominions in the Near East – Anatolia, the Levant and the Arabian peninsula. At the same time, the Habsburgs pioneered the idea of a multinational empire, served by the ceaseless and dutiful diligence of the Emperor Franz Joseph I to his peoples. The Ottomans exalted the service of the sultan to his subjects, to God and to the Muslim community. Both Habsburgs and Ottomans found symbolic ways to make these abstract concepts real to their publics: the state's legitimacy was invested in the public personality of the ruler, unlike other European states which increasingly focused upon the institution of monarchical or republican virtue. It was a risky strategy, because it would not last for ever. The 'good old Emperor' would at some point weaken and die, or just lose his appeal.

Like the most successful advertising, the ideas underpinning these two empires proved more durable than the products they promoted. They often used similar approaches, allowing for the very different populations that they served, and they also tried (with less success) to refine the same ideas for international consumption. They spent considerable state funds to sustain their creation. The largest amounts were spent on flagship projects but they also invested directly in information and propaganda. The Habsburgs often subsidised or licensed commercial projects in the form of memorabilia, ornaments and the like. They centred on the image and character of the self-sacrificing leader, Franz Joseph I, who was made highly visible and the object of state-sponsored publicity material and patriotic shows. The Ottomans, who could not use visual images, which were controversial within a Muslim state, created symbolic objects that represented the sultan's care for his people.³² So when a coffee-shop proprietor in the town of Ankara loyally displayed a portrait of Sultan Abdul Hamid II on its wall (the monarch's portrait was *de rigueur* in even the tiniest hamlet in Austria-Hungary), the report went all the way up to the sultan himself. Quickly, by his order, an embroidered banner was produced bearing only the calligraphic slogan 'Long Live the Sultan' and sent to the shopkeeper; these religiously inoffensive but thoroughly patriotic objects began to appear everywhere in the empire.

This incident in Ankara suggests how much attention was devoted to finding the most appropriate means of influence and persuasion. In Austria, patriotism was expressed by showing the Emperor's (and the immensely popular Empress Elisabeth's) image, at every level from the public to the domestic: public memorials and statues, postcards, porcelain busts for the drawing room, posters and postcards. But the state also produced objects that allowed the people to affirm their participation in the 'loyalty project'. Most substantial was a vast encyclo-paedia in twenty-four volumes, running to more than ten thousand pages, with the title of *The Austro-Hungarian Monarchy in Word and Images* (*Die österreichisch-ungarische Monarchie in Wort und Bild*). The heir to the throne, Crown Prince Rudolf, was behind the project, writing in 1884 to his father, the Emperor, that: 'The study of the peoples living within the boundaries of this empire does not only present a highly important sphere of activity for scholars, but is also of partial use in the development of united patriotism. By the growing recognition of the qualities and characteristics of the single ethno-graphic groups and their mutual and material dependence, *that feeling of solidarity which is to unite all the peoples of the fatherland must be strengthened* [my italics].'³³ The volumes were published in monthly parts between 1885 and 1902 so that even those with quite modest incomes could afford to subscribe. This was more than a normal publishing venture: it was an act of state. 'The editors clearly had a larger agenda of showing cultural plurality as the essence of the

Habsburg monarchy, in line with the motto *Viribus unitis* (With United Strength).' But Ákos Moravánszky made a further important point: 'Utopias are necessary as testing grounds for ideas that will guide future action. The twenty-four volumes of the *Kronprinzenwerk* can therefore be seen as the foundation stones of the utopia of Central Europe, a model that is not based on the modern nation-state principle but that allows multi-ethnicity in the framework of a monarchy legitimized by history.'[34]

'With United Strength' was the Emperor's personal motto, assumed after his accession to the throne in 1848. It was the perfect motif for the multi-ethnic monarchy. In 1898, for his Golden Jubilee celebration (an event shadowed by the murder of his wife, the Empress Elisabeth) his younger daughter, Archduchess Marie Valerie, sponsored a magnificent commemorative volume called *With United Strength: The Book of the Emperor Franz Joseph I* (*Viribus Unitis: das Buch vom Kaiser*). It neatly bridged the gap between the solid, traditional monarchy symbolised by the old Emperor and the spirit of the new age. It showed Franz Joseph I surrounded not just by his court and officials, but by a people happy to be ruled by the 'good old Emperor' – peasants, city dwellers, and all the different nationalities.[35] In one engraving the Emperor greets his young grandchildren, each of them dressed in the traditional costume of a different region. By contrast, the title page was peopled with scantily clad young women, androgynous young men, lithe putti, all in the Secession style, an art form that the Emperor personally found degenerate and appalling.[36] But officially he had to accept it as part of his symbolic role as Father of the Nation.

There were other projects on a very large scale, Ottoman and Habsburg. Both symbolised the dynasties' new sense of mission in a world that they found increasingly alien. The first project (Ottoman) was a desert railway and the second (Habsburg) fabricated a public face of social unity. First, the railway. Abdul Hamid II was by right the custodian of the Muslim Holy Places of Mecca and Medina. Every year he sent a new *mahmal* – the embroidered covering for the Holy Kaaba in Mecca; he was the guardian of the annual pilgrimage as the caliph of all true Muslims. These pilgrims came from all over the Muslim world, many by sea to Jiddah on the Red Sea. But the vast majority converged on Damascus, then travelled in camel caravans towards Medina in the Hijaz. The journey took at least three weeks, and the pilgrim was often at risk from bandits or local tribesmen. The idea of building a railway from Damascus to Mecca had first been mooted in 1864 but had come to nothing. On 1 September 1900, on the twenty-fifth anniversary of his accession, the sultan launched the project to construct a Hamidye Hijaz railway, bearing the Sultan's name, to signify it was his personal project, and to which he subscribed handsomely.[37] But the bulk of the cost was supported by individual contributions from pious Muslims everywhere. Ottoman state officials and army officers were expected to give a percentage of their salaries, while businesses and individuals were also tithed. The task of construction, undertaken by Turkish engineers and the Ottoman army, took eight years to complete as far as Medina. It was to be built and run by Muslims, a shining example of the power of the Islamic community, which owed nothing to the West. It was a potent symbol of the caliph, Sultan Abdul Hamid II's, determination to support and defend the 'True Believers'. The railway opened in 1908, and was promoted throughout the Islamic world as the caliph working on behalf of the Islamic community. The railway also served a valuable military function, allowing the Ottoman army to reinforce its garrisons in Arabia very rapidly. Unfortunately, it came too late: a year after it opened, Abdul Hamid II was deposed by the Ottoman army. The railway line itself was largely destroyed during the Arab Revolt of 1916, and it has never been restored to full operation.

The second project, the Austro-Hungarian monarchy gaining its force through cultural diversity, 'With United Strength', embodied the last and final phase of the old competitive struggle between the Habsburgs and Ottomans; Andre Gingrich's theory of *Frontier Orientalism* provides the most convincing explanation for what actually happened in the last quarter of the nineteenth century and in the early years of the twentieth century. In effect, the Habsburgs transformed the old antagonism into a kind of philanthropic enterprise.[38] Frontier Orientalism developed out of Edward Said's *Orientalism*, first published in 1980, but Gingrich quickly moved beyond it. Frontier Orientalism was not the rigid and immovable structure which Said described as typical of British and French imperialism. It was much more adaptable. In brief, he described a process whereby the 'bad' Muslim who had attacked the frontiers in earlier times was transformed into a 'good' Muslim. Crushing that rival was the 'decisive precondition' for the rise of the Habsburg's *benign* colonial enterprise in Bosnia and Herzegovina.[39]

Gingrich shows how through the centuries the Habsburgs consistently legitimised their rule by reconfiguring their historic destiny relative to the Ottomans. In the fifteenth century they had constructed an imaginary continuity between Charlemagne's founding of the Holy Roman Empire in the year 1000, uniting and saving Christendom, with their own defence of Europe in the sixteenth and seventieth centuries.

> By constructing such a historical continuity, the Habsburg expansion of early modernity, across half of the globe in the 17th century, already could be portrayed as the fulfilment of a historical mission by the courts in Madrid and Vienna . . . This Habsburg construction of continuity, between themselves and Charlemagne – as a precursor and as another Germanic 'ruler of Europe' – of course had its own contemporary purposes, rooted in European and world politics of the 16th and 17th centuries. That first construction, however, was re-invented a second time in the late 19th century, with the decaying empire's re-orientation towards south-eastern Europe. The empire's Balkan 'frontier' became the new referent for a re-invented continuity of an eastern outpost for Catholic Christianity, where 'tamed' Muslims were now loyal guardians against the new 'Slavic danger'.[40]

The Habsburgs always claimed that nothing important ever changed, but in fact they were very innovative. A political 'compromise' in 1867, and the creation of the Dual Monarchy – Austria-Hungary with complete equality between its two constituent elements – had resolved the Hungarian problem; but it rapidly generated another. The Slav populations of the Austro-Hungarian state– Czechs and Slovaks in the west, Croats and Serbs in the south – began to clamour for equal rights with their German and Hungarian compatriots. Behind them stood Russia, the immensely powerful patron of all the Slavs: the Czar was now more threatening than the sultan.

The fear of the Turks had remained powerful over a considerable time, but it was never monolithic. Even during the heyday of this great fear there were Austrians who regarded the Ottomans as worthy and estimable opponents. Already in the seventeenth century, long before the craze for everything Turkish, both men and women had themselves painted in Ottoman costume, and indulged themselves in oriental fantasies. During the eighteenth-century Enlightenment this attitude of ambivalence spread through much of Europe. More and more 'the Turk' began to illustrate human fallibility in a universal rather than in a uniquely wicked *Muslim* fashion. There was also a wry kind of irony. Voltaire's fictional hero Scarmentado, 'a citizen of Candia', recounted the 'comical anecdotes' of his Travels. In France he was offered human flesh for breakfast; in England pious Catholics were blowing up Parliament; in Holland he watched the people cutting off the head of the Prime Minister. 'Touched with pity at this affecting scene, I asked what his crime was, and whether he had betrayed the state?'

'He has done much worse,' replied a preacher in a black cloak; 'he believed that men may be saved by good works as well as by faith. You must be sensible,' adds he, 'that if such opinions were to gain ground, a republic could not subsist; and that there must be severe laws to suppress such scandalous and horrid blasphemies.'

Scarmentado suffered the attentions of the Inquisition in Spain and then set off for Turkey. '"These Turks", said I to my companions, "are a set of miscreants that have not been baptized, and therefore will be more cruel than the reverend fathers the inquisitors. Let us observe a profound silence while we are among the Mahometans.' In Constantinople, unable to attend church, he resolved:

In order to console myself for this loss, I frequently visited a very handsome Circassian. She was the most entertaining lady I ever knew in a private conversation, and the most devout at the mosque. One evening she received me with tenderness and sweetly cried, 'Alla, Illa, Alla.'

These are the sacramental words of the Turks. I imagined they were the expressions of love, and therefore cried in my turn and with a very tender accent, 'Alla, Illa, Alla.'

'Ah!' said she, 'God be praised, thou art then a Turk?'

I told her that I was blessing God for having given me so much enjoyment, and that I thought myself extremely happy. In the morning the Imam came to enrol me among the circumcised, and as I made some objection to the initiation, the cadi of that district, a man of

great loyalty, proposed to have me impaled. I preserved my freedom
by paying a thousand sequins, and then fled directly into Persia, resolved
for the future never to hear Greek or Latin mass, nor to cry "Alla, Illa,
Alla," in a love encounter.'[41]

Voltaire's message was simple: the Turks were no worse than the rest
of humanity. Jonathan Israel makes 'Rethinking Islam' – a 'dissident
complex of ideas about Islam' – a central principle of Enlightenment.[42]

By the 1820s the study of the East in Vienna, which had begun in
1753 with the Empress Maria Theresa's foundation of the Imperial
Oriental Academy for translators, was beginning to influence Austrian
attitudes towards the East.[43] The young Joseph Hammer entered the
Academy in 1788, and made his name with his studies of the Orient.
His career advanced rapidly, with his books published under the
name of Joseph von Hammer-Purgstall, in German and in several
foreign languages. Their influence was profound, and marked a slow
transition in perception: the Ottomans and the East were no longer
a religious abomination but were becoming a historical and cultural
phenomenon worthy of study and understanding.[44]

A spirit of collaboration emerged as the Ottoman empire began to
move purposefully in the direction of the West. The alliance between
France, Britain, the Kingdom of Piedmont in Italy and the Ottoman
empire in the Crimean War against Russia between 1853 and 1856
ended with the Treaty of Paris, in which the Turks were recognised
for the first time as part of the European state system. From that
point onwards, the Ottomans worked purposefully to participate in
international events. In 1863 the Ottoman government held a General
Exposition in Istanbul (on the model of the 1851 Great Exhibition in
London, in which Turkey had participated). It took place in the heart
of the city on the ancient Hippodrome, in front of the mosque of
Aya Sofia. In an annex to the main hall, which displayed the Turkish
products, foreign exhibitors proffered their wares, including the Josef
Werndl arms factory in Steyr. The Ottomans participated in almost
every major international fair thereafter.

In 1873 Vienna put on an International Exposition following the
style of the Paris Universal Exhibition in 1867. The 'eastern' displays
from Egypt, Persia and the Ottoman empire were an outstanding
popular success, particularly the Turkish Pavilion and the Turkish

Coffee House. The Berlin *Illustrierte Zeitung* showed a throng of Austrians mingling amiably with Turks in traditional costume. Three of the exhibits on which the Ottoman government lavished the greatest care were books: one a large volume of photographs of traditional Turkish dress, showing men, women, and children, all presented as a scientific depiction of Ottoman social life; another surveyed Ottoman architecture, and a third was on sights around the Bosporus. This was in keeping with the exhibition's objective that Vienna should be the meeting point of East and West. Arthur von Scala, the celebrated director of the Austrian Museum of Art and Industry, later wrote, 'A new world has been opened to the eyes of the majority of visitors ... They have found irresistible the view that the rich treasures that the East has sent to Vienna ... offer an inexhaustible source of knowledge, a starting point to establish new and prosperous contacts in all direction.'[45] With all these connections – from Hammer-Purgstall and the Oriental Academy, to a network of business and trading links – a kind of synthesis emerged. Austria-Hungary and the East could become natural economic and cultural partners. Jacob von Falke, who had written of the art industry of the future after the Paris exhibition, described the effect of the 1873 Exposition in Vienna: 'It is the Orient which is important to cure the degenerated feeling for colours ... it is the East that will change our taste for colour and will reform the carpets, tapestries and ceramics that we produce.'[46] And not just the applied arts: Gustav Klimt entered the Vienna School of Art in 1876 and throughout his long career his painting showed a distinctly 'Eastern' enchantment with colour and surface, just as Falke had predicted.

This cultural and political connection gradually developed a more political turn as a means to counteract Russian power and influence. Perhaps Austria-Hungary could take over the economic and social transformation of the backward European provinces of Turkey-in-Europe, because of this long connection, previously hostile but now benign. By this means the Habsburgs could fulfil their civilising mission, with the eager collaboration of their former enemies. It was the doctrine of 'my enemy's enemy is my friend'. The 'bad' Muslim using Gingrich's terms, was on the way to being transformed into the 'good' Muslim. Quite suddenly this strategic aspiration became a political reality. In 1878, Austro-Hungarian diplomacy achieved its greatest triumph. The Congress of Berlin was charged with resolving the political turmoil resulting from the Russo–Turkish war of 1877–8, which had caused a collapse of the Ottoman empire in Europe. After some deft negotiation the treaty terms allowed Austria-Hungary to occupy and administer Bosnia, Herzegovina and a strategic strip of land called the Sanjak of Novipazar in perpetuity, although sovereignty formally remained with the Ottoman empire.[47]

Instantly, the old yearnings for eastern hegemony revived, and a force was sent south to take possession of this unexpected windfall. Count Andrassy, the Austro-Hungarian Foreign Minister who had negotiated the transfer, said it could be occupied by two squadrons of hussars and a mounted band. He was wrong. It took four years and, by the end of the occupation, the Habsburg army had suffered over five thousand casualties, and still the countryside was full of armed guerrillas. Before the insurrection broke out, the French consul in Sarajevo had been of the opinion that the rebels 'will probably disperse at the first shot fired from an Austrian cannon'. He was also wrong. Austrian rule was eventually imposed at a huge cost in money and many lives, on both sides. Thereafter, over the next three decades, a vast programme of modernisation was put in motion – and Bosnia-Herzegovina became a flagship for the 'benign' consequences of Austro-Hungarian modernity. In time, the Bosnian and Herzegovinian recruits to the imperial army became famed as the bravest and most resolute soldiers, the incomparable *Bosniaken*, whose jaunty military march 'Die Bosniaken kommen' was a special favourite with the citizens of the Austrian cities. Many communities experienced the quiet, well-behaved and sober Muslim infantry stationed in their midst.[48] One advantage was that the smart soldiers in their red fezzes, closely controlled by military imams and under strict discipline, did not get the citizens' daughters or maidservants pregnant, which is more than could be said for the rest of the Emperor's soldiery.

In their miniature Balkan empire Habsburgs quickly learned the tricks of colonisation. The old ideology of conversion was replaced in Bosnia by a more dispassionate treatment of religious minorities than anywhere else in the Austro-Hungarian monarchy. The trustworthiness of the Muslim Bosnian soldiers in the First World War – the 2nd *Bosniaken* won more medals for bravery than any other unit – further dissipated the old terrors. Vienna's rule over Bosnia finally generated 'the good Muslim, "our" unwavering ally in difficult times'.

This last phase in the long and shifting history, ending with Austria-Hungary's defeat in 1918, completes – or almost completes – the course of Austrian Frontier Orientalism'.[49] Where did it all end? Where it had begun: on the battlefield. The Austrian military became obsessed with the imminent possibility of military catastrophe, and planned for a pre-emptive strike.[50] The fanciful Austrian polycultural approach, 'With United Strength', ended up, as Norman Stone acutely observed, 'as a system of institutionalised escapism, and the chief benefit it conferred upon its subjects was to exempt them from reality'.[51] When the First World War started on 4 August 1914, it was the result of the murder of the heir to the Habsburg monarchy in Sarajevo, shot by a Bosnian nationalist, inspired by the Serb fantasies of history, on the anniversary of the defeat at Kosovo Polje in 1389, where the Battle for Europe had started. The Austrian revenge attack on Serbia was a shambles.[52] The war was a terminal collision between ancient mythologies and current political realities. The line-up on one side was Germany, Austria-Hungary and the Ottoman empire; on the other, Russia, France and Britain, three world imperial powers. The four years of conflict destroyed the German, Austrian, Ottoman and Russian empires, leaving the world to the three democracies: Britain, France and the United States of America. There were many paradoxes that emerged from the cataclysm, but none more unlikely than the emergence of a strong Turkey from the shards of the Ottoman empire, led by a war hero, General Mustafa Kemal, later to be known as *Ataturk*, or Father of the Turks. His portrait is still in every office and school to this day, just as the image of the good old Emperor Franz Joseph I once adorned the buildings of the Austro-Hungarian Monarchy.

Coda

In the 1990s the Haitian social anthropologist Michel-Rolph Trouillot wrote a persuasive (and provocative) book about how history is made. He called it *Silencing the Past*. Early on, he described his intention: 'The book is about history and power. It deals with the many ways in which the production of historical narratives involves the uneven contribution of competing groups and individuals who have unequal access to the means of such production. The forces I will expose are less visible than gunfire, class property, or political crusades. I want to argue they are no less powerful.'

Although in my book there has been a great deal of gunfire (and nothing about either class or property), it is really about what Trouillot describes: two competing groups with unequal access to the means of producing history. In that respect the Habsburgs (and the other western nations involved in the struggle) held the best cards. I have suggested that this history needs to be reconsidered.

During this long struggle between the Ottomans and Habsburgs something unusual happened, which has gone unremarked. For centuries they were the bitterest of enemies. Then they stopped being enemies, even becoming unlikely allies from 1914 to 1918. After that war, commercial ties continued to grow, and in the 1950s Turks began to arrive in Austria as guest workers, as they did in much larger numbers in West Germany. They were not well treated, but virtually no one regarded them as a threat. Now, the west is gripped by fear, and a fresh Battle for Europe promoted as a direct continuation of the old Battle for Europe.

The contrast between what actually happened and these carefully fabricated myths is startling. Once more the Siege of Vienna in 1683 is becoming an inspirational metaphor of perpetual struggle, of West versus East, of Muslim versus Christian, just as it was hundreds of years ago. Once more the event is serving a polemical purpose. Now it buttresses the idea that a new Battle for Europe is being fought. The Turks of the twenty-first century must not be allowed to enter the European Union because this will destroy Christendom. They would succeed where their Ottoman predecessors had failed in 1683.

Those holding these views include very prominent men, among them a former Commissioner of the European Union, Frits Bolkestein, who said very publicly that if Turkey entered the EU, then 'the liberation of Vienna in 1683 would have been in vain'.[1] Cardinal Joseph Ratzinger, later Pope Benedict XVI, also looked to history: 'The roots that have formed Europe, that have permitted the formation of this continent, are those of Christianity. Turkey has always represented another continent, in permanent contrast with Europe. There were the wars against the Byzantine Empire, the fall of Constantinople, the Balkan wars, and the threat against Vienna and Austria. It would be an error to equate the two continents . . . the entry of Turkey into the EU would be anti-historical.'[2]

Against history? This is a very strong claim but Bolkestein and Pope Benedict XIV are not the only people who believe in this fable. The masthead of The Gates of Vienna blog puts it simply: 'At the siege of Vienna in 1683 Islam seemed poised to overrun Christian Europe. We are in a new phase of a very old war.'[3] I have tried to present dispassionately what happened centuries ago. There was, in that time, unimaginable cruelty, savagery and implacable hatred among all the combatants. Yet in the nineteenth century the bitter attitudes that suffused those struggles diminished, and a new kind of relationship developed, which I have also described. The older feelings and attitudes were (and are) still present but they were (and are) definitely in abeyance.

Scouring the darker parts of the past, creating false memories for use as weapons, is a risky business. No one can say what will happen as a result. In the Balkan wars of the 1990s we witnessed many examples of a partial view of the past being invoked for political ends. Mythologised history became the excuse for savagery: ethnic cleansing is one of the most loathsome neologisms of the twentieth century.

Elizabeth Johnson presents perils implicit in the past in her bestselling novel The Historian. The heroine, before she begins her tale, pens a Note to the Reader. It is short but completely to the point: 'As a historian, I have learned that, in fact, not everyone who reaches back into history can survive it. And, it is not only reaching back into history that endangers us; sometimes history itself reaches inexorably forward for us with its shadowy claw.'[4] She is writing about exactly the same territory as I am, the lands stretching from Istanbul in the east to Vienna in the west, from Macedonia in the south to beyond the Carpathians in the north. The history she describes is actually a *myth-history*, not the kind safely contained in libraries and archives, but at large in the world: it is never-ending, potentially as dangerous as a virulent disease. Paradoxically, the antidote to this malign past is the process of history itself: the painstaking analytical, forensic work of uncovering the past, 'as it actually was', and making it known.[5]

The backward look behind the assurance
Of recorded history, the backward half-look
Over the shoulder, towards the primitive terror
T. S. Eliot, 'The Dry Salvages'

Notes

Preface

1. The train had started in Athens and meandered interminably slowly north-westward.
2. The friend was Christopher Duffy, whose knowledge of sieges and siege-craft has no equal. When they dug deeper to make the *U-Bahn*, many artefacts of the older cityscape were discovered. See Wiener Stadtwerke and Elisabeth Hewson, *Zeitmaschine U-Bahn: Eine Reise Jahrtausende Kultur-erfahrungen*. Vienna: C. Ueberreuter, 1994.
3. With, I think, some good advice from the *Land* museum service.
4. There is also a marble cross and plaque on the flat ground by the river.
5. Meeting at the Hungarian Academy of Sciences, 5 September 2005.
6. Except, at last, Virginia Aksan's exceptional *Ottoman Wars*. This deals in great depth with the Ottomans but necessarily relies on secondary material for the Habsburgs.
7. There are two first-rate books in English on the siege of Vienna, one by John Stoye, *The Siege of Vienna*, and the other by Thomas M. Barker, *Double Eagle and Crescent*. Both began with the antecedents to the siege and stopped when it was over.
8. Until the late seventeenth century, the East referred primarily to the Islamic lands to the east and south of Europe; China was then normally called Cathay or Tartaria. But fear of the East was not linked exclusively to Islam. The world-conquering Mongols in the thirteenth century induced a state of terror, as had the seemingly unstoppable Magyars of the tenth century. Earlier still, there were the fearsome tales of the tribal migrations of Central Asia – Huns – 'the tempest of Attila' and the terri-fying 'native valour of the Avars', as chronicled by Edward Gibbon in *The Decline and Fall of the Roman Empire*. From Gibbon in the eighteenth century to Oswald Spengler's *The Decline of the West* in the twentieth century, there has been no shortage of writing about what Gibbon described as 'the greatest, perhaps, and the most awful scene in the history of mankind'.

9. These were the records of the Österreichische Waffenfabriks Gesellschaft, then held by Steyr Daimler Puch, its successor in business, and the records of Technische Militär Administratifs Committe, held in the Österreichisches Staatsarchiv, Kriegsarchiv.

10. Except by Norman Stone, who, in *The Eastern Front*, conclusively explained the deep roots of failure.

Introduction

1. The Ummayad dynasty ruled for a longer period in Spain, but the unity of the Arab world had sundered.

2. Revelation 20: 8.

3. There are known versions of the story in Latin, Greek, Spanish, English, French, German, Syriac, Armenian, Persian, Arab, Hebrew, Coptic, Ethiopian, Serbian, Croat, Czech and Polish. See: Armand Adel, *Le Roman d'Alexandre. Legendaire Medieval*, Brussels: Office de Publicité, 1955, and J. A. Boyle, 'The Alexander Romance in the East and West', *Bulletin of the John Rylands Library* 60 (1977): 13.

4. Edward Gibbon, *The History of the Decline and Fall of the Roman Empire*, p. 224.

5. David J. Roxburgh (ed.), *Turks: A Journey of a Thousand Years*. London: Royal Academy, 2005.

6. Carole Hillenbrand, *Turkish Myth and Muslim Symbol: The Battle of Manzikert*. Edinburgh: Edinburgh University Press, 2007.

7. Cited John Julius Norwich, *A Short History of Byzantium*, p. 240.

8. He was later strangled on the orders of his elder cousin Andronicus.

9. Ertegrul, his father, was the progenitor of the dynasty.

10. Anthony Luttrell, 'Latin Responses to Ottoman Expansion before 1389', in Elizabeth Zachariadou (ed.), *The Ottoman Emirate (1300–1389). Halcyon Days in Crete, I. A Symposium Held in Rethymnon 11–13 January 1991*, pp. 119–34. Rethymnon: Crete University Press, 1993.

11. Norman Davies, *Europe: A History*. Oxford: Oxford University Press, 1996, p. 386.

12. Selim passed on the sense of destiny to Suleiman. 'It has been revealed to me that I shall become the possessor of the East and West, like Alexander the Great . . . I am a king, son of a king, descended through twenty generations of kings.' In *Ibn Iyas. An account of the Ottoman conquest of Egypt in the year A.H. 922 [AD 1516]* translated from the third volume of the Arabic chronicle of Muhammed ibn Ahmed ibn Iyas, an eyewitness of the scenes he describes, by W. H. Salmon. London: Royal Asiatic Society, 1921, p. 91. Cited in Hakan T. Karateke and Maurus Reinkowski (eds), *Legitimizing the Order*.

13. Caroline Finkel, *Osman's Dream*, p. 117, citing Dariuz Kolodziejczyk, *Ottoman–Polish Diplomatic Relations (15th to 18th Century): An Annotated Edition of Ahdnames and Other Documents*. Leiden: E. J. Brill, 2000.

14. Geoffrey Parker, 'The Place of Tudor England in the Messianic Vision of Philip II of Spain', *Transactions of the Royal Historical Society* 12 (2002): 167–221.

15. Ibid.

16. Perhaps it was a response to Charles's pressure? See Rhoads Murphey, 'Suleyman I and the Conquest of Hungary: Ottoman Manifest Destiny or a Delayed Reaction to Charles V's Universalist Vision', *Journal of Early Modern History* 5 (2001): 197–221.

Chapter 1

1. They embodied the 'savage and destructive spirit' which was how Thomas Malthus described the nomads of Scythia and the steppes, from whom the Ottomans were reputedly descended. See Thomas Robert Malthus (1766–1834), *An Essay on the Principle of Population: A View of its Past and Present Effects on Human Happiness; with an Inquiry into Our Prospects Respecting the Future Removal or Mitigation of the Evils which It Occasions*. London: John Murray, 1826. Sixth ed, book 1, ch. 7.

2. A number of sources suggest that it was unclear whether a war had been planned, but on both occasions that the sultan's *tuğ* were planted – in 1663–4 for the campaign on the Styrian border and in 1672 for the Khotin campaign in Poland – war had followed.

3. See Ogier Ghislain de Busbecq (ed.), *The Turkish Letters of Ogier Ghislain de Busbecq*, p. 150.

4. Nurhan Atasoy. Otag-i Hümayan, *The Ottoman Imperial Tent Complex*, Islanbul: MEPA/Aksoy, 2000.

5. Ibid., p. 229.

6. At the imperial summer palace at Edirne there was a second set of work rooms and stores.

7. The roof piece of one marquee studied by Atasoy weighed more than 300 kilos.

8. See C. T. Forster and F. H. B. Daniell (eds), *The Life and Letters of Ogier Ghislain de Busbecq, seigneur of Bousbecque, knight, Imperial ambassador.* London: C. K. Paul, 1881, vol. 1, p. 218.

9. Luigi Ferdinando Marsigli, *L'Etat Militaire de l'Empire Ottoman*, ch. XVIII: Du Bagage.

10. See Forster and Daniell, *The Life and Letters*, vol. 1, p. 155.

11. See Godfrey Goodwin, *The Janissaries*, p. 40.

12. See Forster and Daniell, *The Life and Letters*, vol. 1, pp. 86–8, 153–5, 219–22, 287–90, 293.

13. See Busbecq (ed.), *The Turkish Letters of Ogier Ghislain de Busbecq,,* p. 147.

14. Ottoman poets liked the anthropomorphic imagery of wild animals, and in this case the empire was like a lion. It was a good metaphor. Lions are lazy, and slow to rouse; building the war camp, which grew each day on the Çyrpeci Meadow, was the first outward and deliberate sign of Ottoman arousal.

15. Baron von Kunitz, *Diarium Welches der am Türckischen Hoff und hernach beym Groß-Wezier in der Wienerischen Belaegerung gewester Kayserl.* Vienna: 1684.

16. Edward Luttwak, *The Grand Strategy of the Roman Empire from the First Century A.D. to the Third.*

17. Strictly speaking, it was the Grand Duchy of Lithuania which abutted the Ottoman lands.

18. For example, the janissaries were using volley fire at the same time (or before) it was used in the west. See Günhan Börekçi, 'A Contribution to the Military Revolution Debate: The Janissaries' Use of Volley Fire during the Long Ottoman–Habsburg War of 1593–1606, and the Problem of Origins', *Acta Orientalia Academiae Scientiarum Hung.*, vol. 59 (4) (2006): 407–438.

19. See Gábor Ágoston, *Guns for the Sultan*, p. 93.

20. See Anton Dolleczek, *Monographie der k.u.k. österr.-ung. Blanken und Hand-feuerwaffen*, pp. 52–3. The 'Spanish Riders' were used by the Prussians against the Swedes at the Battle of Fehrbellin.

21. Knolles' description. See Address to the Reader in Richard Knolles, *The Generall Historie of the Turkes from the first beginning of that Nation to the rising of the Othoman Familie . . .*

22. This is not to diminish the achievement of the great contemporary travel writers like George Sandys. But Asli Cirakman rightly distinguishes between those who wrote without ever visiting the Ottoman lands and travellers (like Sandys) who actually saw with their own eyes. I would add the third category, which could be called expatriates, those who spent long periods in another culture; they formed a different set of impressions.

23. He had attended, as an imperial envoy, the marriage in Winchester between the King of Spain, Philip I, and Queen Mary of England.

24. The most recent edition was published by Louisiana State University Press in 2005.

25. See Alexandrine St Clair, 'A Forgotten Record of Turkish Exotica', *The Metropolitan Museum of Art Bulletin. New Series* 27, no. 9 (May 1969): 411–23.

26. But Ezel Kural Shaw points to the essential limits of that experience. She observes that 'The examination, analysis and evaluation of

foreigners' accounts of the Ottoman empire require the removal of two obstacles, or veils, first by a realization of the assets and limitations of the observer, imposed by his cultural and linguistic background as well as by his personality, and second by an understanding of the complexity of Ottoman society.' Ezel Kural Shaw, 'The Double Veil: Travelers' Views of the Ottoman Empire, Sixteenth Through Eighteenth Centuries'.

27. Nicolay was appointed the *Cosmographe* to the court of Henri II in 1566, and he had translated (from the Spanish) the famous volume *L'Arte de Navegar* on the art of navigation by Pedro de Medina in 1569, two years after his own travels were published by the same publisher, Rouille, in Lyons.

28. See Nicolas de Nicolay, *The nauigations, peregrinations and voyages, made into Turkie by Nicholas Nicholay, Daulphinois of Arfeuile . . . conteining sundry singularities which the author hath there seene and obserued: deuided into foure bookes, with threescore figures, naturally set forth as well of men as women, according to the diuersitie of nations . . . with diuers faire and memorable histories, happened in our time; Translated out of the French by T. Washington the younger.* London: T. Lawson. 1585. 82. This is the English translation of the 1577 edition published in Antwerp. Nicolay's book, *Les quatre premiers livres des Navigations et Peregrinations Orientales . . . Avec les figures au naturel* first appeared in 1567/68. It also appeared in German (1572 and 1577) and Italian (1576 and 1580).

29. For example, also the images of the heretical Muslim sects, especially the virginal Calenderi, with monstrous rings inserted through their penises.

30. Nicolay, *Navigations*, pp. 126–7.

31. For example, Francesco Sansevino derived his *deli* for his *Informatione* from the copperplate engraving after page 144 in the 1568 Lyon edition of Nicolay. See Bronwen Williams, 'Reflecting on the Turk in Late Sixteenth-Century Picture Books', *Word & Image* 19, nos 1 and 2 (Jan.–June 2003): 38–57.

32. See C. J. Heywood. 'Sir Paul Rycaut, a Seventeenth-Century Observer of the Ottoman State: Notes for a Study', in Ezel Kural Shaw and C. J. Heywood, *English and Continental Views of the Ottoman Empire 1500–1800*, pp. 37–55.

33. Epistle to the Reader in Paul Rycaut, *The present state of the Ottoman Empire . . .*

34. Ibid. Epistle Dedicatory.

35. Busbecq, like his twentieth-century diplomatic descendants, produced a long Advice once he had left his embassy and returned home. He wrote 'about a method how to manage war against the Turks'. His answer was to copy them: create a standing army, recruit and train the best of the nation.

36. To find any equivalent in the terror stakes we need to come into our
    own era, to the mature Stalinist Soviet Union. Rightly or wrongly, the
    European states to the west of the Iron Curtain were terrified by the
    power and menace of Russia – by its overwhelming military strength,
    its political dominance in international politics, and above all its ideo-
    logical challenge to all forms of religion and to western democratic
    principles. Fear of Russia did not stem from any particular event: Stalin's
    Russia did not have to do anything to be feared: its very existence was
    malign and threatening.

Chapter 2

1. Naib-i-Sultanat.
2. See Miguel de Cervantes, *Don Quijote*, ch. 1.
3. See Colin Imber, *The Ottoman Empire, 1300–1650. The Structure of Power*.
   London: Palgrave Macmillan, 2002, pp. 120–23.
4. Franz Babinger, *Mehmed the Conqueror and His Time*, pp. 376–9.
5. Mustafa Naima, *Ravzatü'l–Hüseyn*, 6, 336. Cited in Caroline Finkel,
   Osman's Dream, p. 259.
6. For the progress see Caroline Finkel, *Osman's Dream*. On the potency of
   symbolism see G. Necipoğlu, *Architecture, Ceremonial and Power*, pp. 151–2.
7. For the *verilmistir* of the Ottoman sultans see http://www.
   osmanli700.gen.tr/english/miscel/ranks.html.
8. Finkel, *Osman's Dream*, p. 271.
9. See Sieur Le Croix, *The wars of the Turks with Poland, Muscovy, and
   Hungary: from the year 1672, to the year 1683*, pp. 23–4.
10. Ibid.
11. See Nurhan Atasoy, *A Garden for the Sultan*, pp. 222–9.
12. The ancient Roman city of Hadrianopolis (renamed Edirne) had been
    the first city of the Ottoman's empire in the west.
13. It is easy to see this in the Yildiz complex constructed by Sultan Abdul
    Hamid II, which was built after the accidental destruction of the Edirne
    Saray during the war with Russia in 1875. Now being reconstructed,
    Yildiz reflects much of the Ottoman love of gardens.
14. See Giovanni Benaglia, *Relatione del viaggio fatto à Constantinopoli*,
    pp. 68ff.
15. See *Evliya Chelebi Seyatnamesi*, vol. 2. Istanbul: Yapi Kredi Yayinlar,
    pp. 255–6.
16. See Rhoads Murphey, *Ottoman Warfare, 1500–1700*, p. 136.
17. See Gábor Ágoston, *Guns for the Sultan*.
18. The phrase is that of Felix Kanitz, who travelled widely in the Balkans
    between 1858 and 1889. But it is a common western trope of the Ottoman

legacy to Europe. See Robin Okey, 'Central Europe/Eastern Europe. Behind the Definitions', *Past and Present* 137 (1992): 114.

19. This description is taken from Alan W. Fisher, *The Russian Annexation of the Crimea, 1772–1783*, pp. 16–17.

20. Qu'ran 2: 187.

21. Light-coloured horses were less favoured on campaign, because they provided more visible targets.

22. It is now more common and correct to call them *Tatars*, but this misses the powerful connection which westerners imputed between the Tartars and the word 'Tartarus': the infernal regions, described in the *Iliad* as being situated as far below Hades as heaven is above the earth, and by later writers as the place of punishment for the spirits of the wicked. According to the Greek poet Hesiod, a bronze anvil falling from heaven would take nine days and nights to reach earth, and an object would take the same amount of time to fall from earth into Tartarus, a dank, gloomy pit, surrounded by a wall of bronze, and beyond that a three-fold layer of night. See Martha Thompson at http://www.pantheon.org/articles/t/tartarus.html.

23. The title James Chambers gave to his book on the Mongols. Modern studies suggest the Nogai Tartars retained the essence of the Mongol style of warfare.

24. Thomas Spalatensis, *Historia Salonitana*, c 36. MGH SS ... vol. 17. Hanover: 1861, cited in Pál Engel, *The Realm of St Stephen*.

25. Matthew of Paris, *Chronica Maiora*. See Robert Kerr, **GENERAL HISTORY and COLLECTION of VOYAGES and TRAVELS, ARRANGED in SYSTEM-ATIC ORDER:** *Forming a Complete History of the Origin and Progress of Navigation, Discovery, and Commerce, by Sea and Land, from the Earliest Ages to the Present Time*, 1811, vol. 1, ch. 6 – Travels of an Englishman into Tartary, and thence into Poland, Hungary, and Germany, in 1243.[1] Hakluyt. I. 22.

26. This was the 1698 campaign. See L. J. D. Collins, 'The Military Organization and Tactics of the Crimean Tatars, 16th–17th Centuries', in Vernon J. Parry and M. E. Yapp (eds), *War, Technology and Society in the Middle East*, pp. 266–76.

27. See Jacques Margaret, *The Russian Empire and Grand Duchy of Muscovy: A 17th-Century French Account*, translated and edited by Chester S. L. Dunning. Pittsburgh, PA: University of Pittsburgh Press, 1983, p. 45.

28. One reason for the success of the Tartar horse may have been their diet. There were two types of Turkmen horses: one stocky with a shaggy coat, the other the slender Turkmen 'heavenly, blood sweating horses' prized by the Chinese. These survive today as the Akhal-Teke as the direct descendants of the second type; however, Tartar horses

were probably a mixture of the two types. Central Asian tribesmen used to 'feed their horses by a mixture of dry lucerne, mutton fat, and fried dough cakes'. This high protein and low bulk diet reduced their dependence on fresh grass or dry fodder, essential for most European horses. See www.turkishculture.org on horses. In their standard treatise, J. H. Walsh and I. J. Lupton described the Tartar horse as 'fast and untiring, and of the most hardy nature, so that they can support themselves on a quantity and quality of food upon which even our donkeys would starve'. See *The Horse, in the Stable and the Field*, London: Routledge, 1861, p. 25. There was a plentiful supply of mutton fat in an Ottoman war camp, from the rations for the troops. I am very grateful to Donna Landry for steering me in the right direction on this topic.

Chapter 3

1. Franz Babinger, *Mehmed the Conqueror and His Time*, p. 323.
2. Leopold Toifl and Hildegard Leitgarb, *Die Türkeneinfälle in der Steiermark und in Kärnten vom 15 bis zum 17 Jahrhundert*, pp. 6–12.
3. Gerhard Stenzel, *Von Burg zu Burg in Österreich*. He confronted the new young Emperor Charles V who had his own imperial dreams, which brought him into direct conflict with France and Suleiman I. The Ottoman advance has to be related to the 'forward' policy of Charles V. See Rhoads Murphey, 'Suleyman I and the Conquest of Hungary: Ottoman Manifest Destiny or a Delayed Reaction to Charles V's Universalist Vision', *Journal of Early Modern History* 5 (2001): 197–221.
4. Ferenc Szakály, 'Nándorfeáhérvár [Belgrade], 1521: The Beginning of the End of the Medieval Hungarian Kingdom', in Géza Dávid and Pál Fodor (eds), *Hungarian–Ottoman Military and Diplomatic Relations in the Age of Suleyman the Magnificent*, pp. 68–9.
5. Ibid.
6. Topkapi Palace Museum, *Nehzetu'l-Ahbar der Sefer-i Sigetvar*, pp. 1568–9.
7. Ferenc Szakály, 'Nándorfeáhérvár [Belgrade], 1521'.
8. This was the contemporary term, and perhaps the first instance of the 'Kleinkrieg'. But in this case these were often professional soldiers rather than the guerrillas of the Spanish irregular war against Napoleon Bonaparte.
9. Vauban, 1670, cited by Geoffrey Parker, 'The artillery fortress as an engine of European overseas expansion 1480–1750', in James D. Tracy (ed.), *City Walls*, p. 392.
10. They had learned their fighting skills against the Swedes, the Danes and the French.

11. Günhan Böreçki, 'A Contribution to the Military Revolution Debate: The Janissaries Use of Volley-fire during the Long Ottoman–Habsburg War of 1593–1606 and the Problem of Origins', *Acta Orientalia Academiae Scientarium Hung* 59 (4) (2006): 407–38.

12. The Tartar tactic of 'swarming' has been rediscovered and adapted to the situation of twenty-first-century warfare. See Sean J. A. Edwards, *Swarming on the Battlefield*.

13. This term, developed in US strategic and political science, refers to a state's capacity to impose its will by force or threat of force on the far borders or beyond a distant frontier.

14. They did not, as many newspapers and pamphlets asserted in an orgy of wish-fulfilment, recapture the town Zrinyi's ancestor had defended so courageously. See G. EténYi Nóra, 'Szigetvár 1664. évi ostroma'. Egy téves hír analízise – és a Zrínyi-hagyomány. Történelmi Szemle, 1999. 1–2. XLI. 209. There is an English abstract.

15. This is well analysed in Rhoads Murphey, *Ottoman Warfare, 1500–1700*, pp. 122–9.

16. I use 'Habsburg' here as shorthand. In fact the army comprised the Austrian regiments, an imperial contingent from the Rhineland and a detachment of French noble volunteers.

17. Montecuccoli was blamed by Miklós Zrinyi for not being more active in attacking and then pursuing the Ottomans. Hungarian historians have on the whole followed this line. But the Italian commander was right: he did not have the men to engage in pursuit, as it was the only force capable of protecting the frontier. This was one reason for the hurried truce, also damned by the Hungarians who felt they had been abandoned.

18. There is no record of the Tartars ever capturing a town of twenty thousand people.

19. See Henry Marsh, *A new survey of the Turkish Empire and Government . . .*, pp. 62–6.

20. Notably the *akincis* and *delis* who still accompanied the army, but were of little serious use in combat.

21. On contemporary Ottoman projects for reform, see Gabriel Piterberg, *An Ottoman Tragedy*. On internal changes within the power structure of the dynasty see Leslie P. Peirce, *The Imperial Harem: Women and Sovereignty in the Ottoman Empire*. Oxford: Oxford University Press, 1993. Notions of 'decline' were just as common in Spanish seventeenth-century culture, and *arbitristas* promoted a wide range of plans for reform. The second part of Vicente Palacio Atard, *Derrota, Agotamiento, Decadencia, en la España del Siglo XVII*. 2nd edn. Madrid: Ediciones Rialp, 1956, deals with the theme of more general moral decay.

22. Paul Rycaut, *The History of the Turkish Empire from the year 1623 to the Year 1687*. London: Thomas Basset, 1687, p. 1.

23. Ziad Elmarsafy, writing on Rycaut as a source for Racine's play *Bajazet*, makes the case precisely: 'What seems to bother Rycaut is the parallel between the Rome of the early Principate and the seventeenth-century Ottoman empire, especially the apparent correlation between their prosperity and inherent viciousness.' See Ziad Elmarsafy, '"O Homines ad servitutem paratos!": Bajazet and the scandal of slave rule', *Romantic Review* 7 (November 2000).

24. Rycaut, *The History of the Turkish Empire from the year 1623 to the year 1687*. The Epistle to the Reader.

Chapter 4

1. See Johannes Sachslehner, *Wien Anno 1683*, p. 53.

2. Katalin Plihál, 'The First Printed Map of Hungary', *The Hungarian Quarterly* XLIII, no. 170 (Summer 2003) http://www.hungarian quarterly.com/no170/7.html.

3. See *A Letter from an eminent Merchant in Constantinople to a Friend in London* . . .

4. See Rhoads Murphey, *Ottoman Warfare, 1500–1700*, pp. 21–2. The march from Edirne to Esztergom in 1666 took 119 days, of which 67 were days of rest. On average the army would be lucky to make much more than twelve miles a day under good conditions.

5. Cited in Murphey, *Ottoman Warfare*, p. 20. This is taken from an anonymous Ottoman account of the Battle of Varna in 1444, and these words are supposedly spoken by the Christian leaders. But the Tartar's campaign season was also based on the availability of forage

6. See Warren S. Walker and Ahmet E. Uysal, 'An Ancient God in Modern Turkey: Some Aspects of the Cult of Hizir,' *Journal of American Folklore* 86 (1973). See http://khidr.org/hizir.htm.

7. See Giovanni Benaglia, *Relatione del viaggio fatto à Constantinopoli*, p. 100 seq.

8. This is my surmise, because the documents covering this episode either do not exist or were revised after the event to blacken the character of Kara Mustafa. The one document that supposedly makes the situation clear is from an unreliable source, not actually present at the event. However, while the book was at press, I read the new study by Marc David Baer, *Honoured by the Glory of Islam. Conversion and Conquest in Ottoman Europe*. New York: Oxford University Press, 2008. Baer has researched extensively in the Ottoman archives and

texts, and his important study of Mehmed IV's rule now makes me much more confident that my conjectures here are soundly based.

9. I believe that the traditional view – Mehmed IV's feebleness and Kara Mustafa's incredible greed – are inherently implausible, given both the information available and its context. See Walter Leitsch, 'Warum wollte Kara Mustafa Wien erobern?' *Jahrbücher für Geschichte Osteuropas* 29, part 4 (1981): 494–514.

10. Peter Meienberger, *Johann Rudolf Schmid zum Schwarzenhorn als kaiserlicher Resident in Konstantinopel in den Jahren 1629–1643*, p. 118.

11. Of course, once the great attack failed, history was rewritten and the sultan portrayed as wisely dubious from the outset and latterly wholly innocent of his duplicitous servant's machinations.

12. See Caroline Finkel, *Osman's Dream*, p. 288. She is citing Silahdar (Swordbearer) Findikli Mehmed Aga's story of the dream in his memoir.

13. Suleiman I was 'the mighty annexer of the Realms of War to the Realms of Islam'. See Colin Imber, 'The Ottoman Dynastic Myth', *Turcica* XIX (1987): 7–27.

14. Ibid.: 21.

15. See Andrew Wheatcroft, *The Habsburgs*.

16. Peter F. Sugar, 'Major Changes in the Life of the Slav Peasantry under Ottoman Rule', *International Journal of Middle East Studies* 9, no. 3 (October 1978): 297–305.

17. András Mócsy, *Pannonia and Upper Moesia: A History of the Middle Danube Provinces of the Roman Empire*, translation edited by Sheppard Frere. London: Routledge & Kegan Paul, 1974.

18. This is a phrase used in Bak and Kiraly's collection as an epigram to describe the period of the Habsburg–Ottoman contest for the possession of Hungary.

19. This problem applies to both the Habsburg and the Ottoman narratives, but Gabriel Piterberg, *An Ottoman Tragedy*, can be helpful in approaching the Habsburg records as well.

20. See Paul-Henry Chombart de Lauwe, *La culture et le pouvoir*. Paris: Stock, 1975; and *Images de la culture*, 2nd edn, Payot, 1970, p. 15. Chombart de Lauwe was describing the anarchic qualities of many great modern cities, which existed as a set of boundaries between the settled and the transient.

21. This is the world perfectly and inspirationally described by Cecilia Holland in her novel *Rákossy*, published in 1967, reissued 2006.

22. See Hans Schiltberger, *Reisebuch* (facsimile of the original 1476 edition), Elisabeth Geck (ed.). Wiesbaden: Pressler, 1969.

23. Grein's story echoes that of Martin Guerre, as told by Nathalie Zemon Davies in *The Return of Martin Guerre*. Cambridge, MA: Harvard University Press, 1984.

24. Dr Pál Fodor of the Hungarian Academy of Sciences remarked to me in 2005 that while there was considerable knowledge of Ottoman atrocities in Hungary, down to places, to dates, and, sometimes, to the names of the victims, this was not invariably the case.

25. John Smith. *The true travels, adventures, and observations of Captaine Iohn Smith, in Europe, Asia, Affrica, and America from Anno Domini 1593 to 1629 . . .*, chs XI and XII.

26. See Almut Höfert, *Den Feind beschreiben: 'Türkengefahr' und europäisches Wissen über das Osmanische Reich 1450–1600.*

Chapter 5

1. On 13, 17, 18, 20 May, when the janissaries set out for the north.

2. See Edward Brown, 'The General Description of Hungary', in *A brief account of some travels in divers parts of Europe . . .*, p. 3.

3. Loeb translation, *Life of Caesar*, 1919.

4. See Henry Neville, **PLATO REDIVIVUS** *or a* **DIALOGUE CONCERNING** *Government*, . . .

5. 'Habitus' was first used in this sense by Norbert Elias in *The Civilising Process*, vol. 2. Oxford: Blackwell, 1982, and in *The Court Society*. Oxford: Blackwell, 1983. But Pierre Bourdieu's work, based on his work on the Kabyle house, where its physical elements were in a constant state of meaningful transition, is more what I have in mind here. See Pierre Bourdieu, *Outline of a Theory of Practice*. London: Cambridge University Press, 1977.

6. It remains rare to yoke the Ottomans and Habsburgs in this kind of tandem; it was rare to make the connection, although the German historian Leopold von Ranke did so, primarily with the Spanish Habsburgs, in his *The Ottoman and the Spanish Empires, in the Sixteenth and Seventeenth Centuries*, published in 1837.

7. See Stephane Yerasimos, 'The Imperial Procession: Recreating a World's Order', n.d. http://www.geocities.com/surnamei_vehbi/yerasimos.html.

8. John P. Spielman, *Leopold I of Austria*, pp. 35–6.

9. John Stoye, *The Siege of Vienna*, p. 31.

10. For one contemporary account see Jeremias Cacavelas, *The Siege of Vienna by the Turks in 1683 . . .*, pp. 29–37; and Johannes Sachslehner, *Wien Anno 1683*, pp. 85–8.

11. See K. Köhler, *Die orientalische Politik Ludwigs XIV: ihr Verhältnis zu dem Türkenkrieg von 1683: mit einem einleitenden Kapitel über die französisch-türkischen Beziehungen von Franz I. bis zum Tode Mazarins.* Leipzig: K. F. Koehler, 1907, pp. 74–5. Cited in Stoye, *The Siege of Vienna*.

12. Johannes Jacob von Weingarten, Fürsten-Spiegel. Prague, 1673. Cited in Maria Goloubeva, *The Glorification of Emperor Leopold I in Image, Spectacle and Text*, p. 159.

13. See, for example, 'A short memorial of the most grievous sufferings of the ministers of the Protestant churches in Hungary by the instigation of the popish clergy there and of the release of such of them as are yet alive, nineteen of them having died under the cruelties of their persecutors, and obtained the glorious crown of martyrdom'. London: William Nott, 1676.

14. Ibid. 'An appendix of the state of the Churches in Hungary and Transylvania', p. 21.

15. See Victor von Renner, *Wien im Jahre 1683*, pp. 64–5.

16. Even less if they followed the southern route towards Graz and crossed the River Raab at St Gotthard, as in 1664. That was unlikely, given the superstitious memory of the great defeat.

17. There were a whole set of legends about red and golden apples in Turkish and Islamic legend.

18. *The Koran*, translated by N. J. Dawood. Harmondsworth: Penguin, 1979, p. 334.

19. Gaetan Guillot, 'Un témoin italien de la Guerre des Impériaux contre les Turcs 1683', *Revue d'histoire diplomatique* 28 (1914): 163–16.

20. See Stoye, *The Siege of Vienna*, p. 84, citing Franz-Anton Edler von Guarient, *Codex Austriacus ordine alphabetico compilatus, das ist: eigentlicher Begriff und Innhalt aller unter deß Ertzhauses zu Oesterreich . . . einlaufenden Generalien.– Wienn . . . 6 vols Vienna: Voigt, vol. 1: 394–6, and vol. 2: 396–1. I have not been able to check the references myself.

21. For Count Harrach's account in his diary, see Ferdinand Mencik (ed.), 'Ein Tagebuch während der Belagerung von Wien im Jahre 1683', in *Archiv für steirische Geschichte* 86 (1899): 205–52.

22. This was to be headed by Rüdiger von Starhemberg and the elderly Count Caplirs.

23. His long and anguished letter to Marco d'Aviano expresses his feelings very clearly. See Onno Klopp, *Corrispondenza epistolare tra Leopoldo I . . .*, pp. 23–4. Letter 27: Leopold to Aviano. Passau, 18 July 1683.

Chapter 6

1. *Auff, auff Ihr Christen*. This was the title of a pamphlet by the famous preacher Abraham à Sancta Clara, by coincidence published in the city on 7 July 1683.

2. It did them little good, since many were caught by the Tartars on the road west. See John Peter a Valcaren, *A relation or diary of the siege of Vienna*, p. 11.

3. Ibid., p. 15.

4. Josef Mathias Trenkwald, *Der Einzug Herzog Leopold VI in Wien*, 1872, Kunsthistorisches Museum.

5. In 1547 a city map showed 150 large gardens; by 1600, they had all been built over. See Robert Rotenberg, *Landscape and Power in Vienna*, p. 34.

6. As seen in the bird's-eye maps of the period.

7. See the map by Bonifazius Wohlmut.

8. Later called the Ottakringbach.

9. Edward Brown, *A brief account of some travels in divers parts of Europe . . .*

10. Vincenzo Scamozzi, *L'idea della architettura universale; divisa in xii. Libri*. Venice: published by the author, 1615, p. 191.

11. Nichole Hochner, 'Louis XII and the Porcupine: Transformation of a Royal Emblem', in *Renaissance Studies* 15 (2001): 17–36.

12. Thomas M. Barker, *Double Eagle and Crescent*.

13. There is an argument that Sebastian de Vauban developed his system of attack from the Ottoman techniques of attacking a bastioned fortress.

14. See Martha Pollak, 'Representations of the City in Siege Views of the Seventeenth Century: The War of Military Images and their Production', in James D. Tray (ed.), *City Walls: The Urban Enceinte in Global Perspective*. Cambridge: Cambridge University Press, 2001, 605–46

15. Caroline Finkel, *Osman's Dream*, pp. 267–9, cites Evliya Çelebi likening it to 'the Day of Judgement' and he lists it among the six great defeats of the dynasty. See also Evliya Çelebi [Tchelebi], *Les Guerres des Turcs*, for the full account of the battle.

16. There was one small, angled rampart, built up from a section of the original wall, the 'Spaniard', covering the Burgtor.

17. Georg Rimpler's works were later collected and reprinted by a Saxon military engineer, Captain Ludwig Andreas Herlin, in 1724: *Sämmtliche Schriften von der Fortification (etc.)*. A descendant of Rimpler has produced a useful study of his work and reputation: Kurt Rumpler, *Festungsbaumeister Georg Rimpler und die Zweite Türkenbelagerung*, 2007, at members.kabsi.at/familienforschung/Rimpler.pdf.

18. See Burcu Özguven, 'A Palanka: A Characteristic Type of the Ottoman Fortification Network in Hungary', in M. Kiel, N. Landman and H. Theunissen (eds), *Proceedings of the 11th International Congress of Turkish Art*, Utrecht, 34 (2001): 1–12.

19. More recent fortresses had casemates, strengthened below ground areas that would prevent enemy sappers from getting close to a wall or exploding charges beneath it.

20. See Jan Pieter van Vaelckeren, *Vienna à Turcis Obsessa à Christianis Eliberata*. See http://www.uni-mannheim.de/mateo/camenahist/ vaelckerni/jpg/s005.html. The shortened English edition was entitled *A relation or diary of the siege of Vienna written by 'John Peter a Valcaren', [a Flemish] judge-advocate of the Imperial army; drawn from the original by His Majesties command*. London: William Nott and George Wells, 1684. I have preferred to use this version because it is graphically and vividly translated from the original Latin.

21. The Poles were Prince Lubomirski's horsemen, notorious for their wildness, and under contract to the Emperor. They had previously fought with the Hungarian rebels.

22. Valcaren, *A relation or diary of the siege of Vienna*, pp. 31–2.

23. Richard F. Kreutel, *Kara Mustafa vor Wien*, pp. 13–14.

24. Valcaren, *A relation or diary of the siege of Vienna*, p. 27.

25. See Jean de Labrune, *The life of that most illustrious prince, Charles V, late Duke of Lorrain and Bar, generalissimo of the imperial armies, rendered into English from the copy lately printed at Vienna, written by a person of quality, and a great officer in the imperial army*. London: Randal Taylor, 1691.

26. See Özguven in Kiel, Landman and Theunissen (eds), pp. 1–12.

27. Nor do twentieth-century events like Stalingrad provide much help, because modern weapons are so very different in their power and range.

28. Valcaren, *A relation or diary of the siege of Vienna*, p. 42 599.

Chapter 7

1. At one point Thököly's troops captured Bratislava but were soon driven out by the citizens, supported by Lorraine's troops, who routed them on 29 August.

2. See Valcaren, *A Relation or diary of the siege of Vienna*, p. 70.

3. See Gábor Ágoston, *Guns for the Sultan*, pp. 68–70.

4. Valcaren, *A Relation or diary of the siege of Vienna*, p. 49

5. Ibid.

6. Ibid., p. 85.

7. Paul Nettl and Theodore Barker, 'Equestrian Ballets of the Baroque Period', *Musical Quarterly* 19, no.1 (January 1933): 74–83.

8. Cited in Victor von Renner, *Wien in Jahre 1683*, p. 361.

9. It has been argued that an assault on the walls facing Leopoldstadt island would have been an easier approach, but that would have meant that the Turks would have had to storm the walls across open ground through the mud of the Danube. Western officers at the time agreed

that the attack on the Burg was the correct approach.

10. Revelation 20: 7–8.
11. Qu'ran 21: 97.
12. Valcaren, *A Relation or diary of the siege of Vienna*, p. 84.
13. Ibid., p. 67.
14. For the events of 4 September the best accounts are Johann Georg von Hoffmann, *Relation du siège de Vienne par un officier de la garnison*, in Ferdinand Stöller, *Neue Quellen zur Geschichte des Türkenjahres 1683 . . .*, pp. 136–7, and the Conte Francesco Provana di Frosaco, whose *relation* was first printed by Henri Marczali in *Revue de Hongrie* 3 (1909). Thomas M. Barker, whose translation is used here, suggests that 'Hoffmann' was misidentified and the renowned Sardinian officer is the source of both documents.
15. Valcaren, *A Relation or diary of the siege of Vienna*, pp. 87–8.

Chapter 8

1. Valcaren, *A relation or diary of the siege of Vienna*, p. 95.
2. See Javed, cited in H. A. Reed, The Destruction of the Janissaries by Mah'mud II in June 1826.' Unpublished Ph.D. thesis, Princeton University, 1951, p. 323.
3. Akdes Nimet Kurat, *The despatches of Sir Robert Sutton, Ambassador in Constantinople, 1710–1714*, p. 66.
4. Laudon to Joseph II, 22 September 1788, cited Duffy, *Military Experience*, p. 244.
5. Later historians talked in terms that it was beyond the Turks' capacity to hold the city, which was at the farthest extent of their strategic 'reach'. All this was true in theory, but they would not be so easy to remove in practice, especially since (as Field Marshal Laudon later observed) they would fight to defend a pile of shattered ruins.
6. Pufendorf under the pseudonym of Severinus de Monzambano, *De statu imperii Germanici /ad Laelium Fratrem, dominum Trezolani, Liber unus*. The Hague, 1667.
7. Voltaire, *Essai sur l'histoire générale et sur les moeurs et l'esprit des nations*, ch. 70, 1756.
8. Figure cited by Hochedlinger, *Austria's Wars of Emergence*, p. 157. There are a number of other estimates, some inflated for political reasons, but his overall total is probably the most reliable.
9. The reason for the Hanoverian lack of response was that the duke was afraid of an attack on him, and, although his army was large, he could not afford to denude the defences of his duchy.

10. Great efforts were also made to recruit the Great Elector of Brandenburg to the cause, but principally because his army of thirty thousand was the best in the Empire.

11. This was the only bridge across the river between Krems and Vienna.

12. Richard Brzezinski, *Polish Winged Hussar*, pp. 16–17.

13. Not with all. He was an inveterate enemy of Hermann of Baden, the chair of the Imperial War Council.

14. In 1683, in celebration of his victory at Vienna, the Emperor Leopold I ordered a great church to be built on the Kahlenberg as the point from which symbolically the great victory had been launched. But when the church was opened in 1693, he decreed that the mountain should thereafter bear his more august name, becoming the Leopoldsberg. At the same time, to the confusion of subsequent generations, he transferred the name of Kahlenberg to the nearby Josephsberg.

15. From W. C., *The Siege of Vienna: a poem*. London. H. Hills, June, 1685.

16. See Richard Kreutel (ed.), *Kara Mustafa vor Wien*, pp. 109–10, 'of incalculable strength, with cavalry and infantry, as well as 200 large and small cannon'.

17. D'Aviano was a Capuchin monk, and hence, in his grey cassock, literally the *éminence grise* behind the Emperor's thoughts and decisions. He experienced all the difficulties and hardships faced by the troops. See his letter from the battlefield in Onno Klopp, *Corrispondenza epistolare tra Leopoldo I imperatore . . .* , pp. 29–30, 11 September 1683.

18. See Kreutel (ed.), *Kara Mustafa vor Wien*, p. 76.

19. See Thomas M. Barker, *Double Eagle and Crescent: Vienna's Second Turkish Siege and its Historical Setting*, p. 330.

20. Quoted in Brzezinski, *Polish Winged Hussars*, p. 46. Kochowski's history was published as *Commentarius belli adversus Turcas ad Viennam, et in Hungaria anno 1683 gesti ductu et auspiciis* at Crakow in 1684.

21. See Brzezinski, Polish Winged Hussars, pp. 43–50.

22. See [François-Paulin] Dalerac, *Polish manuscripts, or, The secret history of the reign of John Sobieski, the III. of that name, K. of Poland 1700*, pp. 97–8.

23. Ibid., p. 100.

Chapter 9

1. See Kerstin Tomenendal, *Das türkische Gesicht Wiens*. Most of the evidence of contact comes from the eighteenth century, but there are traces for the seventeenth. Tomenendal dates the coffee craze from the embassy of Kara Mehmed Pasha in 1665.

2. The last known of many variants before the nineteenth century was

printed in Vienna in 1597 by Gregor Huber. Copy in National Széchényi Library, Budapest.

3. See *The Bondage and Travels of Johann Schiltberger*, trans. J. Buchan Telfer. London: Hakluyt Society, series 1, no. 58, 1879.

4. In addition to the cash from Rome, he ordered local bishops and monastic orders to contribute from their resources, potentially a far more lucrative source for the Habsburgs and other Catholic rulers. These Catholic funds were then used to pay for contingents from Protestant states with expert and highly trained professional armies.

5. Michael Hochedlinger rightly uses the term 'reconquista' but without making any specific links with Habsburg ideology. See Hochedlinger, *Austria's Wars of Emergence*, p. 167.

6. Dominique Carnoy, *Réprésentations de l'Islam dans la France du XVIIe siècle: la ville des tentations*, pp. 86–90. The full title was *Le bouclier de l'Europe, ou La Guerre Sainte, contenant des avis politiques & Chrétiens, qui peuvent servir de lumière aux rois & aux souverains de la Chrétienté, pour garantir leurs estats des incursions des Turcs, & reprendre ceux qu'ils ont usurpé sur eux. Avec une relation de Voyages faits dans la Turquie, la Thébaïde & la Barbarie.*

7. Cited in Thomas M. Barker, *Double Eagle and Crescent*, p. 339.

8. See [François-Paulin] Dalerac, *Polish manuscripts: or The secret history of the reign of John Sobieski, the III. of that name, K. of Poland 1700*, p. 363.

9. Leopold prided himself on his stately lack of emotion, but the Poles expected something different. It is very unlikely that he intended any snub to his allies.

10. See 'The Ancient Identity of Hungarians'. http://www.imninalu.net/myths-Huns.htm.

11. See Fred Hamori, 'The Legend of the Turul Hawk', http://users.cwnet.com/millenia/turul.htm.

12. See Emilio Lovarini (ed.), *La Schiavitù del Generale Marsigli sotto i Tartari e i Turchi da lui stesso narrata*, p. 59 seq.

13. This gargantuan text was Marsigli's *Danubius Pannonico-Musicus, observationibus geographicis, astronomicis, hydrographicis, historicis, physicis perlustratus*, The Hague 1726.

14. Nominally in Ottoman hands, the garrison was small, and to the northeast lay Transylvania, a half-hearted ally of the Turks, but hostile to the Habsburg embrace.

15. He did not take the city by storm, as the Habsburg mercenaries sold it to the Turks.

16. See Sir Paul Rycaut, *The History of the Turks . . .* , pp. 125–6.

17. The collection grew over time, with 100 pieces given by his uncle Hermann of Baden. In 1771 his son August Georg made a Turkish

Chamber to house these exotic objects; but in 1877, the then ruler carried them off to Karlsruhe to form a collection of 'Turkish curiosities'. They have been in the Badisches Landesmuseum since 1920.

18. Rycaut, *The History of the Turks* . . ., p. 127.
19. Ibid.
20. See Gábor Ágoston, *Guns for the Sultan*, p. 136.
21. The Emperor Leopold rejoiced in this signal victory to d'Aviano, saying it was not as had been anticipated in Vienna: 'il qual luogo però non trovano così distrutto e di pari resistenza, como habbiamo supposto a Vienna'. See Onno Klopp, *Corrispondenza epistolare tra Leopoldo I imperatore* . . ., p. 33. Letter from Leopold to d'Aviano. Linz, 24 October 1683.
22. Hammer has a slightly different version, with the meeting and execution taking place around midnight. See *Histoire de l'Empire Ottoman*, vol. 12, pp. 154–6.

Chapter 10

1. Jean de Préchac, *The grand vizier, or, The history of the life of Cara Mustapha, who commanded the Turkish army at the siege of Vienna in the year 1683*. It was first published in French and translated into German, Italian and Dutch, as well as English.
2. Rycaut, *The History of the Turks* . . ., p. 127.
3. Caroline Finkel, *Osman's Dream*, p. 289, citing Silahdar Tar'rihi.
4. Leopold's inclination was towards completing the conquest, but the threat of France in the west was strongly in his mind, because of Habsburg dynastic interests in the Low Countries, and because of his position as German Emperor. He wrote to d'Aviano on 23 January 1684 from Linz: 'In somma, Padre mio, io son tutto in questa guerra – ma solo non posso bastare.' D'Aviano wrote back on 13 February that the war of Reconquest would have 'grandissimi avvantaggi per bene di tutti la Christianità'. The Pope himself thought it was 'per bene del Christianismo'. See Onno Klopp, *Corrispondenza epistolare tra Leopoldo I imperatore* . . . , pp. 35–8. Letter 41 and Letter 43. Leopold echoed the same idea in his letter to Aviano of 10 April: 'il bene della Christianità tutta . . . un'opera da Dio solo, e non humana, e certo che da questa risultaranno beni molti per tutta Christianità.' Ibid., 10 April, Linz, page 39. Letter 65.
5. Johann Abelinus, Johann Philipp Merian, **THEATRI | EUROPAEI | CONTINUATI** | *Zwoelffter Theil/* . . ., p. 624 seq.
6. Paul Rycaut, *A true and exact relation of the imperial expedition in Hungaria, in the year 1684*, p. 6.

7. Ibid., p. 4. Perhaps he was reading the situation of 1699, after the Battle of Zenta a decade earlier.

8. Ibid., p. 7.

9. Ibid., p. 11.

10. Ibid., p. 13.

11. It was said that the citadel was taken by subterfuge, after the sultan's army had driven off a Habsburg army attempting to take the citadel from Hungarians. 'But the king of Germany, Hungary's neighbour, the unbeliever named Ferandus [Ferdinand] who, cursed djaur [infidel] as he is continually at war with the followers of Islam and has always been a vengeful rebel would have liked to become King of Hungary. There- fore his unbelieving brother named Karlo [Charles V], allied to the King of Ispania [Spain] and with the support of other unbelievers of depraved lives, assembled a huge army from the provinces that are hotbeds of terror, and placed guns and weapons on his innumerable boats on the Danube. The cursed one named Perenyi, one of the Hungarian magnates, also joined him. Moving with all these forces he took power for himself in Hungary and laid siege to the city of Buda.' See Geza Perjes, *The Fall of the Medieval Kingdom of Hungary*, p. 301. http://www.hungarian-history.hu/lib/warso/warso18.htm.

12. Gábor Ágoston, *Guns for the Sultan*, p.154.

13. Onno Klopp, *Corrispondenza epistolare tra Leopoldo I imperatore* . . . , pp. 41–2. From d'Aviano to Leopold. 14 June 1684. With the army. Letter 49.

14. Ibid., pp. 23–4. Letter 27: Leopold to Aviano. Passau, 18 July 1683.

15. Ibid., p. 132. In Letter 150, its writing scarcely legible, he wrote to Leopold on 2 September 1686: 'Lodato Iddio e Maria! Buda fu presa per assalto . . . Vero miracolo di Dio, mentre non credo sino morti cento de'nostri. Scrivo in fretta.'

16. See Rycaut, *A true and exact relation of the imperial expedition in Hungaria, in the year 1684*, pp. 23–4

17. Ibid., p. 32.

18. Ibid.

19. Ibid., p. 45.

20. Rycaut, *A true and exact relation of the imperial expedition in Hungaria, in the year 1684*, suggests 25,000 – a huge proportion of the total force.

21. Ibid., p. 153.

22. Anon, *An historical description of the glorious conquest of the city of Buda* . . . , pp. 5–7.

23. Mark L. Stein, *Guarding the Frontier*, pp. 29–59.

24. JS [John Shirley], *A true account of the heroick actions* . . . .

25. Peter Canyi, 'The Importance of Nové Zámky during the Habsburg–Ottoman War,' *Slovak Journal of Political Sciences* (2/2003) at http://www.ceeol.com.

26. For the 1663 siege and surrender by the Habsburg garrison, 'An exact narrative of the remarkable occurrences of the siege of Newhausel', in Anon, *A brief Accompt of the Turks late expedition . . .*, pp. 12–18.

27. Ibid., p. 18.

28. For a compelling fictional account of this kind of war on the frontier, see Cecilia Holland, *Rákossy*. Although the historical context is generalised, the book catches the nature of conflict with remarkable precision. Géza Gárdonyi, *Eclipse of the Crescent Moon: A Tale of the Siege of Eger, 1552.* Budapest: Corvina, 1991, first published in 1899, fictionalises a real event in a more traditional manner.

29. See JS, *A true account of the heroick actions . . .*, pp. 13–15.

30. Ibid., p. 21.

31. He was seized by the Ottomans and taken in chains to Edirne for failing to support them with sufficient energy and zeal.

32. The hope of enlisting the Persian Shah in this anti-Ottoman enterprise came to nothing, but a serious attempt was made by Leopold's envoy to launch a war on the eastern border of the Ottoman empire.

33. The Emperor Leopold conceded a small part of Silesia and the deal was sweetened by a substantial subsidy.

34. Louis XIV certainly thought so, on the basis of extensive military intelligence. See Richard Place, 'The Self-Deception of the Strong: France on the Eve of the War of the League of Augsburg', *French Historical Studies* 6, no. 4 (1970): 465.

35. Moritz von Angeli, 'Die Eroberung von Ofen und der Feldzug gegen die Turken in Jahre 1686', *Mitteilungen des K.K. Kriegsarchiv* (1886): 15–18.

36. See *An historical description of the glorious conquest of the city of Buda . . .*, p. 8.

37. Ibid., p. 12.

38. Ibid., p. 14.

39. This was where the Habsburgs erected their guns after 1848 to overawe the citizens of Buda.

40. *An historical description of the glorious conquest of the city of Buda . . .*, pp. 20–23, especially 9 July

41. Ibid., p. 26.

42. The siege journal recorded that every night the 'besieged repaired with gabions and palisades, the wall that secured the castle'. See ibid., 14 July, p. 27.

43. Ibid., p. 33.

44. Ibid., p. 40.
45. Ibid., p. 51.
46. His intuition was confirmed by intercepted letters to the Grand Vizier from the pasha of Buda that entreated him to relieve the city, but, whatever happened, he was determined to hold out 'to the last extremity'. See ibid., p. 54.
47. Ibid., p. 62.
48. Ibid., p. 66.
49. Ibid., p. 66.

Chapter 11

1. See Karl Vocelka, *Geschichte Österreichs. Kultur-Gesellschaft-Politik*. Wien, 2002, p. 141. But the term has come to have a more generalised and diffuse meaning, as in *einem 'Heldenzeitalter' der österreichischen Stadt-und Landesplanung*, 'the heroic age of town and regional planning'.
2. Peter Krenn and Walter J. Karcheski, Jr, *Imperial Austria. Treasures of Art from the State of Styria*, p. 14. This was the total in the 1629 inventory and it kept on growing, to more than 100,000 items. One hundred suits of cuirassier armour were added in 1683 alone.
3. See Michael Hochedlinger, *Austria's Wars of Emergence*, pp. 78–92.
4. Ibid., p. 7.
5. See Janos Barta, 'Habsburg Rule in Hungary in the Eighteenth Century', in *Hungarian Studies Review*, 2001. *Hungary 1001–2001: A Millennial Retrospection*.
6. A portrait of Prince Eugene was advertised in the *Daily Courant*, 18 August 1708. 'This Day is Publish'd, Prince Eugene's Prayer, with his Character and Picture curiously Engraven on a Copper-Plate, handsomely Printed on a Broadside, fit to be put into Frames, and hung up in all Families; which Prayer for its singular Excellency has been admir'd by all Nations and Translated into all Languages, and ought to be preserv'd with the Author's Immortal Glory to all succeeding Generations. Price 3d. Sold by J. Morphew near Stationer's-Hall [London].'
7. C. H. L. George describes how: 'The fame of Charles V's victory at Buda also made its way into the advertising section on the back page of The London Gazette. Map and print seller John Oliver placed three advertisements for products related to the siege. On 9th August he advertised a map described as "an Exact Delineation of the Famous Siege of Buda", on 13th September he promoted a mezzotint portrait of Charles

V and on 1st November he placed a notice for "A curious Delineation of the Storming of Buda". On the 4th and 7th October His Majesty's printer Henry Hills advertised "An exact Description of the City of Buda" and on 28th October the stationer Richard Palmer inserted a notice for a map of Hungary. On 21st October the medal maker George Bower advertised "A Medal of the Duke of Lorrain, with a Reverse representing the Figure of the Christian Religion triumphing over the Crescent". Only thirteen newspaper advertisements for medals were placed in the later Stuart period which suggests that the presence of this notice is evidence for the strength of English response to the siege.' See C. H. L. George, *Topical Portrait Print Advertising in London Newspapers and The Term Catalogues*. Durham University, 2005, ch. 1.

8. Paul Rycaut, *The history of the Turks*, p. 136.
9. Derek McKay, *Prince Eugene of Savoy*. London: Thames & Hudson, 1977, p. 43.
10. Nicolas Henderson, *Prince Eugen of Savoy*, p. 40, citing Instruction to Eugene from the Imperial War Council 5.7.1697, in A. Arneth, *Das Leben des Kaiserlichen Feldmarshalls Guido von Starhemberg*. Vienna: Carl Gerold und Sohn, 1853, pp. 187–8.
11. The best basic account in English is in McKay, *Prince Eugene of Savoy*, pp. 41–8, but a lot of the incidental detail is in A. Arneth, *Prinz Eugen von Savoyen*, vol. 1, pp. 98–111.
12. Rycaut, *The history of the Turks*, p. 555.
13. On Tverda, see the UNESCO World Heritage proposal http:// whc.unesco.org; on Brod, see the local site http://www.tzgsb.hr/ pg008.htm; for Petrovaradin, a history at http://www.veljkomilkovic. com/OtvrdjaviEng.htm. Doxat was unfortunate enough to be executed for surrendering a fortress to the Turks in 1738; Marsigli narrowly avoided execution but was cashiered for the premature surrender of a fortress – during the War of the Spanish Succession.
14. See Hochedlinger, *Austria's Wars of Emergence*, pp. 308–9. The reasonable enough explanation he gives is that the sultan 'might enter [a] war on the Prussian side'.
15. See Onno Klopp, *Corrispondenza epistolare tra Leopoldo I imperatore* . . .
16. See Christopher Duffy, *The Military Experience in the Age of Reason*, pp. 268–93.
17. Maurice de Saxe, *Mes Rêveries*. Ed. Jean-Paul Charnay, Paris: Economica, 2002.
18. This was de Ligne writing in his guise as Prince Eugene. The struggle at the breach in the wall at Belgrade may have been 'Eugene', but the concern for the conscripted Jews was pure 'de Ligne', who had written

for legal rights and protection for Jews, in which Eugene had no interest. Charles Joseph, Prince De Ligne, *The Life of Prince Eugene: from his own Manuscript*, 1812, p. 7.

19. In *Musikalischen Rüstkammer auf der Harfe*. See http://ingeb.org/Lieder/prinzeug.html

20. See P. A. La Lande, *Histoire de l'Empereur Charles VI* . . . vol. 2, pp. 562–4.

21. The best modern published account of the war in English is in Karl A. Roider, *The Reluctant Ally*, pp. 94–172. Much of this, however, is given over to the complex diplomacy, but Roider has made excellent use of the MS report on the war by Johann Georg Brown, a massive work in five volumes, held in the Kriegsarchiv. The best contemporary account is in the last volume of P. A. La Lande, *Histoire de l'Empereur Charles VI* . . .

22. See Archdeacon William Coxe, *History of the House of Austria* . . ., p. 210. Coxe travelled widely in Europe in the 1770s and early 1780s. He stayed in Vienna and Budapest in 1794.

23. Joseph G. Rosengarten, 'The Earl of Crawford's Ms History in the Library of the American Philosophical Society', *Proceedings of the American Philosophical Society* 42, no. 174 (May–Dec. 1903): 397–404. For the full version of Crawford's experience, the ur-text is in his MSS papers at the American Philosophical Society, but these documents were erratically used by a distant kinsman of the earl, Richard Rolt, for pp. 160–209 of his *Memoirs of the Life of the late right Honourable John Lindesay*. The four volumes of manuscripts contain a much wider range of Crawford's military experiences; and he writes better than Rolt.

24. The details of this medical diagnosis are in Rolt's volume, but the sketch maps are to be found only in the Crawford MSS.

25. The traveller was Franz Baron von Gudenus, in his twenties at the time. Cited in Roider, *The Reluctant Ally*, p. 160.

26. Cited in Karl A. Roider, *Austria's Eastern Question*, p. 186.

27. Rolt, *Memoirs of the Life of the late right Honourable John Lindesay*, pp. 160–209.

Chapter 12

1. In this sense it was different from the cases included in Eric Hobsbawm and Terence Ranger's classic edited volume, *The Invention of Tradition*. Cambridge: Cambridge University Press, 1992.

2. 'The Victories of Duke Charles V of Lorraine' are now KHM inventory

T. IX and consist of nineteen pieces from 'The Liberation of Pressburg' to 'The Submission of Transylvania'.

3. Parts of Prince Eugene's war diaries also survive in the Austrian archives.

4. Charles V, Duke of Lorraine, *Lotharingiai Károly hadinaplója Buda visszafoglalásáról*, p. 427 seqq. The diary is written in a number of different hands, in French, Italian or German, depending on the native language of the diary writer; the content is indexed pp. 455–64.

5. *Political and Military Observations, Remarks and Maxims of Charles V, late Duke of Lorrain, general of the Emperor's Forces. From a Manuscript left by him and never printed before*. London: J. Jones, 1699, p.122.

6. Ibid., p. 126.

7. Ibid., p. 134.

8. Ibid., p. 148.

9. Braubach described how there was a special collection at Schlosshof of a cycle of paintings designed to ensure his posthumous fame. He does not name the artist, but the paintings are undoubtedly the Huchtenburgs. See Max Braubach, *Prinz Eugen von Savoyen: eine Biographie*. Munich: R. Oldenbourg Verlag, 1963–5, vol. 5, p. 79.

10. See Matthias Pfaffenbichler, 'Das barocke Schlachtenbild: Versuch einer Typologie', *Jahrbuch der Kunsthistorischen Sammlungen in Wien*, Bd 91 (1996): 37–110.

11. Ibid.: 92–116.

12. Equally, the production of a tea service and garniture from the Meissen factory may or may not have had his approval. See Maureen Cassidy-Geiger, 'Repraesentatio Belli, ob successionem in Regno Hispanico. A Tea Service and Garniture by the Schwarzelot Decorator Preissler', *Metropolitan Museum Journal* 24 (1989): 239–54. The whole field of Eugene 'memorabilia' awaits proper research.

13. Du Mont, *Batailles gagnés par le Serenissime Prince Fr. Eugene de Savoye sur les Ennemis de la Foi . . . .*

14. Salomon Kleiner. Résidences mémorables de l'incomparable Heros de nôtre Siecle: Répresentation exact des Edifices et Jardins de Son Altesse Serenissime Monsigneur Eugene François . . . Contenant les Plans, Elevations et Veües de la Maison de Plaisance de son Altesse Ser. située dans un de faubourgs de Vienne . . . Le tout levé et designé par le Sieur Salomon Kleiner Ingenieur de son Altesse Electorale de Mayence. Augsburg: Verlegung Jeremias Wolffs seele Erben. 1731: 'Vue du Grand Escalier'.

15. Ibid., 'Chambre de Parade et Audiences'.

16. Ibid., 'Bibliothèque' and 'Cabinet'.

17. Title page Kleiner, *Résidences mémorables de l'Incomparable Heros de nôtre Siecle . . . .*

18. She was never Empress, refusing to be crowned Empress-Consort, and did not attend her husband's imperial coronation.

19. At the time it was the only Order in Europe solely and exclusively established to reward courage on the battlefield. The Prussian order *Pour le Merité* was awarded to civilians as well as military officers, until 1810 when it was made an exclusively military order.

20. He admitted as much to his elder daughter and confidante, Christine: 'It seems to me that I have made Prince Eugene say what we should have done for the defence of Vienna [in 1809].' Cited in Philip Mansel, *Prince of Europe. The Life of Charles-Joseph de Ligne*. London: Phoenix, 2005, p. 379.

21. The Austrian historian Peter Stachel has described how 'Prince Eugene' was made into a secular patron of the country and a mythical protective spirit of the Fatherland. After the end of First World War and the demise of the dynasty, the Italian prince, without a drop of German blood in his veins, suddenly became a German national hero. From 1932, the Austro-fascists pushed on with a 'patriotic' drive in education. The *edle Ritter* ballad appeared in many school songbooks and there was a tremendous focus on Prince Eugene throughout the clerical fascist government right up to the Nazi takeover in 1938. The new 1935 elementary school ABC first reader began A stands (unsurprisingly) for *Austria*, C for *Christianity* and the young child was taught: 'Austria is a Christian state'. E was simply *Prinz Eugen*, H was for *heroes of the homeland*, 'who fought and offered their lives for the homeland'; V stood for *Volk und Vaterland* (People and Nation) 'whom we love as much as our parents'. But all this was framed not within the Jew-hating of German textbooks of the same era but instead with a focus on the Turk as the enemy.

The new secondary school curriculum of 1935 introduced a new topic: *Fatherland Studies*. It suggested the approved basic themes for courses: 'Austria as a pillar of Catholic culture in Europe', 'Austria as a bulwark against the Turks'. Older children were taught that post-Habsburg Austria was heir to the old empire's mission in the east, and that Austria had always defended Christendom against the onslaught of the Turks, and also brought civilisation to the East. In the principal Austrian teacher's journal *Die österreichische Schule*, a contributor wrote that no one, certainly no school child, should ever forget the events of 1683, when 'Austria, Vienna and Styria withstood the Turks . . . stood firm – and [as a result] the peoples of the West live on'. Even after the German takeover in 1938, Prince Eugene remained in high favour. The Nazi *Book of the German Ostmark*, published in 1938, proclaimed 'Prinz Eugen's German Victories'. See Carla Esden-Tempska, 'Civic Education in

Authoritarian Austria 1934–38', *History of Education Quarterly* 30, no. 2 (1990): 187–211.

22. See Stachel: 'In Germany Eugene was proclaimed a forerunner of the Nazi policy of conquest in the east. The great majority of the 22 novels about Prince Eugene, published in German in the period 1932–1941, more or less corresponded to this tendency. His name was given to a heavy battle cruiser of the German navy (1938).

23. *Prinz Eugen, der edle Ritter* was still in the reader *Lesebuch fur Mittelschulen*, vol. III, in 1952. He had by then been purged of any connection with German victories, and freed from association with the SS *Prinz Eugen* division recruited in 1942 from the German minorities of south-east Europe. See Werner Suppanz, *Österreichische Geschichtsbilder*, pp. 176–8.

24. Henderson, *Prince Eugen of Savoy*, p. 289.

25. *New York Times*, 4 November 1918. Archives at http://query.nytimes.com.

26. A note on the past and memory: An individual's memory is limited to his lifetime, and the lifetime of those who have had a direct connection with him; a society can 'remember' in a collective sense over a very extended period. Two German Egyptologists, Jan and Aleida Assmann, with John Czaplicka, in 'Collective Memory and Cultural Identity', *New German Critique* 65 (1995): 125–33, have taken the idea forward from the French philosopher and sociologist Maurice Halbwachs who first approached the topic in 1925. Jan Assmann talks of individual memory which is 'communicative', knowledge and attitudes transmitted conversationally from person to person. But that process cannot go much farther than three or four generations – about a century. Beyond that there is 'cultural memory' which is more of a theory than a description of actual practice. It is the kind of interpretation widely used by archaeologists and anthropologists and less common among historians. Assmann describes 'fixed points' that create and sustain cultural memories. These might be 'fateful events of the past, whose memory is maintained through cultural formations (texts, rites, monuments) and institutional communication (recitation, practice, observance)'. These memories are radically edited and simplified. As Assmann puts it: 'redundant elements are discarded, and a clear and robust cultural message is created for onward narration'. Whatever is to be 'remembered' is very different from the individual memory which is often random, confused and imprecise. Aleida Assmann, in 'Soziales und kollektives Gedächtnis', to be found at http://www.bpb.de, has described how 'Cultural memory preserves the store of knowledge from which a group derives an awareness of

its unity and peculiarity . . . In a positive "we are this" or a negative "that's our opposite" sense.' But in practice things do not always work out. It is incredibly difficult to maintain this sense of 'we are this' and 'that's our opposite' over the long term. Religious faiths – Judaism, Islam and Christianity – have been relatively successful; but even there the dissident *enemy within* is often a greater threat than the *enemy outside*. Protestants have hated Catholics and Sunni have hated Shia with greater virulence than the other antagonist. Over the long term there has never been a solid and consistent line of 'them' and 'us'. Whatever is most dangerous is most feared.

27. This process is described in a short but important book by the philosopher John Lear. In *Radical Hope: Ethics in the Face of Cultural Devastation.* Chicago, IL: University of Chicago Press, 2006, he describes the process by which his subject (the Cree Indians), the roots of their culture based on success in war and honour destroyed, survived the period when, in the old terms, 'nothing happened'. The Cree survived on the basis of a 'prophetic dream' and, I argue, that was also true of the Habsburgs and the Ottomans.

28. Cited in Mansel, *Prince of Europe*, p. 279.

29. Letter to Prince Paul Esterhazy, Austrian ambassador to London, 2 December 1828. See G. de Bertier de Sauvigny, *Metternich and His Times.* London: Darton, Longman and Todd, 1962, p. 247.

30. C. A. Bayly, *The Birth of the Modern World, 1780–1914. Global Connections and Comparisons.* Oxford and Malden, MA: Blackwell, 2004, pp. 61–75.

31. The developing nation states, big and small, increasingly used the same methods of celebration and *ralliement* but often rather crudely. They had something to celebrate, but in return they were circumscribed by reality and current events: the British found it hard to accommodate the 'Indian Mutiny' of 1857, France was convulsed by the humiliating defeat of 1870, imperial Russia was rocked by Japan's stunning military triumph and then the revolution of 1905.

32. This whole process has been exceptionally well covered by Selim Deringil, *The Well-Protected Domains*. His work is based on primary sources, and he does not present the visual evidence. The role of the Hijaz Railway is detailed in William Ochsenwald, *The Hijaz Railway*.

33. Regina Bendix demonstrates how hard it was to achieve these patriotic motives in reality. Regina Bendix, 'Ethnology, Cultural Reification and the Dynamics of Difference in the *Kronprinzenwerk*', in Nancy Wingfield (ed.), *Creating the Other*.

34. Ákos Moravánszky, *Competing Visions*, p. 4.

35. Daniel Unowsky notes that the editor, Max Herzig, wanted to show the world 'how the first in the empire day after day worries over his people and is the first at work'. Daniel L. Unowsky, *The Pomp and Politics of Patriotism*, pp. 105–11.

36. He had, however, a high opinion of Klimt's traditional painting in the Burgtheater and the Kunsthistorisches Museum, awarding him a personal prize.

37. Muhammad A⁻rif, *The Hejaz Railway and the Muslim Pilgrimage*.

38. 'The Austro-Hungarian Midwife' of modernity, in Marko Attila Hoare, *The History of Bosnia: From the Middle Ages to the Present Day*. London: Saqi, 2007, p. 69.

39. 'The mytho-historical meta-narrative of Frontier Orientalism basically claims [that] the bad Muslim and Oriental attacked and seriously endangered our frontier, as in the Turkish wars at the dawn of modernity ... At the beginning of modernity, the bad Muslim was a serious rival and threat to "our" existence. Crushing that rival is portrayed as the decisive precondition for the subsequent rise of Habsburg colonial expansion.' This key theory was developed by Andre Gingrich in 'Frontier Myths of Orientalism: The Muslim World in Public and Popular Cultures of Central Europe', at the 3rd Mediterranean Ethnological Summer School in Slovenia in 1996. I am very grateful to Professor Gingrich for his kindness in sending me a copy. The paper was published in English in the proceedings of that conference in 1998, as 'Frontier Myths of Orientalism: The Muslim World in Public and Popular Cultures of Central Europe' in Bojan Baskar and Borut Brumen (eds), Mediterranean Ethnological Summer School, Piran/Pirano Slovenia 1996, vol. 2, Ljubljana: Instiut za multikulturne raziskave, pp. 99–127. The text later appeared in a slightly revised form in German with notes and bibliography as *Grenzmythen des Orientalismus. Die islamische Welt in Öffentlichkeit und Volkskultur Mitteleuropas*, in Erika Mayr-Oehring and Elke Doppler (eds), *Orientalische Reise: Malerei und Exotik im späten 19. Jh.* Wien: Wien Museum, 2003, pp. 110–29. He returned to the topic in *Kulturgeschichte, Wissenschaft und Orientalismus. Zur Diskussion des 'frontier orientalism' in der Spätzeit der K.u.K Monarchie*, in Johannes Feichtinger, Elisabeth Großegger, Gertraud Marinelli-König, Peter Stachel and Heidemarie Uhl (eds), *Schauplatz Kultur – Zentraleuropa. Transdisziplinäre Annäherungen. Moritz Csáky zum 70. Geburtstag gewidmet* (Gedächtnis – Erinnerung – Identität 7). Innsbruck: Studienverlag, pp. 279–88. Frontier Orientalism has thus existed on the fringes of the Ottoman–Habsburg for more than a decade, but has never made the impact among historians that I believe it deserves.

40. See Andre Gingrich, *Immigration Politics* (1996) and *Grenzmythen des Orientalismus* (2003), passim.

41. 'The History of the Travels of Scarmentado' (1756), a satire by Voltaire.

42. Jonathan Israel, *Enlightenment Contested. Philosophy, Modernity, and the Emancipation of Man, 1670–1752*. Oxford: Oxford University Press, 2006, pp. 615–30.

43. Kerstin Tomenendal, *Das türkische Gesicht Wiens. Auf den Spuren der Türken in Wien*. Böhlau Verlag: Wien, 2000, pp. 63–6.

44. The 'Austrian-style' Orientalism has been surveyed by Eugene Sensenig-Dabbous, 'Will the Real Almásy Please Stand Up! Transporting Central European Orientalism', *Comparative Studies of South Asia, Africa and the Middle East* 24 (2004): 163–80. Hammer-Purgstall had a great popular success but many (jealous) scholars considered him a charlatan.

45. Arthur von Scala, *Österreichische Monatsschrift für den Orient*. Number 1. 15 January 1875. 1–2. Translated by Rainald Franz in his article '"A Treasure Trove": The Hamzanama and the Austrian Museum of Art and Industry 1873–1900'. See John Seyller (ed.), *The Adventures of Hamza. Painting and Storytelling in Mughal India*. Smithsonian Press, 2002, pp. 285–7.

46. Josef von Falke, *Die Kunstindustrie auf der Wiener Weltaustellung*. Vienna: Carl Herold, 1873, p. 25, based on a translation by Rainald Franz, *vide sup*.

47. In 1908 Austria-Hungary annexed the provinces, on the excuse of Abdul Hamid's removal from power.

48. Noel Malcolm, *Bosnia: A Short History*, p. 143.

49. Andre Gingrich: 'The meta-narrative of Austrian Frontier Orientalism thus connects periods and socio-political systems that have little if anything to do with each other, in order to construct a timeless border mission. Charlemagne's medieval outpost against the east, the Ottoman defeats before Vienna of 1529 and 1683, and Habsburg antagonisms with Serbia and Russia of the late 19th and early 20th centuries all are superficially and artificially connected through the mytho-historical narrative of Frontier Orientalism, and through its dual register of the good and the bad Oriental.'

50. Norman Stone, 'Army and Society in the Habsburg Monarchy', *Past & Present* 33 (1966): 95–111.

51. Norman Stone, *The Eastern Front*, p. 71.

52. 'Like the Habsburg Monarchy itself, Austro-Hungarian plans for the war were neat and desirable on paper, but remote from the practical world. The initial battles were lost virtually before they began: a quarter of the army spent the first weeks of the war in a state of directionless confusion, shuttling between the two fronts; ending up as passive and exhausted spectators on both.' Norman Stone, unpublished paper, 'The Mobilisation of the Austro-Hungarian Army 1914', personal communication.

Coda

1. 'Islamic Europe?' *Weekly Standard*, 4 October 2004 issue: When Bernard Lewis speaks . . . by Christopher Caldwell, vol. 10, issue 4.
2. Cited in the Christian Science Monitor posted 22 April 2005, updated 15.15 p.m. at http://www.csmonitor.com/2005.0422/dailyUpdate.htmn. The Italian text of two speeches on the topic, one in *Le Figaro* and the other in *Giornale del Popolo*, can be found at the website of Il Cannocchiale, 25 December 2005 http://lux.ilcannocchiale.it.post/788434.html.
3. http://gatesofvienna.blog.com/
4. Elizabeth Johnson, *The Historian*, Boston, MA: Little, Brown, 2005, p. ix.
5. 'wie es eigentlich gewesen' – the words of Leopold von Ranke, the first architect of modern history.

Bibliography

Unpublished Manuscripts

Unpublished MS draft of Luigi Ferdinando de Marsigli, *Stato Militare dell' Imperio Ottomanno*, in Italian, with additional material not used in the published text and drafts of illustrations by the author. Livrustkammeren [Royal Armoury], Stockholm

Unpublished MSS of John Lindsay, Earl of Crawford, American Philosophical Society, Philadelphia, PA, USA

Contemporary Printed Sources

These are the most useful of the contemporary books I have used, listed by author, or by the first word of the title for anonymous works. They are part of a much larger body of material examined, which has been assembled for the Printed Images Research Consortium project Imaging Orientalism 1480–1830. As a result many have woodcut or engraved images within the text. I have tried to use the contemporary English language translations wherever possible, if only because of the seductive vitality of the language. The title page first appeared in the sixteenth century, and often contained an extensive text outlining the content of the work. This makes referencing the works difficult: the title of one of these books extends to fourteen lines. Reluctantly, I have shortened some of the titles, but the extended list is available from me at The Centre for Publishing Studies, University of Stirling, Scotland, FK9 4LA, United Kingdom; email ajmw1@stir.ac.uk

A Brief Accompt of the Turks' late expedition, against the Kingdome of Hungary, Transylvania, and the hereditary countries of the Emperour: together with an exact narrative of the remarquable occurrences at the Siege of Newhausel. Translated out of Dutch. London: Hodgkinson and Mab, 1663

A Letter from an eminent Merchant in Constantinople to a Friend in London: giving

an exact relation of the Cavalcade of Sultan Mahomet the Fourth, present emperour of the Turks, as he marched out of Constantinople for the invasion of Christendome, and the siege of Vienna. London, 1683

A prospect of Hungary and Transylvania . . . whereunto is added an historical narration of the bloody wars amongst themselves and with the Turks. London: William Miller, 1664

An historical description of the glorious conquest of the city of Buda, the capital city of the kingdom of Hungary, by the victorious arms of the thrice illustrious and invincible Emperor Leopold I. under the conduct of his Most Serene Highness, the Duke of Lorraine, and the Elector of Bavaria. London: Robert Clavell, 1686

A Prospect of Hungary, and Transylvania: with a catalogue of the kings of the one, and the princes of the other; together with an account of the qualities of the inhabitants, the commodities of the countries, the chiefest cities, towns, and strongholds, rivers, and mountains. Whereunto is added an historical narrative of the bloody wars amongst themselves, and with the Turks; continued to this present year 1664. London: William Miller, 1664

A relation of whatever has happened in Germany since the descent of the Turks into Hungary till the raising of the siege of Vienna. Printed at Cologne and reprinted . . . in London. London: H. Bonwick, 1684

A true and exact relation of the great victory obtained by General Schults over Count Teckely in the Upper Hungaria, on the 20th of Septemb. 1684. Together with an account of the battle between the Duke of Lorraine and the Serasquier Bassa before Buda. London: Thomas Snowdon, 1684

A true and exact relation of the imperial expedition in Hungaria, in the year 1684: wherein is contained an impartial and full account of the siege and defence of the city of Buda: as also, the most remarkable actions from day to day of the Elector of Bavaria: with an accurate delineation of the aforesaid siege collected and brought together with great care by a chief military officer there. London: R. Taylor, 1685

A brief accompt of the Turks' late expedition against the Kingdom of Hungary translated out of the Dutch. London: Richard Hodgkinson, 1663

A True and particular relation of the victory obtained by the Christian armies against the Turks at Barkan, the ninth of October, 1683. London: Samuel Lowndes, 1683

A true relation of the great victory obtained by the Christian army over the Turks near the mountain Harsan in the neighbourhood of Syclos, from the camp of Electoral Highness of Bavaria near Barnowar the 14th of August, 1687. London: Samuel Carr, 1687

John Bancks, *The history of Francis-Eugene Prince of Savoy: . . . Containing, the military transactions of above thirty campaigns, made by his Serene Highness in Hungary, Italy, Germany, and the Low-Countries. . . . By an English officer, who served under his Highness in the last war with France.* London: 1754

[Charles-Joseph, Prince de Ligne], *Memoirs of Prince Eugene of Savoy, written by himself [or rather, by Charles-Joseph, Prince de Ligne]. Translated from the . . . French edition, containing all those passages . . . suppressed by order of the French government. Second edition, with an introduction and notes, etc.* London: Henry Colburn, 1811

Glaubwürdiges Diarium und Beschreibung dessen was Zeit währender Türckischen Belagerung der kays. Haupt und Residenz-Stadt . . . Von einem kayserl. Oficier, so sich vom Anfang biss zu End darinnen befunden/warhafftig verzeichnet und zusammen getragen. Regensburg: Paul Dalnsteiner, 1683

Herrliche Creutz-Beuthe, der Christen, welche von denen barbarischen Feinden des Creutzes Christi, den Türken, an den Wallachischen Gräntzen. Nuremberg: L. Loschye. 1683

Primeras noticias, venidas por Paris, de la derrota que las armas alemanas, mandadas por el señor principe Eugenio de Saboya dieron a los Turcos. Seville: F. Garay, 1716

Pannoniæ Historia chronologica: res per Ungariam, Transylvaniam iam inde a cõstitutione regnorum illorum . . . Icones geüinæ regum, ducum & procerum eiusdem militiæ [drawn by Jean Jacques Boissard]. Tabula . . . Omnia in æs eleganter incisa & recens euulgata per Theodore de Bry. Frankfurt on Main: Theodore de Bry, 1596

La Vie de Charles V Duc de Lorraine et de Bar et Generalissime des Troupes Imperiales Divisce en cinq livres. Amsterdam: Jean Garrel, 1691

Des grossen Feld-Herrns Eugenii Herzogs von Savoyen. Nuremburg: Christoph Riegel, 1739

Count Taafe's letters from the Imperial Camp to his brother the Earl of Carlingford. London: William Abbington, 1684

L'Ombre de Charles V Duc de Lorraine consultée sur l'état present des affaires de l'Europe. Cologne: Pierre Marteau, 1693

Giovanni Benaglia, *Relatione del viaggio fatto à Constantinopoli: e ritorno in Germania, dell' Illustrissimo Sig. Conte Alberto Caprara, Gentilhuomo della Camera dell' Imperatore e da Esso mandato come Internuntio Straordinario, e Plenipotentiaro per trattare la continuatione della Tregua . . . Descritta da Giovanni Benaglia.* Bologna: Per gli HH. di Gio. Recaldini, 1685.

Gio Giacomo Dionisi, *Nella vitoria riportata dall armi Cesaree sopra gli Ottomani a Zenta.* Verona, 1718

R. P. Boucher, *Le Bouquet sacré ou le voyage de la Terre Sainte.* Rouen: Seyer, 1745

Edward Brown, *A brief account of some travels in divers parts of Europe: viz Hungaria, Servia, Bulgaria, Macedonia, Thessaly, Austria, Styria, Carinthia, Carniola, and Friuli.* London: Benjamin Tooke, 1685

[François-Paulin] Dalerac, *Polish manuscripts: or The secret history of the reign of John Sobieski, the III, of that name, K. of Poland.: Containing a particular account of the siege of Vienna, and some circumstances in relation to the raising of it; not before made known to the world.* . . . London: H. Rhodes, 1700

Louis Demay, *A discourse, historical and political, of the War of Hungary, and of the causes of the peace between Leopold the First, Emperor of the Romans, and Mahomet the Fourth, Sultan of Turkey. Translated in English.* [by Sir James Turner]. Glasgow: Robert Sanders, 1669

M. Dumont and M. Rousset, *Histoire Militaire du Prince Eugene de Savoye, du Prince et Duc de Marlborough et du Prince de Nassau-Frisem ou en trouve un detail des principales Actions de la derniere Guerre & des Batailles & Sieges commandez par ces troix Genereux. Enrichies de Plans necessaries. Tome Premier Par M. Dumont, Baron de Carelscroon, historiographe de Sa Majeste Imperial, augmente d'un Suppliment, M. Rousset.* 3 vols. The Hague: Isaac van de Kloot, 1729

Du Mont, *Batailles gagnés par le Serenissime Prince Fr. Eugene de Savoye sur les Ennemis de la Foi, et sur de L'Empereur et de L'Empire, et en Hongrie, en Italie, en Allemagne, et aux Pais-Bas, dépeintes et gravées en Taille-douce par le Sr Jean Huchtenburg, peintre très Célèbres á La Haye, avec les Explications Historiques par M. J. Du Mont, Conseiller & Historiogr. de Sa Majesté Imperiale & Catholique.* The Hague: Pierre Gosse and Rutgert Ch. Alberts, 1725

Comte de Girecour, *Essai sur l'Histoire de la Maison d'Autriche.* Paris: Mouthard, 1778, 6 vols

Eberhard Happel, *Der Ungarische Kriegs-Roman, Oder Außführliche Beschreibung, Deß jüngsten Türcken-Kriegs.* . . . *Mit schönen Kupffern gezieret.* Ulm: Matthäus Wagner, 1685, 6 vols

Johann Christian Herchenhahn, *Die Belagerung von Belgrad unter der Anführung des Prinzen Eugen: eine Galerie historischer Gemälde.* Leipzig: Wengandschen Buchandlung, 1788

Salomon Kleiner, *Residences memorables de l'incomparable Heros de nôtre Siecle: Representation exact des Edifices et Jardins de Son Altesse Serenissime Monsigneur Eugene Francois . . . Contenant les Plans, Elevations et Veües de la Maison de Plaisance de son Altesse Ser. située dans un de faubourgs de Vienne. Le tout levé et designé par le Sieur Salomon Kleiner Ingenieur de son Altesse Electorale de Mayence.* Augsburg: Verlegung Jeremias Wolffs seele Erben, 1731

Salomon Kleiner, *Representation des Animaux de la Menagerie de S.A. S Monsigneur le Prince Eugene François de Savoye et de Piemont . . . avec plusieurs plantes etrangeres du dit Jardin, le tout dessigne par le Sieur Salomon Kleiner Ingenieur.* Augsburg: Verlegung Jeremias Wolffs seele Erben, 1734

Richard Knolles, *The Generall Historie of the Turkes from the first beginning of that Nation to the rising of the Othoman Familie . . . Together with the lives and conquests of the Othoman Kings and Emperours, etc.* London: A. Islip, 1603

Jean Laurent Krafft, *Histoire Génerale de l'Auguste Maisone d'Autriche.* Brussels: la veuve de G. Jacobs, 1744, 3 vols

Baron von Kunitz, *Diarium Welches der am Türckischen Hoff und Groß-Wezier in der Wienerischen Belaegerung gewester Kayserl. Resident . . . Baron von Kunitz eigenhändig beschrieben . . .* Vienna, 1684

P. A. La Lande, *Histoire de l'Empereur Charles VI. . . . contenant ce qui s'est passé de plus mémorable en Europe, depuis sa naissance jusque à sa mort, etc.* The Hague, 1743

Sieur Le Croix, *The wars of the Turks with Poland, Muscovy, and Hungary: from the year 1672, to the year 1683. Containing a particular account of several transactions in those wars not taken notice of in the history of the Turks. Written in French by the Sieur Le Croy, Secretary to the French Embassy at the Porte. Translated into English by Mr Chaves.* London: R. Basset, and F. Fawcet, 1705

Le Croy, *An account of the Turks wars with Poland, Muscovy and Hungary.* London: J. King, 1711

Allain Manesson Mallet, *Les Travaux de Mars, ou l'Art de la Guerre. Divisé en Trois Parties. . . . Avec un ample détail de la Milice des Turcs, tant pour l'Attaque que pour la Deffence. Ouvrage enrichi de plus de quatre cens Planches gravées en Taille-Douce. Dedié au Roy.* Paris: Chez Denys Thierry, 1684–5, 3 vols

Henry Marsh, *A new survey of the Turkish Empire and Government in a brief history deduced to the present time and the reign of the now Grand Signior Mahomet IV the present and fourteenth emperor, with their laws, religion and customs. As also an account of the siege of Newhausel.* London: 1663

Luigi Ferdinando Marsigli, *L'Etat Militaire de l'Empire Ottoman: ses progres et sa decadence, par M. le Comte de Marsigli, de l'Academie Royale de Sciences de Paris, et de Montpelier, de la Societe Royale de Londres et Fondateur de l'Institute de Boulogne, ouvrage enrichi de Planhes en taille douce.* Amsterdam and The Hague: Pierre Gosse, Jean Neulme, 1732

Henry Neville, **PLATO REDIVIVUS or A DIALOGUE CONCERNING** Government, *Wherein, by Observations drawn from other* **KINGDOMS** *and* **STATES** *both Ancient and Modern, an Endeavour is used to discover the present* **POLITICK DISTEMPER** *of* **OWN** *with the* CAUSES, *and* **REMEDIES***. The Second Edition, with Additions.* London: S.I.

Jean de Préchac, *The grand vizier, or, The history of the life of Cara Mustapha, who commanded the Turkish army at the siege of Vienna in the year 1683, containing his rise, his armours in the seraglio, his great warlike actions, and the true reason of his undertaking the siege of Vienna, with the particulars of his death in Belgrade. Written originally in French by a Person of Quality [Jean de Préchac] and now translated . . . by Francis Philon.* London, 1685

Richard Rolt, *Memoirs of the Life of the late right Honourable John Lindesay, Earl of Crauford and Lindesay.* London: Henry Kopp, 1753

Paul Rycaut, *The present state of the Ottoman Empire containing the maxims of the Turkish Politie, the most material points of the Mahomatan religion, their Sects and Heresies, their Convents and religious Votaries, their Military*

Discipline, with an exact computation of the Forces both by Land and Sea, illustrated with divers Pieces of Sculpture, representing the Variety of Habits amongst the Turks. . . . Printed for John Starkey and Henry Brome, at the Mitre between the Middle-Temple-Gate and Temple Bar in Fleet Street, 1668

[Sir] Paul Rycaut, *The history of the Turks: beginning with the year 1679: being a full relation of the last troubles in Hungary, with the sieges of Vienna, and Buda, and all the several battles both by sea and land, between the Christians, and the Turks, until the end of the year 1698, and 1699: in which the peace between the Turks, and the confederate Christian princes and states, was happily concluded at Carlowitz in Hungary, by the mediation of His Majesty of Great Britain, and the States General of the United Provinces: with the effigies of the emperors and others of note, engraven at large upon copper, which completes the sixth and last edition of the Turks: in two vol. in folio by Sir Paul Rycaut; kt. eighteen years consul at Smyrna now his Majesty's resident at Hamburg and fellow of the Royal Society.* London: Robert Clavell and Abel Roper, 1700

Schimpfflicher, *Abzug des Türkischen Feld Herrns oder Gross Vexiers von der kaiserlichen Residenzstadt Wien in Oesterreich. Neben einer kurzer Beschreibung seines ganzes Lebens/geführten Krieges.* Vienna: 1684

JS [John Shirley], *A true account of the heroick actions and enterprises of the confederate princes against the Turks and Hungarian rebels, during the last glorious campaign but more particularly the siege and taking of Newhausel. Together with the defeat of the Turkish army near Gran. To which is added the flight and seizure of the grand rebel, Count Teckely, by the Turks; and the manner of his treatment.* London: William Thackery, 1686

John Smith, *The true travels, adventures, and observations of Captaine Iohn Smith, in Europe, Asia, Affrica, and America from Anno Domini 1593 to 1629: his accidents and sea-fights in the Straights: his service and strategems of warre in Hungaria, Transilvania, Wallachia, and Moldavia, against the Turks, and Tartars: his three single combats betwixt the Christian Armie and the Turks: after how he taken prisoner by the Turks, sold for a slave, sent into Tartarias : his description of the Tartars, their strange manners and customes of religions, diets, buildings, warres, feasts, ceremonies, and living: how hee flew the Bashaw of Nalbrits in Cambia, and escaped from the Turkes and Tatars.* . . . London: Thomas Slater, 1630

J. B. Tavernier, *A New Relation of the inner part of the Grand Seignor's Seraglio containing remarkable Particulars never before exposed to publick view.* London: R.L. and Moses Pitt, 1677

[Mr] Travestin, *An account of the Imperial Proceedings against the Turks with an exact Diary of the Siege of Newheusel and its Taking, and also a relation of all the noted performances of the Imperialists in all parts as it was taken from the beginning of the Summer's campaign till the 27th of August. As it was taken by Mr Travestin, an English Gentleman who was all the while Resident in the Army* at *Newhausel and now in the imperial army. . . . With an exact map of the town and the works of the besiegers.* London: Sam Crouch, 1685

Thomas Troughton, *Barbarian Cruelty.* Exeter: W. Lowndes, 1788

John Peter a Valcaren, *A relation or diary of the siege of Vienna. Written by John Peter a Valcaren, Judge-Advocate of the Imperial Army. Drawn from the original by His Majestie's command.* London: William Nott and George Wells, 1684

[Valcaren?] *Journal: or, A most particular account of all that passed in the late seige of Vienna written by a principal officer, who was in the town during the whole time of the seige, and sent by authority to the Imperial Commissioner at the Dyet of Ratisbonne. Translated out of High-Dutch by His Majestie command.* London: H. Rogers and M. Gylliflower, 1684

Jan Pieter van Vaelckeren, *Vienna a' Turcis obsessa, a' Christianis eliberata, sive Diarium obsidionis Viennensis.* Brussels: 1684

Johannes Petrus a Vaelckeren, *Vienna a' Turcis Obsessa, a' Christianis Eliberata: Sive Diarium Obsidionis Viennensis, Inde à sexta Maii ad decimam quintam usque Septembris deductum.* Vienna: Leopoldi Voigt, 1683

Johann Peter von Vaelckeren, *Vienne assiegée par les Turcs, et delivrée par les chrestiens, ou, Journal du siege de Vienne: depuis le 6. de May de l'année 1683 jusqu'au 15. de Septembre de la mesme Année composé en Latin par Pierre à Vael-ckeren avec des figures.* New edition. Brussels: Chez Lambert Marchant, 1684

Johannes Petru[s] Vaelckeren, *Wienn von Türcken belägert, von Christen entsezt anjetzo aus dem Lateinischen ins Teutsch übersetzt von dem Authore selbst.* Linz: Rädlmayr, 1684

Secondary sources and modern editions

Zygmunt Abrahamowicz, Vojtech Kopčan, Metin Kunt, Endre Morosi, Nenad Moačanin, Constantin Serban and Karl Teply, *Die Türkenkriege in der historischen Forschung.* Vienna: Franz Deuticke, 1983

Isabella Ackerl, *Von Türken belagert – von Christen entsetzt: das belagerte Wien 1683.* Vienna: Österreichischer Bundesverlag, 1983

Fikret Adanir and Suraiya Faroqui, *The Ottomans and the Balkans: A Discussion of Historiography.* Leiden: E. J. Brill, 2002

Yusef Agha, 'Account of the mission of Yusef Agha written by himself.' Translated from the Turkish by the Ritter Joseph von Hammer (from the *Transactions of the Royal Asiatic Society of Great Britain and Ireland*, vol. III. London: Royal Asiatic Society, 1833)

Gábor Ágoston, 'Muslim Cultural Enclaves in Hungary under Ottoman Rule', *Acta Orientalis Academiae Scientarum Hungariae* XLV (2–3) (1991): 181–204

— *Guns for the Sultan: Military Power and the Weapons Industry in the Ottoman Empire.* Cambridge: Cambridge University Press, 2005

Virginia H. Aksan, *An Ottoman Statesman in War and Peace: Ahmed Resmi Efendi, 1700–1783*. Leiden: E. J. Brill, 1995

— *Ottoman Wars: An Empire Besieged*. Harlow: Pearson Longman, 2007

— and Daniel Goffman, *The Early Modern Ottomans: Remapping the Empire*. Cambridge: Cambridge University Press, 2007

Benedict Anderson, *Imagined Communities: Reflections on the Origins and Spread of Nationalism*. Revised edn. London: Verso, 1991

Sonia P. Anderson, *An English Consul at Smyrna: Paul Rycaut at Smyrna, 1667–1678*. Oxford: Clarendon Press, 1989

Moritz von Angeli, 'Die Eroberung von Ofen und der Feldzug gegen die Türken im Jahre 1686'. Mitteilungen des K.K. Kriegsarchiv, 1886

Muhammad Ārif, *The Hejaz Railway and the Muslim Pilgrimage: A Case of Ottoman Political Propaganda*. Edited by Jacob Landau. Detroit, MI: Wayne State University Press, 1971

Alfred Ritter von Arneth, *Prinz Eugen von Savoyen. Nach den Handschriften Quellen der kaiserliche Archive*. 3 vols. Vienna: Wilhelm Braumüller (k.k. Hofbuchhändler), 1864

Neal Ascherson, *Black Sea: The Birthplace of Civilisation and Barbarism*. London: Jonathan Cape, 1995

Nurhan Atasoy, *A Garden for the Sultan: Gardens and Flowers in the Ottoman Culture*. Istanbul: Aygaz, 2002

— 'Ottoman Garden Pavilions and Tents', *Muqarnas* 21 (2004): 13–19

— Otag-i Hümayan, *The Ottoman Imperial Tent Complex*. Istanbul: MEPA/Aksoy, 2000

Esil Atil (ed.), *Turkish Art*. Washington, DC: Smithsonian Institution Press, 1980

— *Süleymanname: The Illustrated History of Süleyman the Magnificent*. Washington, DC: National Gallery of Art, 1986

— 'The Story of an Eighteenth-Century Ottoman Festival', *Muqarnas* 10 (1993): 181–200

Aziz S. Atiya, *The Crusade of Nicopolis*. London: Methuen, 1934

Nebahat Avcioğlu, 'Ahmed I and the Allegories of Tyranny in the Frontispiece to George Sandys Relation of a Journey', *Muqarnas* 18 (2001): 203–26

Franz Babinger, *Mehmed the Conqueror and His Time*. Edited by William C. Hickman and translated by Ralph Mannheim. Princeton: Princeton University Press, 1978

Jean-Louis Bacqué-Grammont, 'Recherches sur le quartier de Tophane et l'artillerie ottomane, I. Textes et images commentés', Paris: Editions Adrien Maisonneuve, 1999

Marc David Baer, *Honoured by the Glory of Islam: Conversion and Conquest in Ottoman Europe*. New York: Oxford University Press, 2008.

János M. Bak and Béla Király (eds), *From Hunyadi to Rákóczi: War and Society in Late Medieval and Early Modern Hungary*. New York: Social Science Monographs, Brooklyn College Press, 1982

Alexander Balisch, 'Infantry Battlefield Tactics in the Seventeenth and Eighteenth Centuries on the European and Turkish Theatres of War: The Austrian Response to Different Conditions', in Jeremy Black (ed.), *Warfare in Europe, 1650–1792*. Aldershot: Ashgate, 2005

Ivo Banac, *The National Question in Yugoslavia: Origins, History, Politics*. Ithaca, NY: Cornell University Press, 1974

Mario Baratta-Dragono, *Prinz Eugen von Savoyen in der Publizistik seiner Zeit*. Dissertation, University of Vienna, 1960

Richmond Barbour, *Before Orientalism. London's Theatre of the East, 1576–1626*. Cambridge and New York: Cambridge University Press, 2003

Thomas M. Barker, *Double Eagle and Crescent: Vienna's Second Turkish Siege and its Historical Setting*. Albany, NY: State University of New York Press, 1967

— *The Military Intellectual and Battle: Raimondo Montecuccoli and the Thirty Years War*. Albany, NY: State University of New York Press, 1975.

— *Army, Aristocracy, Monarchy: Essays on War, Society and Government in Austria, 1618–1780*. Boulder, CO: Social Science Monographs, 1982

Gustav Bayerle, *Ottoman Diplomacy in Hungary. Letters from the Pashas of Buda, 1590–1593*. Bloomington, IN: Indiana University Press, 1972

Sandor Bene, *Myth and Reality: Latin Historiography in Hungary 15th–18th Centuries*. Budapest: National Széchényi Library, 2006

Bartolome Bennassar and Robert Sauzet (eds), *Chrétiens et Musulmans à la Renaissance*. Paris: Champion, 1998

Jean Béranger, *Histoire de l'Empire des Habsbourg, 1273–1918*. Paris: Fayard, 1990

Lloyd E. Berry and Robert O. Crummey, *Rude and Barbarous Kingdom: Russia in the Accounts of Sixteenth-Century English Visitors*. Madison, WI: University of Wisconsin Press, 1968

N. H. Biegman, *The Turco-Ragusan Relationship*. The Hague: Mouton, 1967

Nancy Bisaha, *Creating East and West. Renaissance Humanists and the Ottoman Turks*. Philadelphia, PA: University of Pennsylvania Press, 2004

Urs Bitterli, *Cultures in Conflict: Encounters between European and non-European Cultures, 1492–1800*. Translated by Ritchie Robertson. Cambridge: Polity, 1989

Tim Blanning, *The Pursuit of Glory: Europe 1648–1815*. London: Allen Lane, 2007

John W. Bohnstedt, *The Infidel Scourge of God: The Turkish Menace as Seen by German Pamphleteers of the Reformation Era*. Philadelphia, PA: Transactions of the American Philosophical Society, vols 58–9, 1968.

George C. Bond and Angela Gilliam (eds), *Social Construction of the Past: Representation as Power*. London and New York: Routledge, 1994

Max Braubach, *Prinz Eugen von Savoyen: Eine Biographie*. 5 vols. Munich: R. Oldenbourg Verlag

Peter Broucek, *Historischer Atlas zur zweiten Türkenbelagerung: Wien 1683*. Vienna: Franz Deuticke Verlagsgesellschaft, 1983

Daniel Brower and Edward J. Lazzerini (eds), *Russia's Orient: Imperial Borderlands and Peoples*. Bloomington, IN: Indiana University Press, 1997

Richard Brzezinski, *Polish Winged Hussar, 1576–1775*. Oxford: Osprey Publishing, 2006

Nedrat Kuran Burçoğlu (ed), *The Image of the Turk in Europe from the Declaration of the Republic in 1923 to the 1990s*. Istanbul: Isis Press, 2000

Andrew Burghardt, *Borderland: A Historical and Geographical Study of Burgenland, Austria*. Madison, WI: University of Wisconsin Press, 1962

Ogier Ghislain de Busbecq, *The Turkish Letters of Ogier Ghislain de Busbecq. Imperial Ambassador at Constantinople, 1554–1562*. Newly translated from the Latin of the Elzevir edition of 1633 by Edward Seymour Forster. Oxford: Clarendon Press, 1927

Jeremias Cacavelas, *The Siege of Vienna by the Turks in 1683, translated into Greek from an Italian work published anonymously in the year of the siege*. Translated from the Greek by F. H. Marshall. Cambridge: Cambridge University Press, 1925

Dominique Carnoy, *Représentations de l'Islam dans la France du XVIIe siècle: la ville des tentations*. Paris: L'Harmattan, 1998

Lavender Cassels, *The Struggle for the Ottoman Empire, 1717–40*. London: John Murray, 1966

Feliz Yenis Cehiricoğlu, 'Ottoman Ceramics in European Contexts', *Muqarnas* 21 (2004): 373–82.

Evliya Çelebi (Mehmed Zilli ibn Dervish), *Narrative of travels in Europe, Asia and Africa in the seventeenth century by Evliya Effendi: translated from the Turkish by the Ritter Joseph von Hammer*. London: The Oriental Translation Fund of Great Britain and Ireland, 1834

Evliya Çelebi [Tchelebi], *La Guerres des Turcs. Recits de Batailles extraits du Livre de Voyages de Evliya Tchelebi*. Translated by Faruk Bilici. Arles: Actes Sud, 2001

Zeynip Çelik, *Displaying the Orient: Architecture of Islam at Nineteenth-Century World Fairs*. Berkeley, CA: University of California Press, 1992

Gunther Cerwinka, 'Die Eroberung der Festung Kanisza durch die Türken in Jahre 1600', in Alexander Novotny and Berthold Sutter, *Innerösterreich 1564–1619*. Graz: Styria, 1967

Olivier Chaline, *La Reconquête catholique de l'Europe centrale: XVIe–XVIIIe. siècle*. Paris: L'Edition du Cerf, 1998

Charles V, Duke of Lorraine, *Lotharingiai Károly hadinaplója Buda visszafoglalásáról*. Edited by Mollay Károly, Nagy László and Kun József. Budapest: Zrinyi Katonai Kiadó, 1986

Kenneth Chase, *Firearms. A Global History to 1700*. Cambridge: Cambridge University Press, 2003

Daniel Chirot (ed.), *The Origins of Backwardness in Eastern Europe: Economics and Politics from the Middle Ages until the Early Twentieth Century*. Berkeley, CA: University of California Press, 1989

Asli Cirakman, *'Terror of the World' to the 'Sick Man of Europe': European Images*

of Ottoman Empire and Society from the Sixteenth to the Nineteenth Centuries.
New York: Peter Lang Publishing, 2001

Peter Coeck, *The Turks in* **MDXXXIII**. *A series of drawings made in that year at Constantinople by Peter Coeck of Aelst and published from woodblocks by his widow at Antwerp in* **MDLIII**; *reproduced with other illustrations, in facsimile, with an introduction by Sir William Stirling Maxwell.* London and Edinburgh, 1873

Laurence Cole and Daniel Unowsky (eds), *The Limits of Loyalty: Imperial Symbols, Popular Allegiances, and State Patriotism in the Late Habsburg Monarchy.* New York and Oxford: Berghahn Books, 2007

L. J. D. Collins, 'The military organization and tactics of the Crimean Tatars, 16th–17th centuries', in Vernon J. Parry and M.E. Yapp (eds), *War, Technology and Society in the Middle East.* Oxford: Oxford University Press, 1975, 257–76.

William Coxe, *History of the House of Austria, from the foundation of the monarchy by Rhodolph of Habsburg to the death of Leopold II, 1218–1792.* London: T. Cadell and W. Davies, 1807

Géza Dávid and Pál Fodor (eds), *Hungarian–Ottoman Military and Diplomatic Relations in the Age of Suleyman the Magnificent.* Budapest: Lórend Eötvös University, 1994

— (eds), *Ottomans, Hungarians and Habsburgs in Central Europe. The Military Confines in the Era of Ottoman Conquest.* Leiden: E. J. Brill, 2000

Grace Davie, *Religion in Modern Europe: A Memory Mutates.* Oxford: Oxford University Press, 2000

Norman Davies, *God's Playground: A History of Poland*, vol. 1. *The Origins to 1795.* Oxford: Clarendon Press, 1982

Roderic H. Davison, 'Turkish Attitudes Concerning Christian–Muslim Equality in the Nineteenth Century', *American Historical Review* 59: 4 (1954): 844–64

Walter B. Denny, 'Quotations In and Out of Context: Ottoman Turkish Art and European Orientalist Painting,' *Muqarnas* 10 (1993).: 219–30

Selim Deringil, *The Well-Protected Domains. Ideology and the Legitimation of Power in the Ottoman Empire, 1876–1909.* London: I. B. Tauris, 1999

Die österreichisch-ungarische Monarchie in Wort und Bild. Auf Anregung und unter Mitwirkung Seiner kaiserlichen und königlichen Hoheit des durchlauchtigsten Kronprinzen Erzherzhog Rudolf. Vienna: Druck und Verlag der kaiserlich-königlichen Hof- und Staatsdruckerei. Alfred Hölder, k.k. Hof- und Universitätsbuchhändler, vols 1–24, 1885–1902

Hichem Djait, *Europe and Islam.* Translated by Peter Heinegg. Berkeley, CA: University of California Press, 1985

Anton Dolleczek, *Monographie der k.u.k. österr.-ung. Blanken und Handfeuerwaffen.* Graz: Akademische Druck u. Verlagsanstalt, 1970 [1896]

Christopher Duffy, *The Army of Maria Theresa.* Newton Abbot: David and Charles, 1977

— *The Fortress in the Age of Vauban and Frederick the Great: 1660–1789.* London: Routledge & Kegan Paul, 1985

— *The Military Experience in the Age of Reason.* London: Routledge & Kegan Paul, 1987

— *Siege Warfare: The Fortress in the Early Modern World, 1494–1660.* London: Routledge & Kegan Paul, 1996

Alphonse Dupront, *Le mythe de croisade.* Paris: Gallimard, 4 vols, 1997

Sean J. A. Edwards, *Swarming on the Battlefield: Past, Present, and Future.* Santa Monica, CA: Rand Corporation, 2000

Ekkehard Eickhoff with Rudolf Eickhoff, *Venedig, Wien und die Osmanen: Umbruch in Südosteuropa, 1645–1700.* Munich: Verlag Georg D.W. Callwey, 1970

Thomas A. Emmert, *Serbian Golgotha: Kosovo 1389.* New York: Eastern European Monographs

Pál Engel, *The Realm of St Stephen: A History of Medieval Hungary, 895–1526.* London: I.B. Tauris, 2001

Regine Erichsen, 'Scoundrel or Gentleman? The Image of the Turk and the German Cultural Mission in Turkey during World War I', in Nedrat Kuran Burçoglu, *The Image of the Turk in Europe from the Declaration of the Republic in 1923 to the 1990s.* Istanbul: Isis Press, 2000

Büşra Ersanli, 'The Ottoman Empire in the Historiography of the Kemalist Era: A Theory of Fatal Decline', in Fikret Adanir and Suraiya Faroqui, *The Ottomans and the Balkans: A Discussion of Historiography.* Leiden: E. J. Brill, 2002

R. J. W. Evans, *The Making of the Habsburg Monarchy, 1550–1700.* Oxford: Oxford University Press, 1979

Suraiya Faroqhi, *Subjects of the Sultan: Culture and Daily Life in the Ottoman Empire.* London: I. B. Tauris, 2000.

Géza Féher, *Turkish Miniatures from the Period of Hungary's Turkish Occupation.* Translated by Lili Halápy. Budapest: Corvina, 1978

Inanc Feigl, Valeria Heuberger, Manfred Pittioni and Kerstin Tomenendal (eds), *Auf den Spuren der Osmanen in der österreichischen Geschichte.* Frankfurt am Main: Peter Lang, 2002

James Fentress and Chris Wickham, *Social Memory: New Perspectives on the Past.* Oxford: Blackwell, 1992

Lázlo Fenyvesi (ed.), *Buda visszavívása 1686* [Siege of Buda Exhibition]. Budapest: Budapesti Történeti Múzeum, 1986

Paula Sutter Fichtner, *Terror and Toleration: The Habsburg Empire Confronts Islam.* London: University of Chicago Press, 2008

Caroline Finkel, *The Administration of Warfare: The Ottoman Military Campaigns in Hungary, 1593–1606.* Vienna: VWGÖ, 1988. Beihefte zur Wiener Zeitschrift für die Kunde des Morganlandes

— 'The Costs of Ottoman Warfare and Defence', *Byzantinische Forschungen* 16 (1991): 91–103

— *Osman's Dream. The Story of the Ottoman Empire, 1300–1923.* London: John Murray, 2005

Alan W. Fisher, *The Russian Annexation of the Crimea, 1772–1783.* Cambridge: Cambridge University Press, 1970

— *The Crimean Tatars.* Stanford, CA: Hoover Institution Press, 1978

Pál Fodor, 'The View of the Turks in Hungary: The Apocalyptic Tradition and the Legend of the Red Apple in Ottoman-Hungarian Context', in Benjamin Lellouch and Stéphane Yerasimos (eds), *Les Traditions Apocalyptiques au tournant de la chute de Constantinople.* Paris: L'Harmattan, 1999

— *In Quest of the Golden Apple: Imperial Ideology, Politics, and Military Administration in the Ottoman Empire.* Istanbul: Isis Press, 2000

Domenico de Franceschi, *Solyman the Magnificent going to Mosque from a series of engravings by Domenico De' Francheschi at Venice in MDLXIII.* Privately printed for Sir William Stirling Maxwell. Florence and Edinburgh: 1877

C. A. Frazee, *Catholics and Sultans: The Church and the Ottoman Empire, 1453–1923.* Cambridge: Cambridge University Press, 1983

Marianne Frodl-Schneemann, *Johann Peter Krafft: 1780–1856.* Monographie und Verzeichnis der Gemälde. Vienna: Herold, 1984

Ibolya Gerelyes, 'Seeking the East in the West: The Zsolney Phenomenon', *Muqarnas* 21 (2004): 139–51

Gertrud Gerhartl, *Die Niederlage der Türken am Steinfeld 1532.* Vienna: Bundesverlag, 1989

Veronika Gervers, *The Influence of Ottoman Textiles and Costume in Eastern Europe, with particular reference to Hungary.* Toronto: Royal Ontario Museum, 1982

Edward Gibbon, *The History of the Decline and Fall of the Roman Empire.* Edited by J. B. Bury. London: Methuen and Co., 1909

Andre Gingrich, 'Frontier Myths of Orientalism: The Muslim World in Public and Popular Cultures of Central Europe', in Mediterranean Ethnological Summer School, Piran/Pirano, Slovenia, vol. 2, ed. Bojan Baskar and Borut Brumen. Ljubljana: Instiut za multikulturne raziskave, 1998, 99–127

Andre Gingrich, 'Immigration Politics, Austrian Millennial Festivals, and the Role of Anthropology'. Paper presented at the Session 'Anthropology and the Politics of Culture in Contemporary Germany, Switzerland, and Austria', Twentieth Annual Conference of the German Studies Association, Seattle

Andre Gingrich and Richard G. Fox (eds), *Anthropology, by Comparison.* London: Routledge, 2002

Daniel Goffman, *The Ottoman Empire and Early Modern Europe.* Cambridge: Cambridge University Press, 2002

— *Britons in the Ottoman Empire, 1642–1660*. Seattle, WA: University of Washington Press, 1998

Maria Goloubeva, *The Glorification of Emperor Leopold I in Image, Spectacle and Text*. Mainz: Verlag Philipp von Zabern, 2000

Godfrey Goodwin, *The Janissaries*. London: Saqi Books, 1994

Jonathan Grant, 'Rethinking the Ottoman "Decline": Military Technology Diffusion in the Ottoman Empire, Fifteenth to Eighteenth Centuries', *Journal of World History* 10, no. 1 [1999]: 179–201

Erwin Anton Grestenberger, *Befestigtes Wien: von der römischen Antike bis zur Gegenwart*. Vienna: Neuer Wissenschaftlicher Verlag, 2002

Kaspar von Greyerz, *Religion and Society in Early Modern Europe: 1500–1800*. London: Allen & Unwin, 1984

Maximilian Grothaus, 'Zum Türkenbild in der Adels- und Volksliteratur der Habsburger Monarchie von 1650–1800', in Gernot Heiss und Grete Klingenstein (eds), *Das Osmanische Reich und Europa, 1683 bis 1789: Konflikt, Entspannung, und Austausch*. Wiener Beiträge zur Geschichte der Neuzeit, Bd 10/1983

— 'Die Türken vor Wien. 1683. Zerstörung eines altes Feindbildes; Notwendige Anmerkungen zur Austellung im Wiener Künstlerhaus', in O. Bockhorn and E. C. Ehalt, Wiener Beiträge zu Kulturwissenschaft und Kulturpolitik. Vienna, 1983

— 'Zum Türkenbild in der Kultur der Habsburgermonarchie zwischen dem 16. und 18 Jahrhundert', in A. Tietze, *Habsburgisch-osmanische Beziehungen*, Beihefte zur Wiener Zeitschrifts für die Kunde des Morganlandes, Bd 13, 1985

— *Der 'Erbfeindt christlichen Nahmens'. Studien zum Türken-Feindbild in der Kultur der Habsburgermonarchie zwischen dem 16. und 18. Jahrhundert*. Ph.D. Dissertation University of Graz, 1986

— 'Eine untersteirische Turquerie, ihre graphischen Vorbilder und ihre kulturhistorische Bedeutung', *Mitteilungen des Instituts für Steierische Geschichtsforschung* 95 (1987): 271–95

— and Karl Vocelka (eds), *Mitteleuropa und die Türken – politische und kulturelle Beziehungen zwischen zwei Kulturkreisen*. Vienna: ÖBV, 1983.

Fatma Muge Göçek, *East Meets West: France and the Ottoman Empire in the Eighteenth Century*. New York: Oxford University Press, 1987

C. Göllner, 'Die Türkenfrage in Spannungsfeld der Reformation', *Südostforschungen* 34 (1975): 61–78

— *Turcica: Die Europäischen Türkendrucke des XVI. Jahrhunderts*. Bucharest and Baden Baden, 3 vols, 1968; 1978

Maurice Halbwachs, *On Collective Memory*. Translated by Lewis A. Coser. Chicago, IL: University of Chicago Press, 1992

John Hale, *The Civilisation of Europe in the Renaissance*. London: HarperCollins, 1993

Charles J. Halperin, *Russia and the Golden Horde: The Mongol Impact on Medieval Russian History*. Bloomington, IN: Indiana University Press, 1985

Shirine Hamideh, *The City's Pleasures: Istanbul in the Eighteenth Century*. Seattle: University of Washington Press. 2007

Joseph von Hammer-Purgstall, *Wien's erste aufgehobene türkische Belagerung, zur dreyhundertjährigen Jubelfeyer derselben, zum Theil aus bisher unbekannten christlichen und türkischen Quellen erzählt*. Pest: Konrad Adolph Hartlebens Verlag, 1829

— *Histoire de l'Empire ottoman: depuis son origine jusqu'à nos jours. Ouvrage puisé aux sources les plus authentiques et rédigé sur des documens et des manuscrits la plupart inconnus en Europe, tr. de l'allemand, sur les notes et sous la direction de l'auteur, par J-J. Hellert*. Paris: Bellizard, Barthès, Dufour, 18 vols, 1835–43

James Hankins, 'Renaissance Crusaders: Humanist Crusade Literature in the Age of Mehmed II', in *Dumbarton Oaks Papers* 49 (1995): 111–46

Hugo Hantsch, *Die Geschichte Österreichs*. Graz: Verlag Styria, 1959, 2 vols

Matthew Head, *Orientalism, Masquerade and Mozart's Turkish Music*. London: Royal Musical Association, 2000

Friedrich Heer, *Der Kampf um die österreichische Identität*. Vienna: Böhlau Verlag, 1981

Klára Hegyi, *The Ottoman Empire in Europe*. Translated by Ildikó and Christopher Hann; illustrations selected by Vera Zimányi. Budapest: Corvina, 1986

Nicolas Henderson, *Prince Eugen of Savoy: A Biography*. London: Weidenfeld & Nicolson, 1964

Valerie Heuberger, Genevieve Humbert-Knitel and Elisabeth Vyslonzil (eds), *Cultures en couleurs/Cultures in colours: The Heritage of the Ottoman Empire and the Austro-Hungarian Monarchy in the Orient and the Occident*. Frankfurt am Main: Peter Lang, 2001

Michael Robert Hickok, *Ottoman Military Administration in Eighteenth-Century Bosnia*. Leiden: E. J. Brill, 1997

Erik Hildinger, *Warriors of the Steppe: A Military History of Central Asia 500 B.C. to 1700 A.D.* New York: Sarpedon, 1997

Historische Schlachten auf Tapissierien aus dem Besitz des Kunsthistorischen Museums Wien. Eisenstadt: Amt der Burgenländischen Landesregierung, 1976

History-Image: Guide to the Exhibition of the Hungarian National Gallery. Budapest: Hungarian National Gallery, 2000

Michael Hochedlinger, *Austria's Wars of Emergence: War, State and Society in the Habsburg Monarchy, 1683–1797*. Harlow: Pearson Education, 2003

Nichole Hochner, 'Louis XII and the porcupine: transformation of a royal emblem', *Renaissance Studies* 15 (2001)

Nicolaus Hocke, *Kurtze Beschreibung, dessen was in wehrender türkischen Belagerung der kayserlichen Residentz Statt Wienn von 7. Juli biss 12. Septembris dess abgewichenen 1683. Jahrs . . . passiret. [with an afterword by Peter Broucek].* Vienna: Wiener Bibliophilen-Gesellschaft. Facsimile edition, 1983

Margaret T. Hodgen, *Early Anthropology in the Sixteenth and Seventeenth Centuries.* Philadelphia, PA: University of Pennsylvannia Press, 1964

Almut Höfert, *Den Feind beschreiben: 'Türkengefahr' und europäisches Wissen über das Osmanische Reich 1450–1600.* Frankfurt am Main: Campus Verlag, 2003

— and Armando Salvatore (eds), *Between Europe and Islam. Shaping Modernity in a Transcultural Space.* Brussels: Peter Lang, 2000

Meike Hollenbeck, 'Die Türkenpublizistik in 17. Jahrundert – Spiegel der Verhältnisse im Reich?' *Mitteilungen des Instituts fur Österreichische Geschichtsforschung* 107 (1999): 111–30

Anna Horvath, 'A Contemporary Ottoman Source on the Wars in Hungary at the End of the 16th Century,' in György Kara (ed.), *Between Danube and Caucasus. Oriental Sources on the History of the Peoples of Central and Southeastern Europe.* Budapest : Akadémiai Kiadó, 1987

Norman Housley (ed.), *Crusading in the Fifteenth Century: Message and Impact.* Basingstoke: Palgrave Macmillan, 2004

Walter Hummelberger, *Wiens erste Belagerung durch die Türken 1529.* Vienna: Österreichischer Bundesverlag, 1976

Ulrike Ilg, 'Die Türkei in der europäischen Literatur und Buchillustration des 15.–19. Jahrhunderts', in Johannes Kalter and Irene Schönberger, *Der lange Weg der Türken. 1500 Jahre türkische Kultur.* Stuttgart: Linden Museum, 2003

— 'Die "Entdeckung" der osmanischen Kultur durch Künstler und Gelehrte im 16. Jahrhundert: Eine humanistische Utopie'. *Zeitschrift für Historische Forschung,* Beiheft 34, Berlin: Duncker & Humbolt, 2005

Charles W. Ingrao, *In Quest and Crisis: Emperor Joseph I and the Habsburg Monarchy.* West Lafayette, IN: Purdue University Press, 1979

Iaroslav Isaevych, 'The Book Trade in Eastern Europe in the Seventeenth and Early Eighteenth Centuries', in John Brewer and Roy Porter, *Consumption and the World of Goods,* vol. 1. London: Routledge, 1993

J. T. Johnson, *The Holy War Idea in Western and Islamic Traditions.* University Park, PA: Pennsylvania State University Press, 1997

Thomas Kaiser, 'The Evil Empire? The Debate on Turkish Despotism in Eighteenth-Century French Political Culture', *Journal of Modern History* 72, no.1 (2000): 6–34

Robert A. Kann, *A Study of Austrian Intellectual History: From the Late Baroque to Romanticism.* London: Thames & Hudson, 1960

— and Zdenek V. David, *The Peoples of the Eastern Habsburg Lands, 1526–1918.* Seattle, WA, and London: University of Washington Press, 1984

Hakan T. Karateke and Maurus Reinkowski (eds), *Legitimizing the Order: The Ottoman Rhetoric of State Power*. Leiden: E. J. Brill, 2005

Thomas DaCosta Kauffman, *Drawings from the Holy Roman Empire*. Princeton, NJ: Princeton University Press, 1983

John Keegan and Andrew Wheatcroft, *Who's Who in Military History*. London: Weidenfeld & Nicolson, 1987

V. G. Kiernan, *The Lords of Human Kind: European Attitudes to the Outside World in the Imperial Age*. London: Weidenfeld & Nicolson, 1969

Charles King, *The Black Sea: A History*. Oxford: Oxford University Press, 2004

Bela K. Kiraly and Gale Stokes (eds), *Insurrections, Wars and the Eastern European Crisis in the 1870s*. Boulder, CO: Social Science Monographs, 1985

Onno Klopp, *Das Jahr 1683: und der folgende große Türkenkrieg bis zum Frieden von Carlowitz 1699*. Graz: Verlagsbuchandlung Styria, 1882

— *Corrispondenza epistolare tra Leopoldo I imperatore ed il P. Marco d'Aviano capucino dai manscritti originali tratta e pubblicata*. Graz: Libreria Styria, 1888

H. G. Koenigsberger, *The Habsburgs and Europe, 1516–1660*. Ithaca, NY, and London: Cornell University Press, 1971

Béla Köpeckzi, *Staatsräson und christliche Solidarität. Die ungarischen Aufstände und Europa in der zweiten Hälfte des 17. Jahrhunderts*. Budapest: Akadémiai Kiadó, 1983

Judith Deutsch Kornblatt, *The Cossack Hero in Russian Literature: A Study in Cultural Mythology*. Madison, WI: University of Wisconsin Press, 1992

C. M. Kortepeter, *Ottoman Imperialism during the Reformation: Europe and the Caucasus*. New York: New York University Press, 1972

Selma Krasa-Florian, *Die Allegorie der Austria: Die Entstehung des Gesamt-staatsgedankens in der österreichisch-ungarischen Monarchie und die bildende Kunst*. Vienna: Böhlau Verlag, 2007

Peter Krenn and Walter J. Karcheski, Jr, *Imperial Austria: Treasures of Art from the State of Styria*. Munich: Prestel Verlag, 1992

Richard F. Kreutel (ed.), *Kara Mustafa vor Wien. Das türkische Tagebuch der Belagerung Wiens 1683, verfasst vom Zeremonienmeister der Hohen Pforte*. Graz: Verlag Styria, 1955. 2nd edn DTV, 1967

— *Im Reiche des Goldenen Apfels. Des türkischen Weltenbummlers Evliya Celebi denkwürdige Reise in das Giaurenland und in die Stadt und Festung Wien anno 1665*. New edn with additional material by Erich Prokosch and Karl Teply. Graz: Verlag Styria, 1987

Kritovoulos, *History of Mehmed the Conqueror*. Translated by Charles T. Riggs. Princeton, NJ: Princeton University Press, 1954

Akdes Nimet Kurat, *The despatches of Sir Robert Sutton, Ambassador in Constantinople, 1710–1714*. Camden Society (Great Britain) 3rd Series; 78. London: Royal Historical Society, 1953

John R. Lampe, *Yugoslavia as History: Twice There Was a Country*. Cambridge: Cambridge University Press, 2000

François Le Begue, *Journal de la première campagne en Hongrie en 1683*, in Ferdinand Stöller (ed.), *Neue Quellen zur Geschichte des Türkenjahres 1683: die zweite Belagerung Wiens durch die Türken*. Aus dem Lothringischen Hausarchiv Innsbruck: Wagner, 1933

John P. LeDonne, *The Russian Empire and the World: 1700–1917*. New York: Oxford University Press, 1997

Walter Leitsch, 'Warum wollte Kara Mustafa Wien erobern?', *Jahrbücher für Geschichte Osteuropas*, vol. 29, part 4 (1981): 494–514

Benjamin Lellouch and Stéphane Yerasimos (eds), *Les Traditions Apocalyptiques au tournant de la chute de Constantinople*. Paris: L'Harmattan, 1999

Mathieu Lepetit, 'Die Türken vor Wien', in Etienne François and Hagen Schulze (eds), *Deutsche Erinnerungsorte*, vol. I. Munich: C.H. Beck, 2003

Alphons Lhotsky, *Das Zeitalter des Hauses Österreich. Die ersten Jahre d. Regierung Ferdinands I in Österreich. 1520–27*. Vienna: Böhlau, 1971

Edward T. Lilienthal, *Preserving Memory: The Struggle to Create America's Holocaust Museum*. New York: Viking, 1995

Hieronymus Löschenkohl, *1753–1807: erste Sonderaustellung. April–Oktober 1959*. Vienna: Historisches Museum der Stadt Wien

Anne-Marie Losonczy and András Zempleni, 'Anthropologie de la "patrie": le patriotisme hongrois', *Terrain. Carnets du Patrimoine Ethnologique* 17 (October 1991): 29–36

Emilio Lovarini (ed.), *La Schiavitu del Generale Marsigli sotto i Tartari e i Turchi da lui stesso narrata*. Bologna: Nicola Zanichelli, 1931

Edward Luttwak, *The Grand Strategy of the Roman Empire from the First Century A.D. to the Third*. Baltimore and London: Johns Hopkins University Press, 1976

Paul Robert Magocsi, *A History of Ukraine*. Seattle, WA: University of Washington Press, 1996

Claudio Magris, *Danube: A Sentimental Journey from the Source to the Black Sea*. Translated by Patrick Creagh. London: HarperCollins, 1990

Ussama Makdisi, 'Ottoman Orientalism', *American Historical Review* 107, no. 3 (June 2002): 768–96

Noel Malcolm, *Bosnia: A Short History*. London: Macmillan, 1994
— *Kosovo: A Short History*. London: Macmillan, 1998

Albert Mas, *Les Turcs dans la littérature espagnole du Siècle d'Or*. Paris: Centre de recherches hispaniques, Institut d'études hispaniques, 2 vols, 1967

Nabil Matar, *Turks, Moors and Englishmen in the Age of Discovery*. New York: Columbia University Press, 1999.

Klaus-Peter Matschke, *Das Kreuz und der Halbmond: die Geschichte der Türkenkriege*. Düsseldorf: Artemis & Winkler Verlag, 2004

E. Mauvillon, *Historie du Prince François Eugene de Savoye Generalissime des Armées de l'Empereur et de l'Empire, enrichie de Figures en Taille Douce*. Vienna: Briffaut, 5 vols, 1741

William Stirling Maxwell (ed.), *The Chief Victories of the Emperor Charles the Fifth, designed by Martin Heemskerck in MDLV*. 1870

Hans Georg Mayer (ed.), *Die Staaten Südosteuropas und die Osmanen*. Munich: Südosteuropa-Gesellschaft, 1989

Mark Mazower, *The Balkans*. London: Weidenfeld & Nicolson, 2000

J. McGarry and B. O'Leary (eds), *The Politics of Ethnic Conflict Regulation*. London: Routledge, 1993.

William McNeill, *Europe's Steppe Frontier: 1500–1800*. Chicago, IL: University of Chicago Press, 1964

J. R. Melville Jones (trans.), *The Siege of Constantinople, 1453: Seven Contemporary Accounts*. Amsterdam: Hakkert, 1972

Konstantin Mihailovic, *Memoirs of a Janissary*. Translated by Benjamin Stoltz. Ann Arbor, MI: University of Michigan Press, 1975

Hanns Leo Mikoletsky, *Österreich: das grosse 18. Jahrhundert von Leopold I bis Leopold II*. Vienna: Austria Edition, 1967

John Mollo, *Military Fashion. A Comparative History of the Uniforms of the Great Armies from the 17th Century to the First World War*. London: Barrie & Jenkins, 1972

Simon Sebag Montefiore, *Prince of Princes: The Life of Potemkin*. New York: St Martin's Press, 2000

Ákos Moravánszky, *Competing Visions: Aesthetic Invention and Social Imagination in Central European Architecture, 1867–1918*. Cambridge, MA: MIT Press, 1998

Gerda and Gottfried Mraz, *Maria Theresia: Ihr Leben und ihre Zeit in Bildern und Dokumentation*. Munich: Süddeutscher Verlag, 1979

Graeme Murdock, 'Death, Prophecy and Judgement in Transylvania', in Bruce Gordon and Peter Marshall (eds), *The Place of the Dead, Death and Remembrance in Late Medieval and Early Modern Europe*. Cambridge: Cambridge University Press, 2000

Mirela-Luminita Murgescu, 'The Turk in Romanian History Text Books (19th–20th Centuries)', in Nedrat Kuran Burçoglu, *The Image of the Turk in Europe from the Declaration of the Republic in 1923 to the 1990s*. Istanbul: Isis Press, 2000

Rhoads Murphey, 'The Ottoman Resurgence in the Seventeenth-century Mediterranean: The Gamble and its Results', *Mediterranean Historical Review* 8 (1993): 186–200

— 'Ottoman Historical Writing in the Seventeenth-century: A Survey of the

General Development of the Genre after the Reign of Sultan Ahmed I (1603–1617)', *Archivum Ottomanicum* 13 (1994): 277–311

— *Ottoman Warfare, 1500–1700*. London: UCL Press, 1999

G. Necipoğlu, *Architecture, Ceremonial and Power: The Topkapi Palace in the Fifteenth and Sixteenth Centuries*. Boston, MA: MIT Press, 1991

Iver B. Neumann, *Uses of the Other: 'The East' in European Identity Formation*. Minneapolis: University of Minnesota Press, 1998

Johann Newald, *Beiträge zur Geschichte der Belagerung von Wien durch die Türken, im Jahre 1683*. Vienna: Verlag Kubasta & Voigt, 1883

David Nicolle, *The Janissaries*. Oxford: Osprey Publishing, 1995

— *Armies of the Ottoman Empire, 1775–1820*. Oxford: Osprey Publishing. 1998

F. Thomas Noonan, *The Road to Jerusalem: Pilgrimage and Travel in the Age of Discovery*. Philadelphia: University of Pennsylvania Press, 2007

David A. Norris, *In the Wake of the Balkan Myth: Questions of Identity and Modernity*. Basingstoke: Macmillan, 1999

John Julius Norwich, *A Short History of Byzantium*. Harmondsworth: Penguin Books, 1997

Wilhelm Nottebohm, *Montecuccoli und die Legende von St Gotthard (1664)*. Berlin: R. Gaertners Verlagsbuchhandlung

William Ochsenwald, *The Hijaz Railway*. Charlottesville, VA: University Press of Virginia, 1980

[The] Ottoman Empire in Miniatures. Istanbul: Historical Research Foundation Istanbul Research Center, 1988

Stephen Pálffy, *The First Thousand Years: A History of the Pálffy Family*. Budapest: Balassi Kiadó, 2008

Geoffrey Parker, *The Army of Flanders and the Spanish Road, 1567–1659*. Cambridge: Cambridge University Press, 1972

— *The Military Revolution: Military Innovation and the Rise of the West, 1500–1800*. Second edn. Cambridge: Cambridge University Press, 1996

V. J. Parry, 'La manière de Combattre', in Vernon J. Parry and M. E. Yapp (eds), *War, Technology and Society in the Middle East*. Oxford: Oxford University Press, 1975

Ivan Parvev, *Habsburgs and Ottomans between Vienna and Belgrade, 1683–1739*. New York: Eastern European Monographs, 1995

Kurt Peball, *Die Schlacht bei St Gotthard-Mogersdorf 1664*. Vienna: Österreichischer Bundesverlag für Unterricht, Wissenschaft und Kunst, 1978

Richard Perger, *Strassen, Türme und Basteien: das Strassennetz der Wiener City in seiner Entwicklung und seinen Namen: ein Handbuch*. Vienna: Franz Deuticke, 1991

Geza Perjes, *The Fall of the Medieval Kingdom of Hungary: Mohacs 1526–Buda 1541*. Translated by Maria D. Fenyo. Highland Lakes, NJ: Atlantic Research and Publications, 1989

Kiril Petkov, *Infidels, Turks and Women: The South Slavs in the German Mind ca. 1400–1600*. Frankfurt am Main: Peter Lang, 1997

— 'The Rotten Apple and the Good Articles: Orthodox, Catholics, and Turks in Philippe de Mézières' Crusading Propaganda', *Journal of Medieval History* 23, no. 3 (1997): 255–70

Yanni Petsopoulos (ed.), *Tulips, Arabesques and Turbans. Decorative Arts from the Ottoman Empire*. London: Alexandria Press, 1982

Matthias Pfaffenbichler, 'Das Barocke Schlachtenbild: Versuche einer Typologie', *Jahrbuch der Kunsthistorischen Sammlungen in Wien* 91 (1996): 37–110

Ingeburg Pick, 'Daniel Suttinger and Leander Anguissola – Die Kartographen von Wien 1683', *Jahrbuch des Vereins für Geschichte der Stadt Wien* 39 (1983): 69–103

Robert Pick, *Empress Maria Theresa. The Earlier Years, 1717–1757*. London: Weidenfeld & Nicolson, 1966

Othmar Pickl, *Die Belagerung und Rückeroberung von Belgrad 1688. Nach dem Kriegs-Tagebuch des kaiserlichen Generalwachtmeisters Graf Siegmund Joachim von Trauttmansdorff*. 1996. http://www.uni-graz.at/geowww/geo/geoweb_magazin_artikel_detail.php?recordID=144

Mark Pinson (ed.), *The Muslims of Bosnia Herzegovina: Their Historic Development from the Middle Ages to the Dissolution of Yugoslavia*. Cambridge, MA: Harvard University Press, 1996

Gabriel Piterberg, *An Ottoman Tragedy: History and Historiography at Play*. Berkeley, CA: University of California Press, 2003

C. Polchmann, 'Das Türkenmotiv in der Barockpredigt', *Franziskanische Studien* 38 (Münster 1956): 212–17

Regina Pörtner, *The Counter-Reformation in Central Europe: Styria, 1580–1630*. Oxford: Oxford University Press, 2001

Georges Poull, *La Maison ducale de Lorraine devenue la Maison impériale et royale d'Autriche, de Hongrie et de Bohème*. Nancy: Presses Universitaires de Nancy, 1991

Géraud Poumarède, *Pour en finir avec la Croisade. Mythes et réalités de la lutte contre les Turques aux XVIe et XVIIe siècles*. Paris: Presses Universitaires de France, 2004

Daniel Power and Naomi Standen (eds), *Frontiers in Question: Eurasian Borderlands, 700–1700*. Basingstoke: Macmillan Press. 1999

Donald Quataert, *The Ottoman Empire, 1700–1922*. Cambridge: Cambridge University Press, 2000

Julian Raby, 'Mehmed the Conqueror's Greek scriptorium', *Dumbarton Oaks Papers* 37 (1983): 15–34

David B. Ralston, *Importing the European Army: The Introduction of European Military Techniques and Institutions into the Extra-European World, 1600–1914*. Chicago, IL: University of Chicago Press, 1996

Oswald Redlich, *Das Werden einer Grossmacht: Österreich von 1700 bis 1740*. Baden bei Wien: Rudolf M. Rohrer Verlag, 1938

— *Weltmacht des Barock: Österreich in der Zeit Kaiser Leopolds I.* Vienna: Rudolf M. Rohrer Verlag, 1961, 4th edn

Victor von Renner, *Wien im Jahre 1683. Geschichte der zweiten Belagerung der Stadt durch die Türken im Rahmen der Zeitereignisse. Aus Anlass der zweiten Säcularfeier, verfasst im Auftrage des Gemeinderats der k.k. Reichshaupt- und Residenzstadt Wien.* Vienna: Verlag con R. v. Waldheim, 1883

Karl A. Roider, *The Reluctant Ally. Austria's Policy in the Austro–Turkish War 1737–1739.* Baton Rouge, LA: Louisiana State University Press, 1972

— *Austria's Eastern Question, 1700–1790.* Princeton, NJ: Princeton University Press, 1982

Georgely Romsics, *Myth and Remembrance: The Dissolution of the Habsburg Empire in the Memoir Literature of the Austro-Hungarian Political Elite.* Translated from the Hungarian by Thomas J. DeKornfeld. Wayne, NJ: Centre for Hungarian Studies and Publications, 2006

Robert Rotenberg, *Landscape and Power in Vienna.* Baltimore: Johns Hopkins University Press, 1995

Gunther E. Rothenburg, Bela K. Kiraly and Peter F. Sugar (eds), *East Central European Society and War in the Pre-Revolutionary Eighteenth Century.* Boulder CO: Social Science Research Monographs, 1982

Clarence Dana Rouillard, *The Turk in French History, Thought, and Literature, 1520–1660.* Paris: Boivin, 1941

David J. Roxburgh (ed.), *Turks: A Journey of a Thousand Years.* London: Royal Academy, 2005

Kurt Rumpler, *Festungsbaumeister Georg Rimpler und die Zweite Türkenbelagerung,* 2007, at members.kabsi.at/familienforschung/Rimpler.pdf

Charles Sabatos, 'Views of Turkey and "The Turk" in 20th-century Czech and Slovak Literature', in Nedrat Kuran Burçoğlu, *The Image of the Turk in Europe from the Declaration of the Republic in 1923 to the 1990s.* Istanbul: Isis Press, 2000

Johannes Sachslehner, *Wien Anno 1683.* Vienna: Styria Pichler Verlag, 2004

Maurice de Saxe, *Mes Reveries,* ed. Jean-Paul Charnay. Paris: Economica, 2002

Anton C. Schaedlinger, *Die Schreiben Süleymans des Prächtigen an Karl V, Ferdinand I, und Maximilian II. aus dem Haus-, Hof und Staatsarchiv zu Wien.* Vienna: Verlag der Österreichischen Akademie der Wissenschaften, 1983

John R. Schindler, 'Defeating Balkan Insurgency: The Austro-Hungarian Army in Bosnia-Hercegovina, 1878–82', *Journal of Strategic Studies* 27, no. 3 (2004): 528–52

J. Schmidt, 'The Egri Campaign of 1596: Military History and the Problem of Sources', *Habsburgisch-Osmanische Beziehungen,* 125–44. Vienna: CIEPO, 1985

G. Schreiber, 'Das Türkenmotiv und das deutschem Volkstum', *Volk und Volkstum. Jahrbuch für Volkskunde*, ed. G. Schreiber Bd 3 (1938): 9–54

— *Raimondo Montecuccoli: Feldherr, Schriftsteller, und Kavalier: ein Lebensbild aus dem Barock*. Graz: Styria Verlag, 2000

Winfried Schulze, *Reich und Türkengefahr im späten 16. Jahrhundert. Studien zu den politischen und gesellschaftlichen Auswirkungen einer äußeren Bedrohung*. Munich: Beck, 1978

Werner Schwarz, 'Repraesentatio Belli – Eine Kupferstichfolge zum Spanischen Erbfolgekrieg aus dem Augsburger Verlag Jeremias Wolff', in *Zeitschrift des Historischen Vereins für Schwaben* 84. Band, Augsburg, 1991, S. 129–184

Robert Schwoebel, *The Shadow of the Crescent: The Renaissance Image of the Turk (1453–1517)*. Nieuwkoop: B. de Graaf, 1967

Wilfried Seipel (ed.), *Der Kriegszug Kaiser Karls V gegen Tunis. Kartons und Tapisserien*. Milan: Skira, 2000

Kenneth M. Setton, 'Lutheranism and the Turkish Peril', *Balkan Studies* 3 (1962): 133–68

— *Venice, Austria and the Turks in the Seventeenth Century*. Philadelphia, PA: American Philosophical Society, 1991

— *Western Hostility to Islam and Prophecies of Turkish Doom*. Philadelphia, PA: American Philosophical Society, 1992

Ezel Kural Shaw, 'The Double Veil: Travelers' Views of the Ottoman Empire, Sixteenth Through Eighteenth Centuries', in Ezel Kural Shaw and C. J. Heywood, *English and Continental Views of the Ottoman Empire, 1500–1800*. Los Angeles, CA. University of California Press, 1972

Stanford Shaw, *The Old and the New. The Ottoman Empire under Selim III*, 1789–1807. Cambridge, MA. Harvard University Press, 1971

Wendy Miriam Kural Shaw, *Possessors and Possessed: Museums, Archaeology, and the Visulisation of History in the Late Ottoman Empire*. Berkeley, CA: University of California Press, 2003

Mary Lucille Shay, *The Ottoman Empire from 1720–1734 as Revealed by the Dispatches of the Venetian Baili*. Urbana, IL: University of Illinois Press, 1944

Gereon Sievernich and Hendrik Budde (eds), *Europa und der Orient. 800–1900*. Bertelsmann, 1989.

Denis Sinor, 'The Mongols in the West', *Journal of Asian History* 33, no.1 (1999)

M. Smets, *Wien in und aus der Türken Bedrängnis, 1529–1683*. Vienna: Gottlieb, 1883

John P. Spielman, *Leopold I of Austria*. London and New Brunswick, NJ: Thames & Hudson, 1977

— *The City and the Crown: Vienna and the Imperial Court, 1600–1740*. West Lafayette, IN: Purdue University Press, 1993

Franz K. Stanzel, *Europäer: Ein imagologischer Essay*. Heidelberg: Universitätsverlag C. Winter, 1997

— (ed.), *Europäischer Völkerspiegel: Imagologisch-ethnographische Studien zu den*

Völkertafeln des frühen 18. Jahrhunderts. Heidelberg: Universitätsverlag C. Winter, 1999

L. S. Stavrianos, *The Balkans since 1453.* New York: Holt Rhinehart and Winston, 1958

Mark L. Stein, *Guarding the Frontier: Ottoman Border Forts and Garrisons in Europe.* London: I. B. Tauris, 2007

Gerhard Stenzel, *Von Burg zu Burg in Österreich.* Vienna: Verlag Kremayr & Scheriau, 1973

Traian Stoianovich, *Balkan Worlds: The First and Last Europe.* Armonk, NY: M. E. Sharpe, 1994

Ferdinand Stöller, *Neue Quellen zur Geschichte des Türkenjahres 1683.* Aus dem Lotharingischen Hausarchiv Innsbruck: Universitäts Verlag Wagner, 1933, in Mitteilungen des Österreichischen Instituts für Geschichtsforschung. Ergänzungs-Band XIII, Heft 1.

Norman Stone, *The Eastern Front, 1914–1917.* 2nd revised edn. London: Penguin, 2004

John Stoye, *Marsigli's Europe 1680–1730. The Life and Times of Luigi Fernandino Marsigli, Soldier and Virtuoso.* New Haven, CT: Yale University Press, 1994
— *The Siege of Vienna.* New edn. Edinburgh: Birlinn, 2000

Walter Sturminger, *Bibliographie und Ikonographie der Türkenbelagerungen Wiens 1529 und 1683.* Graz: Verlag Böhlaus, 1955

Peter F. Sugar, *Industrialisation of Bosnia Hercegovina, 1878–1918.* Seattle, WA: University of Washington Press, 1963
— *South Eastern Europe under Ottoman Rule, 1354–1804.* Seattle, WA, and London: University of Washington Press, 1977
— *A History of Hungary.* Bloomington, IN: Indiana University Press, 1990

Werner Suppanz, *Österreichische Geschichtsbilder. Historische Legitimationen in Ständestaat und Zweiter Republik.* Vienna: Böhlau Verlag, 1998

Paula Fichtner Sutter, *Terror and Toleration: The Habsburg Empire Confronts Islam, 1526–1850.* London: Reaktion Books, 2008

Ferenc Szakály. 'Nándorfeáhérvár [Belgrade], 1521: the beginning of the end of the medieval Hungarian kingdom', in Géza David and Pál Fodor (eds), *Hungarian–Ottoman Military and Diplomatic Relations in the Age of Suleyman the Magnificent.* Budapest: Hungarian Academy of Sciences/Institute of History, 1994

Franz Taeschner, *Alt-Stambuler Hof- und Volksleben: Ein Türkisches Miniaturen-album aus dem 17. Jahrhundert.* Hanover: Orientbuchhandlung Heinz Lafaire, 1925

Marcus Tanner, *Croatia: A Nation Forged in War.* New Haven, CN: Yale University Press, 1997

Victor-L. Tapié, *L'Europe de Marie-Thérèse: du baroque aux lumières.* Paris: Fayard, 1973

Karl Teply, *Türkische Sagen und Legenden um die Kaiserstadt Wien*. Vienna: Hermann Böhlaus Nachfolgers, 1980

[Jean de] Thevenot, *Voyages de Mr. de Thevenot tant en Europe q'en Asie et en Afrique*. Paris: Charles Angot, 1689

Jean-Michel Thiriet, 'La Redécouverte d'un homme de guerre et de lettres: Montecuccoli', http://www.stratisc.org/strat_058_MONTECUCCO.html.

Andreas Tietze (ed.), *Habsburgisch-osmanische Beziehungen. Wien 26.–30. September 1983*. Beihefte zur Wiener Zeitschrift für die Kunde des Morgenlandes, Bd 13. Vienna: Verlag des Verbundes der wissenschatlichen Gesellschaften Österrreichs, 1985

Edward Timms, 'National Memory and the "Austrian Idea" from Metternich to Waldheim', *Modern Language Review* 86 (1991): 898–910

Maria Todarova, *Imagining the Balkans*. Oxford: Oxford University Press, 1997

Leopold Toifl and Hildegard Leitgarb, *Die Türkeneinfälle in der Steiermark und in Kärnten vom 15. bis zum 17. Jahrhundert*. Vienna: Bundesverlag, 1991

Kerstin Tomenendal, *Das türkische Gesicht Wiens. Auf den Spuren der Türken in Wien*. Vienna: Böhlau Verlag, 2002

István György Tóth, *Literacy and Written Culture in Early Modern Central Europe*. Budapest: Central European University Press, 2000

James D. Tracy (ed.), *City Walls: The Urban Enceinte in Global Perspective*. Cambridge: Cambridge University Press, 2001

Daniel L. Unowsky, *The Pomp and Politics of Patriotism: Imperial Celebrations in Habsburg Austria, 1848–1916*. West Lafayette, IN: Purdue University Press, 2005

Nicolas Vatin, *Les Ottomans et l'occident (XVe–XVIe siècles)*. Istanbul: Editions Isis, 2001

Dorothy Vaughan, *Europe and the Turk: A Pattern of Alliances, 1350–1700*. Liverpool: Liverpool University Press, 1954

George Vernadsky and Michael Karpovich, *The Mongols and Russia: The History of Russia*, vol. 3. New Haven CT: Yale University Press, 1953

V. Viuksic, *Cavalry: The History of a Fighting Elite, 650 BC–AD 1914*. London: Cassell, 1993

Karl Vocelka, 'Public Opinion and the Phenomenon of Sozialdisziplinierung in the Habsburg Monarchy', in Charles W. Ingrao (ed.), *State and Society in Early Modern Austria*. West Lafayette, IN: Purdue University Press, 1994

— 'Die inneren Auswirkungen der Auseinandersetzung Österreichs mit den Osmanen', *Südostforschungen* 36 (1977): 13–34

Mara R. Wade and Glenn Ehrstine, '"Der, Die, Das Fremde". Alterity in Medieval and Early Modern German Studies', *Daphnis. Zeitschrift für Mittlere Deutsche Literatur* 33, pt 1 (2004): 5–32

Georg Wagner, *Das Türkenjahr 1664: eine europäische Bewährung. Raimund Montecuccoli, die Schlacht von Gotthard-Mogersdorf und der Friede von Eisenburg [Vasvár]*. Eisenstadt: Burgenländisches Landesarchiv, 1964

Ernst Wangermann, *From Joseph II to the Jacobin Trials: Government Policy and Public Opinion in the Habsburg Dominions in the Period of the French Revolution*. Oxford: Oxford University Press, 1959

Hermann Watzl (ed.), *Flucht und Zuflucht: Das Tagebuch des Priesters Balthasar Kleinschroth aus dem Türkenjahr 1683*. Graz: Hermann Böhlaus Nachf., 1956

Andrew Wheatcroft, *The Habsburgs: Embodying Empire*. London: Penguin, 1995

— *Infidels: A History of the Conflict between Christendom and Islam*. London and New York: Penguin and Random House Inc., 2005

Wien 1529. Die erste Türkenbelagerung. 62. Sonderausstellung des Historischen Museums der Stadt Wien. 4. Oktober 1979 bis 10. Februar 1980. Vienna: Eigenverlag der Museen der Stadt Wien, 1979

Bryan Glyn Williams, *The Crimean Tatars. The Diaspora Experience and the Forging of the Nation*. Leiden: E. J. Brill, 2001

Nancy M. Wingfield (ed.), *Creating the Other: Ethnic Conflict and Nationalism in Habsburg Central Europe*. New York and Oxford: Berghahn Books, 2003

— *Flag Wars and Stone Saints: How the Bohemian Lands Became Czech*. Cambridge, MA. Harvard University Press, 2007

Larry Wolff, *Inventing Eastern Europe: The Map of Civilisation on the Mind of the Enlightenment*. Stanford, CA. Stanford University Press, 1994

Reingard Wutzmann, *Hieronymus Löschenkohl: Bildreporter zwischen Barock und Biedermaier*. Vienna: Edition Tusch: 1978

David Wyn Jones, *Music in Eighteenth-Century Austria*. Cambridge: Cambridge University Press, 1996

Bat Ye'or, *The Decline of Eastern Christianity under Islam. From Jihad to Dhimmitude*. Madison, NJ: Fairleigh Dickinson University Press, 1996

— *Eurabia: The Euro–Arab Axis*. Cranbury, NJ: Associated University Presses, 2005

Stephane Yerasimos, *Les Voyageurs dans l'Empire Ottoman (XIVe–XVIe siècles): Bibliographie Itinéraires et inventaire des lieux habités*. Ankara: Imprimerie de la Société Turque d'Histoire, 1991

Kemal Pacha Zadeh, *Histoire de la campagne de Mohacz par . . . Translated with notes by Pavet de Courtreille*. Paris: L'Imprimerie Impériale, 1859

István Zombori (ed.), *Fight against the Turk in Central Europe in the First Half of the 16th Century*. Budapest: METEM, 2004

Zdzislaw Zygulski, Jr, *Ottoman Art in the Service of the Empire, 16th and 17th Century*. New York: New York University Press, 1992

Index

Abbas I, Shah 56

Abdul Hamid II, Sultan 255, 256, 257, 258, 259

Abdurrahman Abdi Pasha 219, 222, 223

Adrianople see Edirne

Aga, Osman 92

Ahmed, Prince (son of Mehmed IV) 83, 97

Alexander the Great 1, 99, 245, 252

Alexander I, Czar 254

Alexander, Prince, of Poland 183, 185, 193

Alexander Romance 1

Alexius I Comnenus 4

Álmos 194

Alp Arslan 4

Andrassy, Count 264

Anguissola, Leander 130

Arabia/Arabs 1, 2, 3; Revolt (1916) 259

Aramont, Count of 30, 31

armies, Habsburg 18, 61, 63, 65, 66, 70, 100, 105, 114, 164–6, 168, 230, 235–6, 243; cavalry 19, 26–7, 106; dragoons 64; grenadiers 141; hussars 64; musketeers 26, 27, 64, 141, 142; pikemen 25–6, 64, 125; siegecraft 74, 208–9; see also Bavarian, Polish and Saxon armies; weapons

armies, Ottoman 4, 15–16, 18, 43–5, 63–4, 65, 66, 79, 87, 111, 114, 140, 204, 230, 236; akincis (light horse) 19, 53; engineers/sappers 17, 25, 126, 129, 130–31, 141, 148, 149–50, 209; infantry/janissaries 20–22, 23–5, 26, 28, 45–6, 64–5, 75, 101, 142, 143, 163–4, 197, 217, 236, 237; siegecraft 45, 74, 124; sipahis (palace cavalry) 19, 23, 26, 53, 119, 197, 204, 205, 217, 237; war camps 13, 14–17, 23; see also Tartars; weapons

Aşikpaşazade (historian) 85

Ataturk (Mustafa Kemal) xxviii, 265

Athens 8

Attaleiates, Michael 3

Auersperg, Count 116

Austria/Austria-Hungary/Austrians 7, 73, 229, 235, 263–4; troops 134, 138, 230; 'Age of Heroes' 228–9, 245, 249, 250–51, 252–3, 255; Holy Alliance 254; Turkish guest-workers 266; see also Habsburgs; Vienna

Austro-Hungarian Monarchy in Word and Images, The 257–8

Avars 50

Aviano, Father Marco d' 177, 203, 206–7, 211

Babinger, Franz: *Mehmed the Conqueror* . . . 57

Baden, Hermann, Marquis of 113, 130, 203, 211

Baghdad 45, 56; siege (1638) 36, 39

Bahçisaray 47–8

Balkans, the 6, 17, 20, 45, 50, 57, 193; wars (1990s) 267

Banjaluka, battle of (1737) 238

Barkan, 204, 211, 213, 216; battle of (1683) 195, 196, 197, 198, 199, 246

Barker, Thomas 64

Batthyany, Countess 251

Batu, Mongol leader 50–51

Bavaria, Maximilian Emmanuel, Elector of 105, 106; and siege of Vienna (1683) 137, 165, 168, 170; demands command 203; and sieges of Buda 209, 211 (1684), 222, 223 (1686); captures Belgrade (1688) 229

Bavarian army 164, 165, 168, 169, 170, 178, 183, 198; at sieges of Buda 205, 209, 210, 217, 218, 219

Baybars, Sultan 189

Bayezid I, Sultan 89, 189

Bayezid II, Sultan 57

Bayly, Christopher: *The Birth of the Modern World* 255

Bektashi dervish preachers 21

Bela III, of Hungary 4

Belgrade 6, 80; Ottoman defeat (1456) 7, 56, 57; falls to Suleiman (1521) 9, 57–8, 61; Ottoman occupation 43, 45, 67, 80; Ottoman war camp (1683) 86, 87, 97; battles for (1688–9) 229; captured by Prince Eugene (1717–18) 234, 237–8, 240; fortified by Doxat 242; peace treaty and mistakenly surrendered to the Turks (1739) 242, 253; recaptured by Laudon (1789) 243–4; handed back to Selim II 244

Benaglia, Giovanni 23

Benedict XVI, Pope 267

Berlin, Congress of (1878) 263–4

Black Death 55

Blenheim Palace, Oxfordshire 248, 252

Boccaccio, Giovanni: *On the Fates of Famous Men* 4

Bohemia 8, 62, 118, 139, 166, 235

Boissard, Jean-Jacques: *Lives and Portraits of the Turkish Sultans* 28

Bolkestein, Frits 267

Book of Austria 251

Bosnia/Bosnians 5, 57, 87, 202, 232–3, 238, 264

Bosnia-Herzegovina 260, 264

Brand, Hannah: *Huniades, or, The siege of Belgrade* 56

Brandenburg: army 164, 203, 215, 220, 230

Brandenburg, Friedrich Wilhelm, Elector of 203, 215

Bratislava *see* Pressburg

Britain/England 34, 102, 107, 121, 202, 254, 255; Crimean War 261; World War I 265

Brod (fortress) 235

Brown, Edward 98, 99, 123, 126

Brown, Johann Georg 243

Brunswick, Charles, Duke of 253–4

Buda 6, 57; captured by Suleiman (1521) 58; pashas' responsibilities 45, 89; occupied by Suleiman (1541) 224; attacked by Sobieski and Lorraine (1683–4) 193, 195, 196, 204, 205; sieges 205–6, 207–11 (1684), 215–24, 229 (1686); recaptured (1686) 224

Bulgars 50

Bursa 38
Busbecq, Ogier Ghislain de 29, 33, 51; *Letters* . . . 16, 19, 22, 29–30, 41
Byzantines 1, 4–5

Caesar, Julius 99, 193
Calvinists 107–8
Canaletto (Bernardo Bellotto) 252
Candia, siege of (1650–69) 39, 42, 81, 126, 130, 131, 132, 207
Capistrano, John 56
Caplirs, Count 153
Caprara, Count 22–3, 73, 79, 100, 112
Caprara, General Enio 116, 215
Carlos II, of Spain 117
Carpathian Mountains 17, 49
Çelebi, Evliya *see* Evliya Çelebi
Charlemagne, Holy Roman Emperor 7, 260
Charles I, of England 32
Charles II, of England 32, 33, 137
Charles V, Holy Roman Emperor 7, 8, 9, 101; at siege of Tunis (1535) 192, 243, 245
Charles VI, Holy Roman Emperor 228, 238, 239, 240, 242, 252
Chombart de Lauwe, Paul-Henry 89
Christendom/Christians 1, 3; hatred of Ottomans 4, 5, 8–9, 61, 213–14; Catholics v. Protestants 18, 91, 93; in Ottoman army 20, 140; *see also* Crusades
Chyryen, fall of (1678) 41
Conquests of Alexander the Great, The (tapestries) 245
Constantinople *see* Istanbul
Coppin, Father Jean 191, 202
Cossacks 47, 51, 215
Covel, Dr John 14
Crawford, John Lindsay, 20th Earl of 240, 241

Crete 39, 83, 139, 202; *see also* Candia
Creux, Baron 220
Crimea, the 47–8, 51, 202; *see also* Tartars
Crimean War (1853–6) 262
Croatia/Croats 8, 57, 68, 98, 231, 234, 235, 260; horsemen (*pandurs*) 68, 69; at Szigetvár 59–60
Crusades 3, 5, 121, 189–90; *see also* Hungary, Reconquest of

Dalerac, M.: *Secret History* 185
Dalmatia 8, 57
Damascus 114; railway to Mecca 258–9
Danube, River 49, 50, 77, 80; Iron Gates 1, 6, 57; 'Trajan's Bridge' 6; fortresses 81, 86; pontoon bridges 119, 134, 194; and Vienna's defences 122, 127; Barkan–Esztergom bridge 195, 197–8; pontoon bridges restored 205; supply chain to Vienna 208; set as boundary 234
Danube meadows 169
Darda 98, 99, 109
Dardanelles 39
Daun, Field Marshal Leopold von 249
Davies, Norman: *Europe: A History* 6
Degenfeld, General Hannibal von 168
Diodato, Johannes 188
Diogenes Romanus, Emperor 4
diseases 55, 134, 145, 150–51, 210, 243
Doxat, General 239, 242
Drava, River 68, 86, 87, 234; Osijek bridge 68–9, 97–9, 210, 220
Dreimarkstein 173, 175, 179

Dual Monarchy, the 260
Duffy, Christopher 125, 235–6
Dumont, Jean: *The Battles won by the Most Serene Prince Eugene of Savoy* . . . 247, 248–9
Dupigny, Count 154

Edebali (dervish) 85
Edirne (Adrianople) 5, 14, 31, 39, 40, 41, 42–3; Palace 14, 37, 38, 41, 42, 77, 79; Ottoman army's departure from 77–9
Eger, fortress of 60, 67, 213
Eliot, T.S.: 'The Dry Salvages' 11, 269; 'Little Gidding' 225
Elisabeth, Empress of Austria 257, 258
England *see* Britain
Enlightenment, the 261, 262
Erivan, siege of (1635) 36
Esterhazy, Count 106, 214
Esztergom (Gran) 113, 195, 196; captured by Suleiman (1543) 195; siege (1684) 197, 198–9, 211, 213; battle (1686) 214
Eugene, Prince of Savoy 66, 197, 246; at defence of Vienna (1683) 170, 173; orders construction of Linienwall (Vienna) 212; wounded at sieges of Buda (1686) 218; defeats Sultan Mustafa at Zenta (1697) 229, 230–32, 233; sacks Sarajevo 232–3; in War of Spanish Succession 228, 247; defeats Turks at Petrovaradin (1716) 233; recaptures Belgrade (1717) 234, 237–8; last campaign (1737) 240; memorialised by artists 247–9; aggrandizes Belvedere 248; love of animals 248; biography written by de Ligne 249–50; death 251–2; as

Austrian hero 229, 237–8, 245, 250–51
European Union 267
Evliya Çelebi 42, 71, 140

Falke, Jacob von 263
Febure, Michel 191
Ferdinand II, of Habsburg 58, 118, 162, 172
Filibe (Philippopolis) 79–80
Fischa, River 116, 137
Fischamend 137
fortresses, Habsburg *see* Habsburgs
France 66, 102, 166, 191, 254, 255; and Habsburgs 34, 56; and Ottomans 104, 106, 202; War of the Grand Alliance 230, 235; War of the Spanish Succession 228, 229; repulses Prussian army 253–4; Crimean War 262; World War I 265; *see also* Napoleon Bonaparte
Francis I, Holy Roman Emperor (Francis Stephen of Lorraine) 239, 240, 254
Franconia 165; troops 170, 183
Franz Ferdinand, Archduke 265
Franz Joseph I, Emperor of Austria 250, 255, 256, 257, 258
Frederick II (the Great), of Prussia 235, 249
Frederick III, Holy Roman Emperor 7
Froissart, Jean de: *Chronicle* 5
Frondsberg castle 57

George I, of England 165
Germany / German states 7, 33, 52, 72, 191, 254, 255, 256, 265; troops 165–6, 170, 172, 173, 177, 212; *see also* Bavarian army; Brandenburg; Franconia; Prussia; Saxon army

Gersthof 175, 177, 181

Gibbon, Edward: *The History of the Decline and Fall of the Roman Empire* 1, 2, 75

Gingrich, Andre xxvii, 259–60, 263

Giray, Mehmet, Khan 47–8

Giray, Mengli, Khan 53

Gobelins tapestry factory 245

Goltz, General von der 182, 187

Gran *see* Esztergom

Gran, Archbishop of 105

Gränberg 173, 181

Graz 55, 57, 67, 70, 110; Cathedral fresco 55; Landeszeughaus (armoury) 237

Greif, Hans, Lord of 189

Grein, Andreas 90–91

Grinzing xxiv, 180

Grocka, Battle of (1739) 240–42

Guilleragues, Comte de 106

Güns *see* Köszeg

Gustavus Adolphus, of Sweden 64, 102, 126

Györ (Raab) 81, 111, 112, 113, 115, 116, 126, 130

Habsburgs 6–7, 227–8; mutual hatred of Ottomans 84–5, 88–9; wars with France 34, 56; sixteenth-century fortresses 61–2, 66, 67, 80–81, 86, 123–6, 128, 130, 234–5; truces with Ottomans 56, 61, 62, 72, 73, 90; and Thirty Years War (1618–48) 56, 63, 66; similarities with Ottomans 100–3; in nineteenth century 254–8, 263; and Frontier Orientalism 259–60; and World War I 265; *see also* army, Habsburg; Leopold I; weapons

Hadrianopolis *see* Edirne

Hainburg, sack of (1683) 136–7

Halliweil, General 204

Hammer-Purgstall, Joseph 262, 263

Hardegg, Count 168

Hasan, Abaza 38

Heiligenstadt 175, 176, 180

Heissler, Colonel 170, 172

Heisterman, Captain 156

Henri II, of France 30

Henry VIII, of England 34

Hermannskogel 172, 173

Hildburghausen, Field Marshal Prince Joseph von 241

Hillenbrand, Carole 3

Hirtenberg, Ferdinand Charles, Prince of 139, 153

Hizir Ilyas 79

Hochedlinger, Michael: *Austria's Wars of Emergence* 235

'Holy Leagues' 166, 190, 215, 228

Holy Roman Empire and Emperors 6, 7, 164, 254, 260; *see also* Leopold I

Huchtenburg, Jan: *The Battles won by the Most Serene Prince Eugene of Savoy . . .* 247, 248--9

Hungary / Hungarians 2, 4, 6, 17, 42, 49, 88; creation of 50, 194; invaded by Mongols (Tartars) 50; first maps 77; defeated by Ottomans 7, 8, 9, 24, 39, 42, 57–8, 61, 74, 84; Protestants persecuted by Leopold 72, 73, 85, 101, 106–9; Long War (1593–1606) 86; fortresses 42, 62, 66, 80–81, 86, 108; Ottoman campaigns 68–9, 72, 98 (1663–4), 78, 80–81, 98–9, 106, 175, 176 (1682–3); Reconquest of 190–92, 193, 194–5, 202–3, 207, 212, 228, 233, 237, 246; and the Dual Monarchy 260; *see also* Buda; Szigetvár

Huns 50

Hunyadi, John 7, 56
hussars (*husaria*), Polish *see* Polish
army

Ibrahim, Pasha of Buda 176
Ibrahim, Sultan ('the Mad') 35–6, 82
Innocent XI, Pope 104, 166–7, 190,
191, 193, 202, 228
Islam/Muslims xxviii, 2–3, 5, 8–9,
16–17, 84, 263; *see also* Mecca;
Mohammad; Qu'ran
Israel, Jonathan: *Enlightenment
Contested* 262
Istanbul (Constantinople) 4, 5, 30,
31, 41; Hagia Sophia (Aya Sofia)
2, 37, 40, 41; captured by
Ottomans (1453) 5, 6, 7, 46, 56,
84, 124, 135, 136; Suleiman's
mosque 9; Ottoman war camp
(1682) 13–17; Tophane gun
factory 19, 45; Ottoman court
101, 203; General Exposition
(1863) 262; *see also* Topkapi
Palace
Istolni Belgrád *see* Székesfehérvár

Jablonowski, Stanislaw 181, 182, 186
janissaries *see* armies, Ottoman
Jerusalem 3, 6, 8, 189
John VI, Byzantine Emperor 5
Johnson, Elizabeth: *The Historian*
267–8
Joseph I, Holy Roman Emperor 117,
228
Joseph II, Holy Roman Emperor
243, 244
Jurišic, Nikola 59

Kahlenberg, the 170, 172, 173, 174,
175, 177, 178
Kamenets, fall of (1672) 39–40, 81
Kaniza (Nagykaniza) 68, 69

Kara Mustafa of Merzifon, Grand
Vizier: background 82–3; adopated
by Mehmed 83; appointed Grand
Vizier 40, 81, 83; renowned for
courage 83; failings as leader
40–41, 46; and Count Thököly
108, 109; on 1682 campaign 13, 14,
41, 43, 46, 78; plans attack on
Vienna (1683) 80, 81, 82, 83–4, 85,
86, 87, 98, 106; in command of
army 97, 98–100, 103, 110–12, 114,
115, 116; receives severed heads
from Hainburg 136–7; and siege of
Vienna 137, 138–41, 143, 148, 151–3,
161, 162, 175, 176, 177, 179, 180, 182,
183; in retreat 184, 186, 201, 211;
and siege of Esztergom 198–9;
executed 199–200
Karlovac (fortress) 235
Karlowitz, Treaty of (1699) 229, 233,
253
Károly, Alexy: statuette of
Starhemberg 133
Keiserstein, General 134
Kemal, Mustafa *see* Ataturk
Kielmansegg, Count 157
Kipling, Rudyard: 'The Ballad of
East and West' 95
Kittsee, plain of 105, 115–16
Kleiner, Salomon 248
Klimt, Gustav 263
Klosterneuburg, abbey of xxiv, 117,
172, 175
Knab, Archbishop Sebastian 202
Knolles, Richard: *Generall Historie of
the Turkes* 28
Kochowski, Vespasian: *Commentary*
183
Kolin, Battle of (1757) 249
Kolschitzky, Georg Franz 188
Komárno 195, 213; island fortress 81,
111, 126

Königsegg, Count 239–40

Köprülü, Grand Viziers 37, 40;
Ahmed 239, 240, 241, 242; Fazil
Ahmed 38, 39, 40, 67–9, 83; Fazil
Mustafa Pasha 229, 231; Mehmed
34, 37–8, 81

Kosovo Polje, battle of (1389) 5

Köszeg (Güns), siege of (1532) 59,
67

Kunitz, Baron Georg Christoph 23

Lajos, King of Hungary 58

Lamormaini, Wilhelm: *The Virtues
of Ferdinand* 118

Laudon, Field Marshal Ernst
Gideon von 243–4

Lauenberg, Julius Francis, Duke of
173

Lazar, Prince of Serbia 5

Lechfeld, battle of (955) 50

Leitha, River 116

Leopold I, Holy Roman Emperor:
character traits 101, 103; delights
in Court Theatre 149; and the
Wienerwald 171; and the army
18, 70, 100, 104; twenty-year truce
with Ottomans 18, 23, 72, 73;
persecution of Protestant
Hungarians 73, 85, 106–8; alliance
with Sobieski 104, 106; appoints
Duke of Lorraine as commander
104–5; inspects troops 105–6; and
Count Thököly 108, 109; and
Ottoman advance on Vienna 112,
113, 114, 115, 116; abandons city
116–18, 119, 136; calls for military
support 165; helped by Innocent
XI 166; command ignored by
Lorraine 169, 172; tempted by
idea of Reconquest 190–92;
returns to Vienna 193; shows
ingratitude to Sobieski 193; signs

agreement to wage war against
Ottomans 202; influenced by
d'Aviano 203, 207; and assaults
on Buda 211, 215, 216, 222;
appoints Prince Eugene 230;
presented with tapestries by
Louis XIV 245

Leopold II, Holy Roman Emperor
244

Leopold V of Babenberg, Duke of
Austria 121

Leopold VI of Babenberg, Duke of
Austria ('the Glorious') 121

Leopoldstadt island 127, 128, 138,
147

Lepanto, battle of (1571) 73, 166, 190

Leslie, Alexander 139

Leslie, James 139

Leslie, Count Walter 139, 169

Leslies of Balquhain and Fetternear
139

Liegnitz, battle of (1241) 50

Ligne, Field Marshal Charles-
Joseph, Prince de 244, 250, 254

Linz 33, 116, 118, 170

Long Wars (1593–1606) 55, 62, 63, 86,
152, (1683–99) 228

Lorck (Lorichs), Melchior 30

Lorraine, Charles V, Duke of:
appearance 104, 105; character
105, 114–15, 168; military career
104, 133, 139; appointed
commander of Habsburg army
104–5; and siege of Vienna (1683)
110, 113–14, 115–16, 119–20, 134, 135,
136, 145–6, 150, 157, 164; defeats
Ottomans 167–72, 173, 174, 177–8,
179–80, 182, 183; and Reconquest
of Hungary 193, 194, 195–7, 198,
203, 204, 213, 236; besieges Buda
(1684) 205, 206, 207–8, 210, 211;
captures Nóvy Zámky 213, 214;

captures Buda again (1686) 215, 218, 219–24, 229; as Austrian hero 228, 245; military career depicted in tapestries 245–6; military observations 246–7; death 247
Lorraine, Leopold, Duke of 245
Löschenkohl, Johann Hieronymous 243
Louis XII, of France 125
Louis XIII, of France 191
Louis XIV, of France 62, 72, 104, 106, 139, 166, 245
Louis, King of Bohemia and Moravia 8
Louis of Baden see Ludwig Wilhelm, Margrave of Baden
Louvois, François-Michel Le Tellier, Marquis de 191
Lubomirski, Prince 138
Ludwig Wilhelm, Margrave of Baden ('Türkenlouis') 187, 197, 203, 209, 211, 228–9

Magdeburg, siege of (1631) 149
Magyars 50, 107, 108, 194
Mamluk sultanate 3–4, 189
Manuel Comnenus, Emperor 4
Manzikert, battle of (1071) 3, 4, 6
Marcomanni, the 50
Maria Antonia, Archduchess 105
Maria Theresa, Archduchess of Austria 240, 242–3, 244, 249, 262
Marie Valerie, Archduchess 258
Marinoni, Johann Jakob 212
Marlborough, John Churchill, Duke of 228, 248, 252
Marsh, Henry 72
Marsigli, Luigi Ferdinando, Count 16, 112, 115, 140, 151, 176, 195
Matthew of Paris: Great Chronicle 51
Matthias (Corvinus), King of Hungary 7

Maurice of Nassau 64
Maximilian I, Emperor 7, 171
Mecca 31, 258, 259
Medina 258, 259
Mehmed II, Sultan ('the Conqueror'): conquers Constantinople (1453) 6, 7, 40, 46, 85, 124, 224; fails to take Belgrade 9, 56, 57; builds Topkapi 36–7, and Edirne palaces 37, 41; and raids on Styria and Carinthia 56–7; death 57
Mehmed III, Sultan 39
Mehmed IV, Sultan: early life 35, 36, 37–8; character 38, 82, 101; love of hunting 38–9; first campaigns 14–15, 38, 39–40; at Constantinople war camp (1682) 13–14; sets out on campaign 17–18, 22, 41, 42–3, 77–80; motives for attacking Vienna 80–81, 82, 83, 84; relationship with Kara Mustafa 81, 83; hands over command to him 97, 98–9, 103; and Count Thököly 108–9; orders Kara Mustafa's execution 199; hears of alliance of Christian states 202
Mehmed, Kara, Pasha of Diyarbakir 177
Mercy, Count Florimond von 204, 229
Metternich, Prince Klemens von 255
Michaelerberg 181
Michault, Nicholas 29
Mohács, battle of (1526) 9, 58, 185, 229
Mohammad, Prophet 9, 38, 78, 193
Moldavia 55, 67, 109, 140
Mongols 50–51, 89
Montecuccoli, General Raimondo: develops musket rest 27; develops tactics for fighting

Ottomans 64, 236; on pikemen 125; and victory at St Gotthard 69, 70–72, 133; death 100; successors 113, 114

Montecuccoli, Colonel 116

Moravánszky, Ákos: *Competing Visions* 258

Moravia 8, 67, 235

Moson 116

Muhi, battle of (1241) 50

Murad I, Sultan 5, 6

Murad II, Sultan 41

Murad IV, Sultan 36, 37, 39, 81

Muslims *see* Islam

Mustafa, Prince (son of Mehmed IV) 78, 83, 97

Mustafa III, Sultan 229, 230, 231, 232

Myriocephalon, battle of (1176) 4

Nagyhársany, battle of (1687) 229

Nagykaniza *see* Kaniza

Naima, Mustafa 36

Napoleon Bonaparte 46, 66, 170, 249, 254

Neipperg, General 240, 242

Netherlands 34, 107–8, 169, 202

Neuhäusel *see* Nóvy Zámky

Neustift 180

Neville, Henry 100–1

Nicholas V, Pope 7

Nicolay, Nicolas de 30, 33; *Navigations . . .* 30–32

Nicopolis, battle of (1396) 5, 89, 90, 189

Nish 80; capture of (1737) 239

Nitra, River 67, 213

Noah 3, 7

Nogai Tartars 51–2

Novigrád (Neuberg) 213

Nóvy Zámky (Neuhäusel) 42, 67, 113, 194, 211; siege (1684) 213–14

Nussdorf 175, 176; battle (1683) 177–81

Oberdöbling 175, 176, 180, 183

Ödenburg *see* Sopron

Oghuz Khans 3, 85

Ögödey, Great Khan 50

Olivier, Heinrich: painting 254

Olomouc 235

Orhan 4, 5

Osijek 86, 98, 99, 100, 215, 220, 234; bridge 68, 69, 97–9, 210

Osman 4, 36, 85

Osman Pasha 244

Ottoman Turks xxviii, 4, 34; and Byzantine Christians 4–6; hatred of Habsburgs 6–7, 84–5, 88–9; similarities with Habsburgs xxviii–xxix, 100–3; 16th–17th-century eyewitness descriptions of 28–33; 'badlands' and borderlands 88, 89; 'decline' xxviii, 65–6, 74–6, 110, 163, 201–3, 263; tales of atrocities 89–92; in 19th century 254–7; construction of railway 258–9; Austrian attitudes to 259–60, 261–2; World War I 265, 266; and Ataturk 265; and European Union 267; *see also* army, Ottoman; weapons

palanka (blockhouses) 24, 131, 140, 176; Barkan 195, 196, 197

Pálffy, Count 221, 241, 242

Papacy, the *see* Innocent XI, Pope

Paris, Treaty of (1856) 262

Párkány *see* Barkan

Passarowitz, Treaty of (1718) 234, 235, 238, 242, 253

Patras 8

Pécs: Habsburg attack (1664) 68

Peikhart, Father 239

Persia 1, 2, 62, 63, 202–3
Pest 22, 50, 204, 205, 206
Petrovaradin (Peterwardein) 230,
    235, 240; battle of (1716) 233–4
Philip II, of Spain 9
Philippopolis see Filibe
Philippsburg, siege of (1676) 139
Pius V, Pope 166
plague 55, 150–51
Plutarch: Lives 75, 99
Pocahontas 92
Poland, Kingdom of 24, 39–40, 42,
    56, 66, 84, 104, 106; see also Polish
    army; Sobieski, John III
Polish army 113, 166, 167, 169–70,
    171, 172–3, 179, 181, 182, 198, 202;
    hussars (husaria) 19, 167, 174,
    183–6, 188, 195–7; mercenaries 40,
    134, 138
Prague 62, 151
Préchac, Jean de: The grand vizier . . .
    201
Pressburg (Bratislava) 105, 115, 119,
    134, 194, 230, 245
printing, spread of 26, 89–90, 91
Prussia 66, 235, 254; army 203, 235,
    253–4
Pruth, River: battle (1711) 163–4
Pufendorf, Samuel 164
Purbach 90, 91

Qu'ran 1, 15, 49, 111, 155

Raab see Györ
Rába (Raab), River 69–72, 73, 111,
    112, 113
Rabca, River 111
railway, Ottoman 258–9
Rákóczi, Prince Francis II 212
Rakowski: Reveille to worthy sons 183
ravelins 123
Reconquest, the see Hungary

Richard I (the Lionheart), of
    England 121
Richelieu, Cardinal 206
Riegersburg, Schloss 57
Rilke, Rainer Maria: 'Die dritte
    Elegie' v
Rimpler, Georg 113, 130–32, 141
Rohan, Maître de: illustration 4
Romans 1, 2, 6, 21, 75, 88, 97, 99
Rosskopf 172, 173, 176, 179, 181
Royal Academy, London: Turks
    (2005 exhibition) 2
Rudolf, Crown Prince of Austria
    257
Russ, Leander: painting 159
Russia/Russians 34, 46–7, 88; and
    Ottomans 40–41, 66, 84, 256, 263,
    264; and Tartars 48, 51, 202; 19th
    century 46, 254, 255, 256, 260,
    262, 263; World War I 265
Ruyter, Admiral Michiel de 108
Rycaut, Sir Paul xxviii, 32–3, 75–6,
    81, 201–2, 223
Rycaut, Peter 32, 33

Sachsen Lauenberg, Julius Francis,
    Duke of 170
Said, Edward: Orientalism 259
St Andra 172
St Gotthard, battle of (1664) xxv, 38,
    55, 69–72, 73–4, 84, 100, 127, 133,
    231
Saladin, Sultan 189
Salm, Count Niklas 58
Salms, Duke of 209
Salzburg, Archbishop of 166
Sanjak of Novipazar 264
Sarajevo 61, 233, 264, 265
Sarmatians 50
Sauberg, the 172
Sava, River 68, 80, 86, 97, 234
Saxe, General Maurice de 237

Saxon army 165–6, 168, 169, 170,
    178–9, 180, 182, 230
Saxony, John George, Elector of
    165–6, 168, 170, 180
Scala, Arthur von 263
Scalia 203–4
Scamozzi, Vincenzo: *The Universal
    Idea of Architecture* 124
Scherffenberg, Count 147
Schiltberger, Johannes 89–90, 91, 189
Schlosshof (palace) 252
Schmitt, Heinrich: map 127
Schultz, General 134, 215
Schwechat 193
Scythians 2, 50
Seckendorf, Field Marshal Friedrich
    von 239
Selim I, Sultan 7, 9, 57, 74, 97
Selim II, Sultan 36, 42, 54
Selim III, Sultan 244
Seljuk Turks 2, 3, 4, 6
Serenyi, Count 143, 147
Sieniawski, Nicolas Hieronymus 181
Sievering 180
Sigismund I, of Poland and
    Lithuania 8
Silahdar Ali Pasha, Grand Vizier 233
Silesia 203, 235
sipahis see armies, Ottoman
Sistova, Peace of (1791) 244, 253
Slankamen, battle of (1691) 229
Slavs 260
Smith, John 92
Sobieski, John III, of Poland:
    appearance 167; alliance with
    Leopold I 104, 106, 137; and
    Charles of Lorraine 104, 167, 168;
    and relief of Vienna (1683) 164,
    167, 170, 171, 173, 174, 179–80,
    181–6, 192–3, 229; offended by
    Leopold 193; pursues Ottomans
    194; ambushed at Barkan 195–6;

and troops' low morale 198;
    signs agreement with Leopold
    and Doge of Venice 202
Sommervogel, Lieutenant 156
Sopron (Ödenburg) 67, 110
Souches, Colonel Charles de 139
Spain 102, 202, 254
'Spanish Rider' 27
Spielman, John P.: *Leopold I of
    Austria* 103
Stalingrad, battle for (1942) 150
Starhemberg, Count Ernst Rüdiger
    von: appearance 133; military
    background 133, 139; as com-
    mander at siege of Vienna (1683)
    117, 119, 132, 133, 135, 140, 141, 142,
    145, 147, 148, 149, 153, 155, 156–7,
    159–60, 163, 168; receives
    Lorraine 186; gives dinner for
    Sobieski 192; meets Leopold
    193; attacks retreating Turks
    197; and siege of Buda (1684)
    206, 209
Starhemberg, Guido von 218, 229
Stetteldorf, castle of 168
Stone, Norman: *The Eastern Front*
    265
Strattmann, Count 216, 222, 246
Styria 55, 57, 67, 69, 227, 235
Suleiman I, Sultan ('the Magnificent')
    7, 8–9, 35, 41, 42, 85; court 29, 30;
    military campaigns 55, 57–8, 59,
    67, 86, 98, 195, 206; siege of
    Vienna (1529) 46, 58, 74, 86, 121,
    128; death 15, 61; triumphs
    displayed in *The Book of Suleiman*
    36
Suttinger, Daniel 130
Sutton, Sir Robert 163–4
Swabia 165
Sweden 34, 102, 126, 202
Syria/Syrians 45, 87, 114

Székesfehérvár (Istolni Belgrád) 110,
    112
Szigetvár: Ottoman sieges of 59
    (1556), 36, 59–61, 67 (1566);
    attacked by Zrinyi (1664) 68
Szirmay, Istvan 108

Tamerlane 89
tapestries 192, 245–6, 248
Tartars 19, 48–9, 50–52; code of
    honour 74; alliance with
    Ottoman Turks 47, 48, 52–4, 74;
    raids 90, 91; at battle of St
    Gotthard 69, 71; at Nóvy Zámky
    72–3; advance on Vienna (1683)
    87, 110, 111–12, 115, 116, 117; and
    siege of Vienna 135, 136, 139, 150,
    169, 175, 176, 235; defeat Poles at
    Barkan 195–6; attacked by Russia
    202; and sieges of Buda 204, 205,
    221
Tekije: shrine 233–4
Thirty Years War (1618–48) 26, 56,
    62, 63, 64, 66, 70, 126, 139, 149,
    165, 168, 203
Thököly, Count Imre 108–9, 135,
    215
Tilly, Johann Tserclaes, Count 62,
    168
Timişoara (Temesvar) 232, 240
Tisza, River 230–31
Topkapi Palace 13, 14, 36–7, 38, 58;
    gardens 41; library 36
Transdanubia 77, 88
Transylvania 55, 67, 107, 109, 212,
    215, 230, 246
Trenkwald, Josef Mathias: painting
    121
Trouillot, Michel-Rolph: Silencing
    the Past 266
Tulln 169–70, 175
Tunis, siege of (1535) 192, 243, 245

Turhan Hatice Sultan, Khadija 36,
    37, 39, 42
'Türkenlouis' see Ludwig Wilhelm,
    Margrave of Baden
Türkenschanz, the 177, 179, 180, 182,
    183, 184, 186
Turkic-speaking tribes 1–2; and
    Islam 2–3; see also Ottoman
    Turks; Seljuk Turks
Turks see Ottoman Turks

Unterdöbling 175, 176, 180, 183
Urban II, Pope 3

Vaelckeren (Valcaren), Johann Peter
    xxviii, 121, 137–8
Valmy, battle of (1792) 253–4
Vasvár, truce of (1664) 56, 72, 73
Vauban, Sébastien Le Prestre de 62
Venice/Venetians 39, 57, 83, 202, 215,
    228, 233
Vermeulen, Jan 245
Vienna xxiii–xxv, 6, 57, 101;
    Ottoman campaigns against 9,
    58, 74, 86, 121, 123, 128, 131, 136,
    190 (1529), 86 (1532), 66–7 (1663),
    69 (1664), see also Vienna, siege
    of (1683) below; coffee houses
    established 188; Linienwall
    constructed (1704) 128;
    occupation by Napoleonic army
    254; Belvedere Palace 248, 252;
    Heldenplatz 250; Imperial
    Oriental Academy 261–2, 263;
    International Exposition (1873)
    262–3
Vienna, Congress of (1815) 254
Vienna, siege of (1683): Ottoman
    planning and motives 46, 80–82,
    83–4, 85, 86, 87–8, 110; Western
    attitudes to 92–3, 103–4, 266–7;
    advance of Ottoman army

111–12, 114, 115, 136–7; city
defences 100, 113, 120–24, 126–33,
141, 142–3; exodus of citizens 118,
136; arsenal 133–4, 135; garrison
134–6, 206; Ottoman encirclement 137–9, 140; advance of
Ottoman saps and tunnels 141,
142, 149–50, 153; Habsburg
defence of palisade 141–3; battle
at Löbl and Burg bastions 143–4,
145–8, 153–61, 162–3, 164; disease
150–51; food supplies 150, 151;
hanging of deserters 155;
celebration of nativity of Virgin
Mary 162; relief 164–87, see
Lorraine, Charles V, Duke of;
Sobieski, John III; see also
Kara Mustafa; Leopold I;
Starhemberg, Count
Vienna Woods see Wienerwald
Villach, Thomas von: fresco 55
Visegrád 204
Vogelsangberg 173
Voltaire 164; The History of the
  Travels of Scarmentado 261–2

Waldeck, Count Karl von 169, 170,
  193
Wallachia 55, 67, 109, 140, 202
Wallenstein, Albrecht von 62, 168
Wallis, Field Marshal George Oliver
  240–42
War of the Polish Succession

(1733–8) 249
War of the Spanish Succession
  (1704–13) 228, 229
weapons: Habsburg 21, 25–7, 141,
  142, 146, 163, 177, 215; Ottoman
  17, 19, 21, 24, 25, 26, 27–8, 64, 124,
  142, 146, 177, 218–19; Polish 167;
  Tartar 48, 49
Weinaus 175
Weizen [Vác], battles of (1684)
  204–5
Wien, River 127, 171
Wiener Neustadt 121
Wienerwald (Vienna Woods) 49,
  117, 139, 169, 171, 172, 180, 181
Winchilsea, Heneage Finch, 3rd
  Earl of 32
With United Strength: The Book of the
  Emperor Franz Joseph I 258
World War I 264, 265
Wynkyn de Worde 56

Yerasimos, Stephane 102–3

Zápolya, John 58
Zemun: Ottoman war camp (1683)
  86, 97, 99, 109
Zenta, battle of (1697) 229, 231–2,
  233, 240
Zrinvár, siege of (1664) 69
Zrinyi, Miklós 59, 60, 185
Zrinyi, Count Miklós, the Younger
  68, 69, 98